The publisher gratefully acknowledges the gen...

to this book provided by the Robert and Meryl Selig Endowment

Fund in Film Studies, in memory of Robert W. Selig, of the

University of California Press Foundation.

The Fun Factory

Mack Sennett on the Keystone studio lot. The director (operating the camera) is Fred Fishback. Courtesy of the Academy of Motion Picture Arts and Sciences.

The Fun Factory

The Keystone Film Company and the Emergence of Mass Culture

ROB KING

University of California Press

BERKELEY   LOS ANGELES   LONDON

University of California Press, one of the most distinguished university presses in the United States, enriches lives around the world by advancing scholarship in the humanities, social sciences, and natural sciences. Its activities are supported by the UC Press Foundation and by philanthropic contributions from individuals and institutions. For more information, visit www.ucpress.edu.

University of California Press
Berkeley and Los Angeles, California

University of California Press, Ltd.
London, England

Library of Congress Cataloging-in-Publication Data

King, Rob.
    The fun factory : the Keystone Film Company and the
emergence of mass culture / Rob King.
        p.   cm.
    Includes bibliographical references and index.
    ISBN 978-0-520-25537-1 (cloth : alk. paper)
    ISBN 978-0-520-25538-8 (pbk. : alk. paper)
    1. Keystone Film Company I. Title.

PN1999.K4K56   2009
791.43′0973—dc22   2008039252

Manufactured in the United States of America
17   16   15   14   13   12   11   10   09
10 9 8 7 6 5 4 3 2 1

The paper used in this publication meets the minimum requirements
of ANSI/NISO Z39.48–1992 (R 1997) (Permanence of Paper).

For Inie
with love, speed, and thrills

Phantasma

Monstrous shapes are before my eyes. Around me strange sounds arise—gurglings, gaspings, exhalations of the murderer; wheezes, snorts, coughs, groans, shouts, barks, feline laughter. The phantoms in front of me cavort dizzily. They are all gray and shot with light. My head whirls—a thing advances toward me, like a man, but I cannot distinguish its features. It falls! I think it falls, if I see aright in the dimness, and it struggles fearfully to rise. It rises! It falls, more terribly than before! Awful sounds are around me now: I am drowned in a tide of discordant sounds.

The terrible gray shadows whirl faster. I see flying feet, I see the semblance of skirts that are lifted distractingly, I see horrid blows, I see ribald assassination. I see these things, and I do not see them. The horrors have no faces!

This is chaos. Humanity is disintegrating. I am gazing into the dull abyss where everything formed is dissolving into formlessness. The hideous sounds beside me continue. It is good to hear these sounds; it is good to hear a scream, if only to know that another beside one's-self lives—and suffers.

There is nothing before me, now, but insane, mad movement. The colorless maelstrom rushes along like the death of a universe. The nebulae are sun-stabbed more quickly, more frequently; the things that are faceless, though legged and alive, fly wildly, as though pursued by a demoniac hurricane.

I cannot look at the pale mass any more, yet I must look. I am spellbound. I am thonged to the wheels of an optical Juggernaut. My eyes are poniards at my brain, yet I cannot take them from this formless, senseless thing which I cannot understand. The casualties about me increase momentarily; soon I shall be alone, a gray thing like the composite thing before me, formless as the faces that should be and are not, reasonless as their speed—

Thank Heaven, that's over!

May someone kick me all around the block if I ever patronize another Keystone without my spectacles!

—E. B. FREDERICKS, *Photoplay Magazine*, August 1915

Contents

x / Contents

Illustrations

Acknowledgments

My first debt of gratitude is to Sumiko Higashi, for the extraordinary attention she has given my work, for the historical rigor that her own work inspires, and for her many suggestions and detailed reading of this book. I am also deeply indebted to Janet Bergstrom, an incomparable ally and friend, who encouraged and supervised the dissertation on which this is based, and whose generosity and scholarship have provided a model I hope to emulate. Thanks, too, to the other members of my dissertation committee—Thomas Hines, Steven Ross, Vivian Sobchack, and Peter Wollen—all of whom labored gallantly through my roughest drafts. Throughout my efforts, both Tom and Steve lent their astute sensibilities as historians, offering helpful pointers for improving my writing and argumentation. Vivian guided the project at its inception and was a sounding board for my earliest thoughts about Keystone. Later, Mary Francis at the University of California Press took the project on, provided sensitive (and always diplomatic) diagnostics of areas that still needed work, and graciously steered the manuscript through its final rewrites. Working with her colleagues Kalicia Pivirotto and Suzanne Knott has made me wonder if every author has it so good. Many others read or heard portions of my research at various stages. Among them I am especially grateful to Jennifer Bean, Lee Grieveson, Tom Gunning, Charlie Keil, Jonathan Kuntz, Mark Langer, Ross Melnick, Chuck Wolfe, and Josh Yumibe, all of whom have enriched my understanding of early film.

A Mellon Postdoctoral Fellowship at the University of Michigan provided me with the time and opportunity to transform the dissertation into a book draft, and I owe an enormous personal and intellectual debt to two colleagues there, Richard Abel and Giorgio Bertellini. Richard, in particular, has been extraordinarily generous in allowing me to draw upon his own research in local exhibition, and the many hours spent at his and Barbara Hodgdon's kitchen table remain the fondest memories of my time in Ann Arbor.

A variety of archives and their staff have been more than helpful, none more so than the Margaret Herrick Library of the Academy of Motion Picture Arts and Sciences, which was a second home to me during various stages of research. Heartfelt thanks to Barbara Hall, Faye Thompson, Jennifer Romero, Lea Whittington, Matt Severson, Michael Tyler, Robert Cushman, and all the staff at the Core and Special Collections desks for facilitating my work in innumerable ways. Madeline Matz and Zoran Sinobad at the Library of Congress (Motion Picture, Broadcasting, and Recorded Sound Division), the late Graham Melville at London's National Film and Television Archive, Mark Quigley and Rob Stone at the UCLA Film and Television Archive, Brian Meacham at the Academy Film Archive, Elif Rongen-Kaynakci at the Netherlands Filmmuseum, and David Shepard were all generous in making available dozens of Keystone films and images. Geri Laudati, director of the Mills Music Library at the University of Wisconsin-Madison, provided access to the original script for *Tillie's Nightmare.*

As important as the individuals who guided me through the archives are those who aided me as archives in their own right. Thanks, then, to Marilyn Slater, Internet gatekeeper for any and everything related to Mabel Normand; Bryony Dixon, who manages the BFI's Chaplin Project; and Simon Joyce and Jennifer Putzi, for sharing their ongoing research on Jennifer's great-grandfather, Adam Kessel. Also helpful were Ted Maland and Maria Muñoz, who each did important archival groundwork on my behalf during the preparatory stages of this project.

Finally, I should acknowledge debts of a more personal nature: To Frederic and Delphine Brost, who allowed me to housesit at their lovely Granada Hills home during an important year in my writing process. To Zac Fink and Betsy Carver, who taught me hospitality and, most important, gave me reasons not to work all weekend. To my parents and brother, who have understood why I have spent almost a decade poring over crumbling studio documents halfway across the globe, and who have supported and encouraged me every step of the way. But above all to Inie Park, who read and reread every sentence in this book and, in the process, became the Keystone scholar she never wanted to be. Convincing her that my arguments might be right has forced me to clarify my writing and rethink many previously unexamined assumptions. Her love, generosity, and kindness dwarf the spirit in which this book is dedicated to her.

Material from chapter 4 was initially incorporated in "'Made for the Masses with an Appeal to the Classes': The Triangle Film Corporation and the Failure of Highbrow Film Culture," *Cinema Journal* 44.2 (Winter 2005), and an earlier version of chapter 5 appeared as "'Uproarious Inventions': The Keystone Film Company, Modernity, and the Art of the Motor," *Film History* 19.3 (2007).

A note on dates: In what follows I cite the month and year of release of all Keystone films on their first mention in each chapter, except in lists of films where I include a single date citation for multiple titles released within a single month. For non-Keystone films, I cite only the year.

Introduction

In August 1928, the movie fan magazine *Photoplay* published what it billed as "The Best Motion Picture Interview Ever Written": no less than Theodore Dreiser—"The Great American Master of Tragedy"—interviewing Mack Sennett—"The Great American Master of Comedy"—in a unique meeting of minds. A startling confessional on Dreiser's part, the interview's opening paragraphs capture Sennett's reputation at the close of the silent era: "My admiration for Mack Sennett is temperamental and chronic," Dreiser begins. "[T]o me he is a real creative force in the cinema world—a master at interpreting the crude primary impulses of the dub, the numbskull, the weakling, failure, clown, boor, coward, bully." Sennett, Dreiser argues forcefully, belongs in the pantheon of literary comic artistry:

> The interpretive burlesque he achieves is no different from that of Shakespeare, Voltaire, Shaw or Dickens. . . . He is Rabelaisian, he is Voltairish. He has characteristics in common with Sterne, Swift, Shaw, Dickens. . . . Positively, if any writer of this age had brought together in literary form—and in readable English—instead of upon the screen as has Sennett—the pie-throwers, soup-spillers, bomb-tossers, hot-stove-stealers, and what not else of Mr. Sennett's grotesqueries—what a reputation! The respect! The acclaim![1]

This book takes as its subject the motion picture company upon which Sennett's reputation, respect, and acclaim would rest: the Keystone Film Company, a manufacturer of slapstick films between 1912 and 1917. It also takes seriously the cultural importance Dreiser attributed to his films. To do so means rescuing Keystone from nostalgic memories of pie-flinging clowns, knockabout policemen, and haywire automobiles; and it means interrogating its films as vehicles of social consciousness and cultural change. As Dreiser saw it, Sennett was the Rabelais of early twentieth-century American culture, the "greatest creator of joyful burlesque the world has ever known," and a purveyor of "human buffooneries" and "slapstick vigor."[2] But these are homilies that cannot be resolved outside of close examination of the matrix of social forces that shaped Keystone's contribution to American cinema. At the time Sennett launched the studio in 1912, the motion picture industry was in the throes of a drive for respectability—fueled by reformers' ongoing concerns about the moral effects of filmgoing—and was taking steps to upgrade cinema as respectable entertainment for middle-class patrons; yet Keystone's filmmakers unabashedly rejected such refinements, reviving "low" traditions of broad slapstick derived from the popular culture of America's workers. The paradox of this particular conjunction lies at the heart of the present study: the better to understand it, we need to recover the meaning and vitality of turn-of-the-century popular culture; to reveal early film comedy in its shifting capacity for resistance and opposition to the film industry's ideological mainstream; and finally to restore working-class values and traditions to their role in shaping new cultural formations and directions.

COMEDY AND SOCIAL CHANGE

The history of comedy—all comedy, not just on film—is the history of the changing social patterns that produce and permit laughter. This is not simply because comedy requires a frame of social reference but because laughter per se presupposes the experience of social inversion. For Mary Douglas, for example, social change is the precondition of all joking. "[A] joke is seen and allowed when it offers a symbolic pattern of a social pattern occurring at the same time," she writes. "The one social condition necessary for a joke to be enjoyed is that the social group in which it is received should develop the formal characteristics of a 'told' joke: that is, a dominant pattern of relations is challenged by another. If there is no joke in the social structure, no other joking can appear."[3] Laughter thus clusters around points of tension within a given social order, where established patterns and relations are beginning to give way to new patterns, new relations; humor translates those conflicts into jokes and provides an articulation of social contradiction at moments of historic change.

Keystone's five-year career occurred at just such a moment. There is general agreement among historians that significant material change occurred during the decades surrounding the turn of the century. Whether it is a shift from a producer to a consumer economy, the waning of genteel culture and the rise of new managerial classes, the impact of urbanization as both social and sensory phenomenon, the displacement of older work habits by a Fordist regime of mechanized production, the "New Woman" and her challenge to traditional gender ideals—however that change is defined, it is clear that a new order was emerging. One needs to reckon, then, with a fundamental upheaval ("modernity at full throttle," to borrow a phrase of Ben Singer's),[4] a turmoil that not only formed the matrix out of which a new mass culture would be born, but also set the parameters for an enormous proliferation of comic creativity. If the possibility of humor depends upon the presence of a "joke" in the social structure, then turn-of-the-century America was primed for an explosion of comic materials. The market for mirth-making underwent dizzying expansion. Between 1895 and 1906, the number of vaudeville theaters more than doubled, providing more than four hundred venues at which audiences could enjoy a variety of comic acts. Comic strips were introduced to the nation's newspapers in the early 1880s, and joke columns soon became a staple of popular journalism. Beginning in 1895, new amusement parks began to congregate at New York's Coney Island—Sea Lion Park in 1895, Steeplechase Park in 1897, Luna Park in 1903, and Dreamland in 1904. And, until 1908, short comedies constituted over 70 percent of the fiction films enjoyed by working-class audiences in the new storefront nickelodeons.[5]

What did all this hilarity mean? What were its implications for social order? As observers of the time realized, the groundswell of laughter came, not from the drawing rooms of the genteel elite, but from an audience of laborers, recent immigrants, working-class families, and lower-middle-class salaried workers attuned to a new, urban world of popular amusement— "funny entertainment" that sprang "from the soil, like a lusty plant, instead of descending upon us from above," as a *Harper's* writer put it in 1904.[6] In such a climate, discourse on laughter soon became a vehicle for genteel anxieties about social change. For the self-appointed guardians of American culture, the new humor was nothing less than a symptom of civilization's decline. Articles with titles like "The Limitations of Humor" and "The Humor-Fetish" abounded in the nation's magazines as genteel critics struggled to restore order. In 1895, a Columbia professor condemned "The Plague of Jocularity" that he believed was infecting American society. "Instead of that interchange of thoughts, which with all other civilized nations is held to be one of the highest of social pleasures," he complained, "we exchange jokes."[7] Others blamed immigrants for importing a "foreign" sense of humor to American soil. "There's been a great change in the sense of humor in New York," the musical comedy playwright Edward Harrigan commented. "The great influx of Latins and Slavs—who always want to laugh not with you but at you—has brought about a different kind of humor. It isn't native, it isn't New York. It's Paris, or Vienna, or someplace."[8]

Such responses implied a thinly veiled recognition that laughter was a symptom—perhaps even an agent—of social upheaval. But they also implied a commitment to the values of discipline and self-control as preconditions of social order. As a number of cultural historians have observed, the nineteenth-century middle class had developed a moral outlook closely tied to the maintenance of class status and the needs of a producer-oriented economy: self-culture, restraint, and moderation were the cornerstones of that worldview, what the historian Warren Susman termed an ethic of "character," an ideal of "selfhood through obedience" or "fulfillment through sacrifice."[9] Victorian attitudes to comedy were cut from similar cloth: laughter was sanctioned only in moderation, and its value was judged by standards of moral edification and respectful fellow-feeling. Advocates of the new humor might extol the "belly laugh," the "boffo," or the "laugh that kills," but genteel discourse on the comic gravitated toward a different, more contemplative standard: "The test of true comedy," George Meredith declared in an influential 1877 essay, "is that it shall awaken thoughtful laughter."[10] From such a perspective, too much joking could hardly be seen as other than a social impropriety, something to be suppressed. In 1903, a writer for *Atlantic Monthly* wrote of the "hidden danger in a perpetual smile and in a never-ceasing search for the amusing in everything," cautioning that "our keen relish for fun may finally produce a kind of humorous dyspepsia resulting from over-indulgence."[11] Another critic, in an earlier issue of the same journal, spoke out against the "modern fashion of loud and constant laughter in our society" and denounced the current taste in humor on the grounds that it meant "failure to meet the highest claims and issues of life."[12] For such writers, excessive frivolity was tantamount to social irresponsibility.

The genteel assault on laughter was not without important effects, perhaps especially for entertainment entrepreneurs desirous of middle-class approval. The path was set by the vaudeville impresario B. F. Keith, whose efforts to eliminate ribald comedy from his theaters earned his chain the nickname "the Sunday School circuit."[13] From around 1908, filmmakers followed suit, cutting back on comedy productions in favor of more reputable dramatic fare: film comedies declined to a third of all domestic fiction productions from 1907 to 1908 and became even rarer in 1909.[14] (Biograph's production figures reflect the slump: the ratio in 1907 was 83 percent comedies to 17 percent dramas, while in 1908 it became 32 percent comedies to 68 percent dramas.)[15] Even so, the accommodation was never complete; the spirit of the gallery gods could not so simply be suppressed. While purveyors of "high-class" vaudeville were repackaging variety entertainment as a respectable product for middle-class consumption, working-class men found alternative outlets in the scatological comedy available at the growing circuits of burlesque houses. Defenders of popular humor began to answer the challenge of the genteel critique. "There isn't a human being alive who isn't a comedian at heart, who wouldn't get a laugh from his friends, or his wife, or his mother-in-law every day—if he could," the celebrated film comedian John Bunny insisted in 1914. "Making other people laugh is the greatest game in the world—and we are all playing it."[16] The decline in film comedy thus proved short-lived: the emergence of Mack Sennett as a major comic filmmaker, starting in 1911, helped initiate a revival in slapstick production that soon numerically equaled dramatic output. And, as the 1910s continued, the spread of exhibition practices that assigned multiple-reel dramas the role of "feature" attractions also, paradoxically, enshrined slapstick as a necessary supporting act to the longer features.[17] The basic pleasures of comedy became an indispensable part of the evening's entertainment.

If, as T. J. Jackson Lears has argued, the decades surrounding the turn of the century witnessed a "shake-up" in the location of cultural power—the waning of genteel hegemony and the spread of new cultural forms that bubbled up from below—then the growing market for humor was clearly part of that process.[18] It also provides the backdrop against which Keystone's significance must be judged. From its founding, this book will argue, the Keystone Film Company played *the* key role in securing the revitalization of American screen comedy, modernizing the then-disreputable genre of slapstick and defining it as a comic form attuned to the popular values of America's working class. The history of Keystone thus illuminates a major reorientation in American culture.

COMEDY AND CLASSICISM

This is not the kind of approach that has typically been brought to bear either on Keystone or, for that matter, on film comedy more generally. Unfortunately, most existing histories of silent comedy tend to treat their object as a token of nostalgia, a tendency from which even the best studies of Keystone have not been immune. The blame for this lies partly with Mack Sennett himself, whose 1954 autobiography *King of Comedy* (written with the assistance of the journalist Cameron Shipp) openly dismisses historical accuracy in favor of personal myth-making. "No autobiographer . . . ever consented to make a deposition purely for the sake of confessing himself," Sennett writes in its opening pages. "Most of us want to brag, and we'll do it even if we have to invent a few sins to fancy up the account."[19] Subsequent histories of the studio—from Kalton Lahue's *Kops and Custards* (1968) and *Mack Sennett's Keystone* (1971) to Simon Louvish's *Keystone* (2003)—work hard to clear their way through Sennett's tall tales but fail to steer their accounts out of the haze of nostalgia to which the studio and its films have long been consigned.[20] This is not to discount the research of these authors, but it is to criticize an approach that insulates Keystone from the movement of history and, in its worst moments, fetishizes questions of utter irrelevance to an understanding of the studio's role in American culture: Whose idea was it to throw the first custard pie? Why didn't Sennett marry Mabel Normand? (leading Louvish to ask: Was he gay?) Was he involved in the murder of the director William Desmond Taylor?

Formalist academic analyses of slapstick's "difference" from the norms of dramatic filmmaking might well be criticized on related grounds. To the extent that the study of dramatic filmmaking has set the terms of debate in film history, comedy has commonly been classified and explained (away) as one of narrative cinema's principal "others." Most major academic works on comic cinema are thus less concerned with the particularities of its historical determinants than with conceptualizing comedy's distance from classical filmmaking conventions. For Steve Seidman, for example, the dominant tradition of narrative cinema is "hermetic," partaking of a closed narrative structure, while comedy is "nonhermetic," granting the comedian scope for the fictional ruptures that narrative cinema typically seeks to contain (e.g., looks into the camera, direct address, etc.).[21] For Donald Crafton, the gags of early slapstick comedies become a source of narrative "excess"—the pie in the face, the slip on a banana skin, the burst of digressive violence upon which slapstick thrives—that impedes the narrative's development and disrupts the storytelling logic of classical Hollywood cinema.[22] Finally, a number of scholars have shifted the emphasis onto issues of spectatorship, using comedy to challenge spectator theory's preoccupation with the visual sense and its commitment to an idealist notion of the distanced, disembodied gaze. Unlike many dramatic genres, these scholars argue, comedy makes it clear that spectatorship is not in fact so distanced, that the spectator's body is crucially implicated in the viewing process: in comedy, the spectator *laughs,* overwhelmed by a spasmodic loss of bodily control (titters, chuckles, guffaws) that simply does not fit the model of the controlling, all-seeing spectator-voyeur that has dominated theories of classical spectatorship.[23]

The basic insight common to all these approaches—that slapstick differs from the dominant modalities of classical narrative cinema—is discussed in greater detail in chapter 3 of this book. For the present, however, it is worth asking what their analyses suggest about the *history* of film comedy. Characteristic here is the writers' dialectical approach to their definitions: the principles of classical Hollywood cinema serve their arguments as the measure (or thesis) against which comedy is then defined (as antithesis). As a result, however, issues of historical development, of industrial and social context, are typically glossed over, surviving merely as minor modifications in the basic conceptual apparatus: comedy is frozen within the bounds of its own alterity, with scant attention paid to its changing function either as an industrial commodity or as a form of cultural expression. The point is particularly clear in the structural analyses of Seidman, for whom comedy is an essentially stable category, its basic properties being a constant across the films of comedians as historically diverse as Buster Keaton, the Marx Brothers, and Red Skelton.[24] But it is often no less evident in the case of those scholars who approach comedy as a "bodily oriented genre" and treat laughter as solely a physiological response, as though it occurred outside changing historical conditions of appropriateness.[25] Such approaches, in short, are ultimately not dialectical enough: for, having identified comedy's heterogeneity, they then fail to take the further step that would inquire into the social reasons for that heterogeneity.

It is a basic tenet of Marxist historiography that such reasons exist, that there is "always a social basis," as Raymond Williams insists, for cultural forms that are "alternative or oppositional to the dominant elements."[26] Comedy is in the last resort a social gesture, not merely a formal construct; and a fully historical formalism would seek to uncover the stealthy motions of social history in slapstick's much-vaunted difference. "Alternative" cultural forms, for such an approach, may indicate the emergence of new cultural formations, perhaps even the coming to consciousness of new classes. They will always be subject to processes of "incorporation," wherein the dominant culture attempts to absorb them into the cultural mainstream; they will, in the end, be a staging ground for cultural struggle, both an area of resistance to the dominant culture and a site that the dominant culture seeks to appropriate for its own ends. This is not naïvely to equate difference with subversion—there is a distinction, Williams insists, between "alternative" and "oppositional" practices[27]— but it is to insist on the importance of alternative forms as a ground upon which social transformations may be worked out. Any attempt to write the history of film comedy in these terms requires a historiographic frame- work that not only acknowledges comedy's formal differences but also sit- uates those differences in their proper place in the dialogical system of social class. Applied to Keystone, such an approach entails exploring the studio's films as an entry point to a fuller illumination of conditions of cul- tural production and consumption at a time of crisis and transition in turn- of-the-century American society.

COMEDY AND POPULAR CULTURE

Why was Keystone—today mostly remembered for supposedly inaugu- rating a "golden age" in American film comedy—an exemplar of cultural change in the early twentieth century? At what precise confluence of social and cultural forces should the studio's significance be located? In its broad- est strokes, this book places Keystone's development in the context of a major reorientation in the meaning and function of culture in turn-of-the- century America. The complex passage from Victorian culture to the modern era involved, among many other changes, a profound transforma- tion in the relationship between culture and social class, what might be described as the shift from a hierarchical cultural order that reinforced social divisions to a commercially driven "mass" culture that tended to obscure those divisions. It is this trajectory that forms the backdrop for my study of the Keystone Film Company.

One needs to begin here with the recognition that the cultural hierar- chies that everywhere pervaded the Victorian era—and that created the space from which slapstick initially emerged as a style of stage comedy— were, at the turn of the century, still relatively recent concepts, the cre- ations of urban elites who had sought to distance themselves from the tastes and practices of workers and immigrants. Whereas the antebellum ideal had been one of a harmonious, integrative civic life, this had become less and less true during the late nineteenth century, as cultural tastes came to be defined in ways that reinforced social differences. So-called true or highbrow culture became synonymous with the exclusive products of the museum, the opera house, and the concert hall, to be enjoyed and protected by the initiated. Historians have examined the multidimensional power of this development both to cordon off high culture for the edification of the elite and as a basis from which reformers could control the recreation of the lower orders.[28] But it also, crucially, set parameters within which popular forms flourished as an aesthetic and ideological alternative to the dominant culture: forced to inhabit a separate cultural and moral terrain, America's lower classes developed cultural idioms that diverged from, and were opposed to, the practices of the genteel middle class.

Since it is an essential part of my argument that slapstick comedy was one of these idioms, a number of points need to be stressed about this "alternative" culture, as posited in this study. Perhaps most important, this was a *popular* culture in the strict sense suggested by Stuart Hall, that is, a culture rooted in and shaped by the material conditions of what Hall calls the "excluded classes." Popular culture, as Hall describes it, refers to that alliance of classes and forces that constitute the "culture of the oppressed," and it exists in a relation of difference from, and of continuous struggle against, the "culture of the power-bloc."[29] Applied to turn-of-the-century America, such a definition opens up important terrain for considering both the material conditions in which working-class culture had its roots and that culture's function in defining class identity. Key here is the relation between the growth of cheap amusements during the late nineteenth century and the rise of a self-conscious working class. With the depression of 1873 and the spread of unemployment, poverty, and strikes in the years that followed, social contrasts in America had reached an unprecedented pitch. The census of 1890 revealed that, out of 12 million families living in the United States, 11 million earned incomes under $1,200 a year, with the average income for this group a mere $380 (far below the poverty level).[30] Such divergences in income were partly the result of widening rifts within the spectrum of employment itself—specifically, the expansion of a "nonmanual" ("white-collar") workforce located hierarchically above the "manual" working class and the radical transformation of manual labor under the aegis of industrial technologies. The transition from an artisanal to an industrial culture, in particular, had entailed severe restructuring of work habits, resulting in a deskilled labor force subject to tedious factory routine. Meanwhile, unprecedented immigration exacerbated perceptions of class difference: with 13 million "new" immigrants from southern, eastern, and central Europe (excluding Germany) arriving between 1886 and 1925, the social disenfranchisement of workers was increasingly overlaid with an aura of otherness, associated with stereotypes of plaintive Jews, criminal Italians, and dim-witted Slovaks.[31] Labor thus signified inequities that could be, and were, displaced by debates about national belonging.

Yet class relations were never simply a matter of ethnocultural groupings, and class identity cannot be understood simply as an issue of individual income or relation to the means of production. Hall's definition of popular culture as an arena of potential "resistance" implies a perspective that also locates class distinctions in *cultural practice:* what becomes central here is the idea of culture not simply as an articulation of pre-given traditions, but of the active role it plays in defining a sense of class belonging among its consumers.[32] Rather than interpreting the popular culture of America's workers simply as a culture of penury and exclusion, one can see it, then, as a consciously structured system of differences vis-à-vis the dominant ideology, a realm of practices and metaphors that defined class membership by contesting the values of the genteel middle class. The point is well made by Roy Rosenzweig, who interprets the customs of working-class saloon-going—the ethic of mutuality and solidarity that undergirded the phenomenon of "treating," the unrepentant squandering of wages on alcohol—as an alternate, proletarian value system, distinct from the dominant ethos of self-discipline and social mobility.[33]

The decades surrounding the turn of the century present a crucial watershed in this respect, because an array of new commercial amusements arose to give expression to these cleavages. Between 1890 and 1920, the nation's wage earners succeeded in reducing the working week from sixty hours to fifty-one, while the real wages of nonfarm employees rose by 35 percent for the same period.[34] With more time and money for recreation than ever before, blue-collar workers helped shape new types of commercial recreation that extended the challenge to genteel norms. The emerging opposition took many forms, but none more characteristic than the boundary that separated a popular aesthetic of sensation from the genteel culture of sentiment. As a number of historians have suggested, the development of middle-class consciousness had been predicated since the mid-nineteenth century on an idealized notion of femininity as moral guardianship: a broader sentimentalization of middle-class culture emerged that aligned the domestic sphere with uplift and transcendence, as evident in genteel-sentimental fiction, in publications like *Ladies' Home Journal,* and in women's participation in social reform. Such a worldview supplemented the Protestant ethic of industry (embodied in the notion of "character") with a sacralized vision of the home as a space of nurture and renewal, and it became the basis for a feminized concept of culture—what historians have called a "cult of domesticity"—predicated upon spiritual and emotional values as the cornerstones of moral worth.[35]

During roughly the same period, however, the rapid growth of cheap commercial amusements supported an opposed idiom of sensationalism that emphasized, not transcendence, but materiality and corporeality, which observers came to interpret as a response to the deprivations of working-class life. The sensationalism of cheap theater was explicable inasmuch as "dull intellects and feeble wills require the stimulus of sensationalism," Rollin Lynde Hartt argued in 1909. "[T]he Underworld has never achieved that divorce betwixt flesh and spirit which is our Puritan heritage."[36] The Baptist theologian Walter Rauschenbusch explained the "debauchery" of popular culture in a similar vein, seeing it as a reaction to the deadening routine of the workplace: "The long hours and the high speed and pressure of industry use up the vitality of all except the most capable. An exhausted body craves rest, change, and stimulus, but it responds only to strong and coarse stimulation."[37] From the belly laugh of variety entertainment to the "blood and thunder" scenes of cheap melodrama, from the thrills of the amusement park ride to the physical contact of the dance hall, popular forms thus reflected a hunger for intense bodily stimulation that, to genteel tastes, was the very definition of vulgarity. An interest in physical spectacle and stimulation made sensationalism an aesthetic mode that corresponded to an emphasis on laboring bodies and the "embodied relationships that workers have to power," Shelley Streeby observes.[38] The slapstick humor of vaudeville's "nut acts," "bone crunchers," and "facial" and "knockabout" clowns was a part of this culture of sensationalism; and, if its pleasures contradicted genteel emphasis on transcendence, they nonetheless crystallized the embodied orientation of working-class culture and experience.

This was not, it should be noted, a culture whose boundaries were precisely those of class: far from being exclusively aligned with urban workers, popular amusements formed part of a broader "plebeian" culture shared by factory laborers, shopkeepers, and clerical workers alike.[39] (A 1911 statistical survey of New York's vaudeville audience, for example, found it to be 60 percent "working class," 36 percent "clerical," and 4 percent "vagrant," "gamine," and "leisured.")[40] Nor was this culture in any way autonomous, being deeply dependent on commercial dynamics: whether they ran amusement parks, operated dance halls, or owned nickelodeons, recreational entrepreneurs played an important role in the commercialization of working-class leisure in the decades surrounding the turn of the century.[41] Indeed, it was precisely this commercial element that made turn-of-the-century working-class cultural practices so crucial to the formation of modern mass culture. Caught up in the accelerating forces of the marketplace, the world of popular amusements quickly outstripped its original audience and, in the process, produced a new cultural orientation. As Francis Couvares shrewdly observes, "The very 'merchants of leisure' who had emerged from and invigorated local plebeian culture ultimately subverted it by forging the links of a nationwide, centralized mass culture industry."[42] By the 1890s, vaudeville impresarios like B. F. Keith and E. F. Albee were building theater circuits that brought their shows to cities across the country, successfully repackaging the boozy, licentious variety theater of the concert saloon as cross-class entertainment.[43] With the formation of the National League in 1880, baseball shed the disreputability of the "Beer and Whiskey League" of the post–Civil War years and began its transformation into the "nation's pastime."[44] And, during the first decades of the twentieth century, former nickelodeon operators like Carl Laemmle and William Fox rose to become presidents of major film companies catering to nationwide "movie-mad" audiences.

By the onset of World War I, the outlines of a new mass culture had begun to take shape. This culture was guided by the dictates of the market; it sought to integrate, rather than to divide, audiences; and it established the production of cultural goods on a rationalized, assembly-line basis (hence the phrase "culture industry").[45] Where earlier cultural distinctions had served to reinforce class hierarchy, the new system obscured class differences by burying them within widely shared (hence widely profitable) cultural experiences. As Max Weber has argued, the market overrides cultural distinctions, requiring the producers of cultural goods to fuse genres and cross boundaries to achieve the broadest spectrum of appeal.[46] In line with this approach, this book explores the emergence of mass culture as a complex, often unpredictable system of commercial interactions between different cultural forms and traditions. The new mass culture was, I will argue, a culture of aesthetic hybridization, one that fused high and popular categories in the effort to appeal across class lines.[47]

The five-year career of the Keystone Film Company everywhere bears the imprint of these transformations. Keystone brought together a group of filmmakers from immigrant, working-class backgrounds, most of whom came to the studio with experience in popular theater and burlesque. Together, they helped chart new cultural directions. During the studio's early years, they fashioned a style of film comedy formed from the roughhouse traditions of working-class comic theater, and they flouted the Protestant moralism of genteel culture. The world of Keystone's early films was a separate, alternative world, removed from developments in dramatic filmmaking during the early 1910s and opposed to the ideological presuppositions that shaped those developments. While filmmakers like D. W. Griffith and Cecil B. DeMille sought to legitimate cinema for genteel tastes, Keystone defined a more properly popular comic style that addressed the values and concerns of the lower classes.

A history of Keystone can thus illuminate much about the place and role of popular culture at the advent of modern society—in particular how popular forms like slapstick were inscribed with the accents and values of working-class audiences as they negotiated the discontinuities of modern life. Yet Keystone's career also reveals how those accents were ultimately softened and deferred by the emergence of mass culture. Beginning in 1915, significant changes began to occur in the studio's comic style, when the studio was swept up in the formation of new corporate organizations designed to market film to a cross-class audience. Faced with the commercial imperative of having to reach out to a larger public—one that would include both men and women, blue-collar and white-collar viewers, the working and genteel classes—Keystone's filmmakers innovated with comic forms built on mechanical spectacle, sentimental narratives, and the titillating display of the famous "Bathing Beauties." What resulted was a style of comedy that substantially dissolved slapstick's significance as a site for engaging the conflicts and pressures of working-class experience, even as it remained profoundly indebted to the sensationalism of popular comic traditions. Sennett himself insisted on those continuities in his interview with Theodor Dreiser, saying:

> I don't know that there is any actual change in the [kind of comedy] that makes people laugh, although there is some, I guess, in the way it's presented. . . . Fifteen years ago the settings could be cruder than they are today, and a waiter in shirt sleeves and no collar could spill soup down the shirt front of a laborer and get a laugh, and that in some ordinary one-armed place not very nice to look at. Today an American comedy audience seems to want better surroundings or settings. And if the waiter is of the Ritz or Ambassador type, and the customer a gentleman in evening clothes—or a lord—so much the better![48]

Shirtsleeves or evening clothes, laborers or lords: the spilling of the soup remains the same. The development of Keystone's comic style illumines the matrix of both the displacements *and* the continuities linking the culture of America's workers to the emergence of a modern culture industry.

In what follows, then, I ask two principal questions: what were the material connections that bound Keystone's early comic style to the experiences and practices of the turn-of-the-century working class? And how did the development of mass culture transform Keystone's place in the cultural hierarchy of the United States? To explore these issues I address questions of social history and film aesthetics, of economics and cultural theory, drawing on a range of archival material including extant film prints and trade press and newspaper commentary. Aside from these, the study also makes use of collections of studio documents—including personal correspondence, contracts, accounts, and production files—held in the Academy of Motion Picture Arts and Sciences' Margaret Herrick Library and the Wisconsin Historical Society.

My investigation proceeds in two sections, each comprising three chapters. Part I considers Keystone's relation to popular cultural practices in early-twentieth-century America, examining the studio's complex engagement with the values of the urban proletariat (chapter 1) and considering the films' representations of ethnic difference in relation to changing patterns of working-class identity (chapter 2). By way of a case study, the first part ends with an analysis of the studio's only feature-length production, the 1914 six-reel comedy *Tillie's Punctured Romance* (chapter 3). The challenge of the feature-length format for Keystone was how to integrate its trademark disjunctive slapstick with a protracted and continuous story: understanding how Keystone's filmmakers met that challenge sheds light on their indebtedness to popular comic tastes and traditions.

Part II opens with an examination of the studio's incorporation into the Triangle Film Corporation, a production and distribution concern that Keystone joined in 1915 as part of a commercial enterprise to market films for genteel consumption (chapter 4). As I suggest, the troubled history of Triangle holds up a mirror to a far broader cultural reorientation in which the ethical and aesthetic precepts of the genteel classes were undermined by the growth of a commercially-driven culture industry. It also illuminates the tangled, unpredictable hybridizations of "high" and "popular" traditions out of which the new mass culture would be born.

Keystone participated in that birth, and this book concludes by examining two of the studio's most celebrated contributions to the changing cultural landscape: the sensational display of "mechanical contrivances" (chapter 5) and the commercial exploitation of the Bathing Beauties (chapter 6). As a way of framing these changes, the final chapters are informed by Georg Lukács's concept of "reification," that is, the erasure of traditional structures of meaning and social distinctions from mass cultural commodities.[49] Public fascination with technological progress and the spread of modern publicity techniques constituted key topoi of the new mass culture, and they promoted shared modes of perception that obscured recognition of the class differences on which that culture was founded.

Keystone's later films and publicity campaigns register these displacements by submerging working-class cultural traditions and iconography—the realm of popular practices and values on which the studio's earlier output had been founded—beneath a reified display of mechanical novelties and scantily clad female bodies. They thus ironically paved the way, this book concludes, for the ideological rewriting that has continued to shape nostalgic perceptions of Keystone's output.

.   .   .

In titling this book, I have borrowed a phrase used at the time to describe the Keystone studios, but one that also signals my intention to reconcile the interpretation of comedy ("fun") with the study of working-class culture and experience ("factory"). Avoiding both a purely aesthetic interpretation of Keystone's films or a narrow industrial history, I have tried in what follows to develop a topology that ties each of these areas to questions of social formation. Such an approach best clarifies Keystone's significance as a studio that straddled both the popular culture of America's workers and a mass culture that shifted into high gear during the 1910s. But it is also the kind of approach best suited to elucidate this book's central assumption— namely, that understanding laughter is a way of understanding social change. "Our specialty was exasperated dignity and the discombobulation of Authority," Mack Sennett recalled in later years. "We whaled the daylights out of everything in sight with our bed slats. And we had fun doing it."[50] Keystone's clowns did more than simply discombobulate Authority: they pointed the way to a new social order, one that bequeathed descendants to our own time.

PART I

"Satire in Overalls"

The Keystone Film Company and Popular Culture

1. "The Fun Factory"

Class, Comedy, and Popular Culture, 1912–1914

One has to hand this to the Americans: with slapstick films they have created a form that offers a counterweight to their reality. If in that reality they subject the world to an often unbearable discipline, the film in turn dismantles this self-imposed order quite forcefully.

SIEGFRIED KRACAUER, *"Artistisches und Amerikanisches" (1926)*

When, in 1912, the *Moving Picture World* critic W. Stephen Bush lamented the "absence of genuine humor" in a majority of comic films, he was merely making explicit a perception that had long been accepted at the grass-roots level.[1] Feeling short-changed by an industry that had drastically cut back its comedy output since 1908, theater owners had taken to writing to trade journals to voice their dissatisfactions. "There is too much high class drama, which cannot be understood by the average working man," noted one such exhibitor. "A very large proportion seems to thoroughly enjoy the old Essanay slap-stick variety."[2] Filmmakers, too, acknowledged the demand: "Can you write a good comedy?" *Photoplay* asked its readers in October 1912. "Try it, for the producer will pay more attention to it just now than any other."[3] "Comedies, comedies, comedies," a studio scenarist demanded in another issue of the same publication. "Get your scriptwriting readers to try their hand at comedies; we need them, all film producers want them."[4]

No doubt there was reason to be thankful, then, when the formation of a new, all-comedy company was announced that fall. No doubt, too, the new concern would benefit from the perceived weakness of its competition. Within weeks of its first releases, fan magazines were heaping praise on "the good work of the new company," observing that it had become "in a very short time one of the most popular brands on the screen."[5] The Keystone Film Company had been born.

That much—and that much alone—can be stated with confidence. The picture blurs, however, when we ask *why* Keystone proved so popular. The above account might suggest a simple issue of supply and demand; and, in film history, this is how Keystone's early success has usually been interpreted. For Kalton Lahue, Keystone prospered because exhibitors were beginning "to cry out for more and better comedies"; for Eileen Bowser, the company was a "veritable fountain of slapstick" that relieved the drought of previous years.[6] Such an interpretation, valid as far as it goes, leaves untouched the question of content: what was it about Keystone films—as opposed to comedies of other brands—that made them such a success? After all, there *were* other comic filmmakers in the years immediately prior to Keystone's birth, and many of them had achieved considerable popularity by the time Keystone arrived on the scene. The comedies of French manufacturer Pathé Frères continued to score well on the American market during this period, with the comic Max Linder frequently singled out by critics as one of "the world's greatest moving picture comedians" or, more simply, "a sure draw."[7] The Essanay comedian Augustus Carney created the character of "Alkali Ike" in the spring of 1911 and, beginning with *Alkali Ike's Auto* (May 1911), launched a series of popular comedies set in the fictional western town of Snakeville: such was their success that by late 1912, Carney's personal appearances at vaudeville houses were provoking "wild demonstrations on the part of his admirers," and department stores began selling Alkali Ike dolls at $1.50 apiece.[8] Nor was Carney's popularity unchallenged among homegrown comedians and producers. Until his death in 1915, Vitagraph's rotund John Bunny won consistent acclaim for his appearances in domestic comedies, achieving a measure of international fame in the process. Production figures at Biograph likewise reflect a renewed interest in comedy, with comic films accounting for 43 and 48 percent of the studio's fiction output in 1911 and 1912 respectively (compared to a low of 32 percent in 1908).[9]

It was, in fact, at Biograph that many of Keystone's founding members, including the company's head, Mack Sennett, got their start in motion pictures; still, it would not be until their work for Keystone that critics began to speak of a new standard—a breakthrough, even—in comic filmmaking. As *Moving Picture World* claimed only a year after the company's debut: "If you are in communication with any comedy company and the editor has tried to tell you what is wanted, it's dollars to doughnuts that you've been told, 'like Keystone.' "[10] Again, then: *why* Keystone? Years later, Sennett offered a simple answer, situating the studio's success in terms of the culture and values of his audience. "Motion picture audiences," he suggested, "are seldom made up one hundred per cent of tycoons, heroes, or millionaires." For the "common people," he noted, there can be nothing funnier than "the reduction of authority to absurdity," and it was this principle that became the centerpiece of his comedy.[11] An examination of Keystone's comic principles will have to wait until later in this chapter, but Sennett's argument offers a useful starting point for analysis. It is true that motion picture audiences hardly consisted of tycoons and millionaires: a 1910 Russell Sage Foundation survey claimed that fully 78 percent of New York City's moviegoers came from the blue-collar sector; and workers and their families continued to compose the bulk of the moviegoing public at least until World War I.[12] If Keystone's success cannot adequately be described in terms of supply and demand, then it seems appropriate to frame the problem in terms that look to the sociology of cultural production, examining how the studio's films engaged the values and practices of the "common people" of whom Sennett wrote. For the present chapter, this means interpreting Keystone—its films, its mode of production, and extra-textual discourse on the studio—in terms of the material connections that bound it to the culture, values, and experiences of America's urban working class. And it means asking a tiered series of questions leading from the conditions of working-class life to the formal properties of Keystone's output. Who were the key filmmakers and what were their social backgrounds? What was work like at Keystone and how can it be understood in relation to workers' experiences of labor? Where did Keystone position its product relative to film industry developments and how did its output address questions of social hierarchy? What, finally, were the pleasures and meanings that the films offered their working-class audience? The answers to these questions require a close reading of Keystone's early years; but they also promise a historical understanding of slapstick as specifically and structurally connected to turn-of-the-century class formation: at once a "sociology" and an "aesthetics."[13]

"GO DOWN TO THE BOWERY AND START IN BURLESQUE": POPULAR CULTURE AND THE WORKING CLASS

In 1900, a twenty-year-old boilermaker, tired of the debilitating heat and backbreaking toil of his ten-hour-a-day job at the local ironworks, left the family boardinghouse in East Berlin, Connecticut, and journeyed to New York in the hope of finding success at the Metropolitan Opera. Armed with a letter of introduction from the musical comedy star Marie Dressler, the young Irish-Canadian immigrant headed for the offices of David Belasco, then the most celebrated impresario of the Broadway stage. The brief audition that followed left Belasco deeply unimpressed. "Let's be practical about you," Belasco supposedly remarked. "If you won't go home, young man, the best way for you to start is this: go down to the Bowery and start in burlesque. . . . And it strikes me forcefully that burlesque is something you might be uncommonly good at."[14]

Such, in brief, was Sennett's version of his entry into show business, as recounted in his 1954 autobiography *King of Comedy*. The hard facts, recently uncovered by the film historian Simon Louvish, uncover a slightly different narrative, giving the lie somewhat to Sennett's rugged self-image as "The Iron Boy Who Wanted to Sing at the Met" (Louvish's phrase). Sennett's career as a boilermaker seems, in fact, to have lasted all of one year (1897), after which the family moved to Northampton, Mass., where he worked at a pulp mill, remaining there until at least 1901.[15] Yet whatever its embellishments, Sennett's account remains of interest for the glimpse it provides into the cultural milieu of turn-of-the-century New York. American urban culture had, by this time, taken on the aspect of a hierarchically ordered world, in which leisure and recreational pursuits were stratified along lines determined by ethnicity, gender, and, above all, class. Broadway was the mecca of theatrical entertainment for New York's leisured classes, and immigrant workers (whether boilermakers or pulp mill employees) simply belonged elsewhere. Fictitious or not, Belasco's injunction to "go down to the Bowery and start in burlesque" resonates with the force of cultural policing, an attempt to regulate the boundaries linking cultural practice and class status. Sennett himself remembered Broadway as a deeply alienating place, "as far removed from anything in my experience as Versailles from a general store in Vermont." The theatrical stars, he recalled, moved in a world of "tail coats, ermine wraps, and tasteful supper parties that were stimulating to hear about but in which I naturally had no part."[16]

Not that there was no entertainment for urban workers and immigrants. The recreational world of the working class was, however, quite different from the culture of the dominant classes. By the late nineteenth century, a panoply of cheap amusements had developed outside the orbit of the "respectable" middle-class world of concert halls, museums, and the legitimate stage. Temporally distinct from the discipline of the workplace and spatially separate from the responsibilities of home, burlesque houses and saloons offered wage-earning men a refuge from the demands of their daily lives.[17] Dance halls and amusement parks fomented a mixed-sex (or "heterosocial") culture in which young working women experimented with new attitudes toward sexual expressiveness and personal style.[18] A new culture of popular sensationalism—whose forms included dime-novels, "blood and thunder" stage melodrama, and traveling daredevil acts, among others—was supplying working-class and white-collar customers with commodified thrills that vividly contradicted the genteel interpretation of culture as, in Matthew Arnold's words, "the study and pursuit of perfection."[19] To these sites of recreation, another would soon be added, one that would lead to the massive expansion of the filmmaking industry in which Sennett eventually made his name: the crude storefront "nickelodeons" in which immigrant and native-born workers enjoyed short, one-reel movies for the price of a nickel or a dime.

But it was at a burlesque house that Sennett first encountered this milieu, and it proved to be an experience he would remember the rest of his life. A bawdy, variety-style entertainment largely frequented by working men, burlesque appealed to Sennett with the force of revelation. "The round, fat girls in nothing much doing their bumps and grinds, the German-dialect comedians, and especially the cops and tramps with their bed slats and bladders appealed to me as being funny people. Their approach to life was earthy and understandable. They whaled the daylights out of pretension. They made fun of themselves and the human race. They reduced convention, dogma, stuffed shirts, and Authority to nonsense, and then blossomed into pandemonium. . . . [A]s a little guy, as a thoroughly accredited representative of the Common Man . . . , I thought all this was delightful."[20] Here was a form of theater that, as Sennett described it, allowed workers to escape feelings of alienation and exclusion, to laugh at the spectacle of a world in which conventions and hierarchies were gleefully overturned. Sennett had found a theatrical milieu with which he could identify, and soon afterward, he made his debut (as the back end of a pantomime horse, he recalled) at Miner's Bowery Burlesque.[21]

Sennett's pungent description of burlesque provides a useful entry point for our analysis, since it foregrounds relations tying popular humor to the experiences of the urban working class. Physical comedy was, of course, hardly an invention of the New World: in the modern era, its lineage extends back to, and beyond, European street theater of the seventeenth and eighteenth centuries, such as *commedia dell'arte* and forms of carnival. (It was, in fact, English-style clowning that provided the first formalized tradition of knockabout on U.S. soil, following the development of the circus during the Jacksonian era and the popularity of circus clowns like John Gosson.)[22] Knockabout's characteristically American form only emerged in the latter half of the nineteenth century, through contact with the sphere of working-class leisure. Slapstick was paradigmatic of the postbellum culture of working-class sensationalism, at once intensely corporeal and resoundingly opposed to cultivated standards. The clown here assumed a distinctly proletarian stance, speaking to, for, and about the working class: the "nut" comics and knockabout turns that began to appear in concert saloons of the 1860s and 1870s were commonly stage Irishmen, in whose performances tumble-down comedy was combined with songs about labor, strikes, and payday.[23] Vaudeville historian Douglas Gilbert describes the popular performers Needham and Kelly, who did a song-and-clog-dance act ("We can dig a sewer, lay a pipe or carry the hod / . . . We're the advocates of all hard workin' men") that ended in "bumps"—jargon for bruising falls on the head, neck, and shoulders.[24] Physical humor, in such instances, took on the lineaments of a "popular realist" aesthetic, providing a nearly direct translation of workers' embodied relation to labor into forms of comic spectacle.[25]

It was this relation to working-class culture that supported slapstick's full flowering in the 1880s and 1890s, with the massive expansion of the market for cheap amusements. "It was because of the great number of these cheap places of amusement and the impulse that they gave to jig-dancing, the singing of comic songs, and the reproduction of knockabout variety acts among the boys of the town," the *Harper's Weekly* critic James L. Ford wrote in 1904, that there had emerged a "positive mania" for the slapstick style, as pioneered by performers like Weber and Fields and Dick and Sam Bernard.[26] Explanations for that "mania" differed at the time—Ford attributed it to a need for "pure diversion" among those subjected to the pace of modern industry, others saw in it a reflection of "that common calamity of proletarianism, arrested development"—but few disputed its connection to the disreputable tastes of the urban proletariat.[27] Slapstick, in its late-nineteenth-century development, became increasingly incompatible with refinement: one of the familiar clichés of comedy producers seeking "respectability" was the claim that they had excised all rough-and-tumble from their shows. Such humor even became a target of repressive legislation in New York when, for a brief period in late 1907, blue laws were invoked to prohibit Sunday performances of "acrobatic acts, juggling, trained animals, and 'slapstick' acts."[28]

If, then, slapstick differed from the standards of genteel culture, those differences were themselves rooted in the material conditions of working-class life and were significant in large part as a function of class hierarchy. Cheap theater, as a major repository of such humor, became a venue in which performers and audience members could set forth and express, through their bodies, alternate values and standards of comportment. Sennett's own account clearly records the worker's vicarious pleasure in witnessing genteel standards subverted ("convention, dogma, stuffed shirts, and Authority [reduced] to nonsense"). "Amateur nights" meanwhile offered an institutionalized setting in which would-be comics could, in turn, emulate those subversions. Popular comedy thus offered a framework within which workers' fantasies and aspirations took shape, a corporeal horizon for negotiating alienated social relations at the level of direct physical immediacy. In a world where opportunities were limited for people with little education or capital, a career in vaudeville or burlesque even held out possibilities for upward mobility, promising an alternate route to wealth and status: as Minnie Marx, mother of the Marx Brothers, put it, "Where else can people who don't know anything make so much money?"[29] This was a sentiment that would have rung true for the filmmakers and performers who came together to form the Keystone Film Company: one way or another, most of them lay beyond the pale of native-born, middle-class society; one way or another, most arrived at comic careers as a way of throwing off the shackles of social circumstance. Accordingly, a comparison of their early careers sheds light on the lines of intersection that bound the forms of popular culture to the personalities in which they were embodied.

The pattern is exemplified by the early biography of Mack Sennett, the onetime boilermaker who came to Broadway with a self-bestowed name and a keen desire to escape the daily grind. Born Michael Sinnott, the future filmmaker was raised within the immigrant and working-class communities in which popular amusements had their roots, and his childhood experiences left him with a lifelong empathy for the values of working people. Recalling life on the Quebec farm where he grew up, Sennett fondly remembered the boisterous Irish-Canadian wakes in which his uncle would perform "house-shattering jigs" while other men would "'twist the wrist,' straining their ham-sized biceps to see who could force the other man's hand to the table."[30] After moving to the steelmaking town of East Berlin, Connecticut, in 1897, the Sinnott family fell into the pattern of many Irish immigrants in America, abandoning farm life to find unskilled factory work—in young Michael Sinnott's case, a job at the American Iron Works. (Historians of Irish immigrant experience have noted how the Irish were primarily a phenomenon of urban life in the mid-to-late-nineteenth-century United States, where they constituted a large body of urban floating labor, virtually a "new" working class of unskilled immigrants.)[31] There, he formed close associations with fellow ironworkers who lodged at his mother's boardinghouse. They were, Sennett remembered, "big men with appetites, and the quantities of cabbage, meat loaf, fresh hot bread, biscuits, pie, buttermilk, and gallon tins of coffee they consumed were prodigious. . . . In the evening they gathered around the fireplace in the living room to discuss William Jennings Bryan and William Howard Taft, or to play checkers, and cribbage, or to talk shop." Yet his own experience at the ironworks—"struggling, lifting, hammering, and getting burned"— left him unsatisfied and, by his own account, he channeled his aspirations into daily singing lessons.[32]

His newfound operatic ambitions seem to have led him to Broadway some time in early 1902, but brought little of the success he sought. Although there is scant verifiable information about this period in his life, it appears that Sennett failed to progress beyond anonymous appearances as a chorus boy in musical comedies and operettas. The titles listed in his autobiography include *King Dodo* (1902), *A Chinese Honeymoon* (1902), and *Mlle. Modiste* (1906), but much of his chorus work seems to have been performed at the Casino Theatre, a cheap musical comedy house that, according to New York's *Dramatic Mirror*, appealed to "the Tenderloin element."[33] Only once did Sennett receive any kind of credit notice from the theatrical press—for what must have been a fairly inauspicious role as "Servant" in Rida Johnson Young's 1907 hit *The Boys of Company B*.[34]

Sennett's frustrations, as recounted in his autobiography, point to an important ambivalence in his own social attitudes. Imbued with a commoner's distaste for social airs, he was caught between desire for theatrical success and thinly veiled resentment of the privileged world in which Broadway stars moved. Although he later admitted to having been "awed" by Broadway, he nonetheless dismissed the "high tones" of theatrical society as the "kind of thing [that] never did become my métier."[35] He may have wanted to escape his class origins, but he remained profoundly shaped by them. (Even during the years of his Keystone success, he would maintain uncommonly deep ties to his family, helping out his uncle John Foy with a job in the studio carpentry department and sending constant financial support to his mother's farm in Danville, Quebec.)[36] Thus it was that he embraced burlesque—a place where he could become something other than a worker and yet maintain contact with the plebeian culture with which he identified. At Miner's Bowery theater, for example, Sennett performed in comic skits for an audience largely composed of recent immigrants. (In the words of the *Dramatic Mirror*, the Bowery Burlesque was known for "attract[ing] people of all nationalities.")[37] As another source of revenue, Sennett journeyed into the streets themselves with the "The Cloverdale Boys," a street-corner Irish quartet available for hire at "weddings in Brooklyn, funerals in the Bronx, [and] Irish wakes all over town."[38]

Finally, in January 1908, he set about finding work in the still unrespectable medium of motion pictures, offering his services as an actor at Biograph's East Fourteenth Street studio. This time, his persistence would be rewarded: Sennett's career took a decisive turn and, after three years' acting for Biograph, he took over as director of the studio's comedy unit.

Sennett had arrived at Biograph after almost a decade of failure in other forms of popular entertainment; his future colleagues followed different paths, but were similarly motivated by a desire for self-transformation. For Ford Sterling, the road to motion pictures would prove just as circuitous, albeit paved with more success. Born George Ford Stich in La Crosse, Wisconsin, in 1882, Sterling grew up in relatively prosperous circumstances around Texas and in Chicago, where his father George Stich Sr., a second-generation German, worked in the cattle trade. Despite a secure middle-class upbringing—including brief enrolment at Notre Dame College (then a Catholic boarding school)—Sterling seems to have rebelled after his father's death threw the family on hard times: he left home and college at age eighteen and soon joined John Robinson's Circus as "Keno, the Boy Clown." His ensuing career seems to have spanned almost the entire array of popular entertainments—from professional baseball to vaudeville and Mississippi boat shows, from "straight" drama with the Frank Keenan Players to German caricatures in musical comedies such as *King Casey*—eventually bringing him to Sennett's Biograph unit in the spring of 1912.[39]

Other future Keystoners meanwhile took a more direct route into the movies, although they, too, found opportunities for personal reinvention: both Mabel Normand and Henry Lehrman, for example, used their film careers to proclaim new identities that would not be marked by the stigma of their lower-class backgrounds. Born in Vienna in 1886, Lehrman arrived in New York in his early twenties, where he worked as a streetcar conductor and nickelodeon usher before trying his luck in the picture industry. Arriving at Biograph in 1911, he introduced himself as Monsieur Henri Lehrman, lied about his supposedly lengthy experience as a French filmmaker at Pathé Frères, and offered his services for five dollars a day. For the rest of his career, he would jokingly be known by the nickname "Pathé."[40]

With Mabel Normand—of whom more in chapter 6—this play on identities took on yet more protean dimensions. Her father was a carpenter of French-Canadian descent and her mother was of Irish parentage; shortly before her birth, the family moved to the immigrant neighborhoods of New Brighton, Staten Island, where Mabel was raised. But this was not the image of her childhood that Normand would choose to publicize. "Mabel

Normand," claimed a biographical sketch in a 1914 edition of *Motion Picture Story Magazine,* "was born in Boston, Mass., of one of the most aristocratic New England families, her maternal grandfather being Governor of Massachusetts."[41] Alternately, according to a 1920 account, Normand had been "born in Atlanta, Georgia, where she received her education and rudimentary instructions in drawing, her desire to learn to paint and illustrate [taking] her, as a young girl, to New York."[42] Stardom had given Normand the chance to invent herself a more genteel image.[43]

Of the team of Biograph comedians that Sennett had pieced together by 1912, only Fred Mace had had an authentic opportunity fully to pursue the respectable, middle-class lifestyle to which his colleagues frequently pretended. By far the most educated of Keystone's founding members, Mace graduated in 1898 from the University of Pennsylvania as a doctor of dental surgery before deciding to try his luck in musical comedy. Unlike Sennett, Mace found ready success on Broadway, winning acclaim for supporting roles in *A Chinese Honeymoon* (1902, supposedly with Sennett himself in the chorus line),[44] *Piff! Paff!! Pouf!!!* (1904), and *The Time, the Place and the Girl* (1907), and featured in numerous celebrity profiles in the trades and local press.[45] As a member of Broadway's sporting crowd, Mace acquired a cultural style he later brought with him to California. After joining Sennett's Biograph unit in May 1911, he set about establishing himself as a member of the film community's elite, hiring a Japanese valet for his Los Angeles home (which he shared with his parents), building up his collection of first editions, and founding The Photoplayers as a gentlemen's club for the nascent filmmaking community.

In the summer of 1912, these Biograph comedians would come together to form the Keystone Film Company. At a time when more "respectable" motion picture companies aligned themselves with Anglo-Saxon culture and identity,[46] Keystone's founding members brought with them a different legacy, one inseparable from their class and immigrant origins. Even before entering motion pictures, many of them had explored the routes linking ethnic neighborhoods to the institutions of popular culture. At Keystone, they would participate in a series of cultural transformations: they would challenge the genteel Victorianism of the native-born middle class, and, in so doing, would give shape to an emergent mass culture that drew energies from the plebeian world of popular entertainment. During the studio's first years, in particular, Keystone's filmmakers would define a new style of film comedy that appealed to the sensationalist tastes of the popular classes and spoke to their resistance to middle-class values. But before these developments could take place, there were practical matters to attend to: studio facilities would have to be built for the filmmakers to work in, systems of production would have to be set in place. Whatever innovations Keystone's filmmakers achieved would depend upon the mode of production they adopted.

"A PEEP BEHIND THE SCENES": RATIONALIZATION, IRRATIONALITY, AND THE FOUNDING OF THE KEYSTONE FILM COMPANY

In later years, Mack Sennett liked to describe the founding of the Keystone Film Company as an opportunistic scheme hatched by a shady group of street-corner wise guys. "Charles O. Baumann . . . and Adam Kessel," recalled Sennett, "were small-time bookmakers around downtown New York. They would even take twenty-five-cent bets. I began to put money on horses . . . [and] went in debt to Kessel and Baumann for a hundred dollars. . . . Here I was with an impossible-to-pay debt to Kessel and Bauman. I went home by side streets and sent word I was out when they called. I had them barred from the Biograph studio so they couldn't get in there and break my legs." After learning that they had had "some experience with motion picture people," Sennett came out of hiding and proposed a novel means of settlement. "Forget the $100 I owe you," Sennett told them. "And put up $2500 to start a new company. I'll make you rich."[47]

It is a colorful anecdote and, like most of Sennett's stories, it wallows in disreputability at the expense of the facts. Baumann had, it is true, once been a bookmaker, and Kessel had worked as a streetcar conductor, but this had been years earlier.[48] (New York State had, in fact, passed an anti-gambling law in 1908 that made racetrack betting illegal.) They had also acquired much more than "some experience" in motion pictures. Kessel's association with the picture business dated back to 1900, when he had briefly operated a Mutoscope parlor on Brooklyn's Thornton Street (in between jobs as a slot machine operator and a liquor salesman).[49] The pair had first entered partnership in the film industry in 1909 with the purchase of the Empire Film Exchange; and, by the summer of 1912, when they were supposedly threatening Sennett with broken legs, Kessel and Baumann were established as two of the most significant figures in the war of the independent producers against Thomas Edison's monopolistic Motion Picture Patents Company (MPPC).

One way of looking at Kessel and Baumann's careers is to see them as part of the new generation of "merchants of leisure" (Francis Couvares's phrase) who were, at that time, emerging from the working class to forge the links of a new culture of commercial entertainment.[50] Second-generation German immigrants both, Kessel and Baumann had entered the film industry following wide-ranging careers as purveyors of "cheap amusements"; and, like other entrepreneurs from their class, they played a role in challenging and subverting middle-class attempts to gain control of working-class leisure. The battle between the MPPC and the Independents was just such a skirmish, in which the Independents were frequently characterized in the trade press as ghetto junkmen, in contrast with Edison's more respectably "American" organization.[51] Popularly known as the Trust, the MPPC had been founded in December 1908 when Edison persuaded eight other production companies, one importer of films (George Kleine), and Eastman Kodak (the only U.S. manufacturer of raw film) to band together, limiting domestic film production for themselves and restricting distribution and exhibition to licensed exchanges and theaters. Although most exchange owners quickly signed with the MPPC to guarantee a supply of films, a number decided to battle it out, Kessel and Baumann among them. In order to keep the Empire exchange solvent, they chose to go into production for themselves, and, on September 25, 1909, they launched the New York Motion Picture Company (NYMP), a holding organization for their newly inaugurated production company, trademark "Bison." By the following year, the more entrepreneurial independents were moving onto the offensive, raiding Trust companies for top talent, and, here too, Kessel and Baumann were among the first. Carl Laemmle, a German-born Jewish immigrant and former nickelodeon operator, had led the way, luring Florence Lawrence from Biograph to his Independent Motion Picture Company in 1909; but Kessel and Baumann followed suit in 1910, signing several Biograph players (among them, James Kirkwood, Marion Leonard, and Henry B. Walthall) for their new Reliance brand. The formation of Keystone kept to this pattern: having already pillaged Biograph's dramatic talent, Kessel and Baumann now raided its comedy unit, signing up director Mack Sennett and actors Henry Lehrman, Mabel Normand, and Ford Sterling.[52]

This account is perhaps a little too neat. For the factors behind Keystone's creation lay not only in disputes between Trust companies and independents but also in developing fissures *within* the expanding independent sector. In order to combat Edison's Trust, the independents had initially required organization and solidarity: to provide the movement with vital organizational coherence, Kessel and Baumann had joined forces with Laemmle in April 1910 to create the Motion Picture Distributing and Sales Company (Sales Company, for short), a distribution channel for all independent productions. But the growing strength of the independent movement soon made this coalition unnecessary. The first cracks surfaced early in 1912, when Harry E. Aitken, president of the Majestic brand, deserted the Sales Company and formed a new, if short-lived, distribution outlet, the Film Supply Company of America. This breakaway move became a credible threat to the Sales Company's dominance when Aitken subsequently launched a second distribution enterprise, the Mutual Film Corporation, announced to the trade in March, with the aggressive policy of buying up and consolidating independent exchanges. Within months, the independent sector was polarized into warring factions: at one end, those production companies aligned with the rapidly growing Mutual organization; at the other, those affiliated with Laemmle's Universal Film Manufacturing Company, founded in June in response to Aitken's secession.[53] NYMP, meanwhile, found itself at the center of these shifting allegiances. Although Kessel and Baumann's first instinct had been to continue with Laemmle, they performed an about-face a few weeks later and entered into negotiations with Mutual, officially announcing their decision to join Aitken's organization on July 29, 1912. The decision proved significant in the development of American film comedy. Since none of Mutual's production companies (Majestic, Reliance, Thanhouser, and American) were equipped to produce comic films, Kessel and Baumann were assigned the task of launching a new comedy label. Some time at the beginning of July, just days after withdrawing its product from Universal, NYMP entered into arrangements with members of Biograph's comedy unit.[54]

Sennett clearly welcomed Kessel and Baumann's proposal (which gave him a one-third interest in the new company),[55] and he wasted no time in building up a backlog of releases: according to Keystone studio documents, production officially began in New York on July 6, though it is likely that it started a couple of days earlier, during the Fourth of July holiday.[56] After completing a handful of films at NYMP's facilities in New York and New Jersey, Sennett, Lehrman, Normand, and Sterling departed for California, arriving in Los Angeles on August 28 and then journeying out to nearby Edendale to set up operations in the former Bison plant, previously a grocery store (fig. 1).[57] "This makeshift studio was exactly what I needed and where I had pined to make pictures when I first saw Southern California," Sennett later recalled in his memoir *King of Comedy*.[58] As the Keystone company settled into what would be its permanent home, Harry Aitken's publicity apparatus moved into high gear, trumpeting NYMP's first releases through the Mutual program. In both the August 31 and September 7 issues of *Moving Picture World*, Mutual ran a three-page ad

FIGURE 1.   The earliest known picture of the Keystone studios, ca. 1912. The original offices were shared with the Broncho Co. Courtesy of the Academy of Motion Picture Arts and Sciences.

informing exhibitors about release schedules for Kessel and Baumann's three companies, the Bison-101 production unit (renamed Kay-Bee in October) and the new Keystone and Broncho labels.[59] The Keystone Film Company, exhibitors learned, would begin releasing on September 23, with regular weekly offerings of two subjects on a single reel (a "split reel," in industry parlance). According to the initial contract, Mutual agreed to pay Keystone ten cents per foot for thirty-three positive prints of each of the studio's weekly reels—a total of around $3,300 per week, half to be kept by NYMP, half to be paid to Keystone to cover production expenses.[60]

As early advertisements for Keystone reveal, Sennett's Biograph successes were significant in generating interest in the new program. Rather than making claims about the innovativeness of Keystone's films, Mutual's publicity chose to emphasize their continuity with Sennett's previous Biograph productions. "Keystone Films are new in name only," asserted the *World*'s first advertisement for the new concern. "They are produced by the company heretofore with the Biograph Co., and directed by the same man—Mr. Mack Sennett. The quality of these films is well known to exhibitors."[61] Sennett himself was not above exploiting his back catalogue for publicity purposes. For the November release of *At It Again,* for example, Sennett and Mace resurrected the successful "two sleuths" roles first introduced in a number of Biograph comedies, beginning with *$500.00 Reward* (1911). Capitalizing on these earlier successes, publicity for *At It Again* claimed that the film "revives the travesty on Sherlock Holmes, in which Mack Sennett and Fred Mace won unbounded popularity."[62]

Yet behind the confident appeal to past successes lay much deeper uncertainties in NYMP's initial plans for Keystone. For several months, Kessel and Baumann remained unclear about the kinds of films they wanted from Keystone and ambivalent about the way the studio was to be managed. The decision to found a studio devoted exclusively to comedy production was unprecedented at the time, and, for a while, NYMP's management seriously considered adding a dramatic unit at the Keystone lot. An early trade press report, for instance, hinted vaguely that Keystone's weekly release schedule would include a "dramatic reel" supervised by "a director who is coming on in a few days, but whose identity is not to be revealed at this time."[63] Although nothing came of such announcements, they continued to surface periodically until almost the end of the year.[64] Kessel and Baumann also doubted Sennett's ability to run a studio without assistance and arranged for Thomas Ince, then director of NYMP's Bison brand, to keep a watchful eye on the new company.[65]

Ince's involvement is crucial to the present analysis. In inviting his supervision, Kessel and Baumann were placing Keystone within the sphere of influence of a filmmaker who was taking pioneering steps in the efficient organization of film production. Ince was at the forefront of the spread of production-line practices that had begun to take hold in the film industry, the model for which was the departmentalized system of "scientific management" first proposed in Frederick Winslow Taylor's experiments in industrial efficiency (published in 1895 and 1903). Part of a general trend to improve the output of industrial workers, Taylor advocated a hierarchical "line and staff" type of management, time-and-motion studies for improving workers' performance, and the initiation of planning departments that would determine costs and materials in advance of each job. It was just such a system that Ince implemented at his Bison company: as early as June 1912, he split the work staff into two production units and introduced detailed continuity scripts as blueprints to control each unit's work. Ince soon abandoned regular directing and editing chores in favor of a centralized, supervisory role, hiring a Rutgers-educated accountant, George W. Stout, to organize the studio into a more thoroughly departmentalized operation.

This mode of production—what Janet Staiger terms the "central producer" system—marked a sea-change in American filmmaking practice.[66]
And, since Kessel and Baumann had enjoined Ince to keep a watchful eye on
Sennett's fledgling studio, it was only to be expected that Keystone's mode
of production would be cast in the same mold. Ironically, for an ex-iron-
worker who had sought escape from his social circumstance through the
world of show business, Sennett would come to preside over a factory-style
studio system. From the outset, he drew on the expertise of, and even hired,
members of Ince's managerial staff. Sometime around November 1912, for
example, Sennett borrowed Richard V. Spencer from Ince's studio to head
Keystone's scenario department. Described in the trade press as "an old
hand at the game" and a "valuable asset to the Keystone company," Spencer
set to work organizing Keystone's writing staff.[67] He was soon promoted to
general script supervisor for NYMP's West Coast operations, however, and
was replaced at Keystone by Karl Coolidge, a local photoplay writer from
the Ammex Film Company.[68] A second key member of Ince's management
joined Keystone's payroll in the summer of 1913, this time in the person of
George Stout himself, whom Sennett hired as his business manager at $75
a week. Stout's signing was no doubt necessitated by the growing complexity of Keystone's work process as the studio followed Ince's lead in the direction of centralization and departmentalization: already by January, a second
unit had been added under Henry Lehrman's direction, and a third would be
established in the fall under the directors Wilfred Lucas and George Nichols.
(Nichols also apparently directed for Keystone during its earliest months, in
the fall of 1912 and early 1913, although not as head of a separate unit.) As
he had done for Ince, Stout further subdivided Keystone's operations, breaking the studio's functions into ten separate departments and assigning to
each a department head and assistant. With the studio largely under Stout's
organizational management, Sennett, like Ince before him, relinquished
hands-on directorial duties and, at the end of the year, took up a more supervisory position, overseeing pre- and postproduction on all pictures.[69] The
growth of Keystone's management hierarchy was reflected in the studio's
spatial layout. In February 1914, construction began on a two-story admin-
istration "tower" at the corner of the Keystone lot: the top floor housed
Sennett's personal office, affording him complete panoptic surveillance of
Keystone's employees (fig. 2).[70]

The paradox here is that, throughout their careers, Sennett and his filmmakers consistently repudiated their allegiance to this system, preferring
instead to proclaim their carnivalesque defiance of the industrial virtues of
efficiency and work discipline. In a later interview, Sennett came close to

FIGURE 2.   The Keystone studios, ca. 1914. Sennett's tower is visible at the far corner of the lot. Courtesy of the Academy of Motion Picture Arts and Sciences.

denying that the Edendale lot was a workplace at all. "[The way] we ran our studio, there *were* no bosses. We had no signs up—'you can't do this,' 'you can't do that,' 'you can't go in there,' 'you can't go in here.' We didn't have any signs. I wouldn't allow a sign to be stuck up in that studio. . . . There was no big boss. I just happened to be like a referee."[71] He frequently spoke out against rationalization and efficiency experts during his tenure at Keystone. "[I]t might be possible to save lumber bills and gasoline and electric light by system," Sennett noted in one published piece, "[but my] impression is that the whole theory of maximum efficiency is overdone. . . . [Y]ou cannot turn men into machines."[72] Indeed, from the studio's earliest days, Sennett's publicity department worked hard to depict the Keystone lot as a zany counterweight to the rationalization of American industry, a place where the lines separating work and play, productive labor and dynamic disorder, became hopelessly tangled. The mythmaking process began early on, as indicated in a *Moving Picture World* report in October 1912:

> Mack Sennett, director of the Keystone company, tells a thrilling story about a hair raising adventure that occurred to him and Fred Mace this week. The Keystone company was engaged in making a comedy in

Griffith Park. . . . The services of a bear were required in the picture
and Sennett had engaged one from a menagerie. According to his version the bear had a mean disposition and refused to be a motion picture
actor. Instead it took off after Mace and Sennett who started toward the
top of the mountain. . . . They ran out along a point and then discovered that they were on the brink of a precipice 1000 feet high. Behind
them was the on-rushing bear. Ahead of them yawned the chasm.
There were only two things to do, and either one was certain death.
Mace says that they turned back and were devoured by the bear, but
Sennett insists that they leaped. The reader will recall that in the opening sentence of this paragraph it was stated that this adventure had
occurred to Sennett and Mace. One suspects that it occurred to them
when they were trying to figure out something for the press agent.[73]

The studio's bizarre press releases soon acquired a certain notoriety, as suggested by a subsequent report published the following month in the same
magazine:

I have another thrilling adventure which is vouched for by Mack
Sennett and sworn to by Fred Mace. It concerns another daring
escapade of the two Keystone sleuths but as Richard V. Spencer refuses
to guarantee it, and it imposes a greater burden upon the credulity than
the famous bear story did, it seems wise to print only the really essential portions of it which are as follows: "Mack Sennett, the famous
director of the Keystone company who————accompanied by Fred
Mace, the inimitable comedian, who————Both Mace and Sennett will
continue to produce the further exploits of the 'Two Sleuths'————
Sennett————Mace————Sennett."[74]

Notwithstanding the evident skepticism of the *World*'s writers, Keystone
continued its stream of eccentric announcements. During the studio's
first year, bemused subscribers to the *World* learned that Sennett was
claiming the world record for completing a 500-foot film within a single
day; that Richard Spencer had taken to editing scripts while sitting on a
pile of logs; that Fred Mace was hosting wild parties "to the scandaliza-
tion of his neighbors"; and that Ford Sterling had almost fallen victim to
an exploding taxicab.[75]

From its beginnings, then, the Keystone lot was the object of a discourse
that blurred distinctions between the studio's working environment and
the world portrayed in its films. Keystone's mode of production was redefined in terms of its product: the making of slapstick was itself a kind of
comedy—as Sennett would claim in his autobiography, "We lived our
art."[76] So central was this conceit to Keystone's identity that the studio
occasionally released "behind the scenes" films depicting the Edendale lot

as a space of comic disorder and chaos. Advertising copy for the first of these, *Mabel's Dramatic Career* (September 1913), promised exhibitors that the "peep behind the scenes [showing] the Keystone players at work" offered "novelty and real laughs."[77] The "peep behind the scenes" in this film consists of a single minute-long shot in which Mabel, a country girl, auditions at the "Kinometograph Keystone Studios." Rather than offering a plausible representation of an audition, Normand presents what is recognizably a slapstick routine, in which she clumsily and grotesquely approximates the postures of screen acting only to fall flat on her face, to the guffaws of those around her. As in later examples like *A Film Johnnie* (March 1914) and *The Masquerader* (August 1914), work at the Keystone lot is represented in terms of knockabout disorder and slapstick action.

In its carnivalesque affirmation of inefficiency and riotous playfulness, Keystone's publicity apparatus spoke out against the very tenets of industrial rationalization that George Stout and Richard V. Spencer had implemented at the studio. For Keystone's filmmakers and staff, life at Keystone was structured in terms of this very contradiction. The Edendale lot was, as a *Motion Picture News* writer aptly put it in 1914, a "fun factory," at once a place of rationalized labor *and* a place of irrational play.[78] The tower-top office was both a tool of surveillance and a place in which Sennett indulged his eccentricities, such as holding story conferences in an enormous bath or boxing in his office gym.[79] Filmmaking at Keystone was rigidly planned and departmentalized, but it was also spontaneous and opportunistic. If a suitable occasion presented itself, the studio's filmmakers would take comedians out to public events and film their spur-of-the-moment shenanigans. Such was the case on New Year's Day 1913, when Fred Mace and Mack Sennett infiltrated the Pasadena Rose Parade costumed as the "two sleuths," while a Keystone cameraman rushed after them shooting footage that would ultimately materialize in *The Sleuths at the Floral Parade* (March 1913).[80] Later that year, Sennett sent out a group of his comedians to improvise comic scenes on the Edendale lake while it was being drained, making use of their mud-caked antics as the climax for *A Muddy Romance* (November 1913).

There are important reasons why this image of studio labor as "a great big joke"—in the words of Sennett gagman, Felix Adler—was so assiduously propagated throughout Keystone's career.[81] Keystone's discourse about its mode of production constituted an important part of the studio's differentiation practices. By so insistently promoting its eccentricities, Keystone distanced itself from hegemonic ideals of labor efficiency precisely at a time when those ideals were taking hold within the film industry. Indeed, in a context of industrywide gentrification, Keystone's self-image not only represented a rejection of the middle-class work ethic; it also implied allegiance to the attitudes of America's immigrant working class. As the labor historian Herbert Gutman argued in a famous essay, turn-of-the-century immigrant laborers negotiated the discipline and rigor of New World industrial practice by clinging on to "premodern" work habits: drinking and singing on the job, playing games, leaving the workplace for excursions—all were "patterns of opposition" that rejected the legitimacy of the factory system.[82] Industrial rationalization was to be challenged, undisciplined jocularity to be embraced. Publicity on Keystone appealed to precisely these values, offering working-class filmgoers a carnivalesque discourse of work in the absence of hierarchy, without supervision, without a "big boss." There is even evidence that workers may have taken vicarious pleasure from reading about life at Sennett's "fun factory"—at least to judge by an article in a February 1915 issue of *Los Angeles Citizen*, a local labor periodical with a large working-class readership. Titled "The 'Movies' in the Making," the article discusses the growth of new film studios in Los Angeles, using Keystone as its example of how movies are made; yet the picture of filmmaking that emerges is remarkably rosy for a socialist paper, describing an almost utopian reciprocity among Keystone's employees and their unstructured attitude to labor:

> [T]he good feeling that exists among the Keystoneites catches and holds our attention. Everyone in sight is smiling, even old "Dad," the gateman to whom before entering we must fully state our business. . . . On the lawn, directly in front of several dressing-rooms, a society belle is seen throwing a ball to a rough-looking hobo, a blue-coated policeman accepts a cigarette from a masked burglar and many other mixed characters are romping on the grass. A queer sight, you say? No. They are performers, made up and awaiting the call to action. A happy and carefree lot are the photoplayers, who, out in the open away from the restrictions of the legitimate stage, must in some way give vent to their jocular spirits.[83]

Here was an image of labor that surely would have appealed to blue-collar readers whose own working lives gave so little room for venting "jocular spirits."

This rhetorical conjunction of labor and play, and of the effacement of labor *by* play, would become central to what Jennifer Bean has described as the "imagination of early Hollywood," and not only at Keystone. By around 1915, in news articles and fan discourse alike, the West Coast studios were routinely viewed as "utopic places," in Bean's words, where the rationalizing imperatives of capitalism were transformed into "endlessly variegated metamorphosis and play."[84] Keystone was both an early model for and, arguably, the apogee of this fantasy. In a 1916 special issue on the studio, the *Dramatic Mirror* spoke precisely of the exemplary "happiness" on the Keystone lot: "Keystone is one of the most likable studios in the whole industry. You have to camp there for a couple of days at least to realize just what a big and *happy* family these Keystoners are. . . . *Happiness*, good humor, and fun dominate the daily life, work and play of the Keystoner. One of the *happiest* penalties you might receive would be a sentence of a day or more to be spent on the Keystone lot."[85]

Exemplary also was the way Keystone's self-image buttressed the attitudes and values of America's immigrant working class. Themselves largely of working-class, immigrant origin, Keystone's filmmakers envisioned their own labor as a playful release from the rigors of industrial discipline, an image of working conditions that, as the *Citizen* article shows, could be appropriated for the pleasure of working-class readers. For the laboring filmgoers who were the film industry's core audience, such publicity surely functioned as a site of projective fantasy, transforming the Keystone studio into an imaginary space distinct from the rigors of the working day (a "heterotopia," to use Michel Foucault's term).[86] Well-publicized glimpses "behind the scenes" thus established an inverted, carnivalized vision of labor whose meaning was materially grounded in the attitudes and values of America's workers.

Still, it was not in terms of its work process alone that Keystone defined alternatives to the dominant culture. Over the course of its first year, Keystone's filmmakers developed a knockabout comic style that directly opposed the growing "respectability" of motion picture comedy in the early 1910s. What people saw on the screens would pose as much of a challenge to dominant values as what they read about Keystone in newspapers and magazines.

"FARCE COMEDY" AND "COMIC MOTION": KEYSTONE'S EARLY COMIC FORM

In his useful study of the Keystone Film Company, Douglas Riblet observes that the studio's early films reveal striking shifts in their approach to film comedy: while the majority of Keystone's earliest extant releases generally feature "succinct" narratives structured around central pranks and misunderstandings, the bulk of its 1913 output foregrounds an increasingly "unrestrained" and "chaotic" brand of knockabout.[87] These are perceptive observations, and any discussion of Keystone's early comic form will have to take account of this transformation. Yet what is missing from Riblet's discussion is any attempt to account for this development in social and cultural terms: What, for example, were the assumptions underlying these different comic aesthetics? How were certain styles of comedy historically associated with certain classes of audience? What values and experiences were interpreted and expressed by the changing semantic forms of early comedy? To answer these questions requires tracing these forms historically and critically, investigating not only their structural properties but also their association with specific class values and ideologies.

We have already noted, for example, that by the time Keystone released its first split-reel in September 1912, American film comedy was just recovering from what had been a four-year slump. Yet, no less important, these years of quantitative decline were also marked by qualitative change, as film producers struggled to define a more "respectable" comic style capable of appealing to a middle-class audience. Both within and outside of the field of comedy, cinema's drive for respectability had entailed a move into the realm of genteel moral discourse, associated with notions of female moral authority and the idealization of domesticity.[88] Even a cursory glance at comedies of the period shows that they increasingly focused on familial and marital settings as a new basis for comic situations. The process is well exemplified in Biograph's output as it developed under D. W. Griffith, Whereas Biograph's pre-1908 comedies had consisted largely of single, extended gags involving chases, ethnic stereotypes, and sexual titillation, Griffith's emphasis on melodrama contributed to the emergence of "middle-class situation comedies."[89]

The new direction first became evident with the launching in 1908 of Griffith's "Jones" comedy series, centered upon the marital misunderstandings between "Mr. and Mrs. Jones" (John Cumpson and Florence Lawrence); but it soon spread to other comedy manufacturers, such as Vitagraph, where the rowdy antics of its earlier "Happy Hooligan" shorts (starring Vitagraph's co-founder J. Stuart Blackton as the eponymous Hooligan) were replaced by a successful series of domestic comedies pairing John Bunny with Flora Finch.[90] Such films defined their greater respectability vis-à-vis earlier slapstick by drawing on conventional presumptions linking moral propriety to female guardianship; but they also offered a satirical—and decidedly male—protest against those presumptions, representing the domestic sphere as a battleground between nagging wives protecting the "purity" of the home and henpecked husbands pursuing disreputable pleasures in the face of female prohibitions.[91]

Still, more was at stake here than a switch to domestic content: the desire for middle-class appeal also provoked the narrative discourse of screen comedy. It is in this sense that the decline of slapstick needs to be understood as part of a more general reaction against the "cinema of attractions," a term coined by Tom Gunning and André Gaudreault to describe the first decade of film history, when motion pictures featured as an attraction at vaudeville houses and other variety entertainments. This was a cinema that, as described by Gunning, had consistently foregrounded theatrical display over narrative absorption, emphasizing surprise and visual delight at the expense of an unfolding story.[92] Directly presentational in approach, such an exhibitionist aesthetic overlapped with—and, with the nickelodeon boom of 1905 to 1907, was eventually incorporated into—the disreputable culture of working-class sensationalism. The industry's bid for middle-class respectability consequently saw filmic discourse move away from an attractions-based aesthetic in the direction of narrative unity, as exemplified by the socially respectable narrative arts of the novel and the "well-made" play. And nowhere were the implications of this shift more acute than in the case of film comedy. One of the most consistent complaints about early comic films—and one that would later be leveled against Keystone's output—had been their disinterest in story. *Motion Picture Story Magazine*, from its inception in 1911, had consistently pushed filmmakers toward "refined comedy, carrying [a] humorous and logical story," as one article put it.[93] *Moving Picture World*'s leading critic, Epes Winthrop Sargent, likewise repeatedly criticized the "senseless chases" of early comedies, suggesting that gags and comic actions should be "germane to the plot and natural to the situation."[94] Making comedy acceptable to middle-class tastes consequently required a drastic stylistic overhaul: comedy would have to become something other than mere slapstick.

Filmmakers at Biograph and Vitagraph negotiated these demands by drawing on an unexpected inheritance: the "mischief gag," a major genre of comic filmmaking from 1896 to 1905.[95] "Mischief gag" films were short prank narratives (many consisting of only a single shot) that typically followed a straightforward structure of cause and effect: a rascal sets up a prank, to which a second character falls victim. The locus classicus for the genre is, of course, the Lumière brothers' now famous *L'Arroseur arrosé* (1895), in which a mischievous boy manipulates the flow of water in a hose so that a gardener receives a faceful of water. Though unsophisticated, this rudimentary cause-effect structure provided a template that later filmmakers found suitable for extrapolating into longer one-reel subjects. Many of the domestic comedies produced by Biograph and Vitagraph between 1908 and 1915 depend heavily upon this formula, offering extended "mischief-gag" narratives in which characters plot to outwit wayward husbands or nagging wives. A case in point is Vitagraph's *Her Crowning Glory* (1911), which fleshes out the prank through an extended presentation of character motivation. For much of its length, the film charts the comic love of a lonely widower (John Bunny) for his daughter's governess (Flora Finch) and the daughter's equally comic resentment at the alienation of her father's affections. The prank occurs only at the film's end, providing a supervening moment of comic surprise to a character-based situation of escalating hostilities: the daughter takes matters into her own hands and cuts off the governess's hair, which has the desired effect of dampening her father's ardor. An earlier example is D. W. Griffith's *Mrs. Jones Entertains* (1909), one of the director's "Jones" family comedies. Here, Mrs. Jones has invited members of the Ladies Temperance League to a luncheon in her home, much to the frustration of Mr. Jones, who hardly shares their views. His mischievous solution is to spike their drinks. Intoxicated, the leader of the League tries to kiss Jones, and his wife furiously orders the women out of her house.[96]

What is surprising—particularly given his reputation as a filmmaker who reinvigorated the slapstick tradition of film comedy—is that, for the most part, Sennett's initial work at Biograph fell securely within the parameters of this new, more "refined" comic style. Of the eighty-nine split-reel and one-reel films he directed there, many focus on distinctly middle-class characters, settings and situations; and most of his early plots are tautly structured around central pranks or misunderstandings. The same appears to be true of the earliest Keystone productions—including those directed by Nichols and, later, Lehrman—though here the paucity of surviving prints problematizes general claims. Out of forty-nine comedies released between September 1912 and February 1913, only *The Water Nymph* (September 1912), *Stolen Glory, At Coney Island, The Grocery Clerk's Romance* (October 1912), *The Cure That Failed* (dir. Nichols), and *The Deacon Outwitted* (dir. Lehrman, January 1913) survive. Yet, judging from these, it is clear that Keystone's initial output, far from breaking fresh ground, remained heavily indebted to the refinements characterizing Vitagraph's and Biograph's output. The "prank," for instance, remains a central device of narrative closure in both *The Water Nymph* and *The Deacon Outwitted*, where young men fool their fathers into consenting to their marriages. In the former, this is achieved when a dapper young gent (Sennett) persuades his fiancée (Normand) to draw the advances of his flirtatious father (Sterling), eventually embarrassing him into approving their engagement. In the latter, a deacon's son and his sweetheart make themselves up in blackface and trick the deacon into marrying them. A more elaborate rendering is offered in *The Cure That Failed:* here, the basic mischief-gag paradigm is doubled, providing what Riblet labels a "prank/counter-prank" structure, in which the victim of one prank turns the tables by executing a second.[97] Ford Sterling plays a drunkard on whom his wife (Normand) and friends play a trick: one of the friends (Fred Mace) dresses as a woman and tries to convince the drunken husband that the two were married during the previous night's revels. Realizing that he is being duped, Sterling's character feigns despair at his apparent bigamy and pretends to commit suicide. It is only when his friends are subsequently arrested for murder that the husband "revives" to reveal his trick.

There is, then, a strong commitment to narrative values in Keystone's earliest surviving output. As with the respectable style of Griffith's Biograph comedies and the John Bunny Vitagraphs, the mischief gag provides the narrative template, and humor arises through the causal organization of preparation and punch line. Still, this trend toward respectability was hardly uniform, even within Sennett's own filmmaking: already in a number of his later Biograph films, Sennett had experimented with a disconnected, loosely structured format more characteristic of the bawdy style of pre-1908 comic films. Direct ethnic and racial parody had begun to surface in his Biograph films during early 1912, notably *A Spanish Dilemma* and *The Tourists.* Other Sennett films from this period, such as *Neighbors,* revisited the format of old-style chase comedy, a residual comic form of which Griffith's 1909 *The Curtain Pole*—featuring Sennett himself as a drunken Frenchman—had been the last notable example in Biograph's catalogue. If Keystone's earliest output often skirted these tendencies (at least judging from extant prints), they remained an available part of Sennett's repertoire and would come to dominate the studio's releases from March 1913 onward.

Sennett's more boisterous comic bent did not long go unrecognized, even at Biograph. Starting with *The Fatal Chocolate,* released in February 1912, Biograph's management began identifying its comic output as "farce comedy," on the title frames and in the *Biograph Bulletin,* a designation evoking knockabout humor lacking any real validity of plot or characterization.[98] Originally a generic label from late nineteenth-century musical theater, the term "farce comedy" dates back to Nate Salsbury's popular stage productions of the 1870s, and in its earliest appearance, it described revue-style playlets in which a rudimentary narrative situation—generally given in the title, as in, say, *Tourists in the Pullman Palace Car* (1879)—was exploited as a basis for comedy skits and musical numbers.[99] Applied to Sennett's Biograph work, however, it implied a more general return to rough-and-tumble comic formulas marginalized in the film industry's quest for respectability. (As the *Photoplay* critic Raymond Schrock explained in January 1913, "farce comedy" implied "wild action, grotesque makeup and a general free-for-all," as distinct from "good clean comedy" with a "well-defined plot.")[100] And it proved to be a label that Sennett was happy to accept: every Keystone comedy released through Mutual would likewise be identified as "farce comedy" by its title card.

As that label suggests, Keystone's contribution to American film comedy needs to be seen, not in terms of the emergence of new comic forms, but instead as a return to, and extrapolation from, residual comic practices that contested the gentrification of the motion picture industry.[101] It was this approach that formed the basis for developments at the studio following the "prank" comedies of its earliest releases. Particularly notable was the revival of the comic chase as the cornerstone of Keystone's slapstick style. A staple of American (and international) film production since before the nickelodeon era, the chase comedy had nonetheless declined in recent years, reflecting a demand for films of greater narrative sophistication. (In its review of Griffith's *The Curtain Pole, Moving Picture World* wondered why Biograph had decided to follow "the worn-out scheme of foreign producers and introduce these long chases . . . as part of their amusement films.")[102] At Keystone, however, the chase quickly set the pattern for the broad physical humor for which the studio's later films became known. This is clear, for example, in the climax to *Stolen Glory,* the earliest example of a chase among Keystone's surviving films. In this remarkable location-shot sequence, Ford Sterling pursues Fred Mace through what is evidently an actual parade in downtown Los Angeles. The balance of the film's humor is here turned decisively in favor of physical spectacle, with little concern for narrative motivation: the comedy of the chase derives less from its function in the film's plot—which, such as it is, concerns Mace's theft of Sterling's military uniform—than from the spectacle of the genuinely furious paraders, who, in a series of shots, break ranks to shoo the unruly comedians away to the sidewalks.[103]

As articulated in *Stolen Glory,* the chase remains recognizably primitive in format: pursued and pursuer simply follow one another through a linear succession of shots, here interspersed with actuality-style shots of the parade in which no Keystone performers are visible. From at least March 1913, however, the studio's filmmakers began to replace this structure with a more complex patterning—namely, the race to the rescue intercutting between characters in comic peril and their would-be rescuers.[104] This, of course, was a format associated with D. W. Griffith's earlier Biograph films, in which the director's use of parallel editing had pioneered in the suspenseful

FIGURE 3.   The first extant appearance of the Keystone Kops. Frame enlargement from *The Man Next Door* (March 1913). Courtesy of the Library of Congress Prints and Photographic Division.

manipulation of narrative time.[105] In Sennett's hands, however, the form was appropriated as a basis for anachronistic knockabout. Significantly, the first surviving Keystone film to feature a parallel-edited climax—*The Man Next Door*, a split-reel comedy released March 17—is also the first extant appearance of one of the most famous hallmarks of the studio's comedy, the "Keystone Kops," as they would come to be known (fig. 3).[106] Comic policemen were a longtime standard of variety knockabout, even appearing in several early chase comedies, like Edison's *The Little Train Robbery* (1905) and—a French example that Sennett might have known[107]—Pathé's *La Course des sergents de ville* (*The Policemen's Little Run*, 1907). Sennett's innovation in *The Man Next Door* was to combine clumsy cops with the parallel-editing conventions of film melodrama, a comic take on dramatic technique presaging Keystone's more overt parodies from this period (discussed later in this chapter). Soon the association of comic policemen and rescue melodrama became standard strategy at Keystone: of at least fifteen extant prints ending with a parallel-edited rescue released in 1913, eleven feature Keystone's roughhouse cops as the would-be rescuers.[108]

In these sequences, knockabout generally takes a very specific form, in which the cops' tumbledown clumsiness frustrates their efforts at rescue, their incompetence counteracting the temporal urgency required for the rescue itself. *The Man Next Door* provides a paradigmatic example by establishing a contrast between a situation of (apparent) peril and the disorganized inefficiency of the policemen. The peril is established when a wife and her lover (Dot Farley and Ford Sterling) trap the wife's husband (Nick Cogley) in a parlor-room trunk, mistakenly believing him to be a burglar. The wife then phones the police, setting up a parallel-edited climax, as follows:

Shot 36: Exterior police station. Four policemen rush out in a disorderly group.

Shot 37: Parlor. The lover (Ford Sterling) sits on top of the trunk as the husband (Nick Cogley) struggles to get out.

Shot 38: Hallway. The wife (Dot Farley) ends her call to the police and exits to the parlor.

Shot 39: Parlor. The lover hands a gun to the wife and, sitting her atop the trunk, exits to the hallway.

Shot 40: Hallway. The lover picks up the phone.

Shot 41: Road. The police attempt to flag down a speeding automobile. The car races past them, knocking them down.

Shot 42: Hallway. The lover puts down the phone, exiting to the parlor.

Shot 43: Puddle. The police stand before a large puddle blocking the road.

Shot 44: Parlor. The lover enters.

Shot 45: Puddle. As they wade through the puddle, the police are knocked into the water by another speeding car.

Shot 46: Road (as in shot 41). A separate group of policemen unsuccessfully attempts to flag down another passing automobile.

Shot 47: Puddle (closer view). The soaked policemen get to their feet and run out of the puddle the way they came.

Shot 48: Parlor. The lover is sitting atop the trunk. The trapped husband manages to lift the lid and stick out his hand, which the lover promptly bites.

Shot 49: Interior trunk. Close-up of the husband lying in the trunk, cradling his wounded fingers.

Shot 50: Parlor. The lover remains on top of the trunk.

Shot 51: Road (a different location from shots 41 and 46). The policemen rush down the road. One finds an abandoned bike and rides out of shot.

Shot 52: Parlor. The wife is sitting on the trunk. The lover hears the approaching police and exits.

Shot 53: Exterior house. The lover rushes outside and leads the policemen in to the parlor.

Shot 54: Parlor. The police pull the husband from the trunk, much to the embarrassment of the wife, whose adultery is now revealed.[109]

"This half-reel picture, is full of rapid-fire situations, which fortunately are easily understood and bring shouts of laughter," *Moving Picture World* noted.[110] *The Man Next Door* is, indeed, the most rapidly edited of Keystone's extant releases up to this point, with an average shot length of 6.1 seconds (almost doubling the combined average speed of Keystone's previous surviving films).[111] But it is precisely on the question of temporality that the film proves most complex. To be sure, there is the "rapid-fire" rhythm imposed by intercutting, a rhythm that lends precision and purposefulness to the unfolding action; but there is also, within this formal patterning, the erratic movement of the cops, a movement in which the cops' tumbledown incompetence comically defers purpose and precision. Their straggling inefficiency is, in fact, doubly inscribed within the text, defined not only *across* the lines of action, through the contrast with the urgent panic of the adulterers, but also *within* the pacing of the race itself, through the contrast with the automobiles that race past them. In terms of the film's formal properties, the cops' actions are entirely excessive, opening up conflicting temporalities in a film otherwise predicated on the evocation of rhythm and speed.

One way to describe these games with time would be in terms of the various experiences of temporality available in turn-of-the-century America. Such an approach is suggested by Tom Gunning, who interprets D. W. Griffith's innovations in parallel editing in terms of "the split-second timing" of industrial production.[112] On this reading, Griffith's use of editing—the measured alternation between separate lines of action—becomes an emblem of industrial time, invoking the mechanical rhythms of factory labor. But what happens when these insights are applied to *The Man Next Door*? Working-class nickelodeon audiences may indeed have found something "strangely familiar" (Gunning) in the rhythmic divisions of Griffith's films;

but this is hardly the experience of time that the Keystone film conveys. On the one hand, the film's "rapid-fire" intercutting imposes the same rigid, orderly tempo as a Griffith film; but the cops' knockabout incompetence defies that rigidity, refuses order. The spectacle of irrationality is reintroduced within the rationalized rhythms of modern clock time, subverting the drama of rescue by the comedy of the cops' (in)actions, and, in the process, bodying forth comic alternatives to the temporal discipline that workers experienced in their daily lives.

If these slapstick races became a benchmark of Keystone's style, one explanation seems, then, to lie in their capacity to address experiences and fantasies born of the circumstances of native industrialization. Under Taylor's studies in scientific management, the modern analysis of the work-process had, by this time, extended principles of rationalization to the worker's body itself, conceived as a mechanical part incorporated into a factory system and required only to perform precisely standardized actions. At Henry Ford's automobile plant in Highland Park, Detroit, for instance, the assembly line was so organized that workers never had to move from their posts, even to stoop to pick something up. For workers whose own labor thus became a "mechanically objectified 'performance'" (as Georg Lukács wrote in 1922), Keystone's chaotic chases may have supplied compensatory spectacles of disorder, of bodies unable to perform according to the requirements of a task.[113] They visualized comic substitutes for the self-control and discipline necessary to adapt to the conditions of modern working life; and, in so doing, perhaps provided an imaginary refuge in which the dehumanizing impact of industrial labor could be negotiated in a playful manner. There is, in fact, a suggestive homology linking Keystone's chase sequences to work processes on the studio lot. For, just as studio publicity promoted an image of play within an industry subject to the requirements of efficiency and standardization, so the climax of *The Man Next Door* restores a moment of irrationality within the precision of the film's parallel editing. Keystone's carnivalesque resistance to the industrial virtues of discipline and orderliness, its cheerful proclamation of the values of disorder and spontaneity, was articulated at all levels of the filmmaking process, in the action of the studio's films as in publicity on the studio's filmmaking practices.

Evidently there was much here for wage-earning filmgoers to enjoy, and, by the end of the year, the fast-paced capers of Keystone's policemen had become a staple of the studio's product. Trade press reviews of new releases routinely drew exhibitors' attention to Keystone films in which "the cops" appeared, and nickelodeon exhibitors soon began advertising the studio's product in terms of the rough-and-tumble policemen, as at the Bungalow Theater in St. Maries, Idaho, where billboards promoted "the break neck police" as an attraction in the theater's program.[114] But knockabout was hardly limited to the cops' appearances. A rougher style of comedy became generally pervasive in Keystone's films from this period, with characters hitting each other with brooms (in *Love and Rubbish,* July 1913) and bricks (*The Riot,* August 1913), slipping on banana skins (*A Healthy Neighborhood,* October 1913), falling around in mud *(A Muddy Romance),* and other antics.

The visceral effect of such slapstick also formed the center of a number of ongoing developments in Keystone's studio style. From at least as early as the November 1912 release of *A Desperate Lover,* Keystone's filmmakers had begun to employ undercranking as a way of heightening slapstick spectacle. And, by late 1913, George Nichols, director of the studio's third unit, was exploiting editing to accentuate the disjunctive impact of the studio's roughhouse comedy, cutting rapidly as characters and objects are thrown between contiguous spaces. (Charles Chaplin, who performed under Nichols's direction in several films, found this style far from salutary for his more incremental style of comedy. As he complained in his autobiography, Nichols "had but one gag, which was to take the comedian by the neck and bounce him from one scene to another.")[115] Further, as the example of *The Man Next Door* suggests, the manipulation of tempo through editing also became a cornerstone of the studio's style in this period, with cutting notably increasing over the course of the year: between September 1912 and February 1913, the average shot ran just under twelve seconds; between July and December 1913, the length was nearer eight seconds, with the fastest editing reserved for the films' frenzied climaxes.[116] Critics were quick to notice the vital role that editing played in Keystone's comic style. In a 1915 article titled "Tempo—The Value of It," Wid Gunning argued that D. W. Griffith and Mack Sennett were "the two greatest living 'tempo builders' in the business today," noting how Keystone's filmmakers exploited tempo for comic effect. "[I]n almost every good Keystone comedy," Gunning elaborated, "the action goes along smoothly with a few good laughs for about half the length of the film and then suddenly it begins to swing faster and faster, until it is moving at the rate of about a mile a minute with laugh following laugh, just the proper time being allowed each to carry from one to the other. That's 'tempo.'"[117] In later years, Sennett would formulate his approach to comedy under the rubric of "comic motion." "There is one thing that I always contend," he once claimed, "and that is motion. Comic motion." On such an approach,

Sennett explained, comedy attaches not to the ends for which an action is undertaken but to the qualities of the movement itself. "Lloyd Hamilton [a popular comedian for Educational Pictures in the 1920s] had comic motion. He would just walk across the room and, without apparently doing anything, make you laugh. Chaplin would do the same thing."[118]

What Sennett is describing here is the pantomimic virtuosity of these performers; but the approach to comedy embedded in his examples also sheds light on developments in Keystone's early comic form. Whereas Keystone's earliest comedies had tied action to narrative as the mainspring of their humor, its 1913 releases began to privilege action—or "comic motion"—as an attraction in its own right, apart from narrative ends. For industry commentators concerned to elevate film as a cultural product, such developments could only be viewed with an ambivalence that, more often than not, indicated barely concealed moral disapproval. As early as December 1912, one reviewer complained that the undercranking in *A Desperate Lover* made the action difficult to follow: "A very slow camera and consequent speedy entrances and exits are the amusing things in this picture. Fred Mace's disguise may make a laugh or two; but the reason for his disguise is not at all clear nor is the story clear. We should like to tell what it is about; but we don't know."[119] From around March 1913, reviews in *Moving Picture World* frequently noted the primacy of action over plot in Keystone's releases: *A Wife Wanted* (March) was described as "plenty of action and shooting and very little plot"; *Her New Beau* (March) as "more action than plot"; and *Cupid in a Dental Parlor* (April) as "lots of action but a slight plot."[120] Yet for working-class viewers who experienced the wrenching discipline of industrial practice firsthand, these same developments may have functioned similarly to Keystone's crazy chases, actualizing imaginary forms of liberation through the vicarious experience of uncontrollable mobility. For these viewers, Keystone's "sensational" focus on bodily disorder may have made slapstick a meaningful corollary to the embodied nature of their labor; and, if so, then what critics disparaged in Keystone's output was the very imprint of working-class fantasy.

This last point needs to be handled carefully. Such an interpretation must remain purely formal unless supported by empirically oriented considerations concerning Keystone's actual audiences and their responses to these films. Unfortunately, little evidence survives that would allow us to know exactly where the films played during this early period. Until 1913, most local newspapers offered at best only scattered and partial listings, especially in larger cities like New York and Chicago;[121] and smaller theaters would in any case have had insufficient funds to advertise, beyond posting the day's bill outside the theater. What data there are, however, offer tantalizing indications that Keystone's pictures were indeed a staple of the cheaper theaters, that they may even have had a special attraction for wage-earning audiences. Few other studios, for example, received as much attention from the *Los Angeles Citizen*, the city's local labor paper. Special articles on the region's film industry often focused on Keystone, and the *Citizen* routinely singled out theaters at which the studio's "well-known," "excruciatingly funny," and "celebrated" comedies were playing.[122] Indeed, from late 1913, the studio's output seems to have been a common feature on the bills of "cheap" vaudeville houses, whose lower ticket costs made them popular with working- and lower-middle-class audiences. In downtown Los Angeles, Keystone films played at the Empress from October 1913 and the Pantages from September 1914, both of which offered a ten-cent scale of prices and drew their clientele from nearby Main Street—the "'pleasure' street . . . of all the day laborers, the orange grove hands, the fellows who keep Southern California in repairs."[123] In New York, the films proved a long-standing fixture on the bill of Proctor's Twenty-Third Street Theater, a cheap vaudeville house situated in the Union Square entertainment district. The pattern is further reflected in the weekly film listings published in the *Chicago Tribune* from March 1914: although Keystone's films seem to have been a regular attraction at Chicago's five- and ten-cent nickelodeons during the first half of 1914, they were almost never listed as playing at the more prestigious picture houses.[124]

Further evidence suggests that the studio's films found particular favor with the immigrant portion of the working class, at least in smaller industrial cities. In the textile mill town of Pawtucket, Rhode Island, for example, the studio's films played prominently at the Star Theatre to audiences mostly from Polish, Italian, and other working-class immigrant neighborhoods from late 1912 through much of 1913. Within weeks of Keystone's debut there, Pawtucket's local press reported that these "exceptionally funny comedy subjects" were provoking "shouts of laughter." Soon the Star was promoting its Keystone subjects by brand name, promising in its news ads "Big Laughmakers from the Popular Keystone Co." or declaring simply "It's a Keystone."[125] In Milwaukee, a small city with a significant German population, Keystone films proved immensely popular at the Vaudette, a German-owned five-cent picture house. As Mutual's trade journal, *Reel Life*, proclaimed: "'A Keystone comedy for every day of the year' is the motto upon which Otto L. Meister and A. Reiss, owners of the Vaudette Theatre in Milwaukee, Wis., have built up an enormous business."[126] Likewise in Des Moines, where, in December 1912, Keystone films made their local debut at the Elite, a theater catering chiefly to the Scandinavian and Jewish communities of the city's east side.[127] Finally, a similar situation seems to have existed in Toledo—the center of America's glassmaking industry and home to a sizable population of Bulgarian immigrants—where by mid-1913, Keystone's films were "bring[ing] round after round of laughter and an occasional excited scream from the women" at the city's largest picture house, the 1,000-seat Colonial.[128] In fact, the first Toledo theater to advertise a Keystone film by brand name in the local press—the Hart Theatre—was, perhaps not coincidentally, also one that directly targeted working-class audiences by posting regular listings in the local labor weekly, the *Toledo Union Leader.*[129]

Just as Keystone had revived forms of screen comedy first popular at the height of the nickelodeon boom, so too did its films find initial success among those who had constituted the nickelodeons' major clientele—the immigrant and native-born working class. In a context of industrywide gentrification, Keystone was a site of heterogeneity, with neither its output nor its audiences fitting the ideals that elsewhere guided cinema's development. That heterogeneity, this chapter has been arguing, was a function of the studio's multilayered affinity with the attitudes and experiences of America's working class. But it would also take shape in ways that overtly challenged the cinematic practices through which the industry was seeking to appeal to the "better" classes. Beginning in early 1913, a new production trend emerged that underscored the studio's open nonconformity to the ideological mainstream of the contemporary film industry: the "comic melodrama."

"TO BURLESQUE EVERY SERIOUS THING THAT GRIFFITH DID": PARODY AND POLEMIC IN KEYSTONE'S FILMS

On March 29, 1913, *Moving Picture World* announced a new series of Keystone comedies. "Mack Sennett, Fred Mace and the rest of the members of the Keystone company are engaged in putting on a new line of pictures—that is, Sennett says he is producing 'comic melodramas' which is an entirely new form of art."[130] This "new line of pictures" had in fact been launched two days previously, with the March 27 release of *At Twelve o'Clock*, a lost film that directly parodied D. W. Griffith's 1908 *The Fatal Hour.* Griffith's picture—the first of his films, incidentally, to include a parallel-edited finale—had featured as its central attraction the kind of technological contrivance common to the "sensation scenes" of low-priced stage melodrama. While on the trail of a gang of white slavers, a woman detective is captured and tied in front of a gun rigged to fire when a clock strikes twelve. A race to the rescue ensues, in which she is saved just before the eponymous "fatal hour." It was the contrivance of the timed gun that Sennett borrowed for his film, in which a "big Mexican bruiser" (Mace) ties the erstwhile object of his affections (Normand) to a post, directly in the sights of a revolver.[131] But where Griffith's film propelled its narrative trajectory through the precise and irrevocable advance of the clock's deadline, Sennett transformed this temporal structure into comedy, introducing alternate rhythms that subverted its dramatic momentum. According to *Moving Picture World*'s plot summary, the film derived much of its humor by intercutting between the woman's urgent situation and the interminable incompetence of the policemen, who "have all manner of mishaps in reaching the scene."[132] This temporal playfulness seems to have culminated, in the film's climactic moments, in a physical symbol of time's inversion: the woman's boyfriend (Sennett) "finally secures a big magnet, which he sticks through the barred window at one minute of twelve, and . . . pulls the hands back."[133] Time, dramatized by Griffith in its unstoppable forward movement, is, in the Keystone film, rendered comical by its apparent reversibility.

Evidently, Sennett was elaborating upon the games with time that he had introduced in such films as *The Man Next Door*. Yet it was its explicitly parodic engagement with the clichéd sensationalism of melodrama that made the film the noteworthy triumph of Keystone's debut year. "[The Keystone] company," pronounced *Moving Picture World*'s reviewer, "has hit upon an exceptionally good burlesque idea, which is worked out in first-class form. . . . [T]he travesty, which occupies a full reel, is above the ordinary offering of the kind."[134] Although the majority of Keystone's releases had hitherto been split-reel subjects, the comic melodramas—of which *At Twelve o'Clock* was the first—were almost always released as full-reel attractions, receiving considerable coverage in the trade press and even the nation's newspapers. Just weeks after *At Twelve o'Clock*'s release, the syndicated movie columnist Gertrude M. Price described how Keystone was "Mak[ing] Comedy Out of Melodrama"—quoting Sennett's definition of comedy as "the 10, 20, 30 type of melodrama 'burlesqued a bit' "—and trade press ads began overtly to publicize Keystone's output as "broad burlesque[s] on melodrama."[135] Such success is particularly notable inasmuch as these pictures provide the most explicit moment in Keystone's early resistance to the film industry's ideological mainstream. If the developments discussed in the preceding pages expressed this through a *formal* regression to older comic styles, then Keystone's burlesques took aim rather at the ethical *content* of dramatic filmmaking, engaging the sentimental modes of popular melodrama in order to subvert them. A form of ideological rewriting, they parodied the narrative and conceptual conventions through which dramatic filmmakers had sought to conform their films to the ethical precepts of the genteel middle class.

These observations will need to be substantiated through analysis: for the present, Keystone's burlesques can briefly be situated in relation to the broader context of turn-of-the-century American theater. A derivative of the Italian *burlare* (to ridicule), the term "burlesque" refers, in its initial significance, to the tradition of theatrical parody that flourished across Europe from the late seventeenth century on, arriving in America two centuries later. (Historically, this has not been the only meaning of the word, and "burlesque" also refers, of course, to the bawdy, variety-style entertainment that put on leg shows for working-class men, in which Mack Sennett began his performing career.)[136] At the simplest level, burlesque may be defined as a form of theatrical parody that has tended historically to flourish within "belated" societies in which formerly prestigious cultural forms have become desacralized, their ritual functions no longer meaningful for their audiences.[137] Such was certainly the case on the late-nineteenth-century American stage, where the taste for burlesque spread across all classes, from the wage-earning audiences of cheap vaudeville houses to the privileged clientele of New York's premier burlesque theater, the Weber and Fields Music Hall. Burlesque theatrics even passed through the hallowed portals of the genteel home: American middle-class families frequently staged amateur playlets in their parlors, and many of these directly parodied the histrionic acting and narrative conventions of nineteenth-century melodrama.[138] One season's dramatic success would be the following season's travesty, as when the Weber and Fields Music Hall staged *Quo Vass Iss?* in 1900, burlesquing the historical drama *Quo Vadis?* which had just finished its run at the New York Theatre. Nor was it uncommon for a travesty and its "straight" counterpart to be staged concurrently, as was the case in 1898 when New York theatergoers could enjoy the historical romance *Cyrano de Bergerac* at the Garden and then laugh at *Cyranose de Bric-a-Brac* at the Music Hall.[139]

Such rampant burlesquing—in vaudeville as on Broadway, on the stage as in genteel homes—was symptomatic of a deeply carnivalized social situation. The flourishing of burlesque was coterminous with a crisis in cultural authority, as the continuing realities of social division circumscribed genteel attempts to define—and elicit consent to—a coherent hegemonic vision. Under the pressures and upheavals of modernity, genteel culture had entered what one historian has called its "weightless" period, marked by uncertain moral commitments, an experience of fragmentation and change, and a growing sense of unreality.[140] Unsurprisingly, then, a favored target of burlesque playwrights was melodrama, a theatrical form that, from its origins in postrevolutionary France, had sought to reassure bourgeois audiences of just the opposite, of the continued existence of an irrefutable and unchanging moral order. On Peter Brooks's influential reading, the emergence of melodrama in Europe was a response to the uncertainties of modernity—where "traditional patterns of moral order no longer provide[d] the necessary social glue"—offering audiences a compensatory vision of a world governed by a sense of cosmic justice. As such, melodrama had originally performed a quasi-religious duty: it addressed fears of moral collapse by depicting the "apparent triumph of villainy" only to allay those fears with the "eventual victory of virtue."[141] Yet the profounder uncertainties of the American situation largely outstripped melodrama's ameliorative function, and the genre took root on the American stage only alongside a deep awareness that its moral vision was, ultimately, something of a sham. If, in Europe, melodrama had grown out of a revitalized bourgeois culture, the form acquired more disreputable associations in America, where it flourished chiefly in the 10–20–30 cent houses frequented by the working- and lower-middle classes—those dispossessed classes for whom melodrama's vision of moral justice might still have offered solace.[142] From cheap vaudeville to Broadway, a burgeoning tradition of burlesque meanwhile took aim at the genre's underlying moral iconography, presenting a world of comic moral extremism in which dastardly "vilyuns" contended with "poor but honest" mothers bereft of "chee-iuld": the moral terms of melodrama were exaggerated to the point at which they collapsed in preposterous hyperbole.

A paradox emerges, however, when considering the relation between melodramatic theater and early film. A mode of representation associated with the lower orders, melodrama nevertheless provided innovative filmmakers with a repertoire of conventions for delivering comprehensible stories and moral lessons. As such, they served as a valuable resource for filmmakers who wanted to transcend the medium's disreputable origins and align their output with the ethical precepts of the genteel middle class. Theatrical melodrama had, after all, evolved a rigidly codified iconography for articulating traditional moral values, and, regardless of the genre's appeal to working-class audiences, its ideological signals remained rooted in a bourgeois worldview. Nowhere was this more evident than in the early career of D. W. Griffith, a director for whom melodrama provided an important tool in his quest to, as he later put it, "reform the motion picture industry."[143] During a period in which the film industry had come under ever more damaging fire from reformers and vice crusaders, Griffith saw that the motion picture could be used to, in his words, "keep boys and girls along the right planes of conduct."[144] Although critical of charity workers who attempted to impose their values on the underprivileged (as in *A Child of the Ghetto* and *Simple Charity*, both 1910), his early films nonetheless captured the crusading spirit of the Progressive era in their vision of ultimate moral order and social justice.[145] From soon after his directorial debut at Biograph in June 1908, he turned to the ambiguous heritage of melodrama as a repository of techniques for realizing that vision: in Griffith's hands, the spectacular conventions of cheap, "blood-and-thunder" melodrama became strategies for reinvigorating the waning values of American Victorianism.[146]

A case in point here is the director's innovative use of parallel editing to dramatize the "race-to-the-rescue" finales of his films. A cinematic equivalent to the "sensation scenes" of cheap melodrama, these climaxes nonetheless afforded Griffith a means of representing the tenets of Victorian moral discourse. The dualism expressed through Griffith's parallel-edited rescues, which dramatize the contrast between an evil aggressor and imperiled innocence—typically, a woman or threatened family—was precisely delineated in terms of middle-class self-definition, particularly as this was predicated on a sentimental idealization of femininity and the sanctity of domestic space.[147] Visualized as what Griffith called the "battle of human ethics common to all consciousness," the parallel-edited rescue served as the vehicle for a specific social conception aligned with the ideology of genteel domesticity.[148] Time and again, in Griffith's films, the "battle of human ethics" centered upon the shattering of the genteel order by an outside intruder, usually a marginal figure marked as socially or racially different. The climactic race to the rescue of *The Fatal Hour*, for example, is precipitated by the violent abduction of two white women by a Chinese villain and his henchman. In a similar vein, *The Lonely Villa* (1909) exploits parallel editing to arouse identification with a white suburban family whose home has fallen under attack from intruding immigrant burglars.

Mention of *The Lonely Villa* returns us to Mack Sennett, who later claimed authorship of the film's basic story idea.[149] (If the claim has any validity, then Sennett can fairly be accused of plagiarism: *The Lonely Villa* drew heavily on a 1907 Pathé film released in America as *A Narrow Escape*, which in turn was based on André de Lorde's 1901 one-act play *Au téléphone*.)

It was around this time, in fact, that Sennett struck up what appears to have been a fairly one-sided friendship with Griffith, seizing on Griffith's habit of taking evening strolls as an opportunity to advance his own ambitions: "When Griffith walked, I walked. I fell in, matched strides, and asked questions. Griffith told me what he was doing and what he hoped to do with the screen, and some of what he said stuck. I thought things over. I began to learn how to make a motion picture." These walks, Sennett admitted, were "my day school, my adult education program, my university" in picture making. But while he admired the expressive value of Griffith's storytelling techniques, he remained skeptical about the moral agenda that Griffith made them serve, a difference of opinion that he associated with their different backgrounds. "I did not see these factors in the same terms as Griffith . . . I think that being from the South influenced him: his father had been a notable Confederate officer, and [Griffith] had been brought up on tales of Chancellorsville, Manassas, Cold Harbor, and charge the ramparts. He saw stories as mass movement suddenly pinpointed and dramatized in human tragedy." In contrast, "What I saw in his great ideas was a new way to show people being funny."[150]

Sennett also realized that Griffith's techniques could be used to parody the moral themes that his tutor took so seriously. As Sennett explained to a journalist in 1916, his "natural tendency to burlesque every serious thing that Griffith did" became "the turning point of his career."[151] That tendency first expressed itself in Sennett's 1912 half-reel comedy *Help! Help!* which was released while both he and Griffith were still at Biograph. An overt burlesque of *The Lonely Villa*, the film illustrates a fundamental tactic of parody, namely, the comic effect achieved through structural incongruities between an original text and its parodic imitation.[152] *Help! Help!* achieves this through a direct, dialectical engagement with *The Lonely Villa*'s parallel-edited format, evoking the Manichean melodrama of Griffith's film only to reveal, in the closing moments, that all is not as it seems: the moral dualism of Griffith's conception is dissolved in a humorous twist.

The film begins with "Mr. and Mrs. Suburbanite" (as a title puts it) at breakfast in their middle-class suburban home. The wife (Normand) is reading a newspaper report about a spate of local robberies, to which she draws her husband's attention. The husband (Mace) reassures her that all is well and leaves for work. Alone and apprehensive, Mrs. Suburbanite spies two tramps outside her home and, fearful that they are the burglars, locks herself inside her husband's study. The sudden movement of a curtain convinces her that the tramps are jimmying the window, and, in a state of exaggerated terror, she phones her husband for help. What follows is a burlesque race to the rescue in which Sennett cuts between the husband's comic mishaps in his dash homeward and the wife's absurd displays of fear. As in Griffith's film, the husband's first impulse is to race home by automobile (shots 15, 17, 19, 23, 25); as in Griffith's film, the automobile fails to work (27, 29, 31). In *The Lonely Villa*, the husband flags down a horse-drawn carriage, which successfully hurries him home. In *Help! Help!*, the husband attempts to steal a donkey, which obstinately refuses to move (32, 33, 35). Chased away by the donkey's irate owner, Mr. Suburbanite hotfoots it over a field, only to encounter a rifle-toting farmer, who drives him off his land (38). Interpolated with these sequences are shots of the terrified wife staring at the curtain (16), phoning the telephone operator (20, 21, 22), cringing on the floor in a desperate prayer (24, 26, 28), climbing into a trunk (30), and crouching with fear in a series of close-ups from within the trunk (34, 36, 39).[153]

While both Griffith's original and Sennett's parody thus use parallel editing to dramatize basically similar situations, the structure of *Help! Help!* contains a crucial difference. *The Lonely Villa* had conveyed its drama through a three-pronged editing pattern—cutting between threatened family, intruding burglars, and desperate husband. With the exception of two early shots in which the tramps are seen outside the Suburbanites' home, *Help! Help!* excises the intruders from its structure, focusing on only two narrative trajectories—the wife's panic and the husband's pursuit. This careful transformation sets up the final twist— the discovery, upon the husband's arrival, that there were no burglars after all, just a dog playing behind the curtain (40, 41, 42, 43). Where, in *The Lonely Villa*, the invasion of the middle-class home had been real, the urgent rescue justified, here the invasion is imagined, the rescue a waste of time.

In one sense, *Help! Help!* can be seen as an early model of Sennett's tendency to wring humor from the contrast between an (apparently) urgent state of affairs and the bungling inefficiency of the rescuers. But its success as parody also involves a more pointed subversion of Griffith's moral drama. Griffith's focus on the threatened family and the struggle to protect the middle-class home was, as has already been noted, consonant with a genteel worldview that sacralized the domestic sphere as a site of uplift and renewal. Saving the family, as a term of Griffith's narrative form, aligned cinematic technique with the agenda of genteel reformers who associated moral stability with home-grown values and female (wifely, motherly) guidance. Yet it is precisely this ideology that is devalorized in Sennett's film: idealized notions of domesticity and female moral stewardship are comically overwritten by Normand's hyperbolic, gibbering performance until, finally, it is revealed that there was no threat after all, just the mistaken assumption of a highly strung housewife. If *The Lonely Villa* rests on the assumption of domestic sanctity, *Help! Help!* offers a desacralized vision of suburban paranoia: the "Angel in the House" of sentimental cliché has become a fool.

The film thus instantiates a principle that would lie at the heart of Keystone's series of burlesque melodramas: replicate the form of film melodrama but gut it of its moral—and moralizing—meanings. One way of doing that, as the earlier film had revealed, was to suggest a situation of melodramatic peril and then to expose it as simple misunderstanding. Keystone's filmmakers seem to have taken particular delight in placing many of the archetypal icons of genteel virtue in circumstances of wholly imagined danger. Such is the case, for example, in the Lehrman-directed *The Bangville Police* (April 1913), a one-reel film that adapts the burlesque plot of *Help! Help!* to one of the most characteristic tropes of nineteenth-century sentimental literature, the idealization of the rural life as an unspoiled moral economy.[154] Here, a simple country girl (Normand) mishears a conversation between two farmhands and, mistakenly believing that they intend to rob her, barricades herself inside a farmhouse and calls the police. Once again, the mistake is revealed only in the final moments, after the woman has been "rescued." And, once again, the joke is at the woman's expense. From the perspective of the film's conclusion, Normand's country maid seems more a dimwitted rube than an embodiment of feminine sanctity. In other films from the cycle, by contrast, the viewer is in on the mistake from the outset. A case in point is the split-reeler *Hide and Seek* (April 1913). In a comic twist on the climax of the stage melodrama *Alias Jimmy Valentine*, office workers mistakenly believe that a child is trapped in a time-locked vault: the police are called and a race to the rescue ensues. Interspersed among images of speeding police trucks and anxious office workers, the director, George Nichols, inserts a series of shots that reveal to the audience what none of the characters know— namely, that the little girl has simply wandered off to a nearby playground. Parallel editing thus establishes an ironic narrative omniscience, deflating the melodrama before it has begun to get off the ground.

Such narrational tactics can be grouped together as *syntactic* variations on melodramatic form. In each case, these burlesques manipulate the underlying structures of film melodrama, employing editing either to withhold information (in the case of *Help! Help!* and *The Bangville Police*) or to provide ironic commentary (in the case of *Hide and Seek*). Other burlesque tactics, however, took aim at melodrama's familiar iconography, offering *semantic* variations upon the typology of characters through which the genre expressed its ideological vision. By substituting comic alternatives for melodrama's pantheon of country maidens, villainous city gents, and corn-fed heroes, Keystone's burlesques frequently produce effects of ironic distantiation, playing out a melodramatic situation through protagonists devoid of moral resonance. This is most pointed in *A Little Hero* (May 1913), a novelty half-reel comedy in which the melodramatic triad of hero, villain, and victim is transposed into the animal world. The film's parallel-edited climax, in which a heroic dog rescues a bird from the dastardly clutches of a cat, drew wry commentary from *Moving Picture World*: "It is unique and, though a little rough on the cat, will pass muster."[155] Likewise, where Griffith's melodramatic imagination frequently focused on the bravery and innocence of a youthful couple, Keystone's burlesque "mellers" often centered upon overtly farcical visions of young love. In *Barney Oldfield's Race for a Life* (June 1913), for example, the youthful hero (Sennett) is a slow-witted, bashful rube, while his sweetheart (Normand) is a spirited young woman who, in the film's opening sequence, reacts to the humble gift of a daisy with a comically unsentimental scowl.

What distinguishes films like *Barney Oldfield's Race for a Life* and *A Little Hero* is that, while satirizing melodrama's moral iconography, they nevertheless make the most of the genre's formal capacities for suspense. Unlike *Help! Help!* and *The Bangville Police*, these films place their comic characters in situations of quite authentic peril, often playing the formal conventions of melodrama in surprisingly "straight" fashion. *Mabel's New Hero* (August 1913), for example, climaxes thrillingly when Normand's character rescues herself from a runaway hot-air balloon; and *Barney Oldfield's Race for a Life* ends in similarly sensational style with a race to rescue Normand from the train tracks. Griffithian editing structures are carefully and explicitly evoked in such films, not always to ridicule, but to replicate their dramatic momentum: the slow-paced comic scenes of *Barney Oldfield's* opening (average shot length 8.5 seconds) thus yield to a heightening of tempo during the film's parallel-edited finale (average shot length 5.3 seconds), which in turn culminates in a spectacular process shot creating the impression of a hair's breadth escape from the path of a thunderous locomotive (fig. 4).[156] Available evidence on reception and publicity suggests that the films' popularity resided precisely in their ability to fuse comic pleasure with genuine thrills, promoting hybridized viewing experiences that straddled the affective registers of slapstick and sensation melodrama.[157] One exhibitor's report on *Barney Oldfield's Race for a Life*, for instance, indicates the audience's tremendous absorption in the parallel-edited suspense, even while he categorized the film as comedy. "The people stay to see it two and three times," explained Harry D. Carr, owner of the

FIGURE 4.   Frame enlargement from *Barney Oldfield's Race for a Life* (June 1913). Courtesy of the Academy Film Archive, Academy of Motion Picture Arts and Sciences.

Lyric theater in Defiance, Ohio. "I ran it three times last night and am holding it over for tonight. *It is the greatest comedy ever shown in town bar none.*"[158] Advertisements for the films stressed precisely this mixing of generic pleasures, describing *Barney Oldfield's Race for a Life* as "a combination of sensational, thrilling and humorous melodrama" and *For the Love of Mabel* (June 1913) as "a series of thrilling burlesque melodramatic incidents."[159]

In comparison with the formal subversions of films such as *Help! Help!* Keystone's more authentically sensational burlesques admittedly do less to contravene melodramatic convention. Parody, as a satirical practice of imitation, here becomes subordinate to pastiche, as a form of mimicry lacking parody's satiric edge: the melodramatic mode is mobilized less as a target of critique or distanced irony than through a comic self-consciousness that exploits and relies upon melodrama's framework of thrilling affects.[160] Even in such cases, though, a parodic intent remains evident in semantic incongruities of performance and characterization—most notably in Ford Sterling's frequent and deliciously over-the-top portrayals of mustachioed "vilyuns" (fig. 5). Simple exaggeration was, after all, among the most basic

FIGURE 5. Ford Sterling, as melodramatic "vilyun," intruding on a scene of burlesque courtship in *Barney Oldfield's Race for a Life* (June 1913). Production still
courtesy of the Academy of Motion Picture Arts and Sciences.

and familiar of burlesque practices. "There's just a hair's breadth between
melodrama and comedy," Mack Sennett himself explained in a syndicated
interview in 1913. "You can make the latter out of the former by exagger-
ating it a bit."[161] Epes Winthrop Sargent concurred, in a 1914 column on
the "vogue" for travesty, arguing that "exaggeration" was the most potent
weapon in the burlesque filmmaker's arsenal.[162] In a later interview, the
Keystone comedian Chester Conklin likewise explained that all that was
needed to burlesque melodrama was "simply [to] take a dramatic scene and
overplay it."[163] Performances of this kind subverted the iconography of
good and evil upon which melodrama thrived, allowing audiences, in
Sargent's words, to "laugh at the good-natured fun poked at the villainous
villain, the heroic hero and the virtuous heroine," even as they thrilled to
the films' sensational climaxes.[164] In the hands of Keystone's filmmakers,
melodrama's ethical ritual quickly shaded into carnivalesque caricature.

Sargent's reference to a "vogue" is significant, since it indicates that
Keystone's burlesque melodramas quickly spawned imitators at other studios. Already by February 1914, Universal had followed Keystone's lead,

instigating production of comic melodramas at both of the studio's comic divisions (Al Christie's Nestor company and the Joker brand), and the format would remain a staple of slapstick production throughout the silent era.[165] Keystone's burlesques were, unarguably, the studio's most influential contribution to American film comedy during its first year and would become one of its most enduring formulas. As late as 1916, advertisements were still promoting the burlesque melodrama as Mack Sennett's "special formula," proven "to get desired results at all times." " 'Take one perfectly good dramatic plot," one ad explained, "soak in several gallons of fun and laughter, pour in one villain and mix thoroughly, add one favored sweetheart, and stir the contents until it is completely twisted out of shape into a hilarious tangle of fun and frolic.' "[166]

By this time, the institutionalization of the format had, as might be expected, all but annulled its original parodic force (thus tilting the force of the burlesque more decisively toward pastiche). Yet the mischievous vitality of the earlier films cannot be stressed too much. Keystone's early parodies mounted a merry resistance to a mode of melodramatic filmmaking that aligned cinematic form with genteel moral precepts. These films lampooned the moral rhetoric through which filmmakers like D. W. Griffith had sought to refine film melodrama and they desacralized efforts to establish motion pictures as a handmaiden for sentimental and domestic ideologies. They appropriated melodrama's moral iconography, emptied it of its content, and subverted it to the transmission of alternative comic messages. In a context of industry gentrification, they were standard-bearers for the studio's playful disregard for the values of genteel culture.

·　　·　　·

"Popular culture," writes Stuart Hall, "is organized around the contradiction: the popular versus the power-bloc"—and the comic pleasures that Keystone offered consistently engaged that contradiction.[167] In its rejection of the "refined" comic style pioneered at Biograph and Vitagraph, in its self-publicized aversion to the tenets of industrial discipline, in its parodying of cinematic forms that gave voice to genteel moral precepts, Keystone articulated and reinforced the values of a working-class culture that differed from and was antagonistic to the culture of the dominant classes. Themselves largely of humble social origins, Keystone's filmmakers were unapologetic about their affinity with the plebeian culture of America's lower classes: popular amusements provided the essential values and traditions with which they chose operate, and it was with the popular classes that the films found their initial success. In certain instances, in fact, those populist affinities impinged directly on class politics, leading the filmmakers into overt activism on behalf of labor issues: in April of 1913, for example, Mabel Normand toured Los Angeles nickelodeons in what was described in the press as a "Socialist propaganda campaign"; and, by early 1916, Sennett himself was writing publicly on behalf of labor, promoting the educational value of "well constructed dramas, uproarious comedies and current news pictures" for working men and women.[168]

Yet such isolated occurrences should neither be overemphasized nor imply a necessarily political subversiveness to Keystone's early form: certainly, one cannot assume an a priori subversive vector to slapstick, no matter the context in which it was produced. The decisive question, in fact, is not whether Keystone slapstick departed from genteel values—it did— but whether that departure was, in the last resort, held in check. It is well to remember that slapstick comedy of the early 1910s was, after all, an entirely *permissible* rupture of hegemony in an industrial context that had learned to delegate such festive populism to a subordinate role. As Peter Krämer has suggested, the revival of slapstick that began around 1911 was possible only because of the consolidation of exhibition practices that prioritized dramas—whether one-reelers or, increasingly, multiple-reel subjects—as "feature" attractions, in relation to which all other genres (comedies, travelogues, etc.) now served as support.[169] The decline in violent comedy could be reversed by filmmakers like Sennett because the subversion for which slapstick stood was now safely contained by industry practices that accorded preeminence to "feature" dramas. This is why it is important to insist that the liberatory pleasures of Keystone slapstick were primarily vicarious and imaginary, and not politically transformative. Perhaps the most that can be said about the politics of Keystone's early form is that it preserved a subsidiary space for the articulation of value systems that departed from dominant ideologies. If this fell far short of actualizing class conflict, still it offered a symbolic configuration for the values and attitudes of American workers; it was, as the German critic Siegfried Kracauer saw it, a "counterweight" to the discipline of an industrializing society.

Yet the point, taken by itself, hardly accounts for the full conditions of Keystone's early success. Who audiences laughed with and who they laughed at proved to be ideologically charged issues that, over Keystone's coming years, would touch on complex questions at the heart of American working-class experience—questions of ethnic division and class membership. Paradoxically, it was a young Englishman who turned out to be the pioneer.

Enter Charles Chaplin.

2. "Funny Germans" and "Funny Drunks"

Clowns, Class, and Ethnicity at Keystone, 1913–1915

In my time, the person doing the comedy was funny to look at. We dressed funny, and we looked funny.

CHESTER CONKLIN, *interviewed in 1955*

To appreciate properly Charles Chaplin's work at Keystone, we need to begin with events at Edendale in the spring of 1914. On March 7 Carl Laemmle's Universal Film Manufacturing Co. ran a two-page advertisement loudly proclaiming its recent acquisition of Keystone's leading comedian, Ford Sterling. Declaring "A Universal Howl of Joy" at the news that "MR. FORD STERLING has joined the big 'U,'" the ad touted a major coup for Universal—and a major setback for Keystone.[1] In one of Universal's characteristic talent raids, Laemmle had acquired the services of a clutch of Keystone filmmakers, including Sterling, the child actor "Little Billy" Jacobs, supporting player Emma Clifton, the directors "Pathé" Lehrman and Robert Thornby, and the general manager of NYMP's West Coast studios, Fred Balshofer.[2] After nearly eighteen months of unequalled success, Keystone was suddenly thrown into crisis. With the ascent of the movie star system as a means of film industry promotion and product differentiation, Sterling's defection came as a galling blow to Keystone, depriving the studio of its most recognizable performer.[3] He had been "my ace comedian," Mack Sennett recalled, and his resignation "put me in a desperate fix": "We claimed to do the impossible always, but it's impossible to run a comedy studio without a leading comedian."[4]

This was the situation from which Chaplin would begin his rise as the most acclaimed comic of his generation. The departure of Ford Sterling was the catalyst for a substantial reorientation in the kinds of characters portrayed by the studio's performers, a transformation with major implications for understanding how Keystone's clowns spoke to the changing

values and experiences of their working-class audience, and a transformation in which Chaplin played a crucial role. Signed to the studio in
September 1913, Chaplin came to Keystone with a tremendous reputation
in vaudeville circles, and, in the wake of Sterling's departure, he quickly
established himself as the studio's new lead.

Despite the veritable avalanche of writing on Chaplin, few scholars have
attempted to explain his meteoric rise, aside from contrasting his "polished
acting and pantomime" with the "hectic, broad Keystone style."[5] While this
is a significant distinction to make—and one that will be developed here—it
is difficult to think of Chaplin's ascent solely as a matter of pacing and polish.
Also important was his skill in defining a comic persona that addressed problematic questions of class and ethnic identity, during a period of structural
transformation within the ranks of America's workers.[6] Over the course of
his twelve-month stay at Keystone, Chaplin played a key part in securing the
transition from a style of comedy predicated on ethnic stereotyping to a
comic form dominated by themes of social class. Where Sterling's performances had fallen squarely within vaudeville traditions of ethnic impersonation, Chaplin's famous "tramp" tended to appear in situations predicated on
the experience of labor and class conflict. No effective account of this shift
can afford to ignore the broader social backdrop against which it occurred.
Chaplin's phenomenal early success occurred at a cultural moment characterized by discourses of "Americanism" and "assimilation" as ideologies for
repressing ethnic difference. Changes in Keystone's comic characters, this
chapter suggests, represented a coming to terms with the changing significance of ethnicity within working-class culture, as immigrant and native-
born laborers alike gradually came to share a common "American" identity
as workers. A close study of Sterling's and Chaplin's work sheds light on the
dualistic pattern of ethnic identity and class membership that structured
working-class experience in the United States during this period and shows
how that pattern was articulated by Keystone's clowns.

"SLOW-THINKING CITIZENS": CLOWNING AND ETHNICITY ON THE VAUDEVILLE STAGE

No discussion of those changes can proceed without first considering
clowning as part of a broader cultural logic of social categorization and
typology. Historically, the very concept of "clown" has involved marginal-
ity. As Louis A. Hieb has argued, the roots of the term stretch back to two
Old German words, *Klonne* ("clumsy lout, lumpish fellow, a countryman,
rustic, or peasant") and *Klunj* ("a clod, clot, or lump").[7] With its conjoined

emphasis on base matter and the socially peripheral, this etymology is remarkably suggestive of the clown's traditional qualities: the clown is "low" both socially ("rustic or peasant") and physically ("clot or lump"). It is this emphasis on physicality, in fact, that has led several writers to interpret clowning through Mikhail Bakhtin's concept of "grotesque realism," an aesthetic category associated with popular festivity and characterized by an exuberant celebration of the "bodily element." The grotesque body, Bakhtin argues, "is unfinished, outgrows itself, transgresses its own limits. The stress is laid on those parts of the body that are open to the outside world, that is, the parts through which the world enters the body or emerges from it, or through which the body itself goes out to meet the world. . . . The body discloses its essence as a principle of growth which exceeds its own limits only in copulation, pregnancy, childbirth, the throes of death, eating, drinking, or defecation."[8] The image of the body in grotesque realism, Bakhtin insists, always exists in a dialectical relation to its counterconcept, that of the "classical" body: a "completed" or "finished" body, with all protuberances removed. If the classical body denotes the totality to which the dominant culture aspires, then the grotesque body— the clown's body—provides a festive iconography that stands against the sober and oppressive contours of that culture.

While Bakhtin's observations provide a useful general rubric for thinking about the image of the clown, their application to any specific instance needs to be guided by an examination of particular historical conjunctures. This is because what counts as "grotesque" and "classical" at any given moment will be determined by the society in which these categories operate. As new social relations and classifications take form historically, so will there be changes in the ideological location of the grotesque, usually to the benefit of one group over another. The clown belongs to a repertoire of carnival imagery that marks out sites of symbolic intensity within a given ideological field; it stands less for a universalized economy of mischief than as a specific, changing ideological symbol, always structured in relation to new social classifications within its audience.[9] The point emerges clearly from a discussion of vaudeville comedy of the late nineteenth and early twentieth centuries, when ethnic impersonators ranked among the most popular and numerous comic performers. In large part, the persistence of racial and ethnic stereotyping was one of vaudeville's inheritances from the festivities, minstrel shows, and saloon entertainments of working-class culture in the antebellum period. Then, whiteness had served as a rallying-point for white workers to assert their sense of entitlement as they competed on the labor market against blacks and new immigrants.[10] During the 1840s in Philadelphia, street parades were often used as an opportunity for the American-born to construct a non-native "other," whether by clowning in blackface or sporting caricatured versions of German dress.[11] As over 11 million foreign-born newcomers arrived in America between 1870 and the end of the century, vaudeville took over these traditions, providing lower-class urban audiences with a venue for channeling the ethnic tensions they encountered daily at the workplace and in inner-city neighborhoods.[12] From the influx of Germans and Irish in the 1840s and 1850s to the arrival of southern and eastern European Jews at the end of the century, each wave of immigration systematically produced a new ethnic stereotype. In contrast with the "classical" body of white America, the vaudeville stage elaborated an iconography of ethnic grotesquery: characteristic elements of costume and makeup drew attention to the orifices and bodily extensions, from the stage Jew's exaggerated nose and protruding ears to the red whiskers and ruddy countenance of Irish performers.[13] If, as has been argued, American popular culture was shaped through the subjugation of its nonwhite folk, then, by the turn of the century, ethnicity had become one of that culture's principal commodities.[14]

One way to frame these performances would be to see them as a kind of "social gesture" designed to identify and lampoon the undesirable characteristics and behaviors of America's most recent arrivals.[15] But, as David Roediger's fascinating analysis of nineteenth-century blackface suggests, such a reading hardly does justice to the complex layers of fear and desire that mobilized such caricatures. Ethnic and racial stereotyping, Roediger argues, grew so strongly during the nineteenth century because blacks and recent immigrants came to symbolize ways of living that American-born white laborers had given up, but still longed for. As new patterns of capitalist work discipline reshaped the lives of the nineteenth-century labor force, blackface performance became a way for white workers to project onto others the preindustrial behaviors that they themselves had reluctantly abandoned. Rural and shiftless, spontaneous and sexual, dandified and drunk: the stereotyped "coon" embodied a preindustrial past that white workers both scorned and missed. Antebellum stereotypes of the Irish likewise enacted behaviors frowned upon in the new world of wage labor: drinking, brawling, and irregular work habits. So much was this the case, in fact, that undisciplined behavior in the 1830s was often called "acting Irish."[16]

Roediger's model has a broad applicability that makes it useful in this analysis. If antebellum stereotypes gave vent to frustrations born of industrial labor, might not the same be said of later racial and ethnic representations, especially since the rigors of industrialization only intensified in the later period? Certainly, there are tempting parallels, albeit with notable changes of emphasis. Where earlier stereotypes of idle blacks and brawling Irishmen provoked laughter through their deficiency with respect to industrial standards of discipline, later caricatures also mocked those who had too fully internalized those standards. For turn-of-the-century vaudeville audiences, it was often the very *excessiveness* of the immigrant's pursuit of capitalist values that drew ridicule, notably in the case of the miserly stage Jew. Ethnic acquisitiveness also formed the kernel of the tradition of German impersonation, a form of performance popularly known, by corruption of the word *Deutsch*, as "Dutch" comedy. For Sam Bernard, one of the pioneering German impersonators of the vaudeville stage, the tradition of Dutch comedy was at heart a satire of the immigrant's overzealous quest for class mobility. "To me, the funniest thing in New York at that time [the late 1870s and early 1880s] was the German American. He was a pompous, weighty, slow-thinking citizen. Through American influence he had fallen under the spell of a prosperous sign peculiar to that period. It was the spell of the two-pound chain attached to the five-pound watch."[17] Sporting garish frock coats, top hats, watch chains, and—invariably—a closely cropped goatee (known as a *schnurbart*), Dutch comedians ruthlessly parodied the German immigrant's supposedly excessive desire for the trappings of middle-class respectability.[18] Whether through excess or deficiency, the ethnic stereotype enacted behaviors marked as aberrant in the context of a new industrial society.

Thinking about stereotypes in this light allows one to understand what might otherwise remain paradoxical: namely, the appeal they held even for the implicated immigrant audience. Certainly, it would be a mistake to assume that ethnic caricature was wholly inscribed within the prejudices of native whites. Immigrants flocked to see themselves parodied on the vaudeville stage, and German and Yiddish humor magazines often carried caricatural images similar to those in *Puck* and *Judge*.[19] The invidious impetus behind ethnic stereotyping, as a gesture of social exclusion, was also evidently available for appropriation by the immigrants themselves. Perhaps, for the newly arrived, the ethnic clown served a similar assimilative function as for the native, symbolizing gaucheries to be abandoned as they adapted to American industrial society. To laugh at their own stereotype would, on this reading, have been a way for immigrants to reject that "greenhorn" aspect of themselves not yet Americanized: it affirmed commitment to American cultural norms and, as such, appealed to the immigrant's own desire to "fit in," perhaps especially so for second-generation immigrants less attached to ethnicity than their parents.[20]

Such considerations go some way, at least, toward explaining why ethnic parody found a welcome home in film comedy of the nickelodeon era, when immigrants formed a key component of cinema's patronage among the lower classes. At a time when first- and second-generation immigrants commonly accounted for over two-thirds of the blue-collar workforce in northeastern cities, films like *The Finish of Bridget McKeen* (1901) or *Cohen's Advertising Scheme* (1904) doubtless offered a way for filmgoers of all backgrounds to negotiate the interethnic frictions of their daily lives. No doubt also the ethnic stereotype on film exercised the same adaptive role as in vaudeville: an instrument for disciplining a heterogeneous working class to the new industrial morality. The questions, however, concern what film scholars have usually described as a falling off of ethnic stereotyping by the early 1910s. Did the film industry's dependence on an ethnically diverse audience really force a cutback on malicious caricatures during the nickelodeon era? Do the years 1906 to 1908 really mark a decisive turn away from offensive stereotypes, as one historian has contended?[21] Certainly, changes occurred during this period—for instance, a trending toward more sympathetic, sentimentalized depictions of immigrant life, as in Biograph's 1908 *Romance of a Jewess*. Yet it would err too much on the side of benevolence to assume that ethnic caricature retained only a muted presence in comedies of the 1910s. From its founding in 1912, in fact, the Keystone Film Company firmly grounded its slapstick style in the comedy of ethnic impersonation.[22]

Out of 126 comic subjects released in Keystone's first twelve months of operations, 43 (just over one third) can be identified as featuring prominent ethnic or racial characterizations.[23] As on the vaudeville stage, "Dutch," Jewish, and Irish characterizations predominated (appearing in fifteen, ten, and eight releases, respectively), though other races and ethnicities also received burlesque treatment. (A handful of releases included portrayals of French, Spanish, Italian and Native American characters, and at least five featured blackface roles, for example, *The Darktown Belle* [May 1913] and *Rastus and the Gamecock* [July 1913].) During its first year, in fact, Keystone not only depended upon such comedy—it overtly *marketed* its product in these terms, spotlighting the ethnic basis of its comedy with titles such as *Cohen Collects a Debt* (September 1912), *Pat's Day Off,* and *Hoffmeyer's Legacy* (December 1912). Promotional copy for the studio's forthcoming releases frequently pointed up ethnicity as a comic attraction, such as the ad for *The Riot* (August 1913), which promised the hilarious spectacle of a race riot, describing how "Mrs. Kelly upholds the fighting reputation of [her] race" while the "Jews rally to the defense of their fellowman."[24] And when, in May 1913, Mack Sennett began work on

Keystone's first ever two-reel special, *The Fire Bug* (August 1913), he turned to one of the most hackneyed formulas of vaudeville ethnic comedy: the "arson plot," in which a Jew takes out fire insurance on his place of business and then burns it down. "This is a screamingly comical dramatization of the exposure of the 'Arson Trust,'" proclaimed an advertisement, beneath a still showing Nick Cogley and Mack Sennett sporting derby hats and scraggly whiskers, the established iconography of the stage Jew.[25]

The apprenticeship of many Keystone performers in vaudeville and burlesque may have been an important determinant here: in parodying immigrant groups, Sennett and his troupe were simply working within comic traditions with which they were familiar. The Irish backgrounds of some of Keystone's leading players are also likely relevant. Recent debates among historians of race have shown how Irish performers had been at the forefront of late-nineteenth-century traditions of ethnic and racial impersonation, particularly blackface.[26] For Irish workers, whose own "whiteness" was often questioned, vaudeville caricature had been a means of constructing white identities through the staging of difference; it circled the cultural wagons against African Americans and newly arrived immigrants and allowed the Irish to assert their assimilation as whites. By building upon those traditions, Sennett may well have been translating his own ethnic affiliations into slapstick form.

But he was also—and not for the first time—contesting the class-based standards of "respectability" through which the industry sought cultural legitimacy. In the emerging public sphere of mass culture, of which cinema was increasingly a part, ethnic impersonation had come to be deplored as "low" comedy, a style of humor whose association with working-class subcultures placed it beyond the pale for those who sought middle-class acceptability. As *Moving Picture World* editorialized in October 1913, "We have on more than one occasion pointed out the bad taste and business folly of ridiculing nationalities or races as such. . . . The 'comic' picture which has no other claim on the appreciation of an audience than the ridicule heaped upon a certain nationality ought to be barred forever."[27]

Given that early cinema had been such a repository for ethnic stereotypes, critics seeking the betterment of the medium now regularly lambasted what one called the "almost critical ignorance of and prejudice against the inhabitants of other nations" and charged filmmakers with a responsibility to overcome such prejudice.[28] Deeply implicated in working-class modes of discourse and representation, the ethnic stereotype had become an obstacle to cinema's bid for genteel approval. Keystone's continued reliance on such stereotypes thus became a way in which Sennett's studio, once again, sustained slapstick's links to the culture of America's workers. Commentators of the time were certainly attuned to the relation between Keystone's ethnic comedy and the tastes of the working class. As a reviewer for *Moving Picture World* observed, the immigrant characterizations of one of Keystone's earliest releases, *Riley and Schultz* (September 1912), seemed "intended for friends of burlesque."[29] Here, as on the vaudeville stage, ethnic comedy may have continued to focus the tensions and frustrations, the longings and the prejudices of urban workers. Yet, as the career of one Keystone performer suggests, those sentiments were, by the mid-1910s, on the brink of radical change.

"QUEER JUMPS AND COMICAL ANTICS": FORD STERLING AND THE DECLINE OF THE ETHNIC STEREOTYPE

Among the most popular and enduring forms of ethnic caricature, the tradition of Dutch comedy gave rise to one of Keystone's first major stars—Ford Sterling, a Wisconsin-born veteran of circus and popular theater, himself of German descent.[30] Already by early 1913, commentators were singling out Sterling's work for the company, praising the purported realism of his ethnic impersonations and stressing their connection to vaudeville. "The experience gained by Ford Sterling . . . in vaudeville," noted *Moving Picture World* that April, "has stood him in good stead since his advent in silent drama. . . . . [H]is impersonations of German, Hebrew and Irish characters on the screen leaves [sic] little to be desired and marks the true artist."[31]

Although he appeared in numerous ethnic roles, Sterling was most closely associated with his "Dutch" performances, for which he combined traditional costume elements (goatee, top hat, and frock coat) with a handful of idiosyncratic additions, such as outsize shoes and wire-rimmed glasses (fig. 6). While a lack of extant prints makes it difficult to determine when Sterling first employed this characterization at Keystone, it had clearly been established as his recurrent persona by the end of March 1913, during which month he appeared in his Dutch guise four times in succession, in *A Strong Revenge* (March 10), *The Two Widows* (March 13), *The Man Next Door* (March 17), and *On His Wedding Day* (March 31).[32] Variously referred to in the trades as "Schnitzel," "Krause," and "Meyer," Sterling's Dutch persona soon made him a full-fledged picture personality. No other comedian received more reader votes in *Photoplay*'s 1913 popularity contest, and, by the following year, exhibitors were capitalizing on his reputation with billboards advertising "That Funny German" as a key attraction.[33] Such was his popularity that, in early 1914, the Mutual

FIGURE 6.   Ford Sterling in a production still from *Love and Dynamite* (January 1914). Courtesy of the Academy of Motion Picture Arts and Sciences.

organization briefly publicized its *entire* line around Sterling's Dutch character—the first time Mutual had promoted a single performer in this way—in news ads featuring a pen sketch of his persona captioned "See This Funny Fellow in MUTUAL MOVIES."[34]

Fan publicity on Sterling illustrates the extent to which actors' personal identities and their on-screen characters were fused during this early phase in the star system's development. Extratextual discourse on the comedian offered fans a sustained experience of his screen personality, eliding the gap between the humorous exploits of his film characterizations and the purportedly real events of Sterling's daily life. *Photoplay*, for example, began to run droll—and doubtless fictitious—anecdotes recounting Sterling's off-camera misadventures and experiences. A representative example had Sterling offering romantic advice such as: "At a dance try to step on a girl's feet or tear her frock. Then she will forget all about your homely face."[35] At the same time, fans grew increasingly curious about the actor "behind the makeup." Shortly after Sterling's defection to Universal (where his Dutch persona was renamed "Snookie"), *Motion Picture Story Magazine* noted that most fans would fail to recognize the "funniest man in Moving Pictures" if they saw him out of character, and it printed a photo of him *sans* makeup to clarify any uncertainties.[36] A cartoon in an earlier issue addressed the same disparity, offering a caricatured drawing of Sterling in his familiar guise next to a portrait of him "As He Looks in Private Life."[37]

Sterling's burgeoning fame also provoked a significant realignment in the way Keystone's output was organized in relation to its comedians. Where the studio's earlier releases and publicity had generally refrained from foregrounding individual performances, this changed with the popularity of the studio's lead comedian. Nowhere was this more evident than in the announcement of a two-reel special starring Sterling for release on Christmas Eve, 1913. Colorfully titled *Zuzu, the Band Leader*, the film was distributed separately from Keystone's regular schedule of releases and made available to all exhibitors without restriction. While the extensive publicity campaign stressed the "personal direction of Mack Sennett," accompanying photos placed Sterling's performance front and center, showing him clad in bandmaster's regalia and sporting his trademark Dutch makeup.[38] The film itself, though now lost, seems likewise to have been predicated on its star's performative virtuosity. "At the opening," the *Moving Picture World* reviewer George Blaisdell noted, "we see the idolized Zuzu in the center of his most industrious musicians. The band-stand is the roof of a single-story jewelry establishment. In front of him are hundreds of idolizers, among them Mable [sic]." The centrality of Sterling's performance was thus underscored by its metaphoric inscription within the world of the film: the star performer on the Keystone lot, Sterling was first seen in *Zuzu* as a star performer before an admiring audience. This dynamic of performance and spectatorship seems also to have been reinforced by "alternating views of the antic-performing bandmaster and the maid Mable [sic] . . . [who is] smitten with him."[39] That is, Sennett's direction exploited a basic shot–reverse shot structure (the reference of "alternating views") as a way of centering Sterling's/Zuzu's performance within the visual economy of the film. During the film's opening scene, it would appear, narrative situation and editing worked together to initiate a more comedian-centered comedy than was the norm for Keystone at this time.

Though Blaisdell considered it likely to disappoint the "average house," *Zuzu* proved the biggest moneymaker thus far in Keystone's brief history, quickly recouping its $3,000 cost of production. It also played a role in raising the visibility of the Keystone brand name, as, for instance, in Toledo, Ohio, where the film was the first Keystone picture to be advertised in local press listings.[40] Within the first three months of its release, *Zuzu* brought Keystone net profits of $6,871.54, and by April 1915, when the film was eventually withdrawn from circulation, that figure had risen to $10,028.27.[41] As with its only previous two-reeler, *The Fire Bug*, Keystone had banked upon the popularity of its ethnic impersonators as insurance against the financial risk of two-reel production. But where *The Fire Bug* had proven a one-off, *Zuzu* began a permanent shift toward two-reel production. Shortly after the film's release, Keystone's output was increased to three weekly one-reel productions and a two-reel special every month. As reported in the trade press, four new units were added to facilitate the heightened productivity, thereby "bring[ing] the list to a total of seven directors with the accompanying seven companies."[42] Implicitly acknowledging the importance of his star comedians, Sennett also granted several of Keystone's top performers the opportunity of directing their own units, beginning with Sterling himself and Mabel Normand in December.

The enormous popularity of Sterling's ethnic portrayals thus contributed to Keystone's expansion. Yet the factors behind that popularity—specifically, Sterling's perceived originality, as one critic put it, in getting "entirely away from the old style" of ethnic impersonation—also point to ethnicity's important role in shaping the fast-paced physicality of Keystone's early comic form.[43] At the simplest level, the uniqueness of Sterling's ethnic characterizations was consequent upon cinema's limitations as a silent medium: in Sterling's performances, the verbal transgressions of ethnic dialect humor were translated into physical eccentricity. The splintered and ungrammatical patois of vaudeville's ethnic clowns thus found a corporeal equivalent in what one critic described as Sterling's "disregard for the retention of anatomical unity."[44] Certainly, reviewers recognized the comedian's "queer jumps and comical antics" and "extra-gingered animation" as distinguishing features of his comedy; one commentator even complained that Sterling's exaggerated movements in *A Strong Revenge* impaired the accuracy of his ethnic characterizations. ("[This] funny situation," the review began, "suffers from overacting. . . . [Dutch] characters do not make violent gestures with their hands, such as these actors would have us believe.")[45] Commonly noted also were Sterling's remarkable facial contortions, a celebrated hallmark of the comedian's performance style. From at least as early as *Hide and Seek* (April 1913), close-ups of the comedian's contorted visage were a common attraction in his films—invariably reserved for moments of physical pain (as in *Hide and Seek*, when a safe door falls on top of him)—and Sterling quickly garnered a reputation as a "master in the art of facial expression."[46] Advertisements for Sterling's films often prominently featured the comedian's grimacing face: for the release of its first Sterling vehicle, *Love and Vengeance* (April 1914), Universal ran ads featuring no fewer than eight headshots illustrating his famous mugging (fig. 7).[47] The physicalization of Sterling's comic form was also underscored in the formal pacing of his films, in which rapid editing accentuated the spectacle of breakneck motion. In particular, Sterling's self-directed releases experimented with a remarkably swift tempo, seemingly designed to showcase the clown's manic physical presence. Both *Double Crossed* (January 1914) and *A False Beauty* (March 1914)—the only surviving prints of Sterling's self-directed films from 1914—exceed all previous Keystone releases in speed of editing, with average shot lengths of 4.1 and 4.6 seconds respectively (approximately a twofold increase over the cutting rate of Keystone's 1913 films).[48]

In its hyperbolizing of the physical elements of performance, Sterling's comedy thematizes ethnicity as grotesque and eccentric spectacle, inviting a form of spectatorship that implies, in turn, an attitude of social separation. The immigrant becomes the object of a cinematic gaze that constitutes its social superiority by substituting distance for empathy, mockery for identification.[49] A paradigmatic example is *That Ragtime Band* (May 1913), which, like the later *Zuzu*, features Sterling as the conductor of a German marching band, this time vying for Mabel's affections against a rival trumpeter. The film also prefigures *Zuzu* in its reliance on shot–reverse shot editing, here exploited as a means of staging the clown's humiliation beneath the gaze of another, both the characters in the screen story and the spectator watching the film. In an early sequence, for instance, Mabel sits in on the band's rehearsal, while Sterling makes mooning faces at her. The scene is organized around, and made meaningful by, Mabel's amusement at the bandleader's simpering attempts to impress her: three times the film cuts

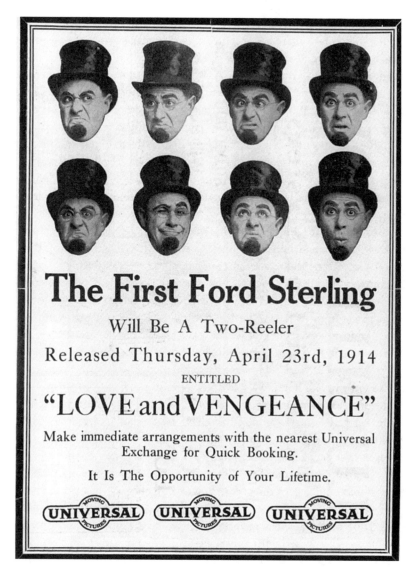

FIGURE 7. Trade press advertisement for Universal's *Love and Vengeance*. From *Moving Picture World*, April 11, 1914.

from a long shot of the band to a close-up of Mabel's sniggering face, inviting the spectator to share her laughter at the German's grotesque posturing.
This formal strategy also provides the basis of the film's final scene, where
a similar handling of the optical field underscores a more aggressive comedy
of humiliation. Here, the band puts on a disastrous show at a cheap vaudeville theater, the film repeatedly cutting between shots of the hostile audience jeering and throwing vegetables and long shots of the band from the
audience's perspective. As in the earlier sequence, the manipulation of point
of view places the film spectator in visual alliance with the fictional audience
and, as a necessary corollary, at a visual and affective distance vis-à-vis the
ethnic clown. As the film prompts laughter at the bandleader's disgrace, so
the pelting he endures reduces him to the purely physical level of sensory-
motor response, leaving him slipping on vegetable debris in the concluding
images. "The 'rough-house' ending," a reviewer for *Moving Picture World*
noted, "will not appeal to a refined audience."[50]

One way to interpret such comedy would be in terms of what Umberto
Eco has called the "comic effect," the hostile laughter invoked by the punishment and humiliation of an "animal-like"—and, in this case, ethnic—
clown. In instances of the comic effect, Eco writes, a social norm is violated
by someone with whom we do not sympathize because he is an "ignoble,
inferior, and repulsive" character.[51] Comic pleasure, in such instances, is
mixed: on the one hand, we vicariously enjoy the clown's transgressive
behavior as a challenge to the repressive power of social order; yet, because
we feel superior to this animal-like character, we laugh also at his consequent punishment and disgrace. It is just such a pattern that structures
Sterling's ethnic performances. Like *That Ragtime Band*, his films generally culminate in the immigrant's humiliation before a crowd of onlookers,
a trope that emphasizes the ethnic clown's culpable and grotesque visibility, inscribing it within the narrative through acts of shaming and exposure. Time and again, the "funny German" is caught in compromising
situations—discovered with another man's wife (*Toplitsky and Co.*, May
1913), unmasked as a social imposter (*His Chum, the Baron*, April 1913),
or exposed as a thief *(Double Crossed)*. Ethnic difference is something to be
exposed, lampooned, and punished; it is what Eco terms "an object of a
judgment of superiority," one that requires the immigrant clown to render
otherness visible as comic display.[52]

.   .   .

Despite his success during 1913, Sterling's Keystone films constituted perhaps the last time that ethnic stereotyping would enjoy such overt presence

in silent film comedy. Although generally recognized as the most talented ethnic impersonator in film comedy, Sterling declined in popularity over the course of 1914. His films for Universal proved disappointing and, chastened by their failure, he returned to Keystone early the following year. Given the large ethnic component of early motion-picture audiences, such stereotyping had always been a somewhat risky proposition: Charles Musser cites the example of the 1907 comedy *Murphy's Wake*, which prompted Irish filmgoers to threaten to destroy the Lyric Theater in Providence, Rhode Island, unless the film was withdrawn.[53] Cinema's growing presence as a form of mass entertainment only made this kind of comedy more problematic in subsequent years. Doubtless those immigrants who had arrived in the closing decades of the nineteenth century had not enjoyed the social security that would have allowed them to protest their portrayal, whether on film or on the vaudeville stage; but this was no longer true by the early 1910s, as second- and third-generation immigrants sought to participate in society on a more equal footing than their forebears. For immigrant audiences who sought assimilation, the "greenhorn" caricature likely still provoked laughter; but the more assimilated those audiences became, the more those stereotypes must have grated: immigrants who espoused middle-class values were tiring of caricatures of themselves in fright wigs and chin whiskers. The old stereotypes that had poked fun at America's recent arrivals, while still visible, now began to recede.[54] Organizations were formed explicitly to oppose the disparagement of immigrant groups, from the tortuously titled Chicago Anti–Stage Jew Vigilance Committee (formed in 1913) to the Anti-Defamation League of B'nai B'rith (1914).[55] Meanwhile, activism of a different kind put paid to the Dutch tradition after a German U-boat sank the British luxury ocean liner RMS *Lusitania* on May 7, 1915, with the loss of almost 1,200 lives, including many Americans, precipitating a wave of anti-German sentiment in the United States. Within this charged political climate, benignly comic representations of Germans were freighted with risk.[56] One of the most celebrated Dutch comics of the vaudeville stage, Al Shean (German-born as Albert Schönberg), fell into temporary critical disfavor after making a passing comment on the war during one of his performances. As one critic complained, "Mr. Shean has the more credible impersonation, has he not—of the German born who is faithful and true to the nation that has adopted him and made him rich? . . . . [But he] is not quite right this fellow, is he, since no one should be talkative for war unless he or his blood is in the war. Should we not have a lot of silence from those who have not undergone the great emotion? Something tells us that we should."[57]

Although its ethnic output was only infrequently a target of explicit censure, Keystone could not long remain insulated from broader pressures. Chicago's police censors gave Sennett's studio an early lesson in the pitfalls of ethnic stereotyping when, in May 1914, they refused a permit to Keystone's *The Peddler,* citing a Jewish caricature as their chief objection: "Permit refused because picture ridicules a Jewish peddler."[58] The ethnic stereotype had in any case become a far less visible presence in Keystone's output following Sterling's departure. Studio policy even formalized the trend when, early in 1915, ethnically neutral character names were announced for the studio's top performers. "Keystone players . . . [are] to be assigned definite names for all productions," reported *Motion Picture News* in January. "Roscoe Arbuckle is to be known as Fatty, Miss Normand as Mabel, Mack Swain as Ambrose, Chester Conklin . . . as Mr. Droppington, and Sid Chaplin [Charles Chaplin's half-brother] as Mr. Gussell."[59] Needless to say, a palpable distance separates names such as Ambrose and Droppington from the earlier Cohens and Schnitzels: eccentricity had begun to substitute for ethnicity as a basis of comic characterization.[60] But it would be wrong to overstate the discontinuity these transformations entailed with respect to Keystone's clowns. A case in point is Mack Swain's "Ambrose" character, a hulking dolt who, adorned with spit curl and bristling mustache, proved to be one of Keystone's most popular fixtures during 1915. Owing little to preexisting traditions of ethnic impersonation, the Ambrose character lacked determinate social identity, appearing in a wide range of roles, from a medieval king in *Ambrose's Lofty Perch* (March 1915) to a factory foreman in *Ambrose's Nasty Temper* (April 1915). Yet ethnicity remained an ambiguous substratum of the character, a secondary element brought to the fore in films such as *Fatty's New Role* (February 1915), where Ambrose appears as a German saloonkeeper, and *Wilful Ambrose* (March 1915), in which Swain plays a German paterfamilias. Other comedians, meanwhile, reworked ethnic iconography while suppressing overt ethnic connotations. Such was the case with the enormous mustache that Chester Conklin sported for his roles as "Mr. Droppington" and "Walrus," which had formed part of his stage makeup during his early career as a Dutch monologist.[61] Originally a marker of immigrant identity, Conklin's mustache became a more universal comic signifier at Keystone, where his trademark characterizations were rarely given an ethnic dimension.[62] The mustache became a visualization of immigrant difference no longer acknowledged as such (fig. 8).

There is an important sense, then, in which the new characters were less replacements for the ethnic stereotype than incomplete markers beneath

FIGURE 8.   Mack Swain as "Ambrose" (left) and Chester Conklin as "Walrus." Courtesy of the Academy of Motion Picture Arts and Sciences.

which the ethnic stereotype could be suppressed: Keystone's comic characters became palimpsests within which traces of ethnicity remained as dormant substrata. More than that, however, they had trajectories that displaced specific ethnic traits in favor of a generalized iconography of "working-class" identity. Characters like Conklin's Walrus, Syd Chaplin's Gussle, and Charles Murray's Hogan consistently appeared in lumpenproletariat roles that assimilated traditions of ethnic impersonation to the representation of class. Concomitantly, the studio's films increasingly derived humor more from comic interactions across class boundaries than from the dynamics of ethnic impersonation. The course of comic performance at Keystone, as will shortly be examined in more detail, was thus to liquidate the comedy of ethnic difference into the comedy of class hierarchy.

Such an evolution indicates that there was more at stake in these changes than immigrant sensitivities. Changes in Keystone's comic characters occurred in the context of working-class formation and can be traced to changing structures of workers' social experience. The older tradition of ethnic stereotyping had assumed an ethnically separatist working class; but, as several historians have observed, those separations began to loosen during the 1910s, as workers of all backgrounds slowly came together to share their leisure time in new sites of commercialized amusement. A new working-class public was being forged out of earlier ethnic and cultural divisions, albeit one in which some degree of separation still marked its communities. The American-born children of immigrant families not only frequented commercial amusements more often than their parents, but, in so doing, were participating in a process of "Americanization" in which ethnic allegiances were now joined by a common sense of class identity. Roy Rosenzweig, for example, has argued that the commercialization of leisure helped foster opportunities for class solidarity across ethnic lines.[63] Meanwhile, at the workplace, the 1910s saw strengthened initiatives toward a "new unionism" that opened union membership to formerly excluded immigrant groups.[64] In the eyes of Chicago School sociologists in the 1920s, such developments suggested the importance of assimilation as a concept for understanding immigrant experience. Ethnic difference, the Chicago sociologist William Isaac Thomas argued in his classic study *The Polish Peasant in Europe and America* (1918–1920), was less a matter of innate, biological distinction than of cultural factors: if the old regime of urban society had been based upon traditional ethnic solidarities, the new order would be organized largely in terms of class.[65]

Of course, not all minority groups were included in this partial equalizing of working-class identities. The reality of African-American segregation was continually reinforced by blackface depictions of racial "otherness" in vaudeville and minstrelsy, as also in Keystone films.[66] The pattern mirrors one noted by most historians of race: namely, that differences understood culturally (as "ethnicity") were perceived as assimilable, while differences classified biologically (as "race") were not.[67] Thus, even as Dutch and Jewish stereotypes disappeared from the studio's output, blackface comedies remained a consistent, if minor, production trend—for example, *A Dark Lover's Play, Colored Villainy* (January 1915), *The Hunt* (December 1915), *By Stork Delivery* (March 1916), and *The Love Comet* (May 1916). One way to interpret the shift from ethnicity to class at Keystone, then, would be to see it as synecdochal for structural changes within a working class gradually constituting itself in terms of whiteness. In a context marked by a hesitantly emerging consensus dominated by concepts of "assimilation" and "Americanization," the studio's new characterizations represented a coming to terms with a more inclusive understanding of white working-class identity. What historians describe as the "whitening" of ethnic groups may have found comic articulation in the ersatz whiteness of clowns who had formerly depicted ethnic types.

There are at least two kinds of questions to be considered with respect to these hypotheses. The first concerns concrete developments on the

Keystone lot: which of Sennett's filmmakers were centrally involved in this transformation? But this issue must in turn be fleshed out by theoretical considerations about Keystone's interaction with its audiences: how did the clown's transformed social identity affect the class address of the studio's films? What patterns of spectatorship might these changes have invited? It is time, in any case, to look at Charles Chaplin's work at Keystone.

"ONE OF NATURE'S OWN NATURALS": CHARLES CHAPLIN AND THE COMEDY OF CLASS

One of the ironies surrounding Chaplin's astonishing rise to stardom is that it began during a period when Keystone sought publicly to downplay the significance of individual stars to the studio style. In the weeks following Sterling's defection to Universal, NYMP's publicity apparatus had launched a thinly veiled attack on Laemmle's organization, releasing a series of pugnacious advertisements that derided corporate dependency on star power. "A HIGHLY ADVERTISED STAR working under a poor director, with a weak scenario, dragging along a mediocre company, are methods that have never been employed by the NEW YORK MOTION PICTURE CORP. to hoodwink the exhibitor," proclaimed the first of these. "Our strength lies in the fact that we have made it a point to get PRODUCERS whom we knew to have great executive abilities in addition to being the World's GREATEST DIRECTORS."[68] A similar ad the following week insisted that "the school is greater than its pupils," and that "defection from its ranks of a few actresses and actors has absolutely no effect upon its firm establishment and steady progress."[69] Keystone's house style, exhibitors were supposed to realize, counted for more than the talent of any single performer.

Despite such proud assertions, it was only to be expected that Keystone's filmmakers invested hopes in Chaplin, their most recent—and, at a starting salary of $150 a week, their most expensive—major hiring. Prior to signing with Keystone in September 1913, Chaplin was already well known—famous, even—within vaudeville circles. A two-year tour with the American company of the famous British impresario Fred Karno had established him as one of the premier stage comedians in the United States, celebrated for his role as "The Inebriate" in the Karno sketch "A Night in an English Music Hall." His very first appearance in a Keystone film—*Making a Living* (February 1914), for which he appeared in his stage costume of top hat and handlebar mustache—had also scored a distinct success. "The clever player who takes the role of a nervy and very nifty sharper in this picture," commented a reviewer for *Moving Picture World*, "is a comedian of the first water."[70] If any of Keystone's performers were poised to take Sterling's place, it was Chaplin.

But what kind of character was he to play? Ford Sterling had built his reputation on ethnic characterizations, and, at the height of the crisis provoked by his departure, Sennett evidently considered whether Chaplin could be fitted into a similar mold. For his performance in *Mabel at the Wheel* (April 1914), the English comedian was clearly asked to impersonate the former star in a tactical attempt to take some of the wind out of Universal's sails. Made up in something loosely resembling Sterling's Dutch costume of chin whiskers, top hat, and tight-fitting frock coat, Chaplin mugged his way through what became an unhappy and quarrelsome production.[71] It would not be by impersonating others that Chaplin helped Keystone out of its crisis. What distinguished him and made him famous was, of course, the tramp, a comic persona first adopted for the filming of *Mabel's Strange Predicament* (February 1914) and which would feature in twenty-seven of his thirty-five Keystone films.[72] Within weeks, the success of his characterization launched him on the dizzying ascent that would make him the world's most recognizable screen performer: already by late March, *Motion Picture News* announced that Chaplin was "on his way to be a comedian of the films of country-wide popularity."[73] By the end of August, Otto Meister, manager of the Vaudette nickelodeon in Milwaukee, reported that the star's films were proving "sure winners"; and, in November the following year, Chaplin was awarded first place in the "male comedian" category in *Motion Picture Magazine*'s "Great Cast Contest."[74]

Such phenomenal popularity could only have emerged at the intersection of several crosscurrents in the development of film comedy during the mid-1910s, chief among which was the vocal disfavor into which ethnic caricature had fallen by this time. For audiences increasingly resentful at stereotyping expressions of ethnic difference, Chaplin provided a comic persona in which ethnic traits were subordinate to lower working-class identity. Where the trade press had commonly used names like "Krause" or "Schnitzel" to refer to Sterling's performances, Chaplin's tramp was described as a more generalized figure, a "goat" or "funny drunk," to quote two examples.[75] And where Keystone's previous comedians fell squarely within established traditions of ethnic costume, Chaplin was acknowledged as a *bricoleur* of those traditions, a borrower who combined distinct elements to create the famous tramp. According to the earliest published account of the tramp's origins—Harry Carr's "Charlie Chaplin's Story," published in *Photoplay* in the fall of 1915—the costume was an amalgam of costume traditions: a shabby derby (traditional accoutrement of the stage Jew), a "long drooping moustache" trimmed down to become the famous "little toothbrush," and a "funny old pair of shoes . . . [that] had been Ford Sterling's."[76] Likely apocryphal, that story remains important for the way it presents Chaplin's tramp as a composite figure: the tramp outfit appears here as a recombination of preexisting paradigms of costuming, an ambiguous visualization of incompatible immigrant characteristics, a hybridized mechanism for obscuring ethnic affiliations.

Despite such indeterminacies, Chaplin's persona was nonetheless a recognizable social figure, one that would have had direct personal relevance for a significant portion of the working-class audience. As a distinct social type—as opposed to a comic stereotype—the tramp was a particularly visible figure within America of the period 1870 to 1920, when, in the wake of the upheavals wrought by the economic crisis of 1873 and the depression of 1893, as many as a fifth of American workers spent some time as transients.[77] Tramping thus formed part of the common work experience of industrial America. But it was also a familiar theme of turn-of-the-century popular culture, where the tramp was a stock character of newspaper strips, dime novels, vaudeville, and early film comedy.[78] (The American Mutoscope and Biograph Co.'s 1897 film *The Tramp and the Bathers* has been cited as the first motion-picture appearance of the comic hobo.)[79] The key to the tramp's popularity, it would appear, lay in creating a figure whose behavior had comic appeal to those approaching it from different class and ethnic perspectives. Thus, from 1900, working-class readers of the popular-priced *New York Journal* could enjoy Frederick Burr Opper's "Happy Hooligan" cartoon strip, no doubt delighting in Hooligan's bumbling confrontations with figures of authority. Yet, also during the same period, the illustrator James Montgomery Flagg developed the comic tramp for a more genteel audience in a series of "Nervy Nat" cartoons published in the magazine *Judge* between 1903 and 1907. What distinguished Chaplin's work within this tradition was his success in bringing the broad caricatures of popular culture closer to the realities of transient working life. Charles Musser has noted how Chaplin's costume exhibits remarkable similarities to the style of dress worn by actual tramps of the late nineteenth century, as documented in the photographic studies of the Connecticut reformer John James McCook.[80] Likewise, his screen vehicles at Keystone generally construct narratives that directly engage the experience of transient labor: each film typically begins with the tramp pottering around in a park or on a street corner, employed as a menial employee, or looking for work. The tramp is defined, not by consistency of occupation, but by the range of his employment, as a waiter (e.g., *Caught in a Cabaret*, April 1914), a dentist's assistant (*Laughing Gas*, July 1914), a vaudeville stagehand (*The Property Man*, August 1914), a piano deliverer (*His Musical Career*, November 1914), or a janitor (*The New Janitor*, September 1914).

Few scholars, however, have teased out the implications of Chaplin's tramp identity as it relates to issues of ethnicity in early comedy. Certainly, one overlooked aspect of the tramping phenomenon—both as social experience and as cultural symbol—was its inscription in debates over working-class ethnic and racial identity. Though immigrants may have made up a substantial portion of the tramping work force (anywhere between a quarter and two-thirds, according to local studies of the time), most contemporary observers tended to associate hoboes with the *native* working class.[81] "I find on the road no immigrant hoboes," a writer for the *Los Angeles Citizen* noted in late 1913. "They are all American-born."[82] Each tramp, another writer noted, "is a real American man . . . good in emergencies, when the ordinary European laborer is likely to be a 'quitter.' "[83]

At a time of public anxiety over the "new" immigration from Catholic and Slavic nations, the tramp had become a site for actualizing ideologies of American whiteness, the very emblem of an "American" working-class racial identity. A minor genre of "life on the road" accounts reclaimed the tramp as the lasting invocation of the frontier spirit, even as the frontier was finally closing. Jack London's 1907 memoir of his youthful hobo experiences, *The Road*, implicitly engages American traditions of mobility in describing the "charm" of tramping life—the "absence of monotony," "an ever changing phantasmagoria" in which the tramp, having "learned the futility of telic endeavor," lives "only in the present moment."[84] Nels Anderson's sociological study *The Hobo* (1923) meanwhile presents the tramp as an avatar of Anglo-American whiteness, the very model of native individualism—"American in the same sense that the cowboy was," in the author's words.[85] Such nativist associations even played out upon the vaudeville stage, where the tramp supplied comic material diametrically opposed to traditions of ethnic impersonation. As the latter fell into disfavor, the tramp became an appropriate icon for containing the contentious implications of ethnic difference within a whiter, more Americanized persona: tramp comedians thus first emerged in significant numbers in the 1890s and 1900s, when a slight decline in ethnic stereotyping had created a space for new, less divisive forms of comic representation.[86] Indeed, so firmly and so fully did tramp comedians take their place on the turn-of-the-century vaudeville stage that critics began pointing to the tramp as the figure that made American vaudeville uniquely American. As a writer for New York's *Dramatic Mirror* baldly put it in 1915, "the tramp comedian is distinctly American— already a sort of tradition like the Pierrot and the clown of the Harlequinade."[87] Caroline Caffin, in her 1914 book on vaudeville comedy, struck a similar note, describing the comic tramp as "a purely American product."[88] Inscribed within discourses of native whiteness, the comic tramp provided a cultural figure from which to construct an American difference.[89]

No doubt Chaplin benefited from such associations. But there was a further major factor behind the comedian's success, one that relates less to matters of social identity than to performance style. By mid-decade, the hyperbolic physicality exemplified by Ford Sterling's performances was becoming increasingly unpopular, and the trade press began openly to attack the "overdrawn acting" of many contemporary comedians.[90] Captain Leslie T. Peacocke, *Photoplay*'s advice columnist for would-be screenwriters, repeatedly warned against comic situations featuring "foolish, childish acting . . . of which the public has now become tired and disgusted."[91] Elsewhere, in the pages of *Moving Picture World,* Epes Winthrop Sargent raised similar objections, parodying such performances in a 1913 essay: "If your leading character is coming down the street, he no longer should walk; he should take it on the run and bowl over a policeman or an apple woman as he nears the camera."[92] Chaplin himself, as recounted in his autobiography, felt uneasy with the hectic posturing of his Keystone contemporaries and sought a different performance style.[93] From the beginning, he introduced a slower pantomime that was in many ways the antithesis of Sterling's frenetic comedy. The long, 95-second opening shot of his debut film, *Making a Living,* provides a quasi-programmatic exhibition of his approach: showing Chaplin panhandling from a dapper gent (the film's director, Henry Lehrman), the shot affords scope for a far more delicate, incremental interplay than was typical of Keystone at the time. Critics in the trade press immediately responded to the new comedian's performance, commending Chaplin for his naturalistic comic style—"like one of Nature's own naturals," according to the review of the film in *Moving Picture World.*[94] The contrast between Chaplin's "polished pantomime" and the frenzied playing of his contemporaries was swiftly established as part of the performer's legend. In *Photoplay*'s 1915 serialization of "Charlie Chaplin's Story," the author, Harry Carr, spoke of "the quaint touch that he brought to what had formerly been pointless horse play": "His rough comedy had in it a touch of real thought. . . . Theretofore most of the comedy effects had been riotous boisterousness. Chaplin, like many foreign pantomimists got his effects in a more subtle way and with less action."[95] That Chaplin's more deliberate style represented a fundamental transformation in comic performance at Keystone cannot be denied. Whereas Sterling's films had tended toward ever-more-rapid editing, Chaplin's work was distinguished by long takes, allowing for finer gradations of performance and more nuanced facial gestures. Chaplin himself was later to recount how he persuaded Sennett not to cut the minute-long opening shot of *Mabel's Strange Predicament,* in which he drunkenly stumbles about a hotel lobby and flirts with the female guests.[96] This strategy of using a long opening take came to be a hallmark of Chaplin's Keystone films—both those directed by himself and those under the direction of others—several of which begin with shots lasting well over a minute (e.g., *His Favorite Pastime,* March 1914; *The Masquerader,* August 1914). His self-directed releases further developed this technique by exploiting the long-take style over the course of entire films, notably in *His Musical Career,* a single-reel comedy consisting of just twenty-seven shots.[97] Also characteristic was Chaplin's ability to engage more complex effects of empathy and involvement than had been the case with Sterling's grotesque Dutch protagonist. Rather than grounding his comedy solely in the expressive possibilities of frenetic action, Chaplin uniquely exploited intervals *between* action that introduced an affective dimension to the performance. This is particularly clear in Chaplin's oft-noted tendency to pause mid-action to meet the camera with his own eyes ("breaking the fourth wall"). Whether a stare of comic befuddlement or an erotic wink, Chaplin's look at the camera reaches for a reciprocity between tramp and audience, beckoning the spectator toward an affective involvement, absent from Sterling's films.

It is here that analysis can return to Umberto Eco's discussion of comedy, touched on earlier. For, if Sterling's comedy is paradigmatic of what Eco terms the "comic effect" (premised on the humiliation of an "animal-like" figure), Chaplin's can be viewed in relation to the complementary category of "humor." As defined by Eco, humor refers to the ambivalent effect achieved when the clown, through still animal-like, also elicits "sympathy" and "tenderness."[98] Where "comic" situations invite the spectator to laugh at the clown's transgression, humor complicates that reaction by opening up a margin for identification. It is precisely such complexity that Chaplin's lumpenproletariat persona provokes, inviting a spectatorship that oscillates between the poles of empathy and ridicule. A vivid example is in *Caught in a Cabaret,* in which Chaplin portrays a saloon waiter who masquerades as a foreign dignitary in romantic pursuit of a society debutante (played by Mabel Normand, who also directed). Here, the film's shifting perspective is inscribed into its narrative form, which traces two corresponding movements across class boundaries: first, when the waiter uses his disguise to gain entrée into Mabel's garden party; second, when Mabel and her rich friends go on a slumming expedition to the saloon, where they discover the "ambassador" waiting tables. During the first movement, the joke is clearly on the wealthy partygoers, who treat the disguised waiter with deference and civility while he binges on cocktails and drunkenly flaunts social codes: the waiter's behavior here is less the "object of a judgment of superiority" (Eco) than a vehicle for spectatorial identification and enjoyment. But it is precisely this identification that is denied in the film's second movement, offering instead a far crueler dynamic of punishment and humiliation. The slumming expedition, as a shift down the social hierarchy, not only reverses the waiter's entry into the world of the elite; it also grounds a quite different comic function for Chaplin's character. Exposed before Mabel's wealthy friends and beaten by his angry boss, it is the waiter who is now the butt of the film's comedy: laughter is directed *at* the working-class clown in his moment of comeuppance.

The film's structure of narrative reversals is distinctive, but *Caught in a Cabaret* neatly encapsulates a common tendency in Chaplin's performances: time and again in these films, class difference is opened up to ambivalent responses, rendered comically intelligible in mutually contradictory ways. On the one hand, Chaplin's tramp was a countercultural force whose social transgressions and anarchic disruption of the workplace doubtless appealed to wage-earning audiences. Yet, as a countercultural force, the tramp generally ended his films at the receiving end of a quasi-ritualistic punishment, alternately apprehended by the law (e.g., *Between Showers*, February 1914), forcibly expelled from a social milieu (e.g., a middle-class home in *His Favorite Pastime*), or, most commonly, pummeled into unconsciousness (e.g., *Laughing Gas*). Accordingly, the tramp seems to have held different meanings for different viewers depending on their social position and class identity. At *Moving Picture World*, for instance, a trade journal that lobbied consistently on behalf of middle-class moral and aesthetic values in film, the character was considered an object of ridicule. "He is a man," one writer noted, "who seldom gives one an opportunity to laugh with him; at the same time, he gives occasion aplenty to laugh at him."[99] Another critic for the same publication praised Chaplin's performances as "delightfully realistic" in depicting "*weaknesses* which any . . . audience is quick to recognize and enjoy."[100] Critics aligned with working-class interests, by contrast, seem to have viewed the tramp less as someone to laugh *at* than as someone to laugh *with,* often describing the comedian in terms implying remarkable fondness and fellow-feeling. A writer for the *National Labor Tribune* clearly appreciated Chaplin's anti-elitist burlesque, praising the tramp as a *"national hero,* whose funny hat, walk, cane, and mustache are now better known than the prayer book."[101] The *Los Angeles Citizen,* another labor periodical, meanwhile paid homage to Chaplin as a *"prince of good fellows,* the man who makes millions laugh."[102]

The fundamental ambivalence of Chaplin's appeal can also be inferred at the level of exhibition. On the one hand, as the testimonies of nickelodeon operators indicate, working-class and immigrant audiences seem to have responded to Chaplin's tramp with unusual enthusiasm, prompting the owners of low-priced theaters to bedeck their lobbies with posters of Keystone's newest star. As *Reel Life,* the house journal of the Mutual Film Corporation, reported in the fall of 1914, the five-cent, German-owned Vaudette Theater in Milwaukee had built up "enormous business" by displaying "banners showing Charlie Chaplin in his numerous rib-tickling roles."[103] Likewise, in November, the manager of the Amuse Theater, a nickelodeon in Dubuque, Iowa, wrote to Mutual requesting information on the comedian. "A better comedian will never be seen before any camera," the exhibitor explained. "Many a button has burst in this house from laughter."[104] (In fact, Chaplin's popularity with the lower classes seems to have provoked a minor backlash, at least to judge from doggerel published in *Police Gazette* calling for a moratorium on Chaplin impersonations: "On ev'ry side we find the man / Who's imitating Chaplin. / . . . Why should he be allowed to come / And put your ev'ning on the bum?")[105] But the burgeoning Chaplin craze was never limited to the nickelodeon audience: when, in December 1914, the managers of Delmonico's restaurant—a mecca of New York nightlife—decided to screen a film as a treat for Christmas customers, they chose *Dough and Dynamite,* a recent Chaplin picture.[106] Likewise, that same month, New York's recently opened Strand Theater ("the ideal temple of the motion picture art," according to *Moving Picture World*) paid a hundred dollars in excess of Keystone's usual rental fee for first-run rights to Chaplin's *His Prehistoric Past* (December 1914).[107] Within a year of his debut in motion pictures, Chaplin had evidently achieved the remarkable feat of a double address, overcoming middle-class disdain for slapstick even as his films extended Keystone's hold on its working-class audience base.[108]

The indices of that popularity were by no means always welcome. By the fall of 1914, unscrupulous exhibitors and exchanges had begun a thriving business in marketing unlicensed "dupes" of the comedian's releases, and Chaplin himself was being courted by tempting offers from Keystone's competitors.[109] (As he wrote his half-brother Sydney around this time, Chaplin had received "all kinds of offers at 500 a week with 40% stock which would mean a salary of or about 1000 a week." "Mr. Sennett is a lovely man and we are great pals," Chaplin concluded, "but business is business.")[110] But Sennett was not slow in turning the Chaplin craze to his advantage. That August, following a series of conferences in New York with his backers, Sennett expanded the studio's production of two-reel comedies from a single monthly release to one every other week. As earlier with Ford Sterling, Sennett banked on Chaplin's name as insurance against the financial risks of this ambitious expansion: not only was Chaplin featured in the first two of these two-reel specials—*Dough and Dynamite* and *His Trysting Place* (November 1914)—but publicity heavily promoted the "inimitable Chas. Chaplin" as their key attraction (fig. 9).

It is worth discussing *Dough and Dynamite* in further detail, since it offers a revealing example of how class difference, in Chaplin's films, was reformulated as cross-class comedy. In *Moving Picture World,* the film was praised as "one of the cleanest ones that Keystone has done," while the reviewer of the *Chicago Tribune* wrote of its attraction for that "large class of nice people who do not like vulgarity in their amusements."[111] By all accounts, in fact, it was this film that set Chaplin on the course of bona fide film stardom. As Harry Carr wrote in 1915, "everyone began talking about the new funny man [following *Dough and Dynamite*]. People who never went to the movies before were drawn by the accounts of the new comedian."[112] According to Chaplin himself, the film, which took nine days to shoot, grossed more than $130,000 during its first year of release, making it the most successful two-reeler in the studio's history.[113]

As Chester Conklin later recalled, the inspiration for *Dough and Dynamite* came during a tram ride with Chaplin after work one day on the Keystone lot. "[One] evening we were riding home on an Edendale street car. . . . I happened to look out the window and here was the bakery and it had a big sign in the window that said 'Baker's helper wanted.' I said, 'Charlie, look at that sign. There's something to work at.' He looked, and he said, 'Oh boy. What we couldn't get out of that flour, that water, that dough. We could get all kinds of gags out of that.' So the next morning, he put up a set and we went to work as a couple of baker's helpers that didn't know anything about baking."[114]

As Conklin's account indicates, the comedy of *Dough and Dynamite* is based in a loosely connected series of dough-related gags, strung together

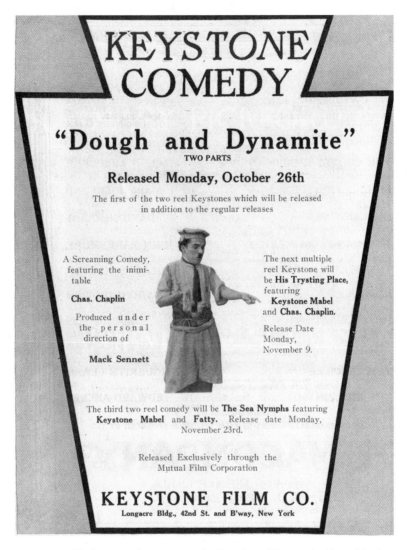

FIGURE 9.   Trade press advertisement for *Dough and Dynamite*. From *Moving Picture World*, October 24, 1914.

by a slight narrative that, one reviewer claimed, "could easily have been told in half a reel."[115] Chaplin and Conklin play teashop waiters who are put to work in the adjoining bakery when the bakers go on strike. In the film's second reel, the strikers hide a stick of dynamite in a loaf of bread;

Chaplin's waiter puts the loaf in the oven, and the bakery explodes. To later historians of film comedy, this narrative has seemed little more than, to quote David Robinson, an excuse for the "fun to be had from sticky dough"; but the original working-class audience would more likely have recognized the film as referencing recent events in the Los Angeles labor movement.[116] Unquestionably, the film's contemporary point of reference was the hard-fought struggle of the city's bakers' unions for better working conditions, widely reported in the local labor press. In what had been the most conspicuous labor crusade in southern California in the early teens, the Jewish and general bakers' unions had joined forces in an ambitious campaign of striking at open shop bakeries. (Small wonder that Conklin spotted a "Help Wanted" sign at an Edendale bakery!) In fact, it was around the time *Dough and Dynamite* went into production, in the late summer of 1914, that the struggle reached its turning point: significant union gains made during this period included an eight- to ten-hour workday and weekly wages from $21, eventually bringing the campaign to a close by year's end.[117]

The bakery setting of *Dough and Dynamite* was, then, far more than an opportunity for fun with "sticky dough": it was a site of intertextuality with current labor issues. Yet, despite this political engagement, the film's handling of its subject remains slippery, to say the least. The picture begins in the teashop, where Chaplin's waiter clears tables, much to the outrage of a top-hatted gentleman, whose food is cleared away before he has a chance to eat it. The first laugh of the picture, then, is directed against class authority, and it is a laugh that the waiter *shares* with the audience, as, turning toward the camera, he openly guffaws at his mistake. Through Chaplin's performance, spectator and waiter are aligned in shared amusement at the cost of a pompous middle-class citizen. This alignment is reinforced in the film's subsequent scene, in which the waiter eyes a buxom female customer. By placing the waiter in the foreground of the image, the composition of the shot allows his erotic gaze to channel the spectator's own relation to the scene, creating a voyeuristic union between waiter and spectator which Chaplin gleefully acknowledges as he winks at the camera (fig. 10). Such scenes are paradigmatic of the film's anti-authoritarian discourse as a whole, pitting the waiter against his customers and inviting the spectator to laugh with—not at—his transgressions: as in the film's opening shot, the waiter time and again wreaks unwitting injury on his respectable customers, dropping a bag of flour on a middle-aged woman, for example, or striking a dapper young man with a plate.

FIGURE 10. Frame enlargement from *Dough and Dynamite* (October 1914). Courtesy of the Academy Film Archive, Academy of Motion Picture Arts and Sciences.

Yet, while these gags offer anarchic commentary on the work ethic, the film avoids a unifying approach to class. Chaplin's waiter is as much at odds with the striking bakers as with his customers, and, in this sense, stands apart from the labor issues engaged by the film's narrative. The film's handling of spatial relations neatly divides the employees into separate factions, setting Chaplin's and Conklin's waiters at a quite literal remove from the bakers. Before the strike, the film structures space in terms of a contrast between above and below, confining the waiters to the ground-floor teashop, the bakers to the basement bakery. During the strike, the relevant spatial contrast is between interior and exterior: here, the waiters move freely within the teashop and bakery, while the strikers remain outside, scheming revenge from the sidewalk. The spatial and ideological distance that separates the waiters from their striking workmates is further mirrored in the spectator's own relation to the action: the film impedes identification with the strikers, drawing on conservative stereotypes to present them as sinister, weasel-faced bomb-throwers.[118]

Given these oppositions, it is useful to see Chaplin's waiter, not as a symbol of working-class interests, but as an intermediary figure within an ambivalent construction of class. In the same breath as the film invites enjoyment of the waiter's anarchic tomfoolery, it also carefully abridges the comic meanings of working-class autonomy, placing the striking bakers beyond the pale of comic representation. The ambiguity is sustained into the second reel, when the strikers hatch, as a title puts it, "A Fiendish Plan." Here, the film uses parallel editing to contrast two kinds of action that, in different ways, express a rejection of the demands of the workplace. On the one hand, there is a series of scenes in which the devious strikers put their vengeful plan into action. In their surprising avoidance of burlesque, these scenes owe more to the moralizing tradition of melodrama than to comedy, particularly when the strikers deceive a trusting young girl into taking a dynamite-laden loaf into the bakery. Intercut with these dramatic sequences, however, are properly comic set pieces in the bakery in which, much to their boss's despair, the two waiters transform the workplace into a chaotic playground. Instead of working, the waiters flirt with their female co-workers, perform virtuoso tricks with trays and plates, and hurl flour and dough at each other.

By alternating between these two lines of action, *Dough and Dynamite* gives vent to an ambivalence that is at once ideological and generic, straddling conservative and anarchic class discourses, melodrama and comedy. The innovative, contrasting structure of the second reel allows the film to incorporate contradictory ideological positions, offering differently accented readings of class conflict: if the scenes of the striking bakers derive from a conservative imaginary of labor radicalism, the bakery sequences offer a comic working-class fantasy in which the alienation of work is replaced by the fulfillment of play. Nor is this ambivalence resolved in the climactic explosion that abruptly—and chaotically—concludes the film. The boss staggers absurdly beneath the debris raining down upon him; the strikers are comically destroyed when the explosion sets off a keg of dynamite in their hideout; and Chaplin's waiter is buried under dough, his face poking through grotesquely in the film's final shot. He, too, thus becomes an object of the spectator's ridicule. All hierarchies, all social differences are erased as each character is implicated within the spectator's laughter.

Unquestionably, the enthusiastic reception accorded the film was in large measure due to Chaplin's performance. In the wake of *Dough and Dynamite*'s success, critics were effusive in describing the "human aspect" of Chaplin's pantomime, stressing "the incongruity of [his] portrayals, his extreme seriousness, his sober attention to trivialities, his constant errors and as constant resentment of what happens to him."[119] But Chaplin was also successful in producing a comedy that articulated opposing perspectives

on class at the level of film form. Here, if Keystone's filmmakers were willing to take it, was an object lesson in double legitimation—in how to
address the collective experiences of America's workers while satisfying
the ideological presuppositions of middle-class filmgoers. Chaplin's work
suggested representational possibilities that not only transcended ethnic
parody but also promised a broader public for Keystone's films.

Yet Chaplin would not remain long at Edendale. After work was finished
on *Dough and Dynamite,* he appeared in only five more films for Sennett
before signing with Essanay in December 1914 for $1,250 a week plus a
starting bonus of ten thousand dollars. His departure was a loss that
Keystone's management would soon have cause to regret. In a letter to
Sennett dated June 4, 1915, New York Motion Picture's vice-president,
Charles Baumann, insisted on the importance of re-signing Chaplin, who
had now become Keystone's major competition in the comedy market.
"We have decided that we can go as high as $3000 a week for Charley
Chaplin if it is absolutely necessary," wrote Baumann. "We are all of the
opinion here that if we have to pay him $3000 a week and he doesn't even
appear in pictures, we have accomplished a great deal by getting him away
from a competing Company, thereby leaving no competition in the field for
the Keystone films." In a muted reference to Sennett's famously strained
relationship with the English comedian, Baumann instructed Sennett to
"be sure to add Charley Chaplin, even if you hate his guts [*sic*], for the
reason that he must be gotten out of the market and competition in that
line killed."[120] Chaplin's Essanay comedies had, ironically, become
Keystone's biggest threat.

"SATIRE IN OVERALLS": KEYSTONE AND THE COMEDY OF CLASS

Whatever stories they told and whatever significance their films held for
their audiences, it is clear that Keystone's filmmakers steered heavily
toward the depiction of working-class characters following Chaplin's
departure. Of the seventy-seven Keystone comedies released during the
first six months of 1915, at least twenty-three can be positively identified
in which the central comic protagonist is a member of the lower classes.[121]
Of these, most took place in settings that working-class viewers would
have experienced firsthand: boarding houses, in *Hash House Mashers*
(January) and *The Rent Jumpers* (April); life "on the tramp," in *Hogan's
Aristocratic Dream* (February); urban tenements, in *A Bird's a Bird*
(February); the factory floor, in *Ambrose's Nasty Temper;* and cheap cafés,

in *A Hash House Fraud* (June), to name but a few. Even Roscoe Arbuckle began to experiment with the tropes of tramp comedy, first assaying a hobo role in *Fatty and Minnie-He-Haw* (December 1914)—which opens with Fatty riding the rails—before appearing as an unusually destitute comic tramp in the assertively titled *Fatty's New Role* (February 1915). Urban working life had evidently become a crystallizing point for a comic style that engaged the culture and experiences of the industry's blue-collar audience base; small wonder that Keystone films gained a reputation as, in *Photoplay*'s words, "satire in overalls."[122]

But Keystone was not long alone in this respect. Several other studios soon began exploiting similar comic material. The years 1915 and 1916, in particular, can be counted as a vogue period for the tramp clown, with the launching of Kalem's successful "Ham and Bud" series, the hobo antics of Cub's "Jerry" films, Rolin's "Willie Work" and "Lonesome Luke" comedies, George Kleine's ten-part "The Mishaps of Musty Suffer," and Universal's "Timothy Dobbs, That's Me" series, along with a host of shorter-lived, if no less colorfully named, characters, like Ino Eatt at Beauty and Weary Willie at Vogue. Animated cartoons took up the exploits of familiar comic-strip tramps, with Happy Hooligan making his first motion picture appearance on the Hearst International newsreel in late 1916 and the odd-job men Mutt and Jeff debuting in cartoons directed by Charley Bowers earlier that year. Nor was the trend exclusive to comedies. At no time in the industry's history would filmmakers be more concerned with working life than in the years leading up to World War I. Between 1911 and 1915, as much as a tenth of the film industry's output revolved around blue-collar protagonists, and many of these films voiced liberal, even radical attitudes that would never again be as freely expressed as during this era of nascent unionization, labor radicalism, and Socialist party success.[123]

Questions arise, however, regarding the ideological attitudes articulated by Keystone's films. What kinds of perspectives did these comedies express, and to whom did they speak? What comic meanings might audiences have drawn from them? These are questions best approached not solely in terms of performance and typology, but by tracing the films' underlying image of society to its origins in class-specific horizons of experience.[124] For what emerged in Keystone's output of this period was a sustained engagement with a social vision with a lengthy heritage in working-class culture; specifically, a vision of a world divided into tramps and millionaires. Contrasts between the lives of the rich and poor had been a defining feature of working-class narrative since at least the mid-nineteenth century—notably in antebellum mysteries-of-the-city novels such as George Lippard's

New York: Its Upper Ten and Lower Million (1853)—but the specific trope of tramps and millionaires had first emerged in the wake of the 1870s depression, finding continued resonance among the popular classes in subsequent decades. (The literary historian Michael Denning cites the example of the preamble to the 1892 Omaha platform of the People's Party: "[O]ur homes are covered with mortgages; labor impoverished; and the land concentrating in the hands of the capitalists. . . . From the same prolific womb of governmental injustice we breed the two great classes— *tramps and millionaires.*")[125] A metaphor for social division, the trope supplied a fictive imagery for articulating the gulf between capital and labor, and it entered popular narrative as a theme of dime-novel fiction in tales like *On to Washington* (1894) and *Young Sleuth and the Millionaire Tramp* (1895). This was not, it should be noted, a representation of class difference in the "realist" sense that characterized muckraking journalism and naturalist fiction; rather, it was an allegorical figure for social hierarchy, an ideological motif articulating workers' experiences of disenfranchisement in a class society. (Denning calls it the "dream-work" of the social, condensing and displacing the dilemmas and antinomies of working-class existence.)[126] But it was also a structure that proved adaptable to comic ends, allowing for numerous comic interactions between its two contrasting poles: on the one hand, tramps, hobos, and misfits; on the other, millionaires, society matrons, and other "respectable" types. At Keystone, that opposition structured even the topography of the comedies, which evolved to become a landscape of mansions and street corners, ballrooms and saloons, swanky restaurants and hash houses. And nowhere was it more consistently articulated than in a series of comedies in which Indiana-born vaudeville veteran Charles Murray appeared as the character "Hogan" (fig. 11).

Murray's work is important in this analysis as a continuation of tendencies initiated in the Chaplin films, both thematically (in their focus on lumpenproletariat life) and formally (in their slow-paced, long-take style). Although his comic persona was clearly intended as Irish ("Hogan" was a common moniker for stage Irishmen), a simple list of film titles indicates that, like Chaplin's films before him, Murray's work was based primarily on class difference, not on divisive portrayals of ethnicity. From December 1914, Murray appeared as Hogan in *The Plumber, Hogan's Annual Spree, Hogan's Wild Oats* (December), *Hogan's Mussy Job* (January 1915), *Hogan the Porter, Hogan's Romance Upset, Hogan's Aristocratic Dream, Hogan Out West* (February), and *From Patches to Plenty* (March). Yet unlike Chaplin's far more diverse work at Keystone, the Hogan comedies were dominated by a single master plot, one that built comedy around the

FIGURE 11.   Charles Murray (left) and Bobby Dunn in a production still from *Hogan's Aristocratic Dream* (February 1914). Courtesy of the Academy of Motion Picture Arts and Sciences.

social and topographical boundaries dividing the disenfranchised from people of wealth. Time and again, Murray's films construct narratives that require him to intrude upon the world of the elite: he is, alternately, an odd-job man hired to fix a leak in a wealthy middle-class household *(The Plumber);* a hotel janitor sent to clean up the rooms of the rich *(Hogan's Mussy Job);* or a tramp who discovers a fortune and gains entrée to a privileged world of polo clubs and swanky cafés *(From Patches to Plenty).*

At the simplest level, these are fantasies of social mobility, appealing to discontented, lower-class elements through scenarios of class inversion and emancipation. Exemplary of this process, *Hogan's Aristocratic Dream* actualizes fantasy as an explicit principle of its narrative, as Hogan—again a tramp—falls asleep and dreams his way back into the courts of prerevolutionary France, envisioning himself as a member of the French nobility. Yet fantasy should not be taken here to imply simple escapism; if the Hogan films can accurately be described as "fantasies of mobility," then they were so in a peculiarly ambivalent sense, their plots fueled by complex layerings of both desire and resentment. Hogan's social mobility not only gives him access to a world of plenty, it allows him to take comic revenge upon elite society. Throughout *From Patches to Plenty*, Hogan playfully wreaks havoc in refined settings, hitting well-to-do ladies with his polo mallet, spraying dinner guests with champagne, devouring a "bird and bottle" supper with undisguised appetite, and bowing with such exaggerated deference that waiters leap away in fright. In *Hogan's Mussy Job*, he attacks a dinner-jacketed hotel guest with a pickaxe and then helps himself to his wine. The ambiguities are immediately apparent: the world of privilege satisfies the laborer in its abundance; but the privileged themselves, their social codes and rules of etiquette, are mocked, flouted, and resisted. But the films' contradictory dynamics go far beyond such basic ambiguities. Hogan's attitude toward the world of privilege may be paradoxical, but so is the spectator's relation to Hogan: like Chaplin's tramp before him, Hogan is a polysemic figure, both a vehicle of fantasy and an "animal-like" object of ridicule. If Hogan's actions pose a critique of the social order, then it is a critique atoned for time and again by punishment and exclusion. *From Patches to Plenty* ends when a group of wealthy diners pummel Hogan out of a swanky restaurant, while in *Hogan the Porter*, the hotel guests gang up to chase him into the city streets. Where the early portions of each film invite us to identify with, and enjoy, Hogan's improprieties, the concluding scenes provoke satisfaction at his ritualized punishment.

Much like the parallel editing in Chaplin's *Dough and Dynamite*, this was a structure combining contradictory ideological positions: class authority is comically repudiated, only to be reasserted by the film's conclusion. With a number of minor modifications, the basic principle can be traced across the work of several of Keystone's comedians, including Roscoe Arbuckle (e.g., *Fatty's Magic Pants*, December 1914), Chester Conklin (*Do-Re-Mi-Boom!* April 1915), and Mack Swain (*Ambrose's Nasty Temper*): in each, a member of the disenfranchised intrudes upon the world of the rich and powerful; in each, that intrusion is answered with punishment or expulsion. Our laughter is twofold: we vicariously enjoy the clown's actions as he flaunts upper-class convention *and* we laugh at him in his humiliation. Keystone's working-class clowns thus exemplified what William Taylor has called the "socially prismatic" characters of turn-of-the-century popular culture—characters who, like the wisecracking Bowery B'hoys or the tearaway comic-strip "Katzenjammer Kids," had comic significance for a range of readers, whether working or middle class.[127] The key to commercial success, Taylor suggests, lay in creating figures capable of integrating alternate visions of cultural hierarchy and of appealing to diverse social needs. Keystone's working-class comedies achieved this through a structure that equivocated between the pleasures of social subversion and satisfaction at the maintenance of social order.

In popularizing comic visions of class difference, Keystone's working-class comedies were thus ironically also shaping forms of cross-class or "mass" representation that displaced the autonomy of popular culture by appealing across traditional boundaries, producing different readings according to social attitudes. One possible response, for example, was proffered by the *Moving Picture World* critic Louis Reeves Harrison, who, inspired by a viewing of Keystone's *Court House Crooks* (July 1915), wrote a lengthy opinion piece on the value of comedy as a medium for critiquing class privilege. Comic visions of social disorder, Harrison insisted, appealed to the fantasies of the disenfranchised by inviting them to laugh at the customs of the dominant classes:

> Poor people become so absorbed in their struggle that their line of thought is cramped by their individual and immediate requirements, but their minds may be reached and powerfully affected through feeling as stirred by the screen story. . . . One effective way to deal with those inherited artificialities of custom which are responsible for injustice to men who deserve better treatment is to hold up to ridicule the heartless stupidity of privilege, affected standards of living among those who have never had the wolf at the door, [and] hypocrisy of those who attempt to create an impression of superiority.

Comedy, ultimately, could provide working-class audiences with a tool for ideological demystification: "Many of us can only get at truth through the process known as *disillusionment*," Harrison concluded. "We must laugh away the cobwebs in our brains before we can reach a state of being able to recognize the truth when it is placed before our eyes."[128]

Yet Harrison's judgment was hardly uncontested. Other, more conservative responses were voiced, responses that celebrated the films, not as liberating visions of social inversion, but as derisory depictions of working-class buffoonery. Harrison himself recognized the humor that sprang from the imbecilic behavior of the studio's proletarian protagonists. In a particularly effusive assessment of Chester Conklin's "Walrus" persona, he heaped praise on the "inanity" of the comedian's portrayals, commending the "inferiority of which his characters are not conscious."[129] Judging by trade press reviews, this was not an uncommon reaction. Clearly, there was pleasure to be had in laughing at Keystone's depictions of working-class culture, as evidenced by the vocabulary that critics used to describe the studio's comic characters—"eccentric," "weakness" (in the sense of "weak-mindedness"), "buffoonery," "inanity."[130] "The majority of scenes take place in and about a factory," a reviewer of *Ambrose's Nasty Temper* noted, "and the characters are, *as would be supposed*, all of the eccentric order."[131]

Again, as with the Chaplin films, this polysemy helps account for Keystone's rising popularity during this period. On the one hand, as Keystone deepened its engagement with the fantasies and experiences of proletarian audiences, the films strengthened their foothold at theaters frequented by the working class. In Los Angeles, the films were firm favorites at houses catering to organized labor. Two of the city's most prominent unionized theaters—the Savoy and the Superba—began exhibiting Keystone's films during the first half of 1915, prompting enthusiastic commentary from the labor press. "It will be good news to Savoy Theatre patrons to know that [the management has] just made a contract for the entire output of the celebrated comedies produced by the Keystone Manufacturing Film Company. . . . Drop in and have a good time."[132] Yet Keystone also made inroads into theaters catering to a more upscale clientele. For the opening of New York's Strand Theater, the manager, S. L. "Roxy" Rothapfel, treated a gala audience to a program featuring an orchestral rendition of "The Star-Spangled Banner," the quartet from *Rigoletto*, William Farnum in the feature film *The Spoilers*—and a Keystone comedy.[133] Throughout late 1914, Sennett's films featured regularly on the Strand's bill, a fact reported with pride in Mutual's *Reel Life* as a "criterion of [Keystone's] quality."[134] Nor was the Strand unique in this respect. In October 1914, *Motography* recorded that "No fewer than four out of five Broadway theaters in a distance of six blocks used Keystone-Mutual comedies last week," including the Broadway, the New York, Hammerstein's vaudeville theater, and the Palace. "An attempt is being made to increase the output of the Keystone-Mutual plant," the report observed, "in order to take care of the business that is indicated by this deserved popularity."[135] By the summer of 1914, theaters nationwide were giving Keystone pictures ever more prominence in local ads, no matter what their class of clientele. Whether in the listings for the Toledo Gaiety (the Ohio city's cheapest vaudeville house) or in ads for the Des Moines Palace (a prestigious 1,100-seat picture palace), the Keystone brand name was a marketable commodity across the theatrical spectrum.[136]

Evidently, Keystone's brand of slapstick was beginning to transcend traditional, class-based patterns of cultural consumption, winning considerable popularity with the small number of middle-class patrons who attended movies during this period. That much, at least, is suggested by a cartoon in *Photoplay* in April 1915 titled "When the Lofty Temples Tumbled" (fig. 12).[137]

When the Lofty Temples Tumbled

FIGURE 12. "When the Lofty Temples Tumbled." *Photoplay*, April 1915. Courtesy of the Academy of Motion Picture Arts and Sciences.

The evident irony of the cartoon lies in the perception that Keystone's popularity was outmatching traditional boundaries that separated "high" and "popular" culture: even stuffed shirts, it suggests, were finding reasons to enjoy Keystone's films. One of those reasons, this chapter has argued, lay in the polysemy of the studio's output, in the capacity of the studio's working-class clowns to reflect and refract the different social discourses through which audiences viewed the films. Keystone's brand of slapstick thus became a remarkable example of a hybridizing mass culture in which diverse groups could find genuine, if partial, representations of their own experiences and outlooks. Buoyed up by this popularity, the studio's filmmakers next began to chart ambitious new courses that would have substantive consequences for the formal parameters by which film comedy was defined.

3. "The Impossible Attained!"

Tillie's Punctured Romance *and the Challenge of Feature-Length Slapstick, 1914–1915*

> These disordered mentalities can't be held to account like cultured
> folk for their shortcomings. They live by minutes, not by years.
> Their thoughts come out in spots, not in streaks. They miss the
> connection between conduct and consequence. In their philosophy,
> human life is as rampant a riot as the wildest of their burlesques—
> chaotic, without reason, guided or misguided by blind fatality. Not
> the hardest or most reiterant of hard knocks will convince them of
> the contrary, for they lack the grasp of sequence.
>
> ROLLIN LYNDE HARTE, *The People at Play: Excursions in the Humor and*
> *Philosophy of Popular Amusements* (1909)

The formal qualities of slapstick comedy were, Sennett believed, best suited to the one- or two-reel format. "We often tried to make a two reeler run into three reels by adding five or six minutes more to it," he later observed. "Well, by golly, it was the toughest thing in the world to do to keep the laugh going that long. About fifteen to eighteen minutes is as far as you can go on one situation. After you pass that you've got to tell a story—a continuous story—and it's difficult to keep them laughing after that amount of time."[1] By the mid-1910s, however, these were difficulties that had to be confronted. The rapidly growing influence of multiple-reel (or "feature") films had begun to pose a challenge to the industrial and financial position of slapstick filmmakers. Whereas earlier in the decade, slapstick's dominant format—the single reel—was the standard commodity throughout the industry, the rising tide of multiple-reel dramas introduced a disparity.[2] Comic filmmakers would have to respond or accept marginalization.

The advent of the feature film was, in fact, a cause for industrywide anxiety. A mode of representation intended to appeal to "better" audiences, the feature film was initially exploited as a format for adapting literary and dramatic works from the genteel cultural tradition, and, as such, constituted a significant development in the industry's relation to cultural hierarchy. But

by 1914, it was evident that the new format would entail equally significant changes for the industry's economic structure.[3] New companies were
formed specifically to handle the distribution of multireel films—Lewis
Selznick's World Special Films Corporation (founded November 1913),
William Fox's Box Office Attraction Company (January 1914), and W. W.
Hodkinson's Paramount Pictures Corporation (May 1914), among others.
New and prestigious "picture palaces" were opened—notably, that April,
the Strand Theater in New York—as exhibition sites for feature programs
catering to a more upscale clientele. Although the outcome of this transitional period remained unclear, the pages of the trade press were filled with
urgent predictions and prognostications. Perhaps, as Carl Laemmle proph-
esized, the public would soon become "satiated with features" and would
return its enthusiasms to variety programs of one- and two-reel subjects.[4]
Perhaps demand for both kinds of product would stabilize in a two-tier
hierarchy of exhibition in which, as augured by the *Moving Picture World*
critic W. Stephen Bush, "One class of theaters will use mostly single reels,
the other will use mostly features."[5] Or perhaps the days of the single-reel
film were numbered. "It seems it is the general sentiment of the people,"
observed one exhibitor. "They want to see features or productions produced in more than one reel."[6]

But these uncertainties were particularly focused for the producers of
slapstick comedies, not least because of a widespread presumption that
slapstick's comic pleasures simply could not be sustained at multiple-reel
length.[7] "Nor do we believe that multiple reel comedy will ever successfully rival the short snappy comedy of a thousand feet," Bush opined. "On
the screen as in the newspaper and on the stage brevity is the soul of wit."[8]
One of the very first multiple-reel comedies—the Ramo Company's three-
reel *This Is the Life* (July 1914)—was condemned on precisely this count.
"[I]n this three reeled Ramo the comedy is too long drawn out to get very
far with any audience," *Variety* noted. "The picture could have been made
in one reel, and then it would have been boring at times. The fewer of these
'comedies' of more than one reel the better."[9] Clearly, the challenge of the
multiple-reel film could not be met simply by "drawing out" the comedy
at the expense of plot. But for slapstick filmmakers eager to exploit the new
format, the alternative was no less problematic—namely, to emphasize
plot at the expense of comedy. As *Motography* reviewer Charles R. Condon
wrote of recent "experiments" in multiple-reel comedy in late 1914, "In
order to sustain interest and continuity, and prevent the picture's becoming a mere jumble of funny complications it has generally been found necessary to sacrifice humor, in places, to allow the plot to be seen and felt."[10]

Considerable interest was generated, then, when it was announced in May that Keystone had begun work on a series of multiple-reel comedies starring the musical comedy star Marie Dressler.[11] "Under any circumstances the venture was a gamble," Sennett recalled in his autobiography; and, although the planned series never transpired, the enterprise did result in *Tillie's Punctured Romance*—the first six-reel comic feature in motion picture history and a film that, on its release, was hailed by *Motion Picture News* as a "masterpiece" of slapstick art.[12] "For any producer to tackle a six reel humorous number was daring, to say the least,[but] the temerity of the makers has been amply justified," the *News*'s reviewer commented.[13]

The language is revealing: multiple-reel slapstick was "daring," it was a "gamble" that required "temerity." In order to reconstruct the nature of that gamble, we need to look closely at the formal parameters of slapstick comedy, to examine how those parameters might have resisted the kind of narrative articulation that a multiple-reel film was assumed to require and, ultimately, to identify how *Tillie's Punctured Romance* overcame that resistance. But the challenge of length was not limited to Sennett's six-reel experiment: also relevant is the standardization of two-reel comedies in Keystone's output and the changes this imposed on preproduction practices. In what follows here, then, I continue my investigation of the dialectic between Keystone's films and popular culture, examining the studio's early comedies in relation to the formal foundations—the gags and pratfalls—of variety and vaudeville humor. By imposing demands for a "continuous story" (as Sennett put it), longer formats challenged the studio's ties to those traditions and forced a greater attention to narrative and plot structure. Understanding how Keystone negotiated that challenge reveals much about the studio's ongoing resistance to broader industry trends, and much about its continued commitment to the tastes of the popular classes.

"TO REVEL IN WILD ACTION":
GAG, NARRATIVE, AND SLAPSTICK COMEDY

Narrative coherence was never one of the defining features of early slapstick. In the words of a contemporary review of one of Keystone's earliest films, *At It Again* (November 1912): "[The performers] succeed in jumbling the plot somewhat, but . . . *the plot is not important.*"[14] The reviewer's observation was astute; it is the gags and comic events that form the main point and appeal of Keystone's early comedies, not the simple plot situations by which their action is propelled. Indeed, in an important essay on early slapstick, Donald Crafton defines the genre precisely in terms of this refusal of storytelling norms. On this analysis, gags are considered a force of narrative disruption, inimical to the logic and clarity of plot: whereas narrative serves as a system for establishing causal links between events, gags tend to obfuscate those links, "misdirecting" the viewer's attention onto pie-smitten faces and other ephemeral moments of slapstick violence. The gags of early comedy are construed as relatively autonomous "attractions," which undermine the coherence of their narrative frame.[15]

Crafton's insightful analysis arguably suffers from its rigid distinction between gags and narrative as inherently opposed systems. Far from being "antinarrative" or "nonnarrative" (Crafton's terms), gags are inevitably articulated in a narrative context, within which they serve a variety of functions. The fact that they *may* constitute digressions should not mask the fact that gags also require narrative preconditions—at the very least, as a consequence of the existence of given characters in a given situation. A more productive definition of slapstick would insist upon the interdependency of comic action and plot, examining how the genre exploits narrative as a system for producing knockabout spectacle. In a 1920 guide for would-be comic screenwriters, the producer Al Christie offered just such a formulation:

> In analyzing even the wildest sort of "slapstick" comedy, you will invariably find at least a trace of fundamental drama. . . . There may have been strange and wonderful mustaches and beards of fantastic shape and unheard-of growth. The facial makeup may have been grotesque, but *invariably there was a basis in conflict.* . . . In every case, in spite of the throwing of pies, the shooting of harmless bullets, the falling of men and women from windows of high buildings only to pick themselves up and run away unhurt—in spite of all these "monstrous and chimerical" happenings, there was in each case a basis of struggle . . . and a foundation of dramatic structure.[16]

While Christie conceded that it is the gags that have priority within the slapstick text, he nevertheless insisted that those gags depend upon, and are produced by, an underlying commitment to narrative values.

What must be stressed, then, is not slapstick's "opposition" to narrative, but rather its indifference to narration—that is, to the task of rendering story material in a way that aids narrative comprehension. Plot elements are not absent, but they are articulated only to the extent that they provide for sequences of slapstick action. This kind of approach is paradigmatic for Keystone's early comedies, and can be illustrated by a sequence from *The Fatal Mallet* (June 1914). The film's "plot," such as it is, concerns the violent to-and-fro between a trio of mashers (Charles Chaplin, Mack Sennett, and Mack Swain) as they battle it out over Mabel Normand's affections. Prior to the sequence in question, two of the rival suitors (Sennett and Chaplin) have discovered a mallet in a barn and, joining forces, decide to use it to dispose of Swain. (Curiously, a hand-painted "I.W.W." sign on the barn door identifies the building as a Wobblies' meeting house.) The ensuing six shots span the distance between this decision and the blow they eventually bestow on Swain's head:

> Shot 79: Exterior barn door. Sennett exits the barn, followed by Chaplin, who playfully taps him with the mallet. Sennett seizes the weapon and strikes back. Chaplin attacks Sennett's head with his cane. Sennett gestures menacingly with the mallet. They leave the shot.
>
> Shot 80: Park (beneath tree). Mack Swain woos Normand.
>
> Shot 81: Park. Chaplin and Sennett enter the shot, Chaplin swinging the mallet. Sennett ducks to avoid being hit.
>
> Shot 82: Park (beneath tree). Swain continues wooing.
>
> Shot 83: Park. Chaplin swings the mallet again, this time hitting Sennett square in the face. Sennett kicks him. They exit the shot.
>
> Shot 84: Park (beneath tree). Chaplin and Sennett sneak up behind Swain and knock him out with a single blow. They doff their hats to Normand and exit the shot, carrying Swain's body.[17]

"[T]he picture, purporting to be nothing other than a mélange of roughhouse happenings, . . . proves that hitting people over the heads with bricks and mallets can sometimes be made amusing," *Moving Picture World*'s reviewer commented.[18] But it also demonstrates a characteristic strategy of Keystone slapstick, the tendency to exploit gaps between the cause-effect chain of narrative (here, between the decision to use the mallet and the execution of the plan) as spaces for impromptu gags and comic performances (here, the bickering blows that the two mashers inflict upon one another). This kind of approach is particularly true of the large number of single-reel "park" films released by Keystone in 1914, in which a park provides a basic locale in which the comedians run off a series of miscellaneous antics. In these films—and *The Fatal Mallet* is a paradigmatic example—plot functions serve as nothing more than linking devices between extended sequences of slapstick byplay and buffoonery. Again, though, this is not "antinarrative" (as Crafton seems to suggest), but a reversal of conventional polarities within narrative—a displacement of plot interest onto intermediary moments of spectacle and display.

In its resistance to narrative values, in its privileging of the digressive byplay and visceral blows of physical comedy, early slapstick was nonetheless more than a site of merely *formal* heterogeneity within cinema of the 1910s: it was an articulation of popular tastes and comic traditions that contradicted the ideological underpinnings of genteel culture. Important work in this area has been undertaken by Henry Jenkins, who identifies two distinct, socially defined comic aesthetics in turn-of-the-century America (briefly touched on in my introduction).[19] The first, genteel view represented traditional Victorian virtues of character and restraint: here, comedy was to serve a serious moral purpose, producing contemplative laughter in middle-class readers. George Meredith provided the watchword for this ideal in a famous 1877 essay "On the Idea of Comedy," where he defined true comedy in terms of "thoughtful laughter" or the "humour of the mind."[20] Such a view stressed narrative as the basic vehicle of humor and emphasized sentiment and fellow-feeling as the distinguishing marks of "refined" comic perception. The stress within this conception was clearly on moderation, in keeping with a Victorian ethic of self-mastery. "Thoughtful laughter is an inner experience—a sort of internal chuckle— which does not display external manifestations. It is the enjoyment of the intellect when situations or characters or sometimes, phrases strike one as happy exhibitions of humor," W. L. Courtney, the distinguished editor of the *Fortnightly Review*, contended as late as 1914.[21] Such a sensibility also served as a mark of individual distinction for members of polite society. "We laugh at farce, we laugh at all kinds of burlesque entertainment, we laugh at pantomimes," Courtney added. "But this kind of laughter could not possibly be called thoughtful and comes more naturally from a vacuous mind."[22]

Yet the ideal of morally purposeful laughter was hardly unchallenged. By the turn of the century, a new comic aesthetic had established itself, one that drew on ethnic, working-class traditions of humor (German and Jewish in particular) and emphasized comic pleasure as a desirable goal in its own right. As defined by the vaudeville historian Albert McClean, this "New Humor" dispensed with the refinements of story-telling technique, emphasizing the compressed joke or gag as its basic structural unit.[23] Shared across a number of media—in popular journalism (where comic strips and joke columns were a staple of newspapers by the turn of the century), in dime joke books (whose number rose from 11 in 1890 to 104 in 1907), and in new humor magazines like *Judge, Life,* and *Puck*—the New Humor was sustained by the growing market for commercial entertainment.[24] And in no field was it more strikingly and dynamically realized than on the vaudeville and variety stage, particularly in the hands of comic monologists like Lew Dockstader, Fred Niblo, and Doc Rockwell. The ideal variety act, the vaudevillian Wilfred Clarke suggested in 1906, was one with "no time for plot": the sequencing of individual jokes, gags, and pratfalls had less to do with narrative coherence than with their sheer cumulative force—the immediate emotional impact they might have on their audience.[25] Closure was less important than a spectacular climax (in vaudeville parlance, a "wow finish"). "The purpose of the sketch," Brett Page wrote in his handbook *Writing for Vaudeville* (1915), "is not to leave a single impression of a single story. It points no moral, draws no conclusion, and sometimes it might end quite as effectively anywhere before the place in the action at which it does terminate."[26] Where advocates of "thoughtful laughter" saw its greatest potential within narrative forms where the melding of humor and sympathy could be carefully achieved, the New Humor exploited the affective immediacy of the gag as the cornerstone of a new, disjunctive comic aesthetic.

Within the field of early film, this distinction was reproduced in a contrast discussed in an earlier chapter—namely, that between slapstick and "situation" comedy.[27] By revitalizing screen farce, Keystone's slapstick style played a significant role in institutionalizing the New Humor in American cinema. Yet the studio's success remained circumscribed—at least during its early years—by critical advocacy of the greater "refinement" of the situation style, as exemplified by the films of John Bunny and Sidney Drew (Bunny's replacement at Vitagraph from 1915). As succinctly defined by Al Christie in his 1920 pamphlet on comedy screenwriting, the term "situation" comedy had "come into common use . . . in order to distinguish between the clean-cut, plausible quality of screen humor and what is known as 'slapstick' comedy." "'Situation comedy,'" Christie explained, "is applied to the one and two-reel subjects in which the characters are dressed as they would be in real life" and in which the "sequence of situations [is] carefully related."[28]

Yet, given the divergent social aesthetics from which the two styles derived, writers also buttressed their definitions with concepts of class hierarchy. "[B]urlesque comedy, of the 'slap-stick' variety, is at present a passionate hobby in photoplayland," William Lord Wright complained in 1914, adding: "Many of these efforts . . . [are] annoying to those who delight in true humor."[29] Even in an article praising slapstick, *Photoplay's* Alfred A. Cohn could attribute the style's popularity to the intellectual failings of the "masses." "For the benefit of those who do not realize the fine distinction between straight comedy and slapstick," Cohn observed, "it may be stated that the latter is more pointed and therefore more apparent and easily understood by the masses than the former."[30] Others found simpler explanations; as Rob Wagner, a socialist teacher and future Sennett publicity man, explained bluntly in 1920, "Rough workers . . . like things that go bang."[31] Slapstick and situation comedy constituted alien aesthetics, not merely because of their distinct formal practices, but because of the ties that bound those practices to the comic traditions of different classes.

"When you see a farce, you expect it to revel in wild action," a *Photoplay* writer argued in 1913. "When you see a good clean comedy, you are first given some semblance of a well-defined plot."[32] The distinction is important in this analysis, because it helps clarify the difficulties Keystone's filmmakers faced in the production of *Tillie's Punctured Romance*. In embarking on that project, Sennett was effectively forcing a confrontation between competing aesthetic impulses. Such a film would require a comic plot capable of sustaining the longer duration; yet, as slapstick, it would subordinate that plot to the demands of comic spectacle. Negotiating between dependency on narrative and resistance to narrative integration, it would "revel in wild action" within the confines of a "well-defined plot." As a close reading of *Tillie's Punctured Romance* suggests, such a film would ultimately be an arena of contention between larger social discourses, a staging ground upon which the disjunctive immediacy of the New Humor would contend against the narrative presuppositions of the situation style. The particular difficulties this entailed were not, however, unique to that picture. Even as work began on *Tillie's Punctured Romance*, Keystone's filmmakers were also adjusting to the demands of two-reel comedy, and in their efforts to standardize two-reel production, they experimented with strategies of comic structure that also shaped their approach to the six-reel project.

"A GENUINE SITUATION IS STICKING AROUND IN IT SOMEWHERE": MODE OF PRODUCTION AND THE TWO-REEL COMEDY

In May 1914, the Keystone scenario editor Craig Hutchison said of the studio's commitment to story values, "The rapidity in which Keystone comedies travel on the screen causes observers to overlook the situations in following the by play. True, we are accused of not having much of a story in our pictures but I think you will find that when the mass of comedy business is scraped away, and the bare plot left exposed, a genuine situation is sticking around in it somewhere. This, however, is usually so skillfully and humorously covered by Mack Sennett's directing, that a careless observer is inclined to overlook it."[33] A tongue-in-cheek sop to middle-class criticism of "plotless" slapstick, Hutchison's assertion neatly captures Keystone's characteristic indifference to narrative clarity and exposition: there is an underlying adherence to narrative, Hutchison wryly asserts, just not a narrative that is recognizable as such.

Yet it was precisely the question of the relationship between "genuine situation" and "comedy business" that exercised the attentions of Keystone's critics over the coming months. By late 1914, reviewers were beginning to comment upon a significant change in the studio's films, a growing attention to story structure that, while never more than partial, mediated between demands for well-plotted comedy and the studio's established slapstick style. Out of fifty Keystone-Mutual releases reviewed in *Moving Picture World* in 1915, at least five received special commendation for well-constructed plots, while only two were faulted for narrative incoherence. (These figures should be compared with those for the previous year, when, out of 101 Keystones reviewed, only three drew praise for story construction, while nine were criticized for their muddled plot lines.) "Although farce-comedies are supposedly written on the . . . cuff, such is far from being the actual case in recent Keystone development," an admiring Louis Reeves Harrison commented in his review of *The Little Teacher* (June 1915).[34]

What lay behind these changes was, arguably, less a sudden desire for respectability than a pragmatic engagement with the greater complexities of the two-reel format. Critical praise for the films' greater story values was more or less simultaneous with the standardization of the two-reel comedy as the studio's principal commodity—first with the introduction of regularly fortnightly two-reelers in October 1914, then with the shift to exclusive two-reel production the following June—and corresponded to a significant transformation in the studio's mode of production. Already, in other studios, the impetus toward longer pictures had led to an expansion in the preproduction process, as companies began employing some form of detailed "continuity script" as a blueprint for planning each film.[35] Yet Keystone had lagged behind industry trends in this respect, adhering to the older practice of the general outline script rather than the more rigorous shot-by-shot continuity. Sennett's supposed aversion to scripts was long a favorite topic of the trade press; as late as the fall of 1914, reporters continued to describe him as "the *only* director who works without a scenario."[36] Although almost certainly spurious, such reports nevertheless indicated real distinctions between Keystone's work process and dominant industry trends: until around mid-1914, Keystone's filmmakers rarely worked from anything more than skeleton outlines of their films, typically no more than a few paragraphs. The studio's earliest surviving preproduction scenario—a one-page outline for *Mabel's Strange Predicament* dated January 10, 1914—deserves quoting in full:

> Husband and wife, and Mabel are staying at same hotel. Mabel is romping with her pet dog in hotel yard when her sweetheart comes on and talks with her. In next set husband and wife are sitting. Wife leaves set for moment to get something. During her absence Mabel's dog's ball rolls into husbands [sic] set. Husband picks it up as Mabel comes on and takes his time in presenting it to her very politely. Wife returning sees and dosn't [sic] like it. Comes on to husband and Mabel and upbraids husband. Lover from first set sees and comes on to husband, wife and Mabel. Recognizes husband as friend and calms the group down somewhat. Wife now takes husband into hotel and Mabel bids lover good bye and also goes into building.
>
> Their rooms adjoin and Mabel as soon as she comes in starts playing with her dog again. The noise penetrates the partition and the wife already harboring a feeling against Mabel exits to complain to the manager about the noise. Meanwhile Mabel has prepared for be[d] and is in her pajamas. In playing with her dog again, the ball rolls out into the public hall. Mabel looks about and seeing no one goes after it. Dog inside room in trying to follow her jumps against door, the spring lock catches and Mabel is locked in hall in her pajamas. At this point drunk comes along and tries to flirt with Mabel. In a panic she tries the next rooms [sic] door and enters husbands [sic] room. Latter is standing at mirror and does not observe her. She hides under bed.
>
> Meanwhile Mabel's lover has taken notion to call and comes to her room. Finds it locked. Looks through key hole and sees Mabels [sic] dog. Passing janitor unlocks door for him and dog emerges. As Mabel is not at home lover decides to call on husband next door. Enters. He and husband hold conversation. Meanwhile in hall Mabels [sic] dog has found her trail and enters and goes to bed wagging tail. Mabel under bed tries to make him go away. Lover and husband notice dog and discover Mabel. Lover starts to beat husband when the three of them hear wife and manager coming. Do not want manager to know seeming scandal, so husband and lover agree to keep quiet. Wife and manager enter. Wife peeved at lover orders him out. He and manager exit. Wife and husband alone. Wife calming down and almost reconciled when she discovers Mabel under her bed in pajamas. Consternation etc.[37]

There is a basic outline of the action; there are also instructions concerning the movement of characters from shot to shot. But this is hardly a "design blueprint" for production. Most tellingly, the document does nothing to account for the visual antics and byplay—in theatrical parlance of the time, the comic "business"—so central to the studio's slapstick form. The scenario merely defines a narrative framework for the comedy, a basic matrix of plot points to be fleshed out by slapstick ad-libbing during production.

For filmmakers committed to the value of comic improvisation and impromptu gagging there was obviously little call for meticulous preproduction work. By late 1914, however, the standardization of two-reel production meant rethinking studio work processes. For one thing, rehearsals became more extensive. A 1915 article, "The 'Movies' in the Making," described the new regimen: the director "rehearses each player in his or her part, always watching the most minute detail and now and then during some bit of difficult action he puts himself in their place and shows just how it should be done. Sometimes the rehearsal will last for 30 minutes to an hour, when but two or three minutes is all the time required to actually take the scene."[38] The growing complexity of the films' narratives also required more exact scripting. By September 1914, scenarios frequently included instructions on shot structure, specifying the use of "flashes" (cutting away to a different set/location), "inserts" (cutting in to a closer view of a person/object), and "cut backs" (cutting between lines of action). The opening paragraphs of the three-page scenario to *He Loved the Ladies* (September 1914) are typical:

> Story opens up with husband and wife in park on bench—Flash to another scene of very pretty girl with her skirts caught on a rose bush, exposing part of limbs, underclothes, etc.
> Flash back to husband who sees this, and starts to flirt. The wife notices the strange actions of her husband—husband sees her—picks up parasol, opens it and puts it in front of wife so as to obscure her view of the girl.
> Husband knocks bee off of wife's nose—it goes into the next set and lands on the girl's nose—girl gets very much excited starts to scream, husbands [sic] exits into girl's set, leaving wife rubbing her nose with powder, etc. She see [sic] husband thru mirror. Wife calls husband back—before he leaves he gives the girl his card—they exchange cards, both find they are stopping at same hotel. Girl leaves to go to hotel. Wife leaves also.[39]

With respect to detail, this is clearly a step beyond the scenario for *Mabel's Strange Predicament*. The ascendancy of narrative values is evident in the attention to exposition, both in the precision of description and in the sequencing of shots. Of course, scope remains for improvised byplay, but what makes the scenario interesting is that it identifies precise places at which those moments are to occur: later sections of the document indicate

numerous pieces of unspecified "business" (to be worked out during filming), such as "biz at table of breaking plate over girl's head," "biz with rope
on roof," and so forth. Gags and narrative are thus construed as separate,
interacting formal systems existing in a specifiable, structured relation to
each other.

This kind of approach would be reinforced by changes in the studio's
work processes when, in early 1915, staff writer Hampton Del Ruth took
over from Craig Hutchison as Keystone's chief scenario editor.[40] Under the
ambitious program of expansion begun by Del Ruth, Keystone scripts were
now routinely subjected to extensive rewriting and generally ran anywhere between five and seven pages in length. As previously, Keystone's
writers identified places for comic "business" within their scenarios; but
they were now also required to compose a "gag sheet"—a detailed list of
comic antics to supply the necessary "biz."[41] One must imagine a process
similar to—although undoubtedly less formalized than—the one that
governed scenario preparation at Sennett's lot in the early 1920s. As
Vernon Smith, Sennett's scenario editor during the later period, described it:

> I would assign two writers to develop [a basic story idea]. All they did
> was tell a story—no gags. . . . When we decided that a yarn was good
> enough, it went to the gag room. . . . A gag conference consisted of
> about six gag men. . . . There was no orderly procedure. The story was
> attacked from all angles by everybody. Anyone who thought up a
> funny situation would not only tell it but act it out at the same time. . . .
> If a stranger had walked in, . . . he might have thought he was in the
> violent ward of an insane asylum.[42]

This two-stage system, as launched by Del Ruth, proved a brilliant adjustment to the demands of the two-reel form, one calculated to supply the
necessary narrative armature without sacrificing the comic spectacle for
which the studio was known. Keystone's staff writers would provide the
former, its gag specialists the latter. Such a system respected the narrative
demands of the longer format *and* it respected the autonomy of the gag:
the tension between comic spectacle and comic narrative was thus institutionalized as the cornerstone of Keystone's preproduction processes. It is
this tension, in fact, that manifests itself in Keystone's 1915 output as the
films' "ideology of form"—a term coined by Fredric Jameson to refer to
the structural divisions produced within a text by the coexistence of several
distinct modes of production.[43] The division of labor during script preparation thus tended to generate significant formal contrasts within Keystone's
two-reel films. The first reel, for example, was very much the province of
the studio's comedians and gag specialists: the scenario staff would do little

more than describe an initial situation and sequence of scenes to be filled out with unspecified gags and comic business. For the second reel, however, they typically constructed more tautly narrativized sequences of events, usually following the studio's familiar pattern of burlesque melodrama. Something of this has already been seen in *Dough and Dynamite* (October 1914), in the transition from the inconsequential tomfoolery of the first reel to the strikers' "Fiendish Plan" in the second. Under Del Ruth, this approach was adopted as the basic template for script preparation. Consider, for example, the enormous scope given to unspecified "biz" in the opening to the scenario for *When Ambrose Dared Walrus* (July 1915):

> Exterior hotel [Mack] Swain and [Vivian] Edwards enter, biz with baggage man on wagon about trunk, exit into hotel. In hotel lobby, [Chester] Conklin on scrubbing, wife at desk, Swain and Edwards enter. Biz at desk. Swain has biz with Conklin's wife, Edwards sees, gets sore and sits down on Conklin. Swain continues biz with [Billie] Brock[well], Conklin bumps Edwards off onto chair, she takes it. Swain is registering. Conklin has love biz with Edwards. Brock at desk gets interested in Swain's name, he gets over he is a big weight man and actor. Swain turns, Edwards and Brock see him, Conklin does not. Conklin has biz with Edward's [sic] ring, Edwards slaps him, Conklin takes it, sees Swain and gets up. Swain bawls him out. Brock tells Conklin to get back to scrubbing, he gets on floor again. Edwards goes to pick up bag, Conklin gets up to help her, Brock and all have biz about bag, Brock, Swain and Edwards exit upstairs. Conklin goes to foot of stairs.

Contrast this with the near total elimination of "biz" in the film's fast-paced climax, in which a conflagration in the hotel lobby prompts a thrilling rescue:

> The Fire department now arrives and starts to hose and water. Biz of Conklin on spout, climbs to Swain's window, gets hit with water and knocked into bed where Edwards is pouting. Swain now breaks in door, sees Conklin on bed and starts to fight. He throws Conklin out window, water hits him and knocks him back on bed again. Swain and he have another fight in which he throws Conklin out window again. Water hits Conklin and carries him to roof. Swain sees him going up and exits to roof after him, Conklin sees this and tells firemen to turn off water, which lets him back down to Swain's room window. Conklin rescues Edwards from the window and slides down the stream.
> Brock on roof with kids calling for help. Swain comes on, does human bridge act to telephone pole. Kids walk across and exit down pole. Brock starts across, Swain's feet slips [sic] and she falls into a net. Swain's hands are burning and he lets go and falls. . . . Ad Lib Finish.[44]

Despite the instruction to "ad lib" the concluding shots—quite typical of Keystone scripts from this period—there is obviously less room here for gags and comic byplay. The scope for "biz" narrows as the action coheres around a melodramatic paradigm.

This two-part pattern served for almost every Keystone release following the move to exclusive two-reel production in June 1915. Of the eleven two-reel films released through Mutual following the new policy, at least eight exhibit this structure.[45] Thus *The Cannon Ball* (June 1915), in which an explosives inspector (Conklin) bumbles around the "Boom Explosives Co." during the first reel before kidnapping the inventor's daughter and provoking a race to the rescue in the second. Thus also *The Battle of Ambrose and Walrus* (August 1915), whose first reel depicts the comic rivalry between two soldiers (Conklin and Swain), while the second hinges on a melodramatic situation in which the general's daughter is rescued from a firing squad. But perhaps the most extreme example of the pattern occurs in Roscoe Arbuckle's *Fatty's Plucky Pup* (June 1915), which bares the device. Here, each reel becomes a separate comedy in its own right. The first half of the film establishes a simple situation—Fatty lives with his mother and is in love with the neighbor's daughter—upon which it elaborates a series of gags: Fatty accidentally sets his bed on fire, drops laundry in a puddle, has a mishap with a hose, and spoons with his sweetheart. The reel ends when Fatty rescues a runaway mutt from a pair of dogcatchers and adopts it for his own. Fade out. The second reel is, to all intents and purposes, a different movie, linked to the first only by its principal characters. Beginning with a title "On a Day's Outing," the reel begins with Fatty, sweetheart, and dog enjoying a seaside excursion, but quickly develops into another Keystone burlesque of D. W. Griffith's 1908 *The Fatal Hour*[46]: the girl is kidnapped by two crooks, taken to a barn, and tied up before a timed revolver. Fatty's pup picks up her trail and proves his pluck in a race to the rescue.

The narrative discourse of *Fatty's Plucky Pup* is evidently not designed for unity. There is nothing necessary in the events of the first reel for an understanding of the second: we do not, for example, need to know *how* Fatty acquires his dog in order to accept the dog's subsequent presence. Narrative development is hostage to the film's structural tensions and divisions. As unusual as this film is, the majority of Keystone's two-reel releases exhibit a similar compromise with narrative values: rather than attempt a comprehensively plotted form, Keystone's filmmakers preferred a more divided approach, shifting from loosely structured "biz" at the films' beginnings to tautly plotted melodramas at the ends. The inventiveness of this strategy was to have met the challenge of the two-reel format without undermining Keystone's indebtedness to the disjunctive formulas of the New Humor. But it also produced an unresolved tension between the demands of slapstick and the demands of narrative, a tension that could—and in the case of *Fatty's Plucky Pup* did—yield disunities within the comic text. This tension lay at the heart of *Tillie's Punctured Romance.*

"WHAT WE WANT IS STRAIGHT GOING ACTION": *TILLIE'S PUNCTURED ROMANCE*

Early in the spring of 1914, Sennett approached Kessel and Baumann to discuss his idea for a move into feature-length production. "I battled with [them] for permission to make the first full-length, or six-reel, motion-picture comedy," Sennett later recalled. "My partners pointed out to me, correctly, that such a picture would not only cost in the neighborhood of $200,000, but demanded a star whose name and face meant something to every possible theatergoer. . . . On top of that, I was reminded, no one had ever made a six-reel comedy. Under any circumstances the venture was a gamble. 'Not a gamble with Marie Dressler,' I said."[47]

Sennett was undoubtedly right. Dressler was one of the preeminent musical comedy actresses of her time. She had featured at the prestigious Weber and Fields Music Hall since 1904, and the successful two-year run of the stage comedy *Tillie's Nightmare* (1910) had cemented her reputation. Sennett surely also realized that Dressler's famously broad performance style would make her a good fit at Keystone. Hardly a beauty by conventional standards, Dressler openly exploited her self-confessed "homely" appearance in her stage performances, soliciting laughter with displays of grotesque, ungainly physicality that contradicted traditional assumptions of feminine grace. Nowhere was this better exemplified than in her role as the eponymous boarding-house drudge of *Tillie's Nightmare,* where Dressler's virtuoso grotesqueries formed the focal point of the show. "The show is dominated by an actress whose main aim is to make herself a monstrosity so she may use ugliness as a bludgeon to wallop the ignorant into blithering and painful laughter," observed a withering review of the show's out-of-town opening in December 1909.[48] "We have observed the lady in many grotesque manifestations," commented another reviewer of the same performance, "but in *Tillie's Nightmare* we think she reaches the heights of homeliness. Occasionally she looks like an amiable sea serpent and again her resemblance is to something prehistoric and unclassified."[49]

By proposing Dressler as the star of his feature-length experiment, Sennett was, in one sense, simply following industry practice. Beginning around 1909, American producers often exploited well-known theatrical actors as marquee attractions for their productions. As a commercial tactic for attracting "better" audiences, this approach had become an industry norm by 1912, when Adolph Zukor launched his Famous Players company with the intent of presenting theatrical actors in film adaptations of their famous roles. Sennett clearly expected Dressler's signing to pay similar dividends with respect to audience appeal. As Dressler later recalled, Sennett and Baumann approached her while she was on rest leave in Los Angeles with the idea of making "good pictures that would take them into first-rate houses." "They thought they could break into first-string theaters if they had my name in the cast," she explained.[50] However, Dressler's own interest in the project lay rather in the opportunity of bringing her "Tillie" characterization to poorer audiences. "[Tillie] was so human, . . . and that is why I have dragged her into the movies," Dressler commented at the time. "Through the screen I am taking her to the human people, the people I could never reach, because they never had the price. . . . I wanted to come to the 'movies' with a 10 cent to 50 cent performance, and I intend to remain with them, watch me."[51] Cultural egalitarianism thus meshed with a desire for prestige to give the planned project significant crossover potential.

Sometime in April 1914, Dressler signed up for twelve weeks work at Keystone at a salary of $2,500 a week (a figure commensurate with her stage salary but more than ten times that earned by Keystone's highest paid stars).[52] According to initial announcements, the original plan was to star her in a series of three- or four-reel comedies under the direction of Mack Sennett, who returned to the director's chair for the project after a four-month hiatus from active filmmaking. As reported by *Moving Picture World* in May, "Marie Dressler . . . will be seen soon in a series of special Keystone Mutual Movie comedies, three and four reels in length. Work of production has been going on for some time under the direction of Mack Sennett . . . and the comedies featuring Miss Dressler will start to appear before the public by the first of July."[53] According to Dressler's autobiography, her deal with Keystone guaranteed her half ownership in the films and stipulated that they would be leased but never sold, that she would receive weekly statements of their earnings, and that her longtime partner Jim Dalton would handle publicity and distribution.[54] (One—no doubt apocryphal—story has Dressler make the further stipulation that she would not work with Roscoe Arbuckle, fearing that he would upstage her in girth. Whatever the merits of this tale, Arbuckle was indeed the only major Keystone star who did not work on *Tillie's Punctured Romance*.)

At some point early in the production process, Sennett abandoned the planned series and set his writers to work on a scenario for a single, longer production. Yet Sennett's own account of the writing of that scenario remains ambiguous.[55] According to his autobiography, an initial plot outline was drawn up during an alcohol-fueled all-nighter involving Sennett himself, Craig Hutchison, Hampton Del Ruth, and a case of champagne. "[W]e got an idea by 2:00 A.M., with three bottles of Mumm's left over. It was Mr. Hutchison who had the moneysaving notion of using the story line of Miss Dressler's stage hit, *Tillie's Nightmare*. We outlined that on not more than two sheets of hotel stationery, had it typed in the morning, and sent it up to the boys in the gag room with orders to make with the funny business."[56] Yet, on the very next page of his memoirs, Sennett makes a slight but important change in the story, claiming that "Hampton Del Ruth and the entire department took *a slim idea* from Miss Dressler's stage play and turned it into *Tillie's Punctured Romance*."[57] This seems closer to the truth: a comparison of the film with surviving scripts of the play reveals no narrative similarities beyond the central character being a naïve country girl named Tillie.

Yet to appreciate fully what the filmmakers did with *Tillie's Nightmare*, we need to pay closer attention to the original stage play. A reworking of the Cinderella myth, the play begins with a lengthy first act depicting Tillie Blobbs's life as a boardinghouse drudge. Under the constant harassment of her bedridden mother, Tillie is hurrying to finish up the housework so that she can go to a vaudeville show with some of the lodgers and her boyfriend Sim Pettinghill ("a small town genius, with Metropolitan aspirations," according to the play's dramatis personae).[58] Since she hasn't had a night off in over a year, this is quite an event for Tillie, and she proceeds to make a spectacle of herself by parading around in an ill-fitting dress designed for the occasion. "She has on a home-made skirt, (rather short) and a shirt-waist. The shirt-waist is a trifle tight and hardly meets in the back."[59] At the last minute, however, Tillie's mother forbids her to go, and her friends leave without her. She sits down to read the paper and falls asleep. End of Act 1.

The remainder of the play is a series of dream scenes in which Tillie visits New York and Paris, marries Sim, embarks on a sea cruise, receives an enormous inheritance, and finances an ill-fated aeroplane prototype, all before a brief concluding sequence in which Sim returns and wakes Tillie up. Rather than advancing a developed narrative, these scenes serve primarily as a springboard for what the *Dramatic Mirror* called "a kaleidoscope of color in constant motion, a potpourri of songs and dances, of spectacular effects . . . embellished with all the fal-de-rol of its specie."[60] They also clearly were designed as showcases for Dressler's virtuoso comic turns. To allow the star free rein for slapstick extemporizing, the original script included instructions for "Specialty (Ad Lib)" sequences, once in a scene in which Tillie gets drunk on a cruise ship, and once in a song after she acquires her inheritance from an English nobleman.[61] Nor were Dressler's performative displays limited to the confines of the play. After the curtain fell on the show's New York debut, she returned to the stage and, in the words of the *Dramatic Mirror*, "sealed her triumph with a musical burletta, 'What I Could Do on the Stage,' in which she travestied Tetrazzini in grand opera, a heavy dramatic episode, and the recent vogue of the Greek and Salome dances."[62]

The narrative of *Tillie's Nightmare* is, it is true, nothing like that of Keystone's film, in which a city slicker lures an innocent country girl to the city, steals her money, and abandons her to her fate. In fact, the "slim idea" that Keystone borrowed for *Tillie's Punctured Romance* came not from the play's framing story, but from the hit song of the show, "Heaven Will Protect the Working Girl." Performed by Tillie during the play's opening scene, the song recounts the story of a "village maid" who receives this advice from mother when she heads for the city: "The city is a wicked place as any one can see, / And cruel dangers' round your path may hurl; / So every week you'd better send your wages home to me, / For Heaven will protect a working girl." In the second verse, the mother's predictions come true, "for soon the poor girl met / A man who on her ruin was intent, / He treated her respectful as those villains always do, / And she supposed he was a perfect gent." When he attempts to seduce her, the country girl remembers her mother's words and, in the concluding chorus, rebuts his advances: "Stand back, villain, go your way! / Here I will no longer stay! / Although you were a Marquis or an Earl. / You may tempt the upper classes, / With your villainous demi-tasses, / But Heaven will protect a working girl."[63]

This is much closer to events in the film, and it is not difficult to see the attraction of these lyrics for Sennett's writers. As earlier argued, Keystone's filmmakers adapted to longer formats by exploiting familiar melodramatic situations as basic narrative armature. The lyrics to "Heaven Will Protect the Working Girl" outline just such a situation: city/country contrasts, urban villains, idyllic country settings, and innocent maidens were among the most hackneyed plot devices of American melodrama, legacies of the genre's characteristic nostalgia for traditional patterns of moral order. Here was material capable of providing a readily comprehensible narrative for Keystone's six-reel experiment.[64]

But this was not the only, or even the most important, element that Keystone borrowed from *Tillie's Nightmare*. For the studio's filmmakers, it was clearly Dressler's comic performance that was the principle dividend in their transaction with the play. Reviewing *Tillie's Punctured Romance* for *Motography*, Charles Condon noted that the film had incorporated elements of Dressler's stage performance: "Marie Dressler, universally known as Tillie, . . . re-enacts on the screen the droll expressions and queer actions which made her famous on the stage in 'Tillie's Nightmare.'"[65] Among the "queer actions" imported from the play were Dressler's grotesque exhibition of homemade dress-wear (which Tillie puts on in the film when she departs for the city), her drunk specialty act (when the city slicker plies Tillie with alcohol at a café), and her burlesque dancing (first in the café scene and later when Tillie hosts a society event). Clearly, in borrowing from *Tillie's Nightmare*, Keystone's filmmakers placed greater value on Dressler's virtuoso grotesqueries than on the play's narrative framework. In fact, in interviews of the time, Sennett took a remarkably dismissive attitude to the film's plot construction, claiming to have "framed the story as I went along," and that he "never use[d] a script." "I find this method has merits," Sennett added, "It gives an elasticity to the plot; we are enabled to take advantage of unforeseen situations and to make the most of them."[66] Despite the spurious claim to have made up the story on the cuff, Sennett's comments reveal much about his tactical approach to narrative values: insofar as the film required a plot, that plot would have to be "elastic" enough to showcase Dressler's performative display. Keystone's selective reworking of *Tillie's Nightmare* set the parameters for such an approach: it provided a rudimentary plot situation (borrowed from the play's hit song) and it provided the necessary moments of comic spectacle (borrowed from Dressler's stage role). This double inheritance would form the springboard for an escalating series of formal and thematic tensions throughout the resulting picture. As the subsequent analysis will show, *Tillie's Punctured Romance* asserted its historical originality as a feature-length comedy against the very standards of well-made narration and cultural uplift that defined the multiple-reel film as a "respectable" product.

. . .

From the outset, the film establishes a playfully deconstructive take on the clichés of cinematic refinement. At the beginning, a title card announces "Marie Dressler," who, seen out of character, steps out from behind a curtain and bows to the camera. A strategy for capitalizing on the legitimacy of stage versus film, such "curtain" openings were not uncommon in feature films of this period (indeed, Cecil B. DeMille's *What's His Name*, released a few weeks before *Tillie's Punctured Romance*, begins in very similar fashion). Taken here, the opening would seem to suggest continuity with Dressler's popular stage successes, a suggestion sustained as a dissolve next transforms the star into her familiar stage persona as Tillie. But the appeal to such safely middle-class registers is immediately undercut when a second dissolve commences the narrative proper, showing Tillie in front of a farmhouse from which her father exits: he kicks her in the posterior and the film is soon launched into an excruciatingly rough style of slapstick, extreme even by Keystone's standards.[67] Kicking, foot-stamping, and even brick-throwing will define the action of the film's beginning.

The formal structuring of the opening reel is, in fact, exemplary of Keystone's throwaway approach to narrative: as in many of the studio's single reel films, plot functions are briefly sketched, serving simply as catalysts for extended sequences of comic spectacle. The film's first six shots serve as the basic narrative setup. Following the initial series of dissolves (counted here as a single shot), four shots depict Tillie's slapstick run-in with her father, ending with them shaking their fists at each other. A title then introduces "A Stranger," seen in the film's sixth shot looking on at the farm from a distance. Wearing a dapper straw hat and carrying a cane, the stranger (Charles Chaplin) turns slowly toward the camera and ponders menacingly as he puffs on a cigarette (fig. 13). He then walks off toward the farm. With remarkable economy, these opening shots not only activate the "city slicker" plot familiar from stage melodrama, they also establish the film's burlesque take on melodramatic iconography. Unlike the country maidens of melodramatic theater, Tillie is hardly a figure of sentimental sweetness and innocence: rather, she is a hulking and homely yokel who, in the film's next shot, strenuously lobs a brick for her dog to fetch (fig 13). Nor is the city slicker particularly slick: the natty impression of his straw hat and cane is humorously belied by his tattered jacket and ill-fitting pants. Still, by way of an initial setup, these brief character introductions are all that is required for the film to launch into full knockabout mode. Tillie now hurls another brick (shot 11), which hits the stranger (12) and knocks him unconscious (14); she runs to help (15), wrestles the stranger to his feet (16), accidentally strikes him in the face (17), and, again accidentally, stamps on his feet (18). The slapstick only ends when Tillie brings the stranger into her home (19), disturbing her father, who looks in from the kitchen (20) as the two begin to flirt (21).

FIGURE 13. The city slicker (Charles Chaplin) contemplates the farm (left); Tillie lobs a brick for her dog to fetch (right). Frame enlargements from *Tillie's Punctured Romance* (December 1914). Courtesy of the Academy Film Archive, Academy of Motion Picture Arts and Sciences.

The following scenes continue this alternation between narrative detail and slapstick spectacle, an approach that defines the opening reel's subsequent development. With the entry into Tillie's home, for example, the film shifts back into a more expositional mode. The stranger is introduced to Tillie's father and discovers that a hefty sum of cash is kept in a kitchen pot; left alone in the front room, he pantomimes his dastardly intention to persuade Tillie to steal the money, then leaves the room to put his plan into action. But this in turn sets off a further fifty-three shots (around five minutes) of knockabout action, in which the stranger, Tillie, and Tillie's father end up pursuing each other around the garden, throwing bricks at one another and falling around, before the stranger eventually catches up to Tillie and commences his persuasion. The reel's concluding nine shots (from the title "Temptation") subsequently restore narrative momentum: the persuasion, the theft of the money, and Tillie and the stranger's departure are dispensed with in little over three minutes of screen time. The second reel then commences with the protagonists' arrival in the city.

Rather than integrate the knockabout into the narrative, the opening scenes of *Tillie's Punctured Romance* pose the two terms in their heterogeneity, switching between the two modes over the course of the first reel. Plot serves primarily to create opportunities within which slapstick byplay may occur; briefly dispensed with, scenes of narrative exposition serve as linking devices for digressive sequences of knockabout action. Common enough in Keystone's one-reel releases, this was nonetheless a daring strategy to announce at the beginning of a six-reel feature, affording little scope for the narrative development that the longer format would seem to require. What is remarkable, then, is that the film sustains this approach well into its second reel, which exhibits the same episodic, modal heterogeneity of the first. The reel opens on an image of unadulterated slapstick, underscoring the sudden change in locale through the chaos of the comic action: Tillie and the stranger are in the middle of a busy road, gesticulating wildly and tumbling around as they dodge the cars that speed past them. Again, however, this segues into brief narrative exposition. A title card announces "The Girl He Left Behind Him," and the film introduces a new protagonist, the stranger's girlfriend (Mabel Normand). Exiting a building (her apartment?), she spots her boyfriend with Tillie and, suspecting infidelity, gives him a firm dressing down.

What distinguishes the second reel is, in fact, less a difference in the interplay of slapstick and narrative than a shift in slapstick registers: the film now moves away from the rapidly edited knockabout of its opening scenes to foreground lengthy, single takes of Dressler's performance. This first becomes evident in a subsequent sequence in a café, in which Chaplin's city gent gets Tillie drunk and steals her money. From the beginnings of her drunken shenanigans to the end of the reel, the film hands center stage to Dressler as she recreates her famous drunk act from *Tillie's Nightmare*—first in five shots of inebriated dancing at the café; then in a brief, seven-shot sequence in which she is carried out of the café and handed over to a policeman; finally in five shots in which she drunkenly skips around the policeman as he takes her away and books her at the local station. Dressler's drunk act had been the most notorious aspect of her stage performance in *Tillie's Nightmare*, prompting conservative critics to complain about "offensive" and "unwholesome" exhibitions that caused "deplorable laughter on the part of a hardened few" while "squeamish observers [averted] their eyes from the stage."[68] Yet for the film, this was to be Dressler's "big scene," as Sennett recalled, and his direction here carefully inscribes her performance as a focus of the viewer's enjoyment. Both in the café and in the street scenes following her arrest, Sennett repeatedly centers Dressler's performance as a source of visual pleasure by cutting away to shots of Chaplin and Normand pointing and laughing (fig. 14).[69] Dressler's presence as grotesque spectacle displaces story development in moments of performative display.

In his astute *Motography* review, Charles Condon summed up the film's attitude to narrative as follows: "The plot [of *Tillie's Punctured Romance*] is a substantial one and if emphasized would become a good comedy-drama, but in its treatment here it merely furnishes *a background for individual action, a frame-work upon which the members of the cast hang*

FIGURE 14.   Tillie dances drunkenly while the city slicker and Mabel laugh at her. Frame enlargements from *Tillie's Punctured Romance* (December 1914). Courtesy of the Academy Film Archive, Academy of Motion Picture Arts and Sciences.

innumerable laugh-provoking mannerisms."[70] Nowhere is this more evident than in the film's first two reels. Rather than develop or complicate the city slicker narrative, *Tillie's Punctured Romance* merely exploits its conventions as a basis for comic spectacle. But such a strategy raises serious problems for the narrative's subsequent progress. If the plot is a mere "background" for sequences of comic action, how is the film to sustain its forward momentum? The difficulty is compounded by the cursory treatment of plot situations: by this point in the film, the major plot functions of the city slicker narrative have been dispensed with—the country maiden has been seduced and taken to the city, her money has been stolen, and she has been abandoned to jail. All that remains is for the city slicker himself to receive his comeuppance—presumably in an extended sequence of slapstick violence—and the narrative will be complete.[71] But this is obviously not a resolution that the film is able to confront at this early stage. Keystone's characteristic avoidance of narrative development has provided no strategy for organizing the plot at any length.

Such is the situation in the film's third reel, in which Charlie and Mabel visit a nearby nickelodeon, having already spent Tillie's money on clothes. The nickelodeon sequence stands at the fault line of the film's narrative dilemma, and is best understood as a displacement that serves a diversionary function with respect to the city slicker plot. Rather than proceed with that plot, the narrative here turns in upon itself, producing a remarkable *mise-en-abyme* at the center of this six-reel film: seated in the nickelodeon, the two protagonists watch a (fictitious) Keystone film, entitled *A Thief's Fate,* and note their own similarities to the characters on the screen. ("A Moving Picture Strangely Shows Them Their Own Guilt and

Its Possible Consequences," declares the intertitle that introduces this sequence.) The film-within-a-film carefully recapitulates the events of the framing story: a city gent brings a naïve country girl to a saloon, where he gets her drunk and robs her. As in the framing plot of *Tillie's Punctured Romance*, the thief's girlfriend appears and registers her suspicions, before he explains his nefarious plan and hands her the money. The film ends when a policeman reveals himself to the criminal couple and leads them away in handcuffs.

Although the opening title for *A Thief's Fate* (visible on the nickelodeon screen) identifies the movie as "farce comedy," this film-within-a-film is clearly played as straight drama. What Chaplin and Normand view on the screen is, in effect, the master plot of which *Tillie's Punctured Romance* is the travesty. Behind this peculiar reversal, however, lies a revealing shift in the text's burlesque strategies. Rather than confront the impending resolution of the city slicker narrative, the film launches a new parody—a burlesque of D. W. Griffith's *A Drunkard's Reformation* (1909), a temperance drama that had depicted the moral reawakening of an alcoholic father who attends a play about the evils of drink. Exemplifying earlier attempts to establish the motion picture as a vehicle for moral sermonizing, Griffith's film had been a landmark in early cinema's inscription in genteel social discourse—a demonstration, according to Tom Gunning, "that *film can be moral*; that watching an edifying drama can have a transforming effect on the spectator."[72] But it is precisely the reformist content of Griffith's original that Sennett's version deflates. Following the Griffith film, Sennett continually cuts between the action on the screen (sometimes shown in the background in long shots of the nickelodeon's interior, sometimes occupying the whole frame) and Mabel and Charlie's alarm at the film's parallels to their own lives. Unlike *A Drunkard's Reformation*, however, the characters' reactions to what they see hardly constitute a moral renewal. Mabel mischievously provokes her boyfriend by pointing out his similarity to the screen villain; Charlie gleefully turns the tables by indicating her resemblance to the villain's girlfriend; both become restless when they notice a mysterious character sitting beside them (played by Charles Parrott); and they flee the theater in panic when they spot a sheriff's badge on his vest. What they have learned from the film is the imminent possibility of being caught, not the moral consequences of their wrongdoing—and, as their continued misdeeds will prove, this hardly counts as "reformation."

Commenting on the episodic structure of *Tillie's Punctured Romance*, the reviewer for *Moving Picture World* described the plot as "nothing but situations."[73] Thus far, the film has hop-scotched across two distinct story paradigms—the city-slicker plot common to stage melodrama and the reform drama of Griffith's *A Drunkard's Reformation*—exploiting each for moments of comic spectacle, and yet deferring the closure that each situation implies. The city slicker steals Tillie's money, but is not caught; he watches a film depicting "a thief's fate," but is not reformed. And, with the nickelodeon sequence completed, there now commences a third situation, one that both shapes the remainder of the film's action and launches a new approach to the challenge of integrating narrative exposition and slapstick spectacle. The film now lifts the burden of narrative progress from the principal protagonists and displaces it onto a secondary group of characters first introduced at the end of the second reel. There, the inebriated and incarcerated Tillie had revealed herself as the niece of "Millionaire Banks"; the police chief had called the Banks mansion to confirm her story; and Tillie had been briefly released into her uncle's custody.[74] Utterly implausible given Tillie's humble station at the film's beginning, this plot twist remains undeveloped until the end of the third reel, where it becomes the basis for a new narrative episode centered on the uncle's misadventures during a mountaineering expedition. Introduced with the title card "Uncle Starts on a Trip to the Summit," the episode initially comprises three brief sequences (two shots, nine shots, and six shots, respectively) intercut with the ongoing antics of the film's principal protagonists. In the first segment, "Millionaire Banks" sets off from camp; in the second, he apparently dies in a fall; and in the third, his guide phones the mansion with the unhappy news. (Three later segments in the fifth reel—each comprising one shot—show the rescue and recovery of the uncle, unexpectedly still alive.)

Early feature filmmakers had occasionally resorted to such bald coincidence as the uncle's mountaineering accident, and it is clear that *Tillie's Punctured Romance* is at one level parodying the similarly unmotivated Alpine demise of the Earl of Kerhill in DeMille's version of *The Squaw Man* (1914). Yet there is additional significance here in the absence of physical comedy from these sequences. Scenes involving the mountaineering expedition are characterized by a dramatic mode of presentation that, despite the parody, contrasts sharply with the film's preceding action. In effect, the film here arrives at a new strategy for organizing the relation between plot development and comic spectacle. To introduce a non-slapstick subplot at this point is implicitly to pass judgment on the film's ability to sustain a coherent story through its current cast of slapstick characters. Thus far, those characters have performed a dual task, both forwarding the narrative and supplying moments of comic display; but the film now uncouples these trajectories, allotting each to a distinct group of characters and social milieu. From the fourth reel onward, there will be a decisive separation between the source of the film's slapstick action (the comic lower-class world of Tillie, the city slicker, and his girlfriend) and the source of the film's plot development (the non-slapstick upper-class world of the millionaire Banks and his retainers). Though the lower-class characters remain the focus of the film, their role in forwarding the narrative is transferred onto the privileged inhabitants of Banks's mansion.

With this move, the heterogeneous aesthetic registers of *Tillie's Punctured Romance* open directly onto the antagonistic dialogue of class difference: the formal interplay of story and slapstick is, from here on out, coded through the interactions between these two socially distinct groups of characters. Banks's mansion becomes the seat of the coordinating energies of narrative: it is the motor of the plot's forward momentum, both source and center of the relay of narrative information that shapes the film's developing action. It is a telephone call to the mansion that confirms Tillie's identity and releases her from jail; it is Banks's retainers who inform Tillie that she is the sole heir of her supposedly dead uncle's fortune; it is a newspaper report of Banks's death that gives the city slicker the idea of marrying Tillie for her inheritance. What this means for the lower-class protagonists, however, is that their previous role as narrative agents is now largely erased, supplanted by their function as comic spectacle within a plot controlled by events within the upper classes. During the mountaineering sequences, for example, the principal characters are involved in nothing more consequential than a series of disconnected run-ins with other characters, first in a number of scenes in a café where Tillie has found a job, later in sequences in a park when Charlie finds out about her inheritance. With the signal exception of Charlie's hasty marriage to Tillie, the film's major protagonists will no longer complete a meaningful plot action in this film.

What does this polarization imply for the remainder of the picture? The forces of narrative order and social authority have now been thoroughly identified; the possibility of narrative resolution would, accordingly, seem to require an act of social control—the rescue of the new heiress by Banks's retainers, perhaps, or their arrest of the city slicker. But this is not what happens in *Tillie's Punctured Romance*. Rather, its final two reels move in the direction of total narrative and social disorder, as plot developments are abandoned to the forces of comic spectacle. By the end of the fourth reel, Charlie has forced Tillie to marry him, and the newlyweds have taken up residence in the mansion. The occasion for the film's final act comes when the couple decides to host a party to celebrate "Their Entrance into High

Society." What follows is an extended slapstick sequence in which the Banks residence, previously the site of social and narrative order, becomes a venue for extraordinarily chaotic scenes of physical comedy. Of all the scenes in the film, the party is not only the longest (occupying most of the fifth reel and some of the sixth), it is also the most devoid of plot developments. Throughout the first two-thirds of the sequence, the film's causal progression stops dead to allow Dressler and Chaplin to perform their specialties—burlesque dancing on Dressler's part, roughhouse violence on Chaplin's. The city slicker, for instance, has repeated run-ins with his upper-class guests: an effete young man who sends Charlie into a paroxysm of homophobic fright; a respectable matron whose dress he accidentally raises to expose her thighs; later, a mustachioed gentleman (Chester Conklin) who physically attacks him when he sits down in his lap. Tillie, meanwhile, tries her hand at tango dancing, and drags Charlie round the floor as she grotesquely mimics the latest dance steps. For these scenes, Sennett subordinates visual style to the demands of foregrounding comic performance: Dressler and Chaplin are kept front and center in the frame, their actions often directed frontally toward the spectator (as in a vaudeville performance); shot lengths remain high (an average of almost 15 seconds), preserving the spatial and temporal integrity of the actors' virtuoso antics. Narrative space becomes performance space and plot development cedes priority to eccentric dancing (fig. 15).

But this is only the beginning of the film's final abandonment of narrative order. Tillie catches her husband spooning with Mabel (who has entered the party disguised as a maid) and the film immediately launches into a rapidly edited chase through the mansion (average shot length 3.5 seconds). Pistol in hand, Tillie bulldozes her way through room after room, smashing down vases, beds, and guests in the process. As the mansion is reduced to chaos, the uncle suddenly returns, recovered from the accident that was thought to have killed him, and orders everyone out of his house. Yet even this gesture of social control is unable to restore the film's coherence: the frenetic action simply moves out of doors, spinning chaotically into the most elaborate chase sequence thus far in Keystone's history. The basic principle here is one of accretion: Sennett multiplies lines of action, building the film toward a climactic tumult of comic spectacle. "Believe me, the work of assembling that last reel was some job," Sennett confessed in interview. "There were over 300 scenes in it, and they all had to be put together logically. . . . Had to have perfect balance and cooperation, and it sure was some work getting it."[75] The actual number of shots comprising the chase is, in fact, closer to half the figure cited by Sennett (159 shots in

FIGURE 15.   Charlie and Tillie dancing at the Banks mansion. Frame enlargement from *Tillie's Punctured Romance* (December 1914). Courtesy of the Academy Film Archive, Academy of Motion Picture Arts and Sciences.

the UCLA/NFTVA restoration); even so, this accounts for a little under a third of the total shots in the entire film.[76] As usual, the Keystone cops appear; but, in this case, there are four separate groups, each with a different mode of transportation—one group in an automobile, one on foot, one in a motorboat, and one in a rowboat. ("The Keystone 'cops' have the riot of their tempestuous, catlike lives," commented one reviewer.)[77] This multiplication increases the scope for intercutting, and the film cuts quickly between the separate pursuits (on the whole, an average shot length of 2.8 seconds from the point at which the uncle ejects the guests). Character after character plunges into the ocean as the chase leads onto Santa Monica pier—first Tillie, then the carload of policemen, two members of the "Water Police" as they launch their motorboat, two more policemen when a wave upsets the rowboat. Three times Tillie is hauled out of the water and dropped back before the police successfully lift her onto the pier.

Accretion, multiplication, and repetition: Sennett evidently conceived the final action as a "wow finish" that would end the picture with a climax of comic spectacle. "What we want is straight going action," he noted in the

Chicago Tribune interview. "We can't stop to go back and we never repeat. . . . We can't go back to the poor old father and mother on the farm. . . . That's the way in 'Tillie's Punctured Romance.' It started with the simple little scene on the farm and then grew from a spring into a brook, into a river, into the ocean."[78] What mattered most to Sennett was not closure, but climax—the "ocean" as both setting and metaphor for a cumulative burst of frenetic action in which plot interest and development are finally swept away. In the end, the film provides only the most cursory of resolutions: there is no attempt to "go back to the poor old father . . . on the farm," no return to Banks and his ruined mansion, no suggestion, finally, of what Tillie's future might hold. In the film's final shot, a drenched Tillie returns her wedding ring to Charlie; Mabel rejects him too; and, doubly spurned, he faints into the arms of a policeman. The narrative ends as Tillie and Mabel embrace, weeping in sympathy over the city slicker's infidelities.

But this is not quite the conclusion of the picture. Two curtains close across the frame, giving the effect of the end of a play. Now out of character, Dressler emerges from behind the curtains, bows to the camera, and calls out to Normand and Chaplin, who join her for the curtain call. As with the film's opening, the final sequence flags Sennett's cultural ambitions for *Tillie's Punctured Romance*, reasserting the film's equivalence to one of Dressler's stage hits. Yet it does so only once again to thwart its own pretensions in a comic about-turn: Chaplin and Normand suddenly disappear through stop-motion substitution, leaving Dressler staring out alone in befuddlement. The trickery of the medium outmatches the legitimacy of *Tillie's* theatrical intertexts as a source of the film's last laugh.[79]

. . .

How, then, does *Tillie's Punctured Romance* resolve the tension between comic spectacle and narrative with respect to the feature-length format? The answer, surely, is that it does not; and in this respect it deserves brief comparison with the later, better-known slapstick features of Chaplin, Lloyd, and Keaton. As Peter Krämer has suggested, the classic comedian features of the 1920s represent less the full flowering of the slapstick tradition than its dilution, a hybridization between traditional slapstick formulas and the demands of the well-made story: films such as *The Gold Rush* (1925), *The Freshman* (1925), and *The General* (1926), Krämer argues, "more or less successfully integrat[e] the persona, the comic and acrobatic performances of the star comedians into seriously presented dramatic story patterns."[80] Yet it is precisely this kind of integration that *Tillie's Punctured Romance* refuses. So far from harmonizing slapstick and story, Sennett adopts a modular strategy in which comic spectacle alternates with, and is segregated from, plot development. Narrative unity is time and again sacrificed as the film skates across different plot situations—a burlesque of the city slicker melodrama, a burlesque of Griffithian reform drama, an inheritance subplot—focusing on the opportunities each provides for comic spectacle and performance, but making little effort to integrate them into a plausible overarching story. Yet the originality of this film is not only that, unlike the later features, it leaves the contradiction between narrative values and comic spectacle unresolved; for, in the process, it also uncovers the meaning of these formal tensions in relation to their basis in class difference. The events in the mansion thus provide an emblem of the text's formal operations at the level of social conflict: the progressive abandonment of story logic to the visceral blows of slapstick spectacle corresponds to the actions whereby the lower classes take hold of Banks's residence and reduce it to bedlam. A skillful negotiation of the narrative demands of the multiple-reel feature, *Tillie's Punctured Romance* successfully pits the popular immediacy of the New Humor against genteel standards of well-made narration; it implies a satiric resistance to the feature format's cultural pretensions; and, ultimately, hypostasizes that resistance in terms of a social antagonism. As early advertisements for the film proudly proclaimed, "The Impossible Attained!"[81]

"SIX THOUSAND FEET OF UNDILUTED JOY": THE DISTRIBUTION AND RECEPTION OF *TILLIE'S PUNCTURED ROMANCE*

There are at least two sets of questions to consider further at this point. The first concerns issues of distribution and reception. Given Sennett's hopes of breaking into "first-string theaters," how did the film's distribution differ from that of Keystone's regular release program? In what kinds of theaters did it play? And how did audiences respond to the six-reel experiment? But these questions lead to another, more complex problem. Why did Keystone release no more feature-length productions after *Tillie's Punctured Romance*? What was the film's legacy for the studio's backers and filmmakers?

After eight weeks of shooting and a further six weeks on editing and postproduction, Sennett left for New York with Thomas Ince on July 25, 1914, to screen the picture for Kessel and Baumann and discuss methods of distribution.[82] "Sennett brought east with him a six-reel comedy," reported *Moving Picture World*, "one on which he had, with all the members of the Keystone Company, put in fourteen weeks. . . . 'I have put into it all that I have got,' he said with emphasis. 'I want to show it before I return to the Coast, and I guess it will be arranged.' "[83] But the question of distribution was not quickly resolved. Although the New York Motion Picture Co. was contractually obligated to release its single- and two-reel releases through Mutual, the same was not true for its feature-length projects. Given the amount of money that Kessel and Baumann had poured into *Tillie's Punctured Romance* ($14,000 on production expenses alone, in addition to Dressler's hefty salary), they took their time fielding distribution offers, eventually selling distribution rights to Al Lichtman's newly founded Alco Film Corporation.[84] Previously one of Adolph Zukor's partners in Famous Players, Lichtman had formed Alco as a combine of exhibitors organized to finance and acquire films in return for a share in profits (it was, in effect, a short-lived precursor to Thomas Tally's later First National Exhibitors Circuit). For a figure variously reported as $70,000 or $100,000, Alco acquired the rights to distribute *Tillie's Punctured Romance* on a states' rights basis, together with twenty-seven initial prints of the picture.[85] For whatever reason, however, the deal did not include rights to the West Coast, which Kessel and Baumann covered by selling nine extra prints directly to big-time vaudeville and motion-picture circuits in the area (at a cost of between $1,500 and $3,000 a print).[86]

The deal with Alco was also briefly delayed when Marie Dressler filed a lawsuit against Keystone in November attempting to block sale of the film. The bone of contention was an alleged verbal agreement granting Dressler's partner Jim Dalton control over the film's distribution and exhibition. "The chief conflict of testimony," reported *Moving Picture World*, "seemed to be as to whether defendant Keystone Co. had declared that Mr. Dalton was just the man to handle the picture and thereafter did not ask him to handle it."[87] Whether there was any factual basis for the allegation is unclear. That Dressler's association with Keystone took such a litigious turn could not, however, have been a surprise to industry insiders. Dalton was an infamously untrustworthy character, notorious for underhanded attempts to bully money out of Dressler's backers. (In the words of the impresario Lee Shubert—who himself had his fingers burned after a dispute over the production of *Tillie's Nightmare*—Dalton was a "blackmailer and a liar" who was "dishonest in trying to obtain money under false pretenses.")[88] Whatever Dalton's part in the suit, the Supreme Court of New York State found Dressler's allegations to be without substance: after reviewing the evidence in early December, Justice Newberger dismissed her application, claiming that "the picture was in good hands and that Miss Dressler's interests were fully protected."[89]

Boosted by a $4,000 publicity campaign, *Tillie's Punctured Romance* finally debuted on December 21.[90] Sennett's hopes of releasing the picture in "first-string" theaters were abundantly fulfilled. In Manhattan, for example, the picture opened at the prestigious New York vaudeville theater on Broadway and 45th Street, where it played as the last act on a special vaudeville bill (including a "four-table high balancing act," Merlin the magician, and the "acrobatic Arabs"). Although the live acts failed to draw large audiences, the same was not true of *Tillie's Punctured Romance*, and "drop-in" crowds flocked to the theater on opening night just to see the picture. "Around 8 o'clock a handful was in," noted *Variety,* "but business picked up by 9:30, though at this juncture the last act was appearing, with the film feature to come."[91] In Los Angeles, the film was shown at the Republic vaudeville house shortly after the management had announced a "new policy" to present the "biggest and best motion-picture productions."[92] Located in the city's downtown entertainment district, the Republic screened the film through late December and January at ten- and fifteen-cents admission, drawing audiences that broke "all [the theater's] attendance records."[93] *Tillie* also broke records at Pittsburgh's thousand-seat Columbia theater, where, at a ten-cent admission price, it did around $2,700 worth of business in its first three days.[94]

Contemporary reviewers shared in the popular enthusiasm. The critic for *Motion Picture News* described the picture as "six thousand feet of undiluted joy," continuing: "If laughing really does put fat on the laugher the population of the United States will take on several tons in weight when this picture goes the rounds. At the private showing case-hardened reviewers, trained to sigh at ordinary humor, laughed until the tears streamed down their careworn faces."[95] Many critics complimented Keystone on sustaining its rapid-paced style within the longer format. "The picture is typically Keystone," noted the *Motography* review, "which fact in itself speaks for its quick action and cyclonic developments."[96] It was "a much enlarged, a de luxe edition of Keystone burlesque," agreed the *Dramatic Mirror*'s critic, which "set a fast pace for a six-reel journey and ended with a sprint."[97] Others acknowledged Dressler's success in matching her performance to the studio's brand of comedy. "Miss Dressler fits into the Keystone type of acting and picture as naturally as if she had acted for years in that fun factory," one reviewer commented.[98] She "fits into the Keystone style of work as to the manner born," another said.[99]

Yet Dressler's glowing reviews failed to soften her and Dalton's anger at the handling of the picture, and, in March 1915, she returned to court in an unsuccessful attempt to appeal the initial decision.[100] Two months later she was in court again, this time bringing a second suit against Keystone to secure an accounting of the film's profits. As *Variety* reported on May 14, "Miss Dressler asserts her understanding was she was to receive a certain percentage of the profit which according to her statement amounts to $122,000 up to date. Of this amount she has received nothing, she says."[101] When the case was eventually settled in August, Justice Alfred Page denied Dressler's contention that there had been misconduct on Keystone's part but directed the studio to provide a full account of her share of the picture's profits within ten days. "These profits were never refused by the Keystone Film Company to Miss Dressler," observed *Motion Picture News*, "but she declined to accept what the court now compels her to accept."[102] Dressler received a $50,000 settlement and promptly filed another lawsuit, this time suing her own lawyer.

Keystone's first and only feature-length project thus ended in an atmosphere of recrimination and vindictiveness. But this was not enough to dampen the filmmakers' enthusiasm for their achievement. Buoyed up by the success of its first multiple-reel experiment, Keystone now sought to match strides with the rest of the industry. *Tillie's Punctured Romance* had proven that multiple-reel slapstick could be a profitable enterprise; small wonder that Sennett and his backers took immediate steps to regularize feature-length production at Keystone. A little over a month after *Tillie's* release, *Motion Picture News* reported that Kessel and Baumann were planning a new "company to make big features, consisting entirely of comedy. . . . Mack Sennett is to be the head of the producing end of the new company, which will use Broadway star comedians and comediennes in the staging of laughmakers, multiple reel size."[103] The same issue of the *News* also contained an advertisement for *Tillie's Punctured Romance* announcing "ANOTHER SMASHING SENNETT FEATURE WITH AN ALL STAR BROADWAY CAST—BIGGER, FUNNIER, BETTER" (fig. 16).[104]

Throughout the following month, reports on the second feature continued to appear, though Keystone's legal run-ins with Dressler seem to have soured the filmmakers on any further hiring of Broadway talent. In place of the projected "All Star Broadway Cast," the new feature would instead use Keystone's own comedians. According to an announcement in mid-February, "Mabel Normand, 'Queen of the Comedies,' is soon to be presented by Mack Sennett in a series of genuine features, not any special line, or on a certain release date, but just as the stories make themselves. Each

MACK SENNETT The Keystone of the Keystone Film Success

Author and Producer of the World's Six Reel Comedy Masterpiece

"TILLIE'S PUNCTURED ROMANCE"

With MARIE DRESSLER

This is a usual scene wherever Mack Sennett's "Tillie's Punctured Romance" is shown.

NOW IN PREPARATION

Another Smashing SENNETT Feature

WITH AN

ALL STAR BROADWAY CAST—Bigger, Funnier, Better

FIGURE 16. *Tillie's Punctured Romance* trade press advertisement. *Motion Picture News,* January 23, 1915.

one is to be complete and different from the rest."[105] The first in the series would also serve as a comeback of sorts for Ford Sterling, who had returned to Keystone earlier that month: "It will be finished within the next four weeks," announced a press notice in late February, "and will serve as a reintroduction of the former Keystone laugh-producer in his happiest mood."[106] Kessel and Baumann, meanwhile, were reportedly in the thick of negotiations for acquiring additional studio buildings to accommodate the new line.

What became of this unrealized project, seemingly so near completion? A couple of brief announcements surfaced the following May—one reporting that the "six-reel feature" was "nearly completed," another that the project "will be finished within the next week"—and then silence.[107] The picture seems to have been abandoned in its very final stages.[108] The reason was undoubtedly a sudden and unexpected shake-up in Keystone's organizational allegiances, marking the beginnings of a new phase in the studio's history.

In a letter dated June 4, Charles Baumann instructed Sennett that the New York Motion Picture Co. would not be renewing its contract with the Mutual Film Corporation, explaining that Mutual's president, Harry Aitken, had come under growing internal pressure to quit his post and was planning "to resign from the Mutual after June 16th."[109] NYMP's management, Baumann explained, had also decided to withdraw its product from the Mutual program and would join Aitken to form a new organization (eventually named the Triangle Film Corporation): Aitken would bring to the project the services of D. W. Griffith, the supervisor and director at his Majestic label, while NYMP would contribute the output of its Kay-Bee and Keystone brands. "Believe me," Baumann confided, "the new scheme is the last thought and the biggest improvement the Motion Picture Industry has ever known."[110] But it was also a scheme in which there could be no place for Keystone's feature plans. All Triangle's feature productions would be handled by Griffith and Thomas Ince, while Keystone would be contracted to supply only two-reel comedies.

Destined to become a ghost in Keystone's history, the second feature project nonetheless constitutes a significant reference point in the development of the slapstick genre. While dramatic filmmakers all but abandoned shorts for multiple-reel productions after 1915, the same route was not followed by comedy studios. But, as Keystone's abortive second feature makes clear, this was not an inevitable consequence of slapstick's inability to sustain the feature format.[111] *Tillie's Punctured Romance* had defied conventional wisdom on the feasibility of feature-length slapstick; and it had done so without concession to the genteel model of "situation"-based humor. Yet Keystone's success in this respect proved short-lived. As the studio prepared to standardize the production of slapstick features, it was caught up in a series of dramatic industry changes. During its three years at Mutual, Keystone had developed an authentically popular comic style that gave shape to the values and aesthetic traditions of its working-class audience; and it had shown its commitment to that style in the face of the unparalleled demands of the multiple-reel format. All this would change under Triangle.

PART II

"More Clever and Less Vulgar"

The Keystone Film Company and Mass Culture

4. "Made for the Masses with an Appeal to the Classes"

Keystone, the Triangle Film Corporation, and the Failure of Highbrow Film Culture, 1915–1917

> Thirty or forty years ago, it would have been generally assumed that the only hope for American society lay in somehow lifting the "Lowbrow" elements to the level of the "Highbrow" elements. But the realism of contemporary thought makes it plain that the mere idealism of university ethics, the loftiness of what is called culture, the purity of so-called Good Government, left to themselves, produce a glassy inflexible priggishness on the upper levels that paralyzes life. It is equally plain that the lower levels have a certain humanity, flexibility, tangibility which are indispensable in any programme.
>
> VAN WYCK BROOKS, "'Highbrow' and 'Lowbrow'" (1915)

To understand Keystone's subsequent career, one must first turn back to 1914, when, in a July issue of *Moving Picture World*, Harry Aitken, president of the Mutual Film Corporation, outlined a social Darwinist vision of the film industry's future. "It must be a survival of the fittest," Aitken asserted. "Those manufacturers who were never fitted for the industry will lose what money they have invested in it and will fall back naturally into the various businesses from which they came. The result will be fewer manufacturers and each making fewer pictures but better ones. . . . It will mean fewer theaters and better ones, fewer patrons at better prices and a general uplifting of the standards." What he envisioned was nothing less than a reorientation of the film industry on a basis of, as he saw it, "quality" as opposed to "quantity." At issue was not simply the nature of the industry's output but its entire organizational basis. "[T]he needs of this business," he wrote, "are better pictures, consequently fewer pictures, and, as a logical result of this, better patronized houses."[1]

The changes Aitken envisioned were indeed far-reaching and testify to an important crossroads in the industry's history. At a time when many leading manufacturers remained unconvinced of the feature film's commercial possibilities, Aitken confidently placed it at the heart of his evolutionary model: "[T]he fittest," he asserted, "is the latest to develop," and the latest to develop was the "plural reel subject." Such films, he believed, might even rid the industry of its disreputable association with immigrant and working-class audiences: multiple-reel pictures would eventually match "the successful theatrical productions [of] today" and prove "of great benefit to the discriminating and appreciative playgoing public."[2] The film industry's future legitimacy, as Aitken saw it, rested upon the standardization of multiple-reel production.

Astute observers would have recognized in that assessment a stark dramatization of key concerns facing industry leaders during this period: Could film be made to appeal to the middle and upper-middle classes? Would the feature film provide the cornerstone of that appeal? Finally, could a "night at the movies" become equivalent to a "night at the theater" for audiences conversant with highbrow culture? At the time of the *World* article, Aitken was already committed to answering such questions in the affirmative. He spent much of late 1914 working as producer on D. W. Griffith's twelve-reel *Birth of a Nation*, a landmark in the industry's cultivation of a middle-class audience. Then, after disputes over the film's financing led to his resignation from Mutual in 1915, Aitken set to work creating a company that, he hoped, would establish an organizational basis for putting his vision into practice. It would be in connection with that company—the Triangle Film Corporation—that the most paradoxical chapter of Keystone's brief history would unfold.

Capitalized at $5 million by the Wall Street investment firm Smithers and Company, Aitken's new project was an early example of the corporate film organizations that began to emerge during the early feature period.[3] A merger between Kessel and Baumann's New York Motion Picture Co. and Aitken's own Majestic label, the Triangle Film Corporation was founded with the aim of exploiting the multiple-reel format for "better" audiences. Early publicity announcements situated Triangle's product within established canons of genteel culture, claiming the corporation's goal to be nothing short of "the reflowering of the story-telling art—a renaissance as remarkable as that of the Elizabethan era or of the literary era of the Grand Monarch in France."[4]

According to the initial plan, every week, Triangle would release one five-reel feature supervised by Thomas Ince (from NYMP's Kay-Bee) and one supervised by D. W. Griffith (from Majestic, renamed Fine Arts under Triangle); each feature would be accompanied by a two-reel Keystone comedy. In a pioneering example of the vertical integration of a major film company, the pictures would be distributed by Triangle's own film exchanges, playing first at a small number of exclusive, Triangle-run "model theatres" (as Aitken chose to call them) before being made available nationwide to independent exhibitors contracted with the company. For the model theaters, Triangle would secure a handful of prestigious locations in major metropolitan centers, charging prohibitively expensive ticket prices of up to $2. "The pictures will be high class enough to play in two-dollar houses . . . [but] will also be suitable to play in houses catering to the masses," Triangle's Vice President Adam Kessel declared. "They will be made for the masses with an appeal to the classes" (fig. 17).[5]

The intent, at least, was clear: to produce motion pictures that articulated "highbrow" cultural values and yet appealed to a cross-class audience. Only a year after its birth, however, the Triangle Film Corporation found itself on the brink of financial disarray, having failed to attract audiences of any class. Already by October 1916, the company was in debt to the tune of over $700,000 and was able to cover operating costs only by taking out more loans.[6] By mid-1917, all three sides of the Triangle—Griffith, Ince, and Sennett—had jumped ship and signed with Paramount, a potent signal of the failure of Aitken's vision.

But Sennett's company bore the brunt of that failure most of all. Prior to Triangle, Keystone's films had been intimately aligned with the values and traditions of working-class popular culture. Now, under pressure from Triangle's high cultural mandate, the studio's filmmakers reconfigured their output, interweaving and hybridizing different aesthetic traditions in ways that illuminate the passage to modern mass culture. Keystone's association with Triangle thus provides an unusually explicit dramatization of those "transformations"—those moments of distortion and reworking—that, as Stuart Hall avers, form an essential part of the history of popular culture, in its constant intersections with the culture of the dominant classes.[7] What resulted, in Keystone's case, were comedies that, in the words of one reviewer, were perhaps "less rousing in [their] appeal to the finer instincts, but nevertheless fully as interesting."[8] Not the least of their interests, this chapter will argue, is the light they shed on the process of cultural intermingling by which working-class cultural values were incorporated into, rather than abandoned by, an expanding commercial public sphere that cautiously embraced popular culture, albeit on terms dictated by older, genteel standards of refinement.

Yet the dissemination of popular forms was only one side of the equation of mass culture. The other lay in the organizational failure of highbrow cultural practice in an era of commercialized leisure—and it is for

OFFICIAL

THE Triangle Film Corporation will distribute productions made under the supervision of D. W. Griffith, Thomas H. Ince and Mack Sennett. Every production will be of the very highest type and each will feature well known stars of the screen and of the stage, whose names will be announced from time to time.

Two five-reel dramas and two two-reel Keystones will be released each week.

As model theatres, indicating the way in which productions of this character can best be shown, the company will itself operate one theatre in several of its most important distributing points; such, for example, as the Knickerbocker in New York. These theatres, in which the prices charged will range from $2.00 down, will be of great service to exhibitors. Aside from the larger cities, it will not be the policy of the company to operate its own houses.

The first week's program, which will have an advance appearance during September, will consist of one five-reel drama produced under the supervision of Mr. Griffith, featuring Douglas Fairbanks; a five-reel drama produced under the supervision of Mr. Ince, featuring Frank Keenan, and a Keystone produced under the supervision of Mr. Sennett, featuring Raymond Hitchcock.

TO EXHIBITORS: Triangle plays will be rented to one good theatre only in each district.

SPECIAL MUSIC FOR EACH PRODUCTION IS BEING PREPARED

FIGURE 17.   Early publicity for the Triangle Film Corporation. From *Motion Picture News,* September 4, 1915.

this reason that it will be necessary first to look at the formation and policies of the Triangle Film Corporation. For what emerges forcefully from Aitken's ill-starred scheme is a decisive shift in the organizational basis of American culture. Genteel hierarchies of cultural traditions, the definition of high culture as distinct from its opposite, popular culture, and the institution of this classification—all became increasingly untenable in an era of commercialized leisure. Grounded as it was in a vision of exclusivity, highbrow culture implied a commitment to ideals of purity that were unable to withstand the for-profit dictates of a modern leisure economy. Triangle's failure accordingly sheds light on a major reorientation in American cultural authority, one in which commerce outmatched gentility as an arbiter of cultural standards, and in which Keystone played an important role, albeit an unexpected one.

"THE EXTERIOR APPEARANCE OF BEING PROSPEROUS": HARRY AITKEN, HIGHBROW CULTURE, AND CONSPICUOUS DISPLAY

Understanding Aitken's new scheme requires us to return once more to the interlocking of cultural practice and class formation in turn-of-the-century America, focusing this time not on popular culture and its divergence from genteel ideals—the background to Part I of this book—but rather on those ideals themselves and their role as tools of social distinction. Triangle's bid to legitimate cinema for the "classes" rested on a notion of cultural hierarchy that, as Lawrence Levine has influentially argued, first emerged out of the efforts of urban elites to maintain authority during the social upheavals of the late nineteenth century.[9] Prior to that, Levine observes, distinctions between "high" and "low" culture were not yet in place: in the antebellum period, art forms such as Shakespearean drama appealed to both popular *and* elite audiences, and popular songs were freely substituted for some arias in American opera houses. Only later, in Levine's view, did theater and opera come to exhibit the divisions between high and popular culture that shaped the cultural landscape of turn-of-the-century America. In an industrializing nation absorbing millions of immigrants and experiencing ever-widening gaps between rich and poor, with fears of foreign-bred radicalism growing apace and reports warning native Anglo-Saxons of the dangers of "race suicide," America's genteel classes imposed distinctions between cultural forms, creating prestigious cultural institutions—such as art museums and opera houses—from which they sought both to reform immigrant and working-class culture and to insulate "pure" culture from the masses. A process of sacralization took place, endowing what would come to be called "highbrow" culture with quasi-spiritual status, while actively denigrating the entertainments of the lower orders.

Levine's well-known account may be faulted for overemphasizing the inward-looking aspects of this phenomenon. To be sure, highbrow culture may well have been an essentially insular ideal, but it also functioned outwardly, offering members of the social elite a highly visible means of asserting membership in a select and exclusive society. It was this latter aspect that Thorstein Veblen captured in his notion of "conspicuous consumption," as formulated in *The Theory of the Leisure Class* (1899). Arguing for the role of "conspicuous leisure" as a means of displaying social respectability, Veblen observed that the cultural choices of America's dominant classes served primarily as "methods of putting one's pecuniary standing in evidence."[10] The development of highbrow cultural practices thus formed part of a broader cultural reorientation toward spending and display as badges of social status. In an era of rapidly rising inflation, many middle-class people had become less concerned with savings and self-denial and more willing to embrace new standards of extravagance.[11] The opening of New York's Waldorf Hotel in 1893 and the consequent growth of elegant public restaurants along Broadway helped to attract America's monied classes to a "society" lifestyle in which older values gave way to new standards of luxury, publicly displayed. The cabarets, nightclubs, and lobster palaces of the early teens offered occasions for conspicuous spending wherein the social formalism of the Victorian era ceded to the newly expressive culture of the upper middle class.[12] Nor was the taste for conspicuous display limited to those who could easily afford it. Economic studies of changing patterns of middle-class consumption pointed to a new middle class of clerical workers who likewise valued spending and comfort as pathways to respectability. A new society of consumers was being born in which wealth and display were inextricably linked to status. "The basis on which good repute . . . ultimately rests is pecuniary strength, and the means of showing pecuniary strength . . . are leisure and a conspicuous consumption of goods," Veblen observed.[13]

Aitken's career and his plans for Triangle were profoundly shaped by the changing climate of middle-class culture. A product of the "old" middle class of propertied landowners, Aitken was born in 1877 in Waukesha, Wisconsin, where he grew up on the farm of his Scots-English father, Elvin Aitken, and his English-born mother, Sarah Jane Hadfield, a pianist at the local church. Years later, in a letter describing his decision to enter the film industry, Aitken identified the traditional virtues of thrift, productive labor, and self-reliance as the crucial elements of his paternal inheritance: "[I] considered Grandfather John Aitken and how he and his father got the money to pay for the farm. They worked hard and practiced thrift. I then discovered that every Aitken relative going from the farm started enterprises, such as a blacksmith shop, a store, a factory, a real estate business, etc."[14] Yet the directions in which this entrepreneurial spirit drove Aitken could not have been predicted: after a brief spell in insurance sales, Harry and his brother, Roy, embarked on a new—and less reputable—career path as nickelodeon exhibitors, opening their first theater in Chicago in 1905. Biographers have suggested that it was Roy's fondness for popular entertainment that led the Aitkens into the picture business, despite its undesirable association with recent immigrants, southern and eastern European Jews in particular.[15] Whatever their motivations, the brothers found tremendous success in their chosen enterprise and by 1912, Harry had formed the Mutual Film Corporation, one of the leading distributors for the growing number of producers working outside the control of the Motion Picture Patents Company.

The Aitkens' respectable middle-class background had at least one important consequence for their careers in America's nascent film industry. Whereas many of the early motion picture moguls found that their status as first- or second-generation immigrants prevented acceptance within the upper social strata, the Aitkens' Anglo-Saxon heritage enabled them to partake in the lifestyle of New York's wealthy elite. In a 1914 letter to D. W. Griffith—then director and supervisor for the Majestic label— Aitken vividly expressed his enthusiasm for society life: "I am having a great time showing your film [*The Escape*] in my apartment to Mr. Irvin Cobb, Otto Kahn, Mary Wilson Preston, Daniel Frohman, editors and society people. This method of presenting them is getting a kind of recognition, which I am sure will be a great boost to you."[16] Despite an upbringing that had emphasized thrift, the Aitkens soon recognized the value of conspicuous display as a strategy for gaining entry into the upper social register. "Of course," noted Roy, "[Harry and I] maintained our rather luxurious apartment on West Fifty-seventh Street and our English butler and his wife. Matt Hosely, our chauffeur, was also on our payroll. . . . [T]he exterior appearance of being prosperous—even though we were not—was very important in our business." As Roy frankly admitted, the brothers "deliberately spent more money . . . than prudence dictated—all for a necessary effect on others."[17]

In short, Harry Aitken understood the significance of money in an era when conspicuous display was a badge of status. Publicity for the Triangle organization consequently cultivated an image of extravagance designed to seduce genteel folk accustomed to equating cost with quality. In the debut issue of the company's exhibitors journal, *The Triangle*, an editorial set the tone by proclaiming that "lavish expenditure is the surest economy."[18] Writing in the same issue, Aitken himself declared "no limit on the sums that might be needed to produce perfect pictures."[19] Nor was this simply a matter of publicity: during their tenure at Triangle, Aitken consistently encouraged his three producers to spend more money than was required to bring costs up to the standard he considered desirable. Whereas a two-reel comedy had previously cost Keystone only around $7,000 in production expenses, Sennett now received flat payments of $20,000 for each of his Triangle releases. Aitken was willing to pour even more exorbitant amounts into Ince's and Griffith's features, peaking in the $58,976 spent on Ince's *Peggy* (1916) at a time when other companies were rarely spending more than $30,000 on program features. Even the average sum spent on Triangle's five-reel productions (about $20,000) was more than twice the costs of its competitors.[20]

It was not in terms of production expenses alone that Aitken aimed to appeal to "better" audiences. By creating a small chain of model theaters with admission set at $2, Aitken sought to establish venues for film exhibition that would provide well-to-do patrons with an occasion to promenade their wealth. Although the initial plan was to open eight to ten model theaters, only three were eventually acquired: the Knickerbocker on Broadway and Thirty-eighth Street in New York, the Studebaker in Chicago, and the Chestnut Street Opera House in Philadelphia, all formerly high-class playhouses. Under the lease of the theatrical magnates Marc Klaw and Abraham Erlanger, the Knickerbocker had from 1911 provided a venue for the stage productions of the Charles Frohman Company. Subleased by Triangle for $85,000 a year, the theater was remodeled into a lavish movie house featuring a thirty-piece orchestra, furnishings that displayed the Triangle trademark, and a troupe of female ushers sporting triangular hats and triangle-embossed lace pantalettes.[21] By charging $2 per ticket, Aitken hoped to make these theaters exclusive cultural institutions that, in the words of *The Triangle*, "the *very best people*" would use "as a rendezvous."[22] Aitken had introduced a $2 admission earlier for the road-show presentation of *Birth of a Nation*, but such prices had never before been asked for regular release programs and were announced to the astonishment of industry commentators. "[Y]ou can take your seat with the assurance that the adjoining one will be occupied by an equally rich, elegant, and aristocratic person," quipped the *New York Times*. "And what a comfort that will be, to be sure!"[23]

After a number of postponements, the first Triangle releases debuted at the Knickerbocker on September 23, 1915, in a gala event bringing together industry leaders with representatives of the New York and European elite such as Otto H. Kahn, director of the Metropolitan Opera House, Ignace Paderewski, and William Randolph Hearst. After a rendition of "The Star-Spangled Banner," Triangle presented Douglas Fairbanks's debut film performance in the Griffith-supervised *The Lamb*, Ince's *The Iron Strain*, featuring the theatrical star Dustin Farnum, and *My Valet*, a four-reel Keystone special, directed by Sennett himself, pairing Mabel Normand with the musical comedy star Raymond Hitchcock. Over the course of the program, noted *Moving Picture World*, the audience "gave frequent applause . . . to evidences of a high order of photography, special effects and characterizations."[24]

Yet, while commentary on the event in newspapers and the trade press was by and large enthusiastic, most reviews sounded a quiet note of dissatisfaction. Few denied Triangle's success in establishing a venue for exhibition that appealed to genteel tastes; nonetheless, critics who had been promised a "reflowering of the storytelling art" found instead what one reviewer described as simply "good average stories."[25] Each of the films, noted the *New York Times*, "is an example of nicely accomplished motion picture photography; no one of them reveals anything amazing or unprecedented in the development of this now hugely popular form of entertainment. Any one who went to the Knickerbocker last evening looking for that must have come away disappointed."[26] The critic for the *Chicago Tribune* reflected the consensus, describing the program as "less of art and more of copy than one wishes to see."[27] Triangle had created a corporate image that embodied genteel propensities for lavish expenditure; it had also created exclusive emporia for the rituals of the wealthy. What was clearly still required was a product that could match up to the moral and aesthetic standards that the middle class expected.

"A BASIS OF HIGH SPECIALIZATION AND INTELLIGENT APPEAL": CULTURAL LEGITIMACY, THE STAGE-STAR EXPERIMENT, AND THE MODEL THEATERS

Herein lay the problem: how could films be made to meet those standards? and, more perplexingly, what would such an attempt imply for Keystone? In an early announcement of the formation of Triangle, Adam Kessel sketched out the company's intentions thus: "The Ince and Griffiths [sic] pictures will be picturizations of the better plays and novels, and original plots, when they are of high standard. For these productions we have already engaged some of the most famous theatrical stars, and are signing up more."[28] Triangle, in other words, would draw on the cultural authority of the theater as a model for legitimating cinema for genteel consumption. Yet Kessel's silence on Keystone is notable, suggestive of the lack of fit between Triangle's high cultural ambitions and the "low" slapstick of Sennett's studio. As events would show, in fact, the gentrification that Triangle sought ultimately jeopardized the popular appeal of Sennett's output. Dramatizing conflicts between popular and high culture, the realization of Aitken's scheme soon proved to be at odds with Keystone's continued success.

The problem emerges clearly from a detailed discussion of Triangle's organizational policies, beginning with the "stage-star" strategy outlined by Kessel in the sketch of the company's plans quoted above. For nowhere was Aitken's predilection for conspicuous spending more evident than in his decision to hire theatrical stars at salaries far in excess of those enjoyed by screen stars of the period; and nowhere did those new signings cause greater difficulties than at Keystone. Once again, Aitken's extravagance provoked astonishment among industry critics, who responded with disapproving grumbles about what one described as salaries "beyond the realms of reasonableness."[29] At a time when stars' weekly earnings had only recently broken the $1,000 mark, Triangle unblinkingly offered from $1,000 to $2,500 for the services of approximately sixty of the nation's top stage players, including Bessie Barriscale, Billie Burke, Frank Keenan, and H. B. Warner.[30] DeWolf Hopper, America's leading exponent of Gilbert and Sullivan comic opera, was signed for a yearly salary of $125,000 to work at Fine Arts; and Sir Herbert Beerbohm-Tree, a British Shakespearean actor described by *Variety* as "the most artistic producer of legitimate plays of the present day," received over $100,000 for thirty weeks' work, also at Fine Arts.[31]

As for Keystone, Aitken invested heavily in musical comedy stars and cabaret headliners such as Willie Collier, Eddie Foy (and his seven children), Hale Hamilton, and Raymond Hitchcock. While none of these comedians can really be described as exponents of highbrow culture, they nevertheless ranked among the brightest luminaries of Broadway. Hale Hamilton, for example, had risen to fame in the title role of George M. Cohan's *Get Rich Quick Wallingford* and had recently starred in *A Pair of Aces* at Broadway's Long Acre Theater.[32] The most successful comic duo of the vaudeville and musical comedy stage, Joe Weber and Lew Fields, signed a three-year exclusive contract with Keystone in June 1915 for over $600,000.[33]

Aitken was banking heavily on the exploitation of theatrical actors as drawing cards for "better" audiences: by signing established stage stars onto its talent roster, Triangle would guarantee—or so the theory went—that its product appealed to genteel theatergoers. There were, of course, precedents for such a strategy, notably the formation of Adolph Zukor's Famous Players company in 1912. Yet, by late 1915, such a policy ran counter to film industry developments, which had seen a burgeoning fan culture give rise to the *movie* star as a key attraction for film audiences. Movie-fan culture had by this time developed sufficient coherence for it to resist such straightforwardly hegemonic bids for cultural "respectability," and Aitken's stage-star experiment immediately foundered on its disregard for the tastes of the industry's existing audience. To take only the most telling example, the sixty-two-year-old Beerbohm-Tree completed just two pictures for Triangle after his much-publicized debut in *Macbeth* (1916) proved a box-office flop. ("It is doubtful if the regular film patrons will care to witness the production," commented one unimpressed reviewer.)[34] Indeed, much of the most hostile trade commentary on the stage-star policy seems to have been expressly reserved for Aitken's most prestigious theatrical signings. In his 1916 review of the year's film performances, Julian Johnson of *Photoplay* offered a particularly merciless assessment: after citing Billie Burke and Beerbohm-Tree as notable screen failures, Johnson culminated his list with a reference to "that delightful gentleman, grand curtain-speaker, and footlight veteran—also that celluloid lemon and shadow ruin—DeWolf Hopper. Let us forbear."[35]

Part of the problem lay in the difficulties Triangle's producers encountered in harmonizing the performances of the stage stars with existing filmmaking practice. This was particularly true at Keystone, where filmmakers struggled to define a comic form that would showcase the Broadway comedians without cost to the studio's trademark slapstick. Here, an initial solution was to keep the Broadway stars at the periphery of the comic action, featured as special attractions, but with no significant role in the narrative. An extreme example can be found in *Fatty and the Broadway Stars* (December 1915), a wittily self-reflexive film evidently designed as a promotional vehicle for the studio's recent signings. Set on the Keystone lot and featuring Mack Sennett in a cameo as himself, the film follows the exploits of a lovelorn studio janitor (Roscoe Arbuckle) as he comically goes about his chores: this basic premise gives rise to a series of disconnected vignettes in which Arbuckle spies on Keystone's stage comedians Sam Bernard, Willie Collier, Joe Jackson, and Weber and Fields as they rehearse comic routines for their forthcoming releases. The stage stars are, in effect, bracketed as elements of spectacle within the framing action, introduced by title cards that reinforce their role as attractions only—"William Collier, Fresh From Broadway," "Sam Bernard In Action," or "Weber and Fields In A Hair Raising Scene."[36] *Her Painted Hero* (November 1915) likewise does little to integrate Hale Hamilton's performance with the narrative, including him merely as the object of Polly Moran's star-struck affections, not as a significant agent within the events of the film. In a review in *Moving Picture World*, Louis Reeves Harrison pinpointed the filmmakers' failure to incorporate Hamilton's performance into the film's action. "[Hamilton] is given a minor role of no importance and no visible characterization, simply a chance to show himself now and then. . . . As 'Her Painted Hero,' he is not featured—he is merely injected."[37]

These difficulties of stylistic cohesion climaxed in the case of Eddie Foy, who flatly refused to participate in the roughhouse antics for which Keystone was best known. In a widely circulated rumor, Foy was said to have walked off the lot when asked to submit to the indignity of a pie in the face for *A Favorite Fool* (November 1915). ("He couldn't see art in a custard pie," a reporter wryly observed.)[38] Apocryphal or not, the story was symptomatic of the difficulties Keystone had in keeping its stage comedians happy: within two months of Triangle's debut, Foy, Hale Hamilton, and Sam Bernard had all left Sennett's studio, having each appeared in only one film. In January, *Motion Picture News* announced that Weber and Fields's *The Worst of Friends* (January 1916) would be their "second and last" Keystone release; and, in March, it was reported that Willie Collier had signed with Ince to appear in "light comedy dramas."[39]

By November 1916, the fate of the stage-star experiment was viewed by one *Photoplay* reporter as an indication of the difficulties to be faced by any company seeking highbrow appeal. "In the future," the writer asked, "will picture plays be turned out as abundantly and as thoughtlessly as tin cans, or will the essentially competitive struggle be continued on a basis of intelligent appeal and high specialization?" Triangle's financial difficulties suggested a pessimistic answer. "This mighty organization, heralded as the invincible directoral [sic] combination, has made great programme material—and has lost the equivalent of Captain Kidd's treasure while doing it."[40] Indeed, despite having staked much of its corporate identity on its prestigious *stage* signings, Triangle had already distanced itself from this policy by mid-1916, when, in a remarkable about-face, it began advising exhibitors to exploit instead its established *film* stars, such as William S. Hart, Roscoe Arbuckle, and Norma Talmadge. (In this way, *The Triangle* asserted, patrons could "get to know the stars and their individual idiosyncracies" and "take a sort of friendly interest in them.")[41] The stage-star experiment may have constituted Triangle's most coherent attempt to forge associations with the cultural practices of the genteel elite; but economic necessity soon forced Aitken to fall back on those performers who had already met with the masses' approval. Commercial considerations had outstripped the authority of highbrow culture.

A strikingly similar story emerges in the case of Aitken's distribution and exhibition policies; and, yet again, it was Keystone that bore the brunt of the policies' problems. In line with the initial plan, Triangle films were to be shown first to patrons of the exclusive model theaters before receiving broad release through exhibitors contracted with Triangle. This two-tier system of exhibition, Aitken hoped, would appeal to the exclusivity of the genteel classes while disseminating high culture to a mass audience. Articulating reformist discourse of the period, Aitken claimed that Triangle pictures could exert a "wonderful civilizing influence," promoting "better understanding between artificially created classes of people."[42] For all his ambitions, however, Aitken grossly overestimated genteel enthusiasm for movies. The "classes" were only just overcoming their ambivalence toward motion pictures: not yet had they embraced regular moviegoing to the extent the model theaters required. Triangle's flagship houses thus floundered as their target audience failed to appear in adequate numbers.

The varying fortunes of the Knickerbocker during this period epitomize the difficulties Triangle faced in creating a commercial basis for the exclusive exhibition of feature films. Although receipts from the theater were initially healthy ($3,000 alone during its opening week), falling attendance forced Aitken to shutter the Knickerbocker's doors as early as January 1916, when he hired the picture palace impresario S. L. "Roxy" Rothapfel to reorganize the theater's operations on a more profitable basis. When even Rothapfel proved unable to reverse the slump—despite reducing the scale of ticket prices to a 50 and 25-cent basis—Aitken unsentimentally cut his losses and withdrew from his flagship theater, selling his unexpired lease to the vaudeville magnate Marcus Loew.[43] The fate of the Knickerbocker was mirrored in the even more spectacular collapses of Triangle's two other showcase houses, Chicago's Studebaker and the Chestnut Street Opera House in Philadelphia, where weekly receipts were rarely enough to break even. In January of 1916, Triangle closed both theaters and began selling off their projection equipment and drapery.[44]

More troubling than the model theaters' collapse, however, was Triangle's failure to attract the industry's working-class audience base to its numerous contract houses, and it was here that Aitken's exhibition strategies hurt Keystone in particular. A substantial hurdle to Triangle's success outside the model theaters was the "program" policy that Aitken insisted on for the distribution of the company's product. Rather than allowing independent exhibitors to compete for individual Triangle titles on an open market, the program policy required theater owners to contract for a full year's slate of releases (a precursor of the "block-booking" arrangement later refined by Paramount). In this way, Aitken hoped, Triangle would nurture a network of independent theaters committed to boosting Triangle's program and to making their theaters "local institutions" for "discriminating recreation seekers."[45] To cover the corporation's vast overhead, however, contracts were offered at unparalleled prices, from over $20,000 per annum in the case of one Pennsylvania theater owner to the fantastic sum of $750,000 paid by W. H. Kemble for two-year exclusive rights to exhibit Triangle films in Brooklyn.[46] Those theaters able to sign up for the Triangle program were consequently either the larger picture palaces located along commercial thoroughfares or the small number of well-appointed movie houses that were beginning to penetrate middle-class residential areas. Despite Aitken's avowed intention to produce films that would appeal to the "masses" as well as the "classes," Triangle's product was effectively barred from the smaller neighborhood theaters where working-class and immigrant audiences preferred to view movies.[47] What this meant for Keystone, moreover, was that its product was effectively shut off from the audiences with whom its films had found their initial success. In Manhattan, for example, Triangle theaters completely bypassed those immigrant areas that, like the Jewish ghettos on the Lower East Side, had contained the thickest concentration of movie theaters during the nickelodeon era. Instead, Triangle's major New York theaters were concentrated along Broadway; first- and second-run houses were located in the major midtown entertainment district between Times Square and Columbus Circle, and subsequent-run theaters were scattered throughout the middle-class neighborhoods of the Upper West Side and the elite areas north of Harlem.[48] Similarly, in Chicago, out of some forty theaters showing Triangle pictures in early 1916, only two were in blue-collar neighborhoods—the Palace and the Thalia, both in the working-class settlements down Roosevelt Road and Blue Island. With these two exceptions, Triangle theaters in Chicago were largely concentrated, on the one hand, in the commercial district bounded by the Loop and, on the other, in the fashionable neighborhoods and commercial centers around Washington Park on the south side and uptown to the north.[49]

Burdened with a theater network that failed to draw sufficient middle-class patrons and shut out the popular audience, Aitken's company began to show growing deficits from June 1916 on (rising steadily to a loss of over $42,000 in the month of October alone).[50] The situation came to a head that fall during four months of tense conferences in New York in which the heads of the company battled over its distribution and exhibition policies. At the heart of these heated exchanges was the question of whether Triangle should continue program booking or allow exhibitors, regardless of contract, to select individual Triangle pictures on an unrestricted, "open" market. Given the damage that program booking was inflicting on Keystone's market share, Sennett lobbied aggressively for open market distribution of his product, eventually persuading Aitken when he threatened to walk out on his contract. (He also got Aitken to raise his weekly salary by $500 and sign over 23,000 shares in the Triangle corporation.)[51] One upshot of the meetings was thus a new distribution policy for Keystone films: those exhibitors contracted with Triangle would continue to have exclusive rights to the Ince and Griffith films, together with a new series of one-reel "Triangle Comedies" (cheaply produced on Sennett's lot using the studio's second-tier performers and filmmakers); but if they wanted the official, brand-name Keystones, exhibitors would now have to pay extra, since they were competing for them against all the other theaters in the area.[52]

Triangle's contracted exhibitors responded at first with confusion, then with fury, realizing that Aitken's organization had broken its obligations by cutting the popular Keystone releases from the regular weekly program. In a letter to Sennett dated January 15, 1917, W. J. Hayes, the manager of a Pennsylvania theater, spoke for many Triangle exhibitors. "In November 1915, we entered into a contract with the Triangle Corporation . . . to furnish us with two features and two comedies a week, paying the somewhat fabulous sum of $425 a week. . . . We boomed the stars, H. B. Warner, Frank Campeau and others, but alas, they proved both meteors on the Triangle program, until finally we had William S. Hart and a number of unknown people about as prominent as the stars in the Milky Way in pictures which had most ungodly names, but which we tried to carry over by putting our Keystone Comedies above the feature." In putting the Keystone pictures on the open market, Hayes claimed, Triangle had shown contempt for its contracted exhibitors: "That [Triangle's] contract . . . called for two comedies a week; that said contract called for a four weeks' notice of discontinuance of said contract.—Pooh!"[53] A letter to Sennett from the manager of a Triangle exchange further illustrates the growing resentment: "Say for instance, you are an exhibitor; you are running Triangle service and paying me $200.00 a week. . . . I ask you to pay me $50.00 or $100.00 more for the Keystones that I have taken away from you. The first thing that enters your mind is that I am double-crossing you. . . . The exhibitor has balked on this. They tell me it is a good way to raise their price and they are absolutely dissatisfied and disgusted."[54]

What these letters revealed was perhaps the last thing Aitken wanted to hear: for all its highbrow credentials, the Triangle Film Corporation had ironically been kept afloat by Sennett's slapstick comedies. By placing the Keystone movies on the open market, Aitken set the stage for a wholesale desertion from the exhibitors' ranks that, by mid-1917, would bring his organization to its knees.[55] Nor did the open market produce the profits Sennett had hoped for: no sooner was the policy put into practice (in February 1917) than Aitken decreed further changes that all but eradicated Keystone's moneymaking potential. Whereas the Griffith, Ince, and Sennett studios had previously received flat-rate payments for their films, they were now paid percentages out of the films' grosses. The theory was that Triangle's producers would thereby enjoy the fruits of each other's successes; in practice, it meant that they all shared equally in Triangle's ever-escalating losses. Despite the popularity of the Keystone films, per picture payments to the studio rapidly declined from the flat rate of $20,000 to an average of less than $14,000.[56] Triangle had become, in Kalton Lahue's apt phrase, a "cross to bear" for its producers: Griffith left in March, followed by Ince and Sennett in June.[57]

"MORE HUMAN THAN USUAL": SLAPSTICK AND SENTIMENT IN KEYSTONE'S TRIANGLE FILMS

Aitken had embarked on a pathbreaking attempt to use highbrow cultural values as the basis of a cinema that would attract both the "class" and the "mass" audience. Yet, as Triangle's career reveals, those values were all-too-easily eroded by a new era of commercial entertainments. The genteel classes had failed to support Aitken's vision, and commercial necessity soon put paid to Triangle's aura of cultural purity and exclusivity. Some light can be thrown on Aitken's difficulties by comparing his policies to the organizational framework that America's genteel classes had typically employed for the distribution of high culture. As Paul DiMaggio argues, the turn-of-the-century elite had been able to satisfy its need for exclusivity only by placing its cultural institutions in the hands of nonprofit organizations. The "purity" of high culture had been maintained by shielding it from the demands of the marketplace; not being economically dependent on mass attendance, cultural institutions such as the Boston Symphony Orchestra did not need to cater to popular tastes.[58] Aitken, however, founded his version of highbrow cinema on an openly commercial footing; the success of the scheme depended upon its ability to reach as large an audience as possible. The cost of Aitken's experiment was thus the very exclusivity he sought. In rapid succession, he was forced to cancel the contracts of the majority of his stage stars, withdraw from the model theaters, and compromise with the policy of program booking—each step a sacrifice of exclusivity in the name of economic necessity. The pattern is one identified by Max Weber: the dynamics of the market require the declassification of culture, forcing cultural entrepreneurs to mix categories to reach the broadest audience.[59]

In fact, Triangle's most consistently popular films—the Keystone comedies—were precisely those that had least to do with Aitken's cultural goals. Given slapstick's traditionally "low" cultural associations, Keystone rested uneasily with Triangle's lofty agenda, a point that was not lost on contemporary observers. In a review of Triangle's debut at the Knickerbocker, one critic noted: "It is curious to see such deft work as [*The Lamb*] in the same program with such primitive slapstick as the Sennett 'comic fillum.' "[60] Yet, as Keystone's remarkably broad popularity attests, these comic "fillums" were evidently able to achieve what Aitken's genteel mandate could not— appeal to the "classes" as well as the "masses." It was slapstick, not sophistication, that satisfied collective desires.

The studio's Triangle output thus participated in a major transformation in American culture. During the 1910s, as Francis Couvares has pointed out, the cultural practices of the genteel middle class were in the process of being deterritorialized by a new arena of commercial leisure with roots in the plebeian world of the lower orders.[61] Keystone's career under Triangle offers an object lesson for understanding that process, providing material evidence of the ways that popular forms were reworked as commercial culture for a cross-class audience. In the case of Keystone, this process cannot adequately be understood through a top-down model of hegemonic incorporation, as though genteel cultural values straightforwardly set the terms to which the studio's output complied; rather, it involved a complex, multidirectional set of interactions between distinct aesthetic traditions and trajectories, a mixing and merging of cultural values that abolished the distinctiveness of "highbrow" and "lowbrow" and, ultimately, helped in the formation of a new, commercially driven mass culture. The confrontation between Keystone's popular energies and Aitken's genteel mandate would thus dissipate the articulation of the cultural divisions from which that confrontation had sprung.

The groundwork for these transformations lay, in the first place, in the radical alteration and expansion of Keystone's production practices. Under Triangle, production time per picture (including scenario preparation, rehearsals, and filming) skyrocketed to an average of sixty days (more than the time spent on principal shooting for *Tillie's Punctured Romance*).[62] Heightened production values meanwhile entailed greater rationalization of studio space. In 1916, a $100,000, four-story administration building was constructed on a site north of the original studio, bringing together studio cafeteria, dressing rooms, technical shop, and wardrobe department. The scenario department, headed by Hampton Del Ruth, was relocated in a bungalow away from the remainder of the studio, while company offices now occupied buildings in the original plant.[63] Never before had Keystone's filmmakers experienced such a degree of specialization and order; the contrast between the old spontaneity of Keystone's early days and the departmentalized system now in place was frequently observed. "In the old days," Sennett noted in July 1916,

> we used to finish up a reel of film in a day or two. I'd set out for loca-
> tions without the slightest idea of what I was going to put my company
> to do when we all got there. . . . We'd make the things up as we went
> along and sometimes it would be good and sometimes it wouldn't.
> Producing comedies in the present (of course, I'm referring to
> Keystones only) is a long and tedious process. . . . When one of my
> directors is finally through with his work, mine commences. My direc-
> tor may turn in four, five or six thousand feet of film in one picture and
> then comes the hardest and best part of it all—cutting.[64]

Despite claiming to edit all of Keystone's pictures, Sennett rarely participated in the day-to-day practicalities of filmmaking under Triangle, delegat-
ing the hands-on task of studio management to John A. Waldron, whom he
hired to replace George Stout in late 1915.[65] As studio manager, Waldron's
first responsibility was to oversee the work of the ever-growing number of
units on the Edendale lot. By March 1916, a total of fifteen units were
reported to be working at Keystone, headed by such directors as Roscoe
Arbuckle, Charles Avery, Clarence Badger, William Campbell, Glen
Cavender, Eddie Cline, Fred Fishback, Ed Frazee, Frank Griffin, Del
Henderson, F. Richard Jones, Charles Parrott, Ford Sterling, and Walter
Wright.[66] In a departure from studio protocol under Mutual—when
Sennett had allowed his lead comedians to direct their own films—
Keystone's new directors were now typically culled from the ranks of the

scenario department (as was the case with Badger, Campbell, and, in July 1916, Harry Williams). Only Arbuckle, Cavender, and, more infrequently, Sterling continued to combine directorial duties behind the camera with comic performances in front. Moreover, since the studio's directors were now more likely experienced writers than performers, their films tended to downplay comic "business" in favor of narrative values and intricately plotted situations. (For example, the use of extended takes of virtuoso comedian performance—a formal element largely introduced by Chaplin and continued in the films of his brother Syd and Charles Murray—simply disappeared as a stylistic option under Triangle.)[67] These new directions were buttressed by Keystone's growing stable of writers, which from 1915 added many noted musical comedy playwrights, vaudeville writers, and journalists. One of the new signings, Frederick Palmer, had started as a dramatic critic for a Rochester daily, worked as a writer in musical comedy, and edited one of the largest theatrical publications on the West Coast, *The Rounder*, before joining Keystone in March 1915. Another, Jean C. Havez, had worked as a press agent for the comedian Lew Dockstader in 1902 before a successful career as a producer of vaudeville acts and musical comedies eventually brought him to Sennett's studio. (He later collaborated on screenplays for a number of Buster Keaton and Harold Lloyd features in the 1920s.) Among other new writers, Clarence Badger and Grace Wilcox also came from journalistic backgrounds, the latter having worked as a society writer for the *Los Angeles Tribune*. Others, such as William Jerome, were among the more successful writing talents of the musical comedy stage. A veteran of some twenty years experience, Jerome had scored significant successes with *Piff! Paff!! Pouff!!!* (1904), featuring Eddie Foy, and *The Ham Tree* (1905), starring the comedy duo of James McIntyre and Thomas Heath (with the young W. C. Fields in a small role).[68]

This was a roster of which Triangle's management was justifiably proud. Calls for experienced writers had long been a refrain among critics demanding the uplift of the film industry, and Triangle's publicity staff lost no time in promoting the new signings.[69] In a two-page spread in a January 1916 issue of *Motion Picture News*, Triangle publicized Keystone's scenario department in terms calculated to appeal to middle-class values, listing the writers' Broadway successes and educational accomplishments. According to the promotional copy, Hampton Del Ruth's "early education was accomplished by a private Italian tutor in arts and literature, followed by an Oxford diploma and a post-graduate course in that institution of learning." Frederick Palmer, meanwhile, "was educated in the public schools of Flushing, L.I., and Rochester, N.Y., and later at Cornell

University" and had "risen to his present position by hard work and concentration."[70]

The hiring of these talents was a crucial tactic in resituating Keystone's
films for Triangle's target audience. In many ways, the musical comedy tradition from which several of them came was diametrically opposed to the
gag-based slapstick of Keystone's Mutual releases. Where the studio's earlier films had capitalized on the aggressive, urban orientation of the New
Humor, musical comedies treated middle-class audiences to exotic,
Orientalist fantasy worlds and lavish spectacle (a famous example being
The Wizard of Oz, first staged in 1903). Where Keystone had derived characters from the gallery of ethnic impersonators and tramp comedians of
vaudeville and burlesque, musical comedy emphasized youthful romance
in plots involving royalty, high society, and mistaken identity. Indeed, in an
interview published in 1904, the "Dutch" comic Sam Bernard—one of
Keystone's future stage stars—had blamed musical comedy for the decline
of theatrical slapstick: "The death of the gag and the passing of slapstick as
a source of fun has been brought about by the present style of musical
comedy."[71]

Symptomatic of changing middle-class mores, musical comedy was a
form that paid lip service to genteel notions of refinement, while featuring
a competing set of values that celebrated luxury and commodity spectacle.
Likewise, Keystone's new writers now emphasized themes of material
indulgence by using settings associated with conspicuous display.[72] In a
radical redefinition of the class dynamics of the earlier productions, the
studio's output shifted attention away from the comic representation of
working-class culture and toward the extravagance of society life. A writer
for *Motion Picture News* spoke approvingly of the "elaborate sets . . . that
have marked [Keystone's output] since the first release on the Triangle program."[73] Thus, to cite a notable example, *The Great Pearl Tangle* (January
1916) was set in the boutique of a fashion designer and featured an exclusive fashion show in which, as a studio publicist insisted, "gowns of real
sartorial importance" were displayed (fig. 18).[74] As a necessary corollary to
these new settings, Keystone's filmmakers and performers also began to
introduce new kinds of comic protagonists: films like *He Did and He Didn't*
(January 1916), *A Modern Enoch Arden* (January 1916), and *A Royal
Rogue* (May 1917) substituted wealthy doctors, lawyers, and European
nobility for Keystone's earlier gallery of tramps and immigrants.

What united these disparate developments was their tendency to evade
the social realities of class. This was directly in line with Aitken's genteel
mandate; for, as has often been observed, gentility in art shied away from

FIGURE 18.   The musical comedy star Sam Bernard (seated left) in a production still from *The Great Pearl Tangle* (January 1916). Courtesy of the Academy of Motion Picture Arts and Sciences.

social problems and lower-class life, preferring an idealization of subject matter to the realism of contemporary urban depictions. (It was in this spirit that William Dean Howells complained in 1891: "The American public does not like to read about the life of toil. . . . What we like to read about is the life of noblemen or millionaires; . . . if our writers were to begin telling us on any extended scale of how mill hands, or miners, or farmers, or iron puddlers really live, we should very soon let them know that we did not care to meet such vulgar and commonplace people.")[75] Such evasiveness was also, however, a symptom of broader film industry trends during this period. Ongoing debates about the regulation of cinema had, in February 1915, resulted in the famous *Mutual* decision in which the Supreme Court ruled against First Amendment protection for motion pictures. The impact of that ruling, as Lee Grieveson has compellingly argued, was effectively to mandate a definition of cinema's public role as "harmless" entertainment, delinked from social or political engagement.[76] At the same time, industry perceptions regarding the changing composition and tastes of audiences were also resulting in changes in the political character of movies. Although class issues hardly disappeared from the screen, producers now commonly assumed that "better" audiences wanted to forget about social problems and instead celebrate the flowering of a new consumer culture.[77]

Keystone's Triangle output suggests all of this quite well. The direct class antagonisms of the studio's Mutual films largely disappear in the Triangle releases, their place supplanted by alternative forms of comic conflict that substitute for the political logic of class difference. The process is vividly exemplified in the narratives of *A Maiden's Trust* (April 1917) and *A Royal Rogue*, both of which derive from one of the most characteristic situations of Keystone's earlier releases—namely, the chaos caused by a working-class character who intrudes upon the social spaces of the elite. In place of the proletarian protagonist, however, the later films substitute a "bogus count" or "fortune hunter" of unspecified class identity who wreaks havoc when he attempts to rob a wealthy household. Similar displacements can be seen in *Better Late Than Never* (February 1916), *His Busted Trust* (November 1916), and *The Late Lamented* (September 1917): here, class conflict is replaced by the contrast between a "starving artist" and an opulent milieu of art connoisseurs and wealthy estates. The opening to *The Late Lamented*, for example, defines its two artists through an iconography of rooming houses and penury previously reserved as signifiers of working-class life. "Harry and Jack are two poverty stricken artists who have not yet arrived," the scenario for this lost film begins. "Everything pawnable has found its way to the pawnshop, and they have nothing left but one suit of clothes each."[78] Yet the social meanings of that iconography are here suppressed, reconfigured by the characters' roles as producers of "high" art. Other films meanwhile reconfigure class difference in terms of the contrast between the simple rural life and the corruption of the city, a common trope of stage melodrama. While Mack Swain's "Ambrose" character had previously been associated with lower-class or ethnic roles within an urban setting, the later Ambrose pictures—for example, *Ambrose's Cup of Woe* (June 1916) and *His Naughty Thought* (May 1917)—more commonly featured the character as a small-town "rube" forced to fend off money-grubbing city villains. What was erased in all these instances was any sense of slapstick's former engagement with social cleavage: much as ethnic difference had earlier been subsumed by Keystone's depiction of class, so class was now subsumed under alternative expressions of difference and opposition.[79]

But the imprint of Triangle's genteel mandate came not simply in the deflection of social themes. Some Keystone films continued to represent the urban poor, and here genteel culture left its trace in the growing sentimentalism of those representations. A dominant paradigm of the late-Victorian literary imagination, the sentimental mode provided Keystone's filmmakers with an ethical iconography tailored to middle-class tastes; but it also required further rethinking of the comic depiction of class hierarchy. It is not difficult to see why this should have been so: sentimentalism has routinely been taken to task by literary historians for its tendency to construe social meanings in ethical terms, its fetishism of the "small" virtues of innocence, victimhood, and passivity and its avoidance of a more authentic social engagement. For sentimental fiction, Michael Denning notes, "the opposition good/not good, sunshine and shadow, rules all action and character. The 'not good' are victims—the prostitute with the heart of gold, the orphan turned tramp, the noble but dying Indian. All can be pitied and all can be forgiven."[80] As an aesthetic mode, sentimentalism corresponded to the moral primacy of the private sphere over the public in genteel thought; and it implied a stress on transcendence, associated with middle-class femininity, that mitigated empirical engagement with social reality. In appealing to this legacy, then, Keystone's filmmakers sought a class transformation that was also aligned with a gendered change, an attempt to translate slapstick into the conventionally feminized discourse of sentimentalism.[81] It is this, in fact, that gives the profound sense of romanticism to the studio's later depictions of the lower classes, a sense nowhere more evident than in the two releases in which Joe Jackson appeared under the direction of Clarence Badger: *A Modern Enoch Arden* (January 1916) and *Gypsy Joe* (March 1916).

One of the stage stars signed by Aitken for the launching of the Triangle program, Jackson came to Keystone having achieved fame as a "tramp bicyclist" in headline performances at New York's exclusive Winter Garden. As a tramp comic, Jackson doubtless seemed a good fit for Keystone, and the studio's filmmakers openly exploited his stage persona as a basis for his films. Not only was he consistently cast in the role of a comic hobo, his pictures also made heavy use of his bicycling skills. (" 'A Modern Enoch Arden' introduces Joe Jackson to Triangle audiences," observed a writer in The Triangle. "The bicycle is used with laughable effect and also to make a rescue when a child is floating away on a disabled motor-boat.")[82] Yet where Keystone's earlier tramp comics had appeared in comic situations predicated on social difference, the plots of Jackson's films were instead organized in moral terms, through the sentimental polarities of "sunshine and shadow" identified by Denning. Although neither A Modern Enoch Arden nor Gypsy Joe is still extant, existing production documents suggest that they paralleled Chaplin's 1915 Essanay films in introducing pathos and romance to the tradition of tramp comedy.[83] This is particularly evident in Gypsy Joe, where preproduction documents reveal a conscious effort to accentuate the romance between Jackson and a gypsy girl played by Dora Rodgers. The "love interest," one unnamed writer noted, "[can] be played up between [Jackson] and Dora, much to the dis-taste of the gypsy chief, who favors [his henchman's] suit for Dora's hand."[84] In the finished film, this produces an unusual focus on the emo-tions and subjectivity of the two lovers: of the eighteen close-ups that pro-duction documents indicate for the film's opening sequence, all but two are of Jackson, Rodgers, or both.[85] Toward the beginning of the film, for exam-ple, Rodgers is introduced by the title "The Belle of the Camp Loves Gypsy Joe," before a cut to a close-up presents her "picking the petals from a flower, doing the time honored 'he loves me, he loves me not.' "[86]

But Gypsy Joe is not only the object of Rodgers's affections; he is also a victim, bullied by a gypsy chief who sends him to kidnap a young orphan girl (Betty Marsh). Neglected and ill-treated by her abusive guardian, the orphan serves as Joe's double in the film's iconography of victimized inno-cence (fig. 19). His natural sympathies prevent him from going through with the kidnapping, and "in a very few moments he becomes very much attached to the child."[87] When her wealthy guardian suddenly appears and begins to scold the young girl, Joe intervenes and pleads for mercy: "Don't Hit Her—Hit Me," reads a title card.[88] Noteworthy here is how the differ-ence in social status—tramp versus guardian—is overwritten by a differ-ence in moral bearing—good father-figure versus bad father-figure. Such associations only become more prominent in the subsequent action, in which the romantic plot combines with the orphan narrative in a sentimental

FIGURE 19.   Tramp as sentimental hero. Joe Jackson and Betty Marsh in a production still from *Gypsy Joe* (March 1916). Courtesy of the Academy of Motion Picture Arts and Sciences.

family drama. Having fled the camp, Joe and his sweetheart rescue the orphan and escape into an idealized realm of nature. The film's concluding shots emphasize the familial allegory: "Joe, Betty and Dora are at last alone," a studio synopsis reads. "The sunset shows Joe and Dora together on a rock, the waves strike them and they run out. FADE OUT."[89] The figure of the tramp in *Gypsy Joe* is thus less a product of social forces than the projection of a sentimental worldview in which victimhood underwrites moral worth.

The pattern is the same in *A Modern Enoch Arden,* a burlesque reworking of a Tennyson poem that had been adapted numerous times on both stage and film (including the Griffith-directed Biograph films *After Many Years* and *Enoch Arden*—1908 and 1911—and a later, Griffith-supervised *Enoch Arden,* directed by W. Christy Cabanne for Harry Aitken's Majestic label in 1915). Drawing from Tennyson's poem its theme of a sailor lost at sea, the Keystone version features Jackson as a middle-class husband and father who is believed drowned in a shipwreck but returns home years later as a tramp. Particularly evident here is the way the tramp is disengaged from social signification: to introduce Jackson's familiar hobo persona as a shipwrecked bourgeois is implicitly to deny its meaning as an emblem of class difference. This, however, is only one step in the film's overall process of displacement. For, after returning home, Jackson next uses his tramp outfit as a disguise to rescue his kidnapped wife and daughter (again Betty Marsh) from a blackmailing lawyer. As a narrative device, disguise emphatically registers the text's abandonment of social meanings: it empties Jackson's tramp persona of social content, leaving behind only the clothes. In the end, following the successful restoration of familial harmony, the film retreats entirely from the social world into an idyllic space of nature, much like the conclusion to the later *Gypsy Joe*. As described in production reports: "Archway water b[ack]g[round] sunset. Joe and wife and baby enter. Fade out."[90]

The sentimentalization of social themes was, in fact, standard procedure in Keystone's early Triangle releases. Aside from the Jackson films, a representative example is found in *A Janitor's Wife's Temptation* (December 1915), Fred Mace's first starring vehicle since his return to Keystone in June 1915. (One of Keystone's founding members, Mace had quit the studio on April 12, 1913 to direct and star in comedies for Harry Aitken's Majestic. When these proved unsuccessful, he returned to Sennett's studio, lured by an undisclosed salary that, according to the trade press, was "equaled by but few motion picture actors.")[91] The film's basic situation might have formed the basis for one of the studio's Mutual pictures: a janitor (Mace) intrudes upon an upscale cabaret and causes chaos among its clientele. But where the Mutual films would no doubt have emphasized the social transgressiveness of his actions, *A Janitor's Wife's Temptation* foregrounds personal meanings. In the first instance, the janitor's actions are motivated, not by comic disregard for middle-class propriety, but by the need to save his family: a highbrow artist is seducing his wife in a back room. But it is the use made of the janitor's infant daughter (yet again, Betty Marsh) that contributes most to the sentimental tone. The sequence in the cabaret is organized around, and made meaningful through, repeated close-ups of Marsh's scared and apprehensive face, a stylistic strategy that construes the action in terms of the impact of family breakdown on an innocent child. In the film's final shot, Marsh brings her parents together again, reuniting them for a concluding kiss.

These innovations in Keystone's comic form were to an extent successful in resituating the studio's films for middle-class tastes. Contemporary critics frequently characterized Keystone's Triangle releases as "free from anything vulgar" (*A Favorite Fool*), "more human than usual" (*Haystacks*

and Steeples, October 1916), or as possessing "unusual features of characterization" (*The Lion and the Girl,* April 1916).[92] The medieval setting of *A
Game Old Knight* (November 1915) put one critic in mind of "light opera,"
and *Oriental Love* (May 1917) drew praise for the "added value in pictur-
esque settings."[93] Other reviews observed the films' narrative values, commenting of *A Royal Rogue* that it contained a "fairly good story besides,
something new in farce" and that *Whose Baby?* (July 1917) "even has a
story to tell."[94] *A Modern Enoch Arden,* the critic for *Moving Picture
World* noted, "has an actual story interest that lifts it out of the realms of
farce . . . to where the audience begins to take an interest in the leading
characters and hope for compensating justice at the end."[95]

All of these phrases and comments represent different responses to
what was essentially a single phenomenon: the hybridizing of Keystone's
comic form with the cultural and aesthetic values of genteel culture. The
emphasis on conspicuous display, the muting of social themes, the introduction of sentiment and pathos: all were strategies calculated to integrate
Keystone's popular energies with the narrative paradigms of the middle
class; all, furthermore, set parameters within which Keystone would define
a new cross-class, or mass-cultural, style. What emerged from this transaction was a slapstick form ambiguously straddling between the culture of
the "classes" and the culture of the "masses," neither fully genteel nor
purely popular. Keystone's late comic form may have transcended divisions between high and low culture, but it did so only by incorporating that
dichotomy into the films themselves.

"MORE IN THE NATURE OF A LIGHT COMEDY THAN SLAPSTICK": THE SWANSON-VERNON FILMS

Nowhere was this adaptation of slapstick to genteel values more evident
than in Sennett's decision, in February 1916, to establish a romantic
comedy unit at Keystone featuring the eighteen-year-old Bobby Vernon
and the sixteen-year-old Gloria Swanson as young lovers. Although the
factors behind that decision remain unclear—Kalton Lahue says only that
the unit was created "at the urging of several of [Sennett's] directors"—it
is reasonable to suppose that the director/performer Charles Parrott was
an instrumental figure in the development.[96] Later to achieve fame as
Charley Chase in Hal Roach comedies in the 1920s, Parrott had previously
appeared in films introducing naturalistic depictions of youthful romance
to Keystone's repertoire—for example, *Hash House Mashers* (January

1915), *Settled at the Seaside* (March 1915), and *The Rent Jumpers* (April 1915)—and was initially signed on to head the new unit. Gloria Swanson would remember him as the unit's creative center and driving force. As she later described her first day on the lot:

> [A] man ran out the door [of a studio bungalow] to shake my hand and introduced himself as Charley Parrott. He took me inside, where a group of men began to clap and cheer as soon as they saw me. A cute young boy ran up to shake hands with me. He said he was Bobby Vernon. . . . [Bobby] explained to me how Mr. Sennett had signed him the week before to be the lead in a new light romantic comedy company. Once Bobby was set for it, everyone had started looking for the right girl.[97]

Despite his likely role in its creation, Parrott did not remain with the unit for long. Dissatisfaction with his weekly $250 salary led him to resign from Keystone in June 1916. Clarence Badger was subsequently brought in as a replacement at the same wage, plus a $300 bonus for every film completed within four weeks. This was top-dollar salary for Keystone's directors, and it suggests the esteem in which Sennett held both Badger's and Parrott's work. (In 1916, Eddie Cline and Fred Fishback received just $100 a week as directors, for example, while Victor Heerman was paid $150.)[98] The Swanson-Vernon unit thus represented a significant investment in studio talent, and Sennett's concern with its success led him to take a close hand in overseeing its first release, *A Dash of Courage* (May 1916). According to Swanson's account, Sennett insisted upon viewing a rough cut of the film once shooting was completed and made notes on possible improvements. "He said he hadn't liked all of the picture, that in fact some of it would have to be done over, but—and he paused—that if audiences didn't find it fresh and funny, they were crazy."[99] Existing documentation supports Swanson's story: the files for *A Dash of Courage* contain the only production documents from this period that include Sennett's own handwritten suggestions.[100] In fact, so encouraged was Sennett by the rough cut that, even before the film's release, he established a second romantic comedy unit pairing Joseph Belmont and Ora Carew under the direction of Carew's husband, Walter Wright.

The Swanson-Vernon unit quickly became one of Keystone's most valuable assets. With the success of the team's first few films, Swanson's starting salary of $65 per week was raised to $115, and the studio began to market the pictures heavily.[101] At the beginning of 1917, Sennett chose a Swanson-Vernon vehicle—*The Nick of Time Baby* (February 1917)—as the studio's first open-market release, evidently banking on the duo's popularity to attract independent exhibitors. Contemporary reviews acknowledged the unit's success in creating a new comic form and praised the filmmakers for avoiding the well-trodden formulas of slapstick comedy. "This comedy is a little off the Keystone color," one critic noted of *The Nick of Time Baby.* "[I]t is more of the nature of a light comedy than slapstick, and contains considerable dramatic interest."[102] Meanwhile, *Haystacks and Steeples*—Swanson and Vernon's fifth pairing—drew praise as an "amusing comedy of a little higher class in some respects than the regular Keystone farce."[103]

Still, it would be a mistake to overstate the discontinuity these films entailed with respect to Keystone's previous output. The use of courtship and romance as a narrative framework had, in fact, first become evident early in 1915—especially, as noted, in a number of Parrott's starring films—and Sennett had supported those efforts by hiring new actors to play "straight" romantic leads. The first of these, Harry Gribbon (or "Silk-Hat" Harry, as he was known at Keystone), had arrived at Edendale in January 1915 with prestigious experience as a lead actor in musical comedies produced by George Cohan and Klaw and Erlanger. Reportedly the first of the studio's comedians to "put on straight make-up," Gribbon was joined two months later by Owen Moore, a popular film star who had made his name in romantic dramas at Biograph and Famous Players opposite his then-wife Mary Pickford.[104] Although none of their films exhibit the romanticism of the later Swanson-Vernon releases, critical response was enthusiastic and showed that romance could be a strategy for appealing to "better" audiences. For the *World* critic Louis Reeves Harrison, for example, Moore's first effort—*The Little Teacher* (June 1915)—provided the occasion for a celebratory report on recent developments in Keystone's output. "'Little Teacher' is one of many [recent Keystone films] which reveal a tendency from ridicule of the inferior, in which primary instincts are held up to ridicule, toward a finer form of humor, such as that which made Dickens popular. . . . . Sennet [sic] will gain ground, rather than lose it, by this gradual change."[105] Small wonder that the studio's filmmakers would return to romantic comedy under Triangle.

But the Swanson-Vernon unit also built on the sentimentality that had marked Keystone's releases from the beginning of the Triangle period. The films are colored by a nostalgia that corresponds precisely to the codes of literary sentimentalism—a longing for what Fredric Jameson terms that "idyllic space of family and child-bride as a Utopian refuge from the nightmare of social class."[106] Where Moore's and Gribbon's films had combined slapstick comedy with narratives of *adult* romance, it was the carefree play-fulness of *childhood* love that formed the cornerstone of the Swanson-Vernon films. Social meanings are thus abandoned to a nostalgic and evasive preoccupation with young love; as Vernon informed Swanson on her first day at Keystone, "We're both supposed to look and act like lovable fifteen in this comedy."[107] Perhaps no single Swanson-Vernon release dramatizes this better than *Haystacks and Steeples,* a film that literalizes evasiveness as a narrative device. The story is essentially one of escape, in which Gloria flees the marriage that has been arranged by her money-grubbing aunt and returns to the farm where she grew up. "My darling granddaughter," reads the letter that Gloria receives at the beginning of the film, "Have you forgotten us at Willow Farm? It's been a long time since you were here. The hired boy is now a man and the little calf a cow."[108] It is in the rural paradise of her youth that Gloria finds refuge from familial and social expectations, discovering in her relationship with the young farm hand (Vernon) a world of romantic self-absorption within a space of nature. "She and Bobby," note the production files for this lost film, "are having a fine time together" (fig. 20).[109] Indeed, the pastoral setting becomes the very element in which the aunt's machinations are unraveled: in a deus ex machina plot twist, a traveling saleswoman chances upon the farm and reveals that she is already married to Gloria's millionaire fiancé. The fiancé's bigamous designs are exposed, the aunt's greed thwarted. "Bobby runs over to Gloria," the studio's synopsis of the film's climax says. "The aunt sees this and tries to keep him away. She starts toward Bobby but the grandmother holds her back while Gloria and Bobby kiss. Fade out."[110]

What the young lovers triumph over, in this film and others, is an adult world in which personal relations have been soured by economic motives. This accounts for the gamut of money-minded villains in their films—the mortgage collector of *Hearts and Sparks* (July 1916), the scheming guardian in *Teddy at the Throttle* (April 1917), and the gang of thieves in *Whose Baby?* But it also helps explain the extraordinary exoticism and abstraction of the film's settings—the pastoral retreat of *Haystacks and Steeples,* the country resort of *A Social Club* (July 1916), the Indian palace of *The Sultan's Wife* (September 1917). If these are films of escape, then they are escapes that lead away, allegorically, from the realities of capitalist existence and toward the realm of childhood fantasy, a protective utopia that deflects the individualism and acquisitiveness of the world outside. Accompanying this retreat is a displacement at the sexual level, notably in three films in which the lovers are accompanied in their exploits by

FIGURE 20. Bobby Vernon and Gloria Swanson in a production still from *Haystacks and Steeples* (October 1916). Courtesy of the Wisconsin Historical Society (Image ID 43918).

"Teddy," a Great Dane. Perhaps the most loaded symbol of the films' sentimentalism, Teddy serves as a substitute for the child that a grown-up sexual coupling might create, a cipher through which the narratives withhold the sexual meanings of the young lovers' romance. This becomes particularly apparent in the concluding shots of those films in which Teddy appears. In the climax to *Teddy at the Throttle,* for example, Teddy rescues Gloria from the path of an oncoming train: Bobby and Gloria embrace around their trusty canine, who stands in for the child that their youth forbids. In *The Nick of Time Baby*, Teddy rescues a kidnapped infant and reunites the boy with his parents: the film again ends as Gloria, Bobby, and Teddy embrace, paralleling the restored family unit, while omitting overt connotations of childbirth.

There is at least one question that merits careful consideration at this point: quite simply, to whom were these films intended to appeal? The extensive publicity given to Teddy—including a *Photoplay* "interview" in July 1917!—suggests his importance as a commodity that could be marketed to a "family" audience of women and children.[111] "This comedy will have a strong appeal for the whole family," a promotional piece on *The Nick of Time Baby* asserted. "One of the star performers is a magnificent Great Dane dog—'Teddy'—who is all but human. The women and children as well as 'Pa' will shriek with delight to see 'Teddy' rescuing a baby from a watery grave; taking him home in his great jaws as tenderly as a mother could carry him in her arms."[112] This emphasis on family also appeared in publicity describing the Swanson-Vernon films in terms of a "real heart interest" that "cannot but appeal to old and young."[113] Such promotional claims indicate a deliberate effort on Keystone's part to appeal beyond its established fan base of working-class men, a development surely not unrelated to the changing demographics of the film audience. Although reliable statistics are difficult to track down, recreation surveys taken at the time show that the percentage of adult male filmgoers had begun to decline in the 1910s; by the end of the decade, W. Stephen Bush would write in the *New York Times* that fully 60 percent of filmgoers were women.[114] The industry had begun to foreground romance as a primary attraction for this growing audience segment, and the Swanson-Vernon films clearly headed Keystone's moves in this direction.[115] "The success of a film is made by the young girl who watches the play and sighs a romantic sigh; she wonders whether she will ever have a lover like the one she sees," Mack Sennett said in a presumably ghost-written opinion piece. "And by the boy who thinks to himself, 'Gee, I wish that was my girl,' as he sees the heroine on the screen."[116]

While this emphasis on romance marked an unmistakable address to a female audience, still it was the idea that these films were respectable fare for middle-class families—suitable for "women and children as well as 'Pa,'" for "young and old," without risk of offense—that was most assiduously promoted, testifying to Keystone's most overt attempt to market its product for genteel tastes. In their idyllic evocations of childhood and play, the Swanson-Vernon films were indeed exquisitely attuned to the changing values of America's middle class. The historian T. J. Jackson Lears offers a productive way of framing this point by describing how new attitudes to childhood in turn-of-the-century culture helped mediate a "crisis" in genteel self-confidence.[117] By the close of the Gilded Age, Lears argues, the formalities of genteel society had become oppressive even to its own members, creating a sense of stagnancy and the belief that intense experience—physical or emotional—was a lost possibility. One result of this was a nostalgic investment in the spontaneity and playfulness of childhood. A protest against the emotional impoverishment of the Victorian era, the valorization of youth and play laid the groundwork for a significant reorientation in middle-class mores. A vision of self-realization associated with childhood, Lears suggests, became the watchword for a transformation in personal ethics (Lears cites the self-help writer Annie Payson Call, who, in 1913, counseled readers to emulate "the healthy baby [who] yields, lets himself go, with an ease which must double his chances for comfort" as a means of managing the frenetic pace of modernity).[118] Veneration of childlike vitality was also embedded in the pursuit of more exuberant standards of behavior, a development linked to changing patterns of middle-class employment. Between 1870 and 1920, the numbers of Americans employed in white-collar, salaried positions rocketed from around 80,000 to over three million, creating a "new" middle-class of young men and women less indebted to the moribund social rituals of the previous era than their elders.[119] Nostalgia for the immediacy of childhood eased adjustment to the routinized and deadening qualities of white-collar employment, providing after-hours escape from the rigors of the workplace: the emphasis on discipline and self-restraint associated with the Victorian ideal of "character" gradually yielded to an emphasis on childlike spontaneity associated with the new middle-class ideal of "personality."[120]

Swanson herself was to be of tremendous importance in transforming the contours of middle-class culture. In Cecil B. DeMille's sex comedies of the early 1920s, such as *Why Change Your Wife?* (1920) and *The Affairs of Anatol* (1921), she embodied the middle-class "New Woman" who pursued extradomestic fulfillment and sexual freedom in the realms of commercial leisure and consumer spending (a phenomenon discussed in more detail in chapter 6). Yet even during her years at Keystone, Swanson was a model for the new ethnic of youthful magnetism, prefiguring the later development of her star image. "She was charming," Clarence Badger wrote of his first meeting with her. "Her face and eyes were unusually beautiful, a kind of winsome, appealing beauty. She radiated *personality*."[121]

Swanson's films with Bobby Vernon likewise spoke directly to the reorientation in middle-class mores. Age versus youth, ritual versus play, tradition versus spontaneity: these are the thematic poles around which the narratives are organized. A common plot structure, for example, contrasts the values of the young lovers' stuffy upper-middle-class parents and their own need to assert their freedom from parental authority. In *Haystacks and Steeples, Teddy at the Throttle,* and *The Sultan's Wife*, a wealthy parent or older relative stands in the way of the couple's romance, insisting upon marriage to someone who might advance the family socially. The tension between the "old" and "new" middle classes crystallizes as a conflict over the meaning of marriage: on the one hand, marriage conceived of as a social act, a strategy by which the couple's genteel parents attempt to secure social status; on the other, marriage as a youthful act of romance and self-realization.[122] The solution to this conflict comes, invariably, in a frenetic race to the rescue in which the lovers' acts of physical daring put paid to parental objections. In both *A Dash of Courage* and *Haystacks and Steeples*, for example, it is Bobby's dynamic rescue of Gloria that yields her parents' favor. In *The Sultan's Wife*, Bobby wins his father's acceptance for his chosen fiancée when the young couple helps depose a villainous Rajah. In the film's final shots, Bobby, Gloria, and Teddy sit triumphantly on the imprisoned Rajah's throne while Bobby's father, a naval officer, stands before them saluting his approval. The energy and dynamism of the young lovers becomes proof of their mutual commitment, and generational conflict dissolves in the affirmation of a new, revitalized middle-class ethic of youth and romance.

Keystone's filmmakers had evidently hit on something new, a comic form predicated on romantic fantasy, featuring exotic and opulent settings, and attuned to the aspirations and values of modern middle-class existence; in short, a style of comedy that capped Keystone's efforts under Triangle to import the appeals of musical comedy into slapstick film. As a number of film historians have observed, these were the precise terms on which the film industry would attract a cross-class audience after World War I, offering films that, like Swanson's subsequent pictures for DeMille, showcased glamorous settings and dealt with the romantic tribulations of the young and wealthy.[123] Sennett himself seems to have recognized that this was a winning formula, and, in subsequent years, he would continue to insist on the value of youthful romance as, in his words, "the surest drawing card for a picture play."[124]

Why, then, did the Swanson-Vernon unit prove so short-lived, producing only nine films before its abrupt termination in the summer of 1917?

Existing documentation reveals that the unit fell apart after Sennett severed connections with Triangle and, on June 29, 1917, signed a three-year
contract with Paramount. Although Sennett renewed contractual options
on Swanson and the director Clarence Badger, Vernon was one of many
performers whom he chose not to bring with him onto the Paramount
label. Unaccountable in retrospect, Sennett's decision left the studio without any actors who could plausibly appear alongside Swanson as a romantic lead. The problem was subsequently compounded when, instead of
looking for a new co-star, Sennett rushed Swanson into immediate production on her first Paramount release. The resulting film, *The Pullman
Bride,* was hastily completed under Badger's direction on September 24,
six days before the release of *The Sultan's Wife,* the final Keystone picture
distributed under Triangle.[125] In terms of plot, the film had much in
common with Swanson's earlier pictures, casting her as a society girl whose
mother forces her to marry a well-to-do businessman. In terms of comic
style, however, *The Pullman Bride* is far more knockabout in tone—a consequence, no doubt, of the decision to cast her with two of the studio's well-
established burlesque comics, Mack Swain and Chester Conklin. The
casting angered Swanson, who resented having to play a foil to, in her
words, "the broadest slapstick comedians in the world." "I continued to be
miserable throughout the shooting of *A Pullman Bride [sic].* . . . I missed
Charley Parrott and Bobby and all the others. . . . [W]hat really bothered
me was that I knew the world of slapstick was not for me. . . . I hated the
vulgarity that was just under the surface of it every minute."[126] Once the
picture was completed, Swanson promptly resigned.

·   ·   ·

The Triangle experiment did not end happily for many, the Keystoners
least of all. The irony was that, in his inability to keep Sennett content,
Harry Aitken ultimately forfeited the very films best able to realize his
hopes of a cinema "made for the masses, with an appeal to the classes."
Where Aitken's highbrow aspirations had proved a dead end, Keystone's
films pointed in new directions, hybridizing genteel aesthetic traditions
with the studio's established slapstick style. Where Aitken had taken genteel culture as a model for the Triangle organization, the Keystone films
reworked and adapted that culture for a cross-class audience. Keystone thus
participated in what has been termed the "desacralization" of genteel cultural tradition, the process by which older middle-class values were redis-
persed within the new commercial mass culture, eventually paving the way
for new categories like "middlebrow."[127] Although the term "middlebrow"

was not coined until the 1920s, the leveling impact of the market on gen- teel standards had long been evident. In many of Keystone's Triangle films, distinctions between "high" and "popular" culture had already begun to disappear in an interpenetration of divergent cultural values and aesthetics. Settings that displayed the opulence of the elite lifestyle, romantic fan- tasies that fused sentimentalism with a cult of youth, and the knockabout action for which Keystone was famous: out of this matrix of divergent impulses the studio's filmmakers successfully reformulated slapstick for a new era of mass entertainment.

Yet despite the ongoing popularity of Keystone's films, the Triangle Film Corporation was itself a failure. And although many factors eventu- ally contributed to the company's collapse, Aitken's persistent financial mismanagement was undoubtedly the major cause. In a telegram to Aitken sent on October 16, 1916, Griffith freely expressed his opinion that Triangle was "the worst managed business in film history."[128] Almost to the end, Aitken poured extravagant sums into the unprofitable policies in which he invested his ambitions. Committed to the value of conspicuous display as a signifier of status, Aitken had raised Triangle's overhead to a level all but guaranteed to wipe out profits. In the words of his brother Roy, Harry's "weakness for immediate expansion" left him unable to "stop and consolidate . . . before moving into new and larger production pro- grams."[129] In fact, Aitken's administrative "weakness" went far beyond the sums he spent on Triangle's behalf: as revealed in a 1921 court action against him, his taste for the high life led him to embezzle some $3 million from the company coffers. If Triangle was Aitken's vision, then it was one he was quite willing to plunder in his personal quest for status.

Looking back a half-century later, Roy Aitken offered somber commen- tary on the fate of his brother's company: "The only purpose of the new financial management of Triangle was to get as much money as possible for the bank investors by cutting costs and by reissuing old Triangle pictures and promoting current productions. . . . To Harry and me, the collapse of Triangle was a soul shaking experience."[130] Despite Harry's hopes, genteel cultural practice could not readily be cashed in the coin of profitable motion pictures. The point is worth emphasizing, if only as a reminder that the film industry of the 1910s was never merely a handmaiden for genteel middle- class ideology. If Triangle's rise and fall can be approached as a microcosm of broader forces within the industry, then the historical model to be kept in mind is one, not of hegemonic incorporation, but rather of a complex barter of specific commercial and class-based interests. Triangle's profound failures and limited successes hold up a mirror to a cultural reorientation in which the ethical and aesthetic standards of the genteel classes were outstripped by the emergence of a profit-driven culture industry. In Keystone's films of the period, some general features of the new pattern emerge clearly, such as the suspension of social themes, the foregrounding of sentimental and romantic values, and the hybridization of aesthetic traditions. The Keystone Film Company was involved in producing the new mass culture; the following chapters focus on its most distinctive contributions.

5. "Uproarious Inventions"

Keystone, Modernity, and the Machine, 1915–1917

The mechanical truth . . . was sometimes first spoken in jest.
LEWIS MUMFORD, Technics and *Civilization* (1934)

In October 1917, the film magazine *Photoplay* published an essay describing a recent "improvement" in slapstick comedy. Whereas "the old slapstick effect" had formerly been achieved with "the familiar pie," Alfred Cohn argued, one studio had, in recent years, developed a new slapstick style centered upon "the super-stunt." The "chief policy" of that studio, Cohn wrote, was "to 'thrill 'em as well as make 'em laugh'" by "hitting the victim with an auto or blowing him up with a bomb."[1] Cohn did not mention the company by name, because he did not have to; any movie fan would have known he was referring to Keystone. Nor was he alone in making these observations. As another critic had noted two years previously, "Almost every Keystone comedy contains at least two or three mechanical or spectacular surprises," adding that "the secrets of many of these would be worth fortunes to less resourceful competitors."[2] Certainly no other aspect of the studio's output ever received equivalent praise. Week after week, reviewers wrote in amazement of what they variously called "mechanical contrivances," "mechanical effects," and "uproarious inventions."[3] From the breakneck pirouettes of "tin lizzies" to more elaborate stunts featuring somersaulting airplanes and spinning submarines, Keystone's participation in the new mass culture emerged most clearly through the theme of modern technology.

One of the things for which Keystone is best remembered is, indeed, mechanical and spectacular surprise; and, like the studio's experiments with romantic and sentimental themes, this too owes its development largely to the studio's Triangle period. Of course, as many historians have noted, the desire to see machine technology, not simply in utilitarian terms, but as a source of pleasure and fascination in its own right provided the basis for a wide range of entertainments during this period, and not only at

Keystone. Whether manifest in the mechanical rides at Coney Island or in the cartoons of Rube Goldberg, in the cult of the automobile or in the public's fascination with cinema itself, technological inventiveness formed the core of an American vernacular tradition whose influence extended across cultural hierarchies and social divisions. As early as the 1840s and 1850s, the language of technical explanation and scientific description had become a form of recreational literature, both in the popular press and in the stories of Poe and Melville, among others; by the turn of the century, new amusement parks like Coney Island were bringing to a head the growing tendency to value technology as spectacle.[4] Technical institutes and engineering schools began to proliferate across the country, from the Massachusetts Institute of Technology (1866) to California's Throop College of Technology (1891). The spirit of inventiveness was also evident in the increased traffic through the U.S. Patent Office: the record of 23,000 patents issued during the decade of the 1850s was equaled if not exceeded every single *year* by the end of the century.[5] These were decades of intense industrialization and technological progress: few people were left unaffected by the speed and scale of change.

Keystone's "mechanical contrivances" clearly belong in this context. Yet, more than mere symptoms of a historical moment, they also provide a touchstone against which to weigh the changing role of popular comedy in an era of unprecedented technological advance. Here as elsewhere, Keystone's filmmakers were creating new comic forms that adapted popular slapstick to the tastes of the growing mass audience for movies. As the *Moving Picture World* critic Louis Reeves Harrison suggested, the success of the studio's "uproarious inventions" lay in their ability to "delight *all* classes," to address fascinations shared by an overwhelming majority of the filmgoing public.[6] Yet where Keystone's similar experiments with romance and sentiment drew on established forms of genteel culture to create a properly "middlebrow" comic form, the studio's haywire mechanical stunts appealed instead to new experiences less indebted to earlier cultural hierarchies. They thus participated in the emergence of a distinctly modern comic form that mediated the meanings of mechanization for a public whose own encounters with technology often betrayed startling uncertainties and ambiguities. Integrating the spectacle of modern machinery into slapstick's carnivalesque ethic of pleasurable disorder, Keystone defined new and appealing images of technology that drew moviegoers into a new world of mass culture. Understanding that process throws into relief the role of technological display in creating new patterns of mass cultural consensus in early-twentieth-century America.

"THEY HAVE NO EXPLANATION—THEY SIMPLY ARE": STUNTS, TRICKS, AND THE OPERATIONAL AESTHETIC

To appreciate their significance, we need first to understand Keystone's mechanical effects as showmanship—that is, as a strategy of product differentiation in an increasingly crowded comedy market. Keystone's box of tricks, in this respect, was the studio lot itself, as rising production budgets enabled filmmakers to develop the resources needed to visualize ever more absurd stunts and sensational scenes. The new direction first became clear in early 1915, when, following a 50 percent budget increase for each film (raising available funds per two-reel picture to around $10,000), Keystone's filmmakers set to work on the pathbreaking *The Cannon Ball* (June 1915)—the studio's first full-fledged example of what might be termed an "effects" comedy.[7] Advertised to exhibitors as "The First Big Mack Sennett Keystone Special" and "The Most Spectacular Comedy Ever Made," *The Cannon Ball* broke new ground for Keystone through its unprecedented concatenation of improbable physical action.[8] At one point, a well-hidden use of piano wires to lift objects up in the air creates a single moving shot in which the villain (Chester Conklin) is doggedly pursued by an errant cannonball; elsewhere, double exposure and piano wires combine to show a policeman flying across rooftops, dragged by a second hurtling cannonball (fig. 21); and, finally, miniature models help create the film's thrilling climax, in which the hero (Charles Arling) uses the cannon to demolish a bridge, sending Conklin tumbling down to the river below. "The Keystone company is in topknotch [sic] form in this number," *Moving Picture World* commented approvingly.[9]

Although the level of attention the film garnered in the trade press was nothing special, it is evident in retrospect that *The Cannon Ball* marked a turning point of sorts for Keystone's filmmakers. Evident also was Sennett's willingness to support these developments, as production budgets were increasingly funneled into the purchasing of new technical tools and gadgetry. Already by the spring of 1915, construction had begun on a $35,000 frame building, housing a 140-by-75-foot open-air stage equipped for stunt work and sensational effects. A 20-by-40-foot water tank at its center would serve Keystone's filmmakers for various purposes over the following years, yielding comic scenes in which rooms filled up with water (e.g., *Ambrose's Nasty Temper*, April 1915) and houses floated out to sea (e.g., *Fatty and Mabel Adrift*, January 1916). The new building also housed a "garage of sufficient size for eight or ten big autos and trucks," supplying storage space for the studio's growing stable of flivvers and police wagons.[10]

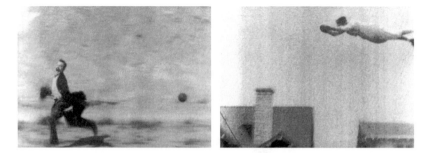

FIGURE 21.   Frame enlargements from *The Cannon Ball* (June 1915). Chester
Conklin is pursued by a cannonball; later, a second cannonball drags a policeman
across the sky. Courtesy of the Academy Film Archive, Academy of Motion
Picture Arts and Sciences.

The process of technical expansion only accelerated following
Keystone's move to Triangle in the fall of 1915. Immediately launched was
a lavish studio upgrade that enabled the purchasing of yet more tools and
contraptions. As *Motion Picture News* reported in November, new "air
equipment" had been purchased for the Keystone plant—specifically, a
"Wright model 'B' aeroplane," which was "in addition to the monoplane
with a Rotary Motor made by Joe Murray of the Keystone publicity
department."[11] That same year, the studio's filmmakers also began work on
an elaborate "panorama" device for the filming of chase sequences—a
rotating painted backdrop in front of which performers would run on a
treadmill. The principle behind this apparatus eventually became the basis
for the most unusual and unique contraption ever to grace Sennett's lot:
the "Cyclorama." An enormous revolving drum capable of speeds of up to
thirty-five miles per hour, the Cyclorama was, one of the studio's child
actors recalled, "like a big merry-go-round in a fun park."[12] In an era of
industrial expansion and rationalization, the Keystone lot had come to
resemble nothing less than a funfair, a carnivalesque reflection of a mechanized world, fully equipped with extravagant and bizarre mechanical
devices (figs. 22 and 23).

By 1916, Keystone had remade itself into an industry leader in innovative special effects and stuntwork, a base from which a number of filmmakers began to experiment with new technologies. Among these was Coy
Watson, a long-standing Sennett employee whose inventive work with
piano wires and other devices earned him the studio nickname "Fire, Wire,
and Water Watson." Other innovations were contributed by Fred W.
Jackman, a cameraman at Keystone since 1913 and the studio's resident

FIGURE 22.   A Keystone airplane filmed against a rotating panorama in *Saved by Wireless* (November 1915). Courtesy of the Academy of Motion Picture Arts and Sciences.

photographic effects specialist (later, also, an effects man on Cecil B. DeMille's 1927 *King of Kings*). But it would be the director Walter Wright who played the crucial role in fusing these disparate innovations into the new, effects-laden approach that became Keystone's hallmark. As a report in *The Triangle* enthused, "Walter Wright is the Keystone's 'trick' director. If you want to make a close-up of an aeroplane 5,000 feet above the sea, or of a man escaping from a sunken submarine, or any little thing of that sort, [Wright] can tell you how to do it."[13] Wright's reputation as the studio's stunt specialist was chiefly established by two films released during Triangle's first months, *Saved by Wireless* (November 1915) and *Dizzy Heights and Daring Hearts* (January 1916), each one an extravagant spectacle of modern machinery, trick photography, and stuntwork. The latter film, in particular, astonished critics with its imaginative use of Keystone's new planes. "[*Dizzy Heights and Daring Hearts*] is a marvelous stunt picture," the *New York Tribune*'s reviewer commented. "Air ships are made to loop the loop, turn turtle, walk on their hind legs and do all the thousand

FIGURE 23. The "Cyclorama," ca. early 1920s. Courtesy of the Academy of Motion Picture Arts and Sciences.

and one tricks incapable of accomplishment except by the aerial fleet used by Mack Sennett."[14] Such effects were, for the most part, accomplished through camera work (notably, a rotating camera); but *Dizzy Heights* also included the most stunning scene of authentic spectacle in Keystone's entire output. For the climax, the studio purchased a two-hundred-foot industrial smokestack at a deserted Inglewood factory and dynamited it for the cameras (an event that drew hundreds of observers).[15] The resulting footage was then cut in with studio-shot footage in which, thanks to deft use of piano wires and a chimney-top set, the heroine appears to fly her plane down and rescue her beloved from atop the smokestack just seconds before it explodes. "Melodrama in its wildest moments has pictured nothing more thrilling than the ascent of the tall chimney and the nerve-tingling incidents of rescue that follow," *Moving Picture World* raved.[16]

To modern viewers watching these films almost a century after their first release, such effects inevitably appear rather obvious, even clumsily so. The important question, however, concerns the films' original audiences: Were *they* aware that camera trickery was involved? To be sure, Keystone's film-makers never denied their use of special effects, and they knew their audiences were savvy enough to differentiate real stunts from trick photography. "Now and then we do a trick film," Roscoe Arbuckle confessed, "but everyone knows it is a trick when they see it—there is no bunk about it."[17] Keystone's special effects, it would appear, evoked pleasure, not because they convinced audiences of their authenticity, but because they inspired wonderment in the representational possibilities of cinema and delight in being "taken in" by skillful trickery. In the eyes of contemporary critics, the Keystone studio seemed like a magician's chest, delighting audiences with trick work that "completely mystifies the uninitiated." The films' special effects were "impossible feats"; they had "no explanation—they simply are."[18] The pleasure of Keystone's "uproarious inventions" was the pleasure of the trick: audiences knew that their eyes were being deceived, yet they delighted in their own mystification.

Recent work by Ben Singer points to a useful comparison here with the "sensation scenes" of turn-of-the-century stage melodrama. As Singer suggests, the elaborate scenography of the popular melodramatic stage—often used to render quite extraordinary spectacles, from Alpine avalanches to hot-air balloon battles—appealed to audiences, not by allowing them to suspend their disbelief (as though they were witnessing something real), but rather, like Keystone, by engaging a "how to" interest in the medium's representational possibilities.[19] Keystone's uniqueness in this respect was, not that it imported this kind of interest to cinema—the "trick" comedies and animations of J. Stuart Blackton, Emile Cohl, and others were the obvious pioneers here[20]—but that it exploited it as key to the studio's brand identity. Sennett and his filmmakers knew that a well-publicized veil of secrecy concerning production methods would not only stimulate audience curiosity but give them competitive advantage over others, like Vitagraph's Larry Semon, who were beginning to experiment with similar effects.[21] A *Photoplay* cartoon from March 1917 represents the Keystone studio as a heavily defended fortress, barricaded against "spies" sent by less resourceful filmmakers (fig. 24). Keystone's trick effects, we are led to understand, are equivalent to state secrets in a time of war: "It's easier to get into Germany than it is to get into the Keystone in these piping times of trick stunts." One also gets a sense of the value Sennett placed on such secrecy from a letter he wrote to Adolph Zukor in December 1917, shortly after leaving Triangle to release his films through Zukor's Paramount Pictures Corporation. "We do our utmost here to keep any and all of our mechanical contrivances a studio secret," Sennett insisted. "Can you imagine, as an

FIGURE 24. "Some of the News That's Fit to Draw." From *Photoplay,* March 1917. Courtesy of the Academy of Motion Picture Arts and Sciences.

illustration, a magician explaining to his audience how a trick is done and then going ahead and doing it? Naturally there ceases to be the required illusion; therefore it is of no interest to the spectators whatever."[22]

It is vital to realize here that, in making these claims, Sennett was placing himself and his filmmakers in a tradition of American entertainers skilled in the practice of pleasurable deception—a tradition encompassing stage illusionists like Harry Houdini and extending back to P. T. Barnum, who had invited mid-nineteenth-century viewers to debate whether his attractions were genuine or hoaxes. This kind of entertainment strategy, labeled the "operational aesthetic" by the historian Neil Harris, was characteristic of an age of intense public fascination with the way things worked, and it appealed to a delight in problem-solving and observing technical operations.[23] Like Houdini's impossible escapes, Keystone's operational aesthetic addressed the amateur's desire to understand technical process at a time when technological advancement far outstripped the average individual's understanding or control. The studio's trick effects invited audiences to examine and debate how they were accomplished—to match wits with Keystone's filmmakers—all the better to "mystify the uninitiated." At Keystone, the spectacle of technology was pervaded by a species of glamour, in the original etymological sense of magical spell.

One can, in fact, see Keystone's operational aesthetic at work in the very structure of the films' comic action. A common tendency, fully developed in the studio's post-1914 output, was to stage elaborate race-to-the-rescue climaxes in which multiplying modes of transportation intersect along chaotic, intersecting paths of pursuit—a car versus a police wagon versus two handcarts versus a runaway safe in *Only a Messenger Boy* (August 1915), a plane versus a yacht versus a car versus a (temporarily) airborne motorbike in *Saved by Wireless*, and a car versus a motorbike versus a bicycle versus two horse-drawn carts versus sprinting policemen in *Thirst* (July 1917), to cite only three variations on this motif. Technology thus became a model for comic action in which narrative logic was replaced by the haywire circuitry of modern technology. In one sense, such sequences continue Sennett's frequent parodies of the race-to-the-rescue melodramas of his former boss at Biograph, D. W. Griffith. Yet, in their absurdist concatenation of mechanical devices, they point also in the direction of cartoonist Rube Goldberg, whose famous "invention" drawings likewise invited the American public to trace nonsensical sequences of cause and effect through the image of the machine.[24] As contemporary reviewers put it, Keystone's rapid, criss-crossing action addressed filmgoers' desire to "follow the lines of interest," only to "bewilder" them with "the rapid succession of the unexpected."[25] The very speed of the action forestalled adequate comprehension. On the whole, the Triangle films were edited far more rapidly than Keystone's previous releases, with an average shot length of around 4.5 seconds, which was simply too fast to follow, at least for the *Moving Picture World* critic Louis Reeves Harrison, who objected: "the movement is very fast, too fast at times for the average spectator" (on *Cactus Nell*, June 1917); "We are lost, in fact, as to the general destination of what is going on" (on *A Dog Catcher's Love*, June 1917); "There is plot enough to supply a high comedy, but it soon becomes submerged in the swift farce, too swift at times" (on *Whose Baby?* July 1917).[26] What Keystone's "uproarious inventions" achieved at the level of spectacle, the studio's "swift farces" accomplished at the level of narrative: both challenged viewers to make active sense of mechanical process, only to submit them to the passive delights of amused befuddlement.

The enormous acclaim this style of comedy received nonetheless suggests how greatly it appealed to the emotional needs of diverse filmgoers. Technological spectacle possessed a mass basis precisely because it addressed interests that were widely shared in a technocratic society; as such, it provided a framework within which Keystone's filmmakers could tailor their output to tastes and enthusiasms linking different classes of audience. Whereas the studio's earliest films had once been disparaged as vulgar fare suitable only for working men and "friends of burlesque" (to quote one condescending review), the display of mechanical process provided Keystone's filmmakers with the key to a quite profound redefinition of slapstick form—a way of adapting low comedy traditions to the tastes of the emerging mass audience for motion pictures.[27] This was a point frequently made in Harrison's *Moving Picture World* reviews, which praised Keystone's stunts and trick work precisely on this count. Appealing to gender-coded notions of respectability, Harrison described the action of *Crooked to the End* (December 1915) as "bound to make some excitable member of any mixed [i.e., mixed-sex] audience hysterical."[28] *Dizzy Heights and Daring Hearts,* meanwhile, was said to contain "marvels of ingenuity which delight all classes."[29] Despite the roughhouse antics of *The Great Vacuum Robbery* (December 1915), Harrison noted elsewhere, even refined viewers would discover much "of real merit" in the film's "original conception of robbing a bank through vacuum tubes."[30] But the point was perhaps put most succinctly in an open letter from one Keystone fan to Mack Sennett, printed in the *Philadelphia Public Ledger*. "Much has been said about the vulgarity of the Keystone comedies, and few people grasp the ingenuity of the mechanical devices," began the writer, who concluded simply: "What could be more clever and less vulgar?"[31] In effect, technological spectacle redeemed physical comedy for a broad, cross-class audience: where once genteel critics had been offended by the "vulgarity" of knockabout comedy, they now were able to celebrate the "ingenuity" of its mechanical devices. The spectacle of modern technology thus formed a crystallizing point for a new mass culture that engaged the interests and experiences of an overwhelming majority of the population.

"THE MOST ASTONISHING BIT OF MECHANICAL TOMFOOLERY THAT EVER HAPPENED": WARFARE, FUNFAIRS, AND FETISHISM

The key word here—the one that crops up time and again in contemporary reviews—is "mystification." What made Keystone's operational aesthetic so popular was, arguably, a conjunction of concerns about the meanings and uses of modern technology, and about the social and human costs of modernity. Perhaps more than any other development in turn-of-the-century culture, the embrace of mechanization was Janus-faced. Already by the 1880s, technological growth in the United States had entered a new phase—a "second industrial revolution," it has been called—spurring a utopian faith in industrial progress, whose monuments included the Brooklyn Bridge and the railroad. Yet the speed of industrialization exacted a stiff price in terms of social discontent, a crisis of discomposure and shock that observers attributed to increased nervous stimulation, what the New York reformer Michael Davis labeled "hyperstimulus."[32] Alongside the din of cheers on behalf of technology as a horn of plenty, there were also more sinister anticipations of technological cataclysm, in which machines were envisioned as instruments of destruction and oppression, as in the techno-logically induced holocaust that closes Mark Twain's 1889 novel *A Connecticut Yankee in King Arthur's Court* or the dystopic vision of future technocracy in Ignatius Donnelly's *Caesar's Column*, published the same year. A succession of titles such as George Miller Beard's *American Nervousness* (1881) and John Girdner's *Newyorkitis* (1901) viewed the pace of the modern technological environment as a disease, whose symptoms included everything from neurasthenia to premature baldness and tooth decay.[33] Modernity appeared to many much in the guise of a jugger-naut, a runaway engine of uncontrollable power that crushed all that stood before its onrush. Whether manifest in late-nineteenth-century paintings of trains thrusting out into a virgin landscape (the "machine in the garden" of Leo Marx's famous study) or in magazine illustrations of streetcars and automobiles leaving streams of injured pedestrians in their wake, the juggernaut provided a template for envisioning the destructive irrationality of a mechanized industrial society.[34]

Against this backdrop of concerns, Keystone's mechanical contrivances remystified technology as a source of pleasure, not anxiety, offering carnivalesque images of out-of-control machinery that bracketed off the more distressing aspects of American culture's encounters with the machine. The point emerges clearly from a discussion of Keystone's 1915 Christmas special, *A Submarine Pirate*, a four-reel comedy whose five-month production period represents the single greatest expenditure of time on any Keystone release.[35] Little known now, *A Submarine Pirate* was in fact the most financially and critically successful of the studio's films outside of its 1914 feature *Tillie's Punctured Romance*. The reviews were unanimously the most positive that any Keystone film had ever received. It was lauded as "quite unusual if not marvelous," "one of the best examples of [Sennett's] art yet shown," and "the most astonishing bit of mechanical tomfoolery that ever happened."[36] According to a report in *The Triangle*, the film even received the unusual distinction of being selected by William Randolph Hearst to show at a high-toned Thanksgiving Day party. "Triangle plays apparently appeal to all classes," the writer smugly surmised.[37]

What appealed to "all classes" was once again the spectacle of a technological process. *A Submarine Pirate* offered viewers an opportunity to see for themselves a "big naval submersible of the latest American type," which, promotional material proclaimed, the U.S. government had loaned Keystone for exterior sequences.[38] The film, it was claimed, "displays submarine work pictorially in such detailed fashion as has never before been seen on the screen. . . . It is like being right in the inside of things to see the views of the interior of the submarine with all its mysterious wires, switches and gears, and to see how a crew prepares to fire the deadly torpedo."[39] Triangle exhibitors, for their part, were advised to bedeck theater lobbies with torpedo and periscope props that would "reflect the characteristics of the movie," while critics, too, boosted the film's technological appeal, praising its display of "interesting methods of handling Uncle Sam's submersibles."[40]

At the time when *A Submarine Pirate* was released, there was indeed exceptional public interest in "submersibles," albeit not for reasons that had much to do with comedy. The sinking of the Cunard ocean liner RMS *Lusitania* by a German U-boat on May 7, 1915, had provoked a widespread outcry that, while it did not precipitate American entry into the war, nevertheless fostered U.S. government support for new defense programs and boosted public anxiety about military preparedness. Almost 1,200 lives had been lost in an incident that newspapers freely described with words like "insane," "madness," and "brutality."[41] This, one would imagine, was hardly fit subject matter for slapstick comedy, especially since two more passenger liners had fallen victim to the same fate within months of the *Lusitania*. The paradox, then, is that a comedy so explicitly grounded in the tragedies of mid-1915 should have proved so enormously popular—even with the U.S. Navy, which announced that it would screen *A Submarine Pirate* for recruiting purposes in light of America's possible entry into the war.[42]

How, then, to transform such events into comedy? The answer offered by *A Submarine Pirate* involved a careful substitution, a rewriting of the associations that had recently accrued to submarine technology. Key here is the motif of technological control as the pivot upon which that reversal turns: the film's progress, stated broadly, is to invert a menacing imagery of technological mastery with a more comic imagining of out-of-control machinery. The film thus begins with what, for Keystone, is an uncharacteristic stylistic flourish: a fade-in on a threatening close-up of a bearded man (Wesley Ruggles) holding a skull—an image whose potent moral weight is underlined by the abstract, chiaroscuro composition.[43] A telegram is delivered, and the man leaves to meet a "mysterious inventor" (Glen Cavender), whom we first see tinkering with a remote-control model submarine. A medium-long shot of the inventor looming over the tiny electronically guided submarine, again in heavy chiaroscuro, provides a programmatic (and, again, unusually dramatic) image of mechanical mastery, defining the inventor as a quasi-demiurgic possessor of technological power. The subsequent scene continues the theme of control, as, over dinner at a hotel restaurant, the inventor instructs his accomplice to take command of a stolen submarine. Transferring his mechanical expertise to his colleague, the inventor explains how to operate the vessel: "These papers and submerging key will give you full command."

If the opening sequences take their tone from the sinister implications of mechanical mastery, the film soon unfolds its comic reversal, when an eavesdropping waiter (Syd Chaplin) steals the "submerging key" and sets off to take command of the submarine himself. From this point on, the characters are thrust into a disorienting mechanical world where they become helpless objects of the technologies they had sought to master. A brief chase sequence, following the theft of the key, launches the film in its new direction: a bomb sends the waiter flying onto a rooftop; two policemen are dragged along behind a speeding automobile; finally, the waiter is picked up by a crane and lowered onto the roof of a passing vehicle. But it is in the ensuing action aboard the submarine (occupying the last two of the film's four reels) that *A Submarine Pirate* turns most decisively upon the characters' comic inability to make technology work for them. Having escaped his pursuers, the waiter now heads off to the shipyard where the vessel is secretly located. A totally technological environment, the interior of the submarine bristles with levers, dials, and wheels, crowded together in claustrophobic, narrowly staged framings. The waiter descends into this interior and there follows a paradigmatic instance of Keystone's operational aesthetic, as a naval officer patiently explains how each instrument functions. Cutting between interior and exterior shots, the film now shows the submarine responding to the waiter's control, submerging and resurfacing as he pushes the levers this way and that. This "Lesson in Submerging" (as an intertitle describes it) served as a key attraction in the film, the point at which—to quote from the film's publicity campaign—viewers were able to witness the craft's "mysterious wires, switches and gears" (fig. 25). Coming at the very center of this four-reel comedy, the scene stages the central confrontation between clown and machine through the display of modes of operation and control, inviting the spectator to view the submarine, not as an instrument of war, but as a source of technical amusement. In effect, the submarine's technology becomes a fetish, precisely analogous to Marx's definition of commodity fetishism as a displacement of desire from human relations onto material objects: substituting for the memory of the *Lusitania*, which contemporary moviegoers surely brought to their experience of the film, *A Submarine Pirate* invites an enchanted fascination with gears, dials, and levers.

It is this substitution upon which the film's success as comedy depends. Foregrounding the vessel's operations over its recent historical uses—technological means over technological ends—the film glosses the submarine as a self-contained space of amusement, the meaning of the technology abstracted from its military purpose. In quick succession, there now unfolds a series of burlesque piratical exploits in which the submarine sinks a passenger liner and then gets caught in a comic battle with a gunboat. Twice the vessel expels the hapless waiter into the surrounding waters, and each time it becomes more a microcosmic amusement park than a machine of war. The first time, the waiter is launched out of the submarine on the end of a torpedo, sending him skimming across the ocean surface in a fashion akin to the then-popular "Shoot-the-Chutes" water slide. In the second instance—the film's final scene—the submarine spins round and round, sending the waiter flying through a porthole: the use of a revolving set here recalls Steeplechase Park's famous "Barrel of Fun," a

FIGURE 25.   The waiter (Syd Chaplin) receives a "Lesson in Submerging." Production still from *A Submarine Pirate* (December 1915). Courtesy of the Wisconsin Historical Society (Image ID 43916).

rotating cylinder that rolled customers off their feet as they entered the park.[44] The film ends with an image of comic mechanical entrapment: a close-up of the waiter mugging frenetically, his head underwater. A coda to the waiter's fate, a fake fish swims into shot and bites him on the nose.

A Submarine Pirate, then, is a film that envisions the submarine less as an instrument of militaristic destruction than as a vehicle for amusing exploits. If part of the fear evoked by the sinking of the *Lusitania* was a sense of technological uncontrollability—the realization that the machines to which people daily entrusted their lives were unable to protect them, that they could even lead them into the paths of other machines in the service of warfare and destruction—then *A Submarine Pirate* negotiated those fears by redefining human subjection to technology as pleasurable spectacle. It is, in fact, possible to see in many of Keystone's effects comedies a similar impulse to engage military machinery in a carnival spirit. *A Submarine Pirate* was, in this sense, only the most notable of several studio releases from the period (late 1915–early 1916) in which "uproarious inventions" overlapped with the technics of world war: thus, *The Cannon Ball*, in which a government inspector visits the "Boom Explosives Co."; *Dizzy Heights and Daring Hearts*, in which rival agents from warring nations vie for the purchase of a new aeroplane; and *Saved by Wireless*, in which a "Minister of War" loses his codebook to a pair of bumbling spies, leading to a frenetic chase by yacht and plane. There is, of course, no little irony in the fact that a war that marked the unprecedented modernization of military technologies also provided inspiration for Keystone comedy. But there is a further sense in which such films crystallized the paradoxical relation between technology and cinematic representation during World War I. As James Latham has shown, references to German military technology in the motion picture trade press actually *declined* during the war, while films that did show scenes of battle tended to emphasize their function as "marvelous" spectacle, apart from any consideration of political ideology.[45] Mass culture's operational aesthetic was thus, among other things, part of a pattern of cultural evasiveness in the face of military technologies whose destructiveness was only rarely acknowledged in the film culture of the time. And, in this sense, what appeared in many Keystone films as an ebullient vision of "uproarious inventions" was perhaps rather a form of aesthetic negotiation that, by shifting attention from ends onto means, onto technical spectacle and process, sought to reposition the devastation of world war under the aegis of carnival.

Viewed thus, Keystone's mechanical contrivances take their place as symptoms of a far broader compulsion within turn-of-the-century culture to revisit technological cataclysm as amusing display. From Currier & Ives lithographs of steamboat explosions to amusement park disaster shows recreating tenement fires and naval battles, a wide range of popular entertainments sought to redefine technological cataclysm according to the pleasure principle. If technology awoke dystopian fears in many, still it could be enjoyed as a source of kinetic sensation and spectacle, as Keystone's comedies make clear. The amusement parks and summer resorts that were becoming big business in America by the early 1900s likewise substituted the thrills of the roller coaster for the traumas of technological devastation. Coney Island's "Leap-Frog Railway," for example, played upon popular fears of railroad accidents by hurtling two electric cars, each filled with up to forty people, toward each other: at the last moment, one of the cars sloped up along a curved set of rails, over the roof of the other and back down behind it. The very technologies that workers encountered at the factory—and that had, in many instances, put them out of work—could be returned to them as forms of commercial pleasure: some amusement park rides were directly inspired by industrial machinery, beginning with Coney Island's 1884 "Switchback Railroad," an early form of roller coaster based on the gravity-powered coal cars used for mining. The logic of such substitutions was succinctly summarized by the modernist artist Joseph Stella, who described Coney Island in terms of "revolving machines generating for the first time, not anguish and pain, but violent, dangerous pleasures."[46] A symbol of the new mass culture, the roller coaster became the dialectical counterpart to the negative perception of technology as juggernaut.

Such amusements anticipate to a degree the themes of Walter Benjamin and other critics who have seen the turn-of-the-century funfair as a key institution for acclimatizing the public to the shocks of modern technology.[47] But they also provide the context against which the meaning of Keystone's "mechanical contrivances" emerges clearly. The psychic principle that could transform a train wreck into a roller coaster was obviously the same as that which could revisit the *Lusitania* tragedy as slapstick comedy. If Keystone and Coney shared a vision of the world as a crazy machine, then this was not because (or not merely because) that vision exploited technology's commercial possibilities as a new source of pleasure, but, more important, because it played a key role, across a range of cultural practices, in transfiguring the experience of modernity and modernization: the "uproarious inventions" of Keystone comedy overlapped with the mechanized thrills of the funfair precisely as homologous sites for negotiating public encounters with new technologies.[48] Particularly suggestive, in this respect, is the intertextuality linking Keystone's "tricks and traps" to popular pleasure machines of the period. The studio's output abounded in images of characters impelled toward absurd extremes of motion by mechanical devices, many of which directly echoed familiar amusement park rides. In *A Scoundrel's Toll* (November 1916), for instance, an impatient boss ejects a youthful inventor from his office by turning on an "automatic pest remover": a conveyor belt transports the young man to a trapdoor, from which he descends "Helter Skelter"–style to the streets below. In *A Game Old Knight* (November 1915)—a medieval period comedy—the protagonist falls through a trapdoor into a mechanized torture chamber (described in production documents as a "knife set") that begins to spin round in the manner of Steeplechase Park's "Human Whirlpool."[49] *Bath Tub Perils* (May 1916) meanwhile provides a surrealist gloss on amusement park water slides: a bathtub conveying a surprised bather careens through a flooded hotel lobby, down a flight of steps, into the streets, along a city reservoir, and out to sea. (The sequence "is as startling in its mechanical effects as it is amusing," Louis Reeves Harrison noted.)[50]

Not that Keystone was the first to exploit the amusement park's cinematic possibilities: Edison's cameramen had made scenic records of Coney Island almost a decade before the founding of Sennett's studio (e.g., *Shooting the Rapids in Luna Park* in 1903), and Edwin S. Porter integrated knockabout comedy with location footage for *Rube and Mandy at Coney Island* (also 1903). Indeed, Coney Island's lasting appeal as a location for early comedies—other titles would include the Vitagraph films *Cohen at Coney Island* (1909) and *Jack Fat and Jim Slim at Coney Island* (1910), among others—testifies to a significant overlap between the pleasures of the amusement park and the pleasures of slapstick: both engaged the body in comic contortions, both liberated it from the normal physical limitations of daily life.[51] Still, at Keystone, the amusement park was more uniquely important as a symbol for the studio's own engagement with the theme of mechanization. The very first film shot under the Keystone label, *At Coney Island* (October 1912), incorporated footage of the park—shot using New York Motion Picture lab facilities located on Coney Island itself—and the studio's filmmakers would have cause to revisit such locations several times in subsequent years: *Settled at the Seaside* (March 1915), *Mabel's Wilful Way* (May 1915), and *The Surf Girl* (July 1916) are notable examples.[52] Nor did amusement parks only supply settings for Keystone films; in several instances, they also shaped the comic dynamics of the films in which they appear, furnishing the mechanical principles of the films' action. Thus, in *The Surf Girl*, the pleasure machines of Santa Monica pier acquire narrative importance, not simply as background, but as active participants in a comedy of female flirtation and unconfined sexuality. Time and again in the film, the amusement park's mechanical devices play a role in undermining male and parental control over the female body. In the opening scene, a brash young man (Al Kaufman) shows off to his girlfriend (Ivy Crosthwaite) on a "test your strength" machine, only to be sent shooting out into the ocean, leaving his sweetheart at liberty to go swimming alone. The process is repeated with a second set of characters, another young woman (Julia Faye) and her stern parents (Glen Cavender and Dale Fuller): as the daughter flirts with a couple of lifeguards, her father first finds himself caught on a conveyor belt at a shooting gallery and later is flushed down a storm drain; the mother, meanwhile, is trapped in an out-of-control roller coaster that races off the tracks, sending her—like the boyfriend and the father before her—hurtling into the ocean. The very machinery of the amusement park cooperates in the liberation of female sexuality.

Yet it would be a mistake to emphasize only the liberatory aspects of the new culture of mechanized pleasure. True, the turn-of-the-century amusement park was in some sense akin to Johan Huizinga's vision of the "ideal playground," a "temporary world within the ordinary world" where "special rules" apply.[53] It was, as contemporary women's historians argue (and as *The Surf Girl* comically suggests), a cultural site that permitted new attitudes toward personal expressiveness, affirming a culture of free-and-easy flirtation that subverted sentimental ideologies of womanhood.[54] It was also a preeminent expression of a new mass culture in which mechanical devices violated conventional expectations of technology and launched fun-seekers into a world of the absurd. Whether at the amusement park or in Keystone comedies, here was a vision of the machine as an exhilarating emancipation from older, genteel standards of behavior and comportment. At the same time, however, it was a vision whose broad appeal cannot be separated from its role as a fetish—both in the Marxist sense of being reified, invested with too numinous a power, and in the Freudian sense of substituting for a less tolerable reality. Keystone had recast physical slapstick as "mechanical tomfoolery," but it had done so through images of technology that mystified mechanical process and sidestepped the often destructive onrush of technological change.[55] At Keystone, as at Coney, the image of the world as a crazy machine was a fetish for the modern era, in which cogwheels, levers, and gears meshed to such exhilarating ends that there remained not the slightest gap for confronting the troubling costs of a mechanized environment.

"IMPERSONATE THE AUTOMAT": A CLEVER DUMMY, ROBOTS, AND THE WORKING CLASS

What role might the machine aesthetic have played in transforming popular comedy's relation to working-class culture? And how, if at all, did the figurative association of machines with pleasure contribute forms of representation that submerged class distinctions in an ostensibly homogeneous mass culture? The fetish character of mass culture was noted by a large number of sociological thinkers in the decades surrounding the turn of the century, although for most, like Thorstein Veblen, this was associated with the circulation of commodities within a consumer economy.[56] Yet there were some for whom the reification of American life was rather to be traced to its technicist tendencies. When the great art dealer René Gimpel toured America during World War I, he discovered a cult of technical effectiveness virtually unknown in Europe, which he implicitly associated with the disenfranchisement of industrial labor, "a materialism that took the form of a cult of the machine that was, strictly speaking, alarming, in makeshift villages no longer centered on a church . . . , but on a factory, a mineshaft, or a railway station, and often deserted overnight."[57] Likewise for Theodor Adorno, America's fascination with "cultic" images of technology—the "technological veil," as he put it—had come to constitute a ritual of mass delusion, a form of disavowal in confronting the consequences of modernity.[58] The ultimate expression of modern culture's technological underpinnings, Adorno wrote in a late essay, was a fascination with "the technical 'how' "—with virtuoso technique and technological achievement—alongside the growing "fatuity of the 'what.' "[59] The image of the machine had its fascinations, to be sure, but they were not fascinations that could easily be translated into social awareness.

The mystique of technology was indeed a particular hallmark of early-twentieth-century American culture, its impact felt across the entire spectrum of cultural production. Diverse and different as it was in form and content, American literary and artistic production of the period shared a growing commitment to an abstract, mechanical conception of force. Writing in 1906, Henry Adams proposed a "Dynamic Theory of History" in which social and political process was now to be apprehended as the development and economy of "forces" and "attractions."[60] In the wake of the Armory Show of 1913, American modernists like Charles Demuth and Joseph Stella seized on the machine as a figure for new aesthetic experiments—and, in the process, abandoned the social focus of earlier Ashcan painters, such as George Bellows and John Sloan.[61] Around the same period, Lewis Hine's famous photographs of factory laborers grew increasingly less concerned with the problem of labor in its social dimension, emphasizing instead the artful symmetries of factory machinery.[62] Whether manifest in Coney Island or at Keystone, in the work of home-grown modernists like Joseph Stella or of visiting Europeans like Francis Picabia, cultural discourse on mechanization represented a disavowal of the social implications of the new technologies and a growing unwillingness to engage the experiences of workers who bore the full brunt of modernity's impact. As Alan

Trachtenberg suggests, America's fascination with the machine dimmed awareness of the radical dehumanization of the workforce that each technological advance represented.[63] One needs to speak, then, of a deterritorialization of the social perspective of Progressive-era creativity by the technicist perspective of modernity. If the machine was a fetish for modernity, then it was a fetish predicated on a displacement of social and political awareness and a muting of reformist discourse on class difference.

More than one cultural historian has observed these changes. Less commonly noted are their implications for the comic sensibility of the new mass culture. As Henry Jenkins has shown, contemporary attitudes to physical comedy had begun to change. Slapstick's low repute as a comic form associated with the cultural traditions of workers and immigrants was superseded by a new appreciation focused instead on the mechanics of its physical action—what George M. Cohan termed the "mechanics of emotion."[64] Under the aegis of a developing interest in reflexology, a pseudoscience of comic "mechanics" came to dominate debates on comedy during this period. Social scientists began to embark on quantitative surveys measuring human receptiveness to jokes and other bits of comic business. Henri Bergson—who was nearly mobbed by his American fans when he spoke at Columbia University in 1912—likewise argued for a mechanistic definition of humor, suggesting that laughter erupted whenever someone behaved in a mechanical way, like a windup person not under intelligent control.[65] Mack Sennett himself contributed to the new discourse in a 1914 interview, which quoted him as describing audience response to slapstick in terms of a "contraction of the . . . zygomatic muscles," a "contraction of the orbicular muscles," and a brightening of the eyes "which results from these muscular contractions."[66] What this actually means—and whether Sennett ever actually said it—is, of course, anyone's guess. But it does indicate the extent to which contemporary discussions of comedy had, by the mid-1910s, joined hands with a technicist vision of culture. Redefined through an abstract language of reflex and mechanical force, popular comic traditions were increasingly disassociated from their origins in working-class and immigrant cultures.

The Keystone Film Company was deeply complicit with the new sensibility. The emphasis on "mechanical contrivances" effectively dissolved Keystone's earlier connection to the culture and values of the lower classes. This was a matter neither merely of the general shift toward genteel settings nor simply of the decline of ethnic and lumpenproletariat clowns noted in the previous chapter. The studio's 1916 releases also saw the emergence of a new comic figure, one that marked the further adaptation of

Keystone's output to modern technics: the tinkerer or inventor. Substituting in part for the studio's earlier gallery of tramps and ethic stereotypes, the new Keystone protagonist was now as likely as not a young inventor who, as romantic lead, successfully rescues his sweetheart from peril with some innovative gadget or other—an "aeroplane life saving device" in *The Love Comet* (May 1916), a "wireless spark plug" in *Hearts and Sparks* (July 1916), or even—more mundanely—a new kind of tram fender in *A Scoundrel's Toll*.[67] Such unions of male know-how and female free-spiritedness seem to have appealed to Keystone's filmmakers as optimistic emblems of the modern era, analogous in many respects to the love relations between independent young women and racecar drivers in several of the studio's earlier films—for example, *The Speed Kings* (October 1913) and *Mabel at the Wheel* (April 1914).[68] But they also mark a significant—and ideologically revealing—switch in the relation of Keystone's protagonists to the means of production: for, unlike the worker, the inventor controls new technologies, rather than being controlled by them.

Here we cannot detail every instance of these changes; but we can look at an archetypical Keystone production of the period and see how the theme of technology problematized representations of class difference. Released in July 1917, *A Clever Dummy* overtly thematizes the relations between inventor, worker, and machine in the modern era. The plot, in which an inventor builds a robot modeled on his janitor and sells it to a pair of vaudeville impresarios, engages several major motifs of the new mass culture: technology, popular spectacle, and their relation to class. From the film's convoluted production history, we can furthermore gain some idea of the difficult process by which Keystone's filmmakers negotiated the theme of modern technology. The gestation period of *A Clever Dummy* was unusually long: the basic story idea seems to have been first formulated in August 1916 during story conferences for a Ford Sterling vehicle (eventually released in April 1917 as *A Maiden's Trust*); its scripting involved creative contributions by at least two directors, Frank Griffin and Herbert Raymaker; principal shooting did not get under way until the following May and was subsequently interrupted when Sennett decided to quit Triangle for Paramount. These long delays and extensive reconceptualizations gave the filmmakers abundant opportunity to experiment with different ideas involving the plot device of a comic robot. Reconstructing that process allows us to trace the chain of displacements underlying Keystone's "uproarious inventions" and to examine, at the level of a single film's production, how technological spectacle entailed the erasure of class as a source of comic meaning.

The story conferences of August 1916 had been dominated by the theme of mechanization, although it would not be until later in the month that the writers began toying with the comic possibilities of a human-like machine. One of the unused ideas for the Sterling film, sketched out in a brief scenario dated August 5, had been for a romantic comedy centered on the romance between an inventor and his landlady's daughter: according to this plot—filed under the generic title "Inventor Story"—the course of true love was to have been obstructed by a scheming lawyer, who sends a "vampire" to seduce the inventor and steal his plans for an "aerial torpedo" (a situation ripe with castration anxiety!). Problems soon arose, however, with the writers' efforts to incorporate the "aerial torpedo" into the film's action: while the earliest outline (August 5) had limited the torpedo's comic duties to a chase finale, later scenarios envisioned a variety of increasingly elaborate possibilities, including a photographic device that would enable the torpedo to "locate and destroy anyone whom it is sent in search of." ("This invention might be in the form of a pig," the scenario bizarrely notes.)[69] An alternative idea, apparently suggested some time in late August or early September, was to change the invention into some kind of automatic maidservant. Unlike the torpedo, an automatic servant could play a more significant role in the comedy, serving simultaneously as a source of mechanical spectacle and a narrative agent. One of the participants in these story conferences, the director Frank Griffin, quickly caught on to the automaton's comic potential, and, in a handwritten note, suggested a further story variation. "This story could be turned into good comedy," he wrote, "by providing the point of a real woman taking the place of an automatic servant and making a character old lady believe it is an automatone [sic]."[70]

The film's comedy, Griffin implied, should derive from the confusion caused by the mutual substitutability of human and machine; and, on September 8, the studio's writers drafted a two-page "Automat Story" based on this principle. Here, the inventor and his sweetheart have already been secretly married by the time the story opens. The complications begin when the young man wires his aunt for money to help complete his new invention—an automatic serving girl "which, by pressing certain buttons and winding up, . . . will perform the functions of the ideal serving maid."[71] The aunt wires back, promising him a major portion of her fortune provided he does not marry without her approval; moreover, she will be stopping by in the near future to inspect his progress with the automaton. "At this juncture," the scenario continues, "the automat . . . catches fire from friction and is destroyed. This places the young man in the position where he has no invention to show his aunt and has no money to make a new invention. . . . Therefore, in order to make the invention over again and keep his wife by his side, he fixes a fake arrangement of small wheels and springs which he fastens around her back . . . and decides to have his wife impersonate the automat."[72] The formal structure of the comic idea thus involved transposing a social relationship (husband-wife) onto a relation of mechanical dependency (inventor-invention): the patriarchal authority of man over woman—embodied in the young hero's relation to the wife he keeps a secret—is transposed onto the dialectic between inventor and invention.[73] Wife and robot are metaphorically interchangeable in their relationship to the film's male protagonist.

The next step in scenario construction would see these displacements transplanted onto a situation defined by class, rather than gender, though this was not a step taken soon. For the time being, the "Automat Story" was abandoned to the studio's unused story files. For whatever reason, Keystone's filmmakers seem to have become uncertain about their story ideas soon after filming began on the proposed Sterling vehicle, eventually halting production in January and jettisoning the inventor premise in its entirety.[74] (The Sterling film was eventually completed in March as *A Maiden's Trust*, with an entirely new plot involving the comic misadventures of a pair of fortune hunters and a stolen necklace.) What brought the "Automat Story" back into development, in May 1917, was a need for a project that could be developed as a vehicle for one of Sennett's recent acquisitions, the screen comic Ben Turpin, signed from Mutual's "Vogue" label two months earlier at the generous starting salary of $200 a week.[75] Rather than putting Turpin to work in the studio's more prestigious two-reel productions, Sennett wanted first to test him in the single-reel "Triangle Comedies" (the cheaply produced, second-tier comedies instituted as part of the deal to release Keystone's two-reel subjects on the open market);[76] and, on May 17, Keystone's writers dusted off the "Automat Story" and redrafted it for the new comedian.

For the "Automat Story" to become a Turpin vehicle, the basic premise would have to be reconceptualized in terms of class. From his first screen appearance back in 1907 (in Essanay's *An Awful Skate*), Turpin had nurtured a distinctly proletarian screen persona, characterized by his outsize coat, battered bowler, scrawny neck, and famously crossed eyes. (Sennett himself would later recall Turpin as a "skinny, strutting little man with a Polish piano player's mane of hair and a neck like a string," and described his "special and universal appeal" as "like Chaplin's . . . the appeal of all undersized gents who stand up against Fate.")[77] By the time Turpin arrived at Keystone in the spring of 1917, his eccentric working-class characterizations had become familiar among audiences, thanks in large part to his stand-out performances as Charlie Chaplin's disheveled companion in the Essanay two-reelers *His New Job* and *A Night Out* (both 1915). Chaplin himself was quoted as describing Turpin as "one of the few really good comedians in motion pictures"; and, in June 1916, *Motography* reported that he was "conceded in the trade to be one of the best slapstick comedians in the U.S."[78]

The new version of the "Automat Story" drafted for Turpin indeed revolves around the theme of class difference. The relationship between inventor and invention, formerly projected onto gender (husband-wife), is here recast in terms of labor (boss-employee). Turpin is cast as a tramp, first seen sleeping in a garbage can. He finds temporary employment as janitor to a wealthy inventor, who enlists his services as a model for a new kind of robot, an "Automatic Man." The janitor, meanwhile, falls in love with the inventor's daughter, who is engaged to her father's young assistant. Further complications accrue when the inventor receives a "letter from the Ancient Order of the Artichokes telling him that they are sending a committee to . . . buy his wonderful invention, which he has just completed of an Automatic Man."[79] The inventor sends the janitor down to the basement to pack the invention in a box; but the janitor decides to pack *himself* up instead, thinking that he can get closer to the inventor's daughter by masquerading as the automaton. Implausibly, the disguise works: the inventor fails to notice the swap and wires the janitor to a control box. Much of the scenario's comedy centers around the ensuing scene, in which the inventor proudly displays the robot's various functions to the visiting committee, while the janitor responds by performing "all sorts of motions." In the midst of these antics, the daughter enters her father's lab and, recognizing the janitor, "denounces him" before the assembled onlookers. Believing that the inventor has been deliberately deceitful, the committee members "let out a holler at being fooled" and prepare to depart. In order to save the deal, the young assistant races downstairs, finds the real automaton, and displays it to the departing committee members, who now agree to purchase the device. The scenario ends with the union of the youthful couple and the janitor's expulsion: "Father gives [the assistant] the girl—Turpin is thrown out of window, landing in a garbage can . . . as at the opening of the picture."[80] Subsequent revisions dated May 18 introduced minor variations upon this outline, but without altering the basic narrative. Of these, the most significant was the decision to replace the committee from the "Ancient Order of the Artichokes" with a pair of theatrical entrepreneurs looking to exploit the "Motoman" as a vaudeville novelty.[81] Following these and other changes, production began on May 21 under director Herman C. Raymaker, who brought principal filming to a close just twelve days later.[82]

A Clever Dummy thus registers the spectacle of technology for a culture that had long valued imaginative intersections of technics and human biology, whether in dime novels like *The Huge Hunter* (1865) (which envisioned a ten-foot "steam man of the prairies") or in sideshow attractions such as Luna Park's 1916 exhibit "The Human Dynamo" (where a woman was bound with metal bands and charged with electricity, all in the name of "interesting experiments").[83] Yet the particular interest of this scenario lies in the way it engages this motif in relation to class. As Peter Wollen has argued, the imagery and literature about robots that springs up during this period can be understood as a figure for the position of the worker in a Taylorist system: erasing distinctions between man and machine, the fictive imagination of robots and automata offered a "metaphorical extension" of the factory worker's subjection to a rationalized system of industrial production.[84] Applied to a reading of *A Clever Dummy*, Wollen's point helps clarify the role played by the repeated slippages and alignments between human and mechanical realms. It clearly matters, in this light, that it is the janitor—rather than one of the other, more affluent characters—who provides the model for the automaton and adopts the automaton's identity as disguise. For the disguise can thus be read as the narrative figure for this metaphoric trope, suggesting a kinship between worker and robot that the film conveys early on when the janitor stands next to the "Motoman" in vivid parallel (fig. 26).

Such metaphoric overtones remain subdued, however, in a film that exploits the automaton primarily as a technological curiosity. For the janitor's adoption of a robotic disguise in fact marks a significant displacement of the film's social themes. Prior to this point in the film, the comic effect of Turpin's performance has lain chiefly in his interactions with social "betters" (hitting his boss with a brick, knocking over a top-hatted gent, etc.); henceforth, the comedy resides instead in the janitor's mechanical masquerade. The disguise changes the janitor from a social being into an abstract robotic image that, for the remainder of the film, exists primarily in the realm of the mechanical and the spectacular. This is nowhere clearer than in the film's major set piece, the inventor's demonstration of the janitor-automaton to the vaudeville impresarios: here, long shots emphasize Turpin's impersonation of a machine—a parody of the Orientalist choreography then in vogue in sophisticated circles—while the inventor is shown operating the control panel in the background. Mise-en-scène associates technical cause (the control panel) and supposed effect (the "automaton's" movements) in the production of comic displays of machine-like behavior; at the same time, a series of cutaways to the astonished theatrical magnates underscores the janitor's exclusive function as spectacle. Keystone's operational aesthetic here effectively forestalls

FIGURE 26.   Proletariat redesigned as automaton. Ben Turpin (left) and
James DeLano in a production still from *A Clever Dummy* (July 1917).
Courtesy of the Academy of Motion Picture Arts and Sciences.

the social discourse of the framing comic narrative: whereas the class dynamics of the film's earlier sequences depended principally on *narrative* action
(specifically, comic interactions across the class divide), the scene of the janitor's masquerade resides, by contrast, in *spectacle*. The flow of action is repeatedly frozen in moments of technical contemplation, as the text's operational
fascinations immobilize the janitor as pure mechanical display.

These are points to be developed shortly. For the present, analysis must
return to the film's convoluted production history. For, even though the
"Automatic Figure" story had now been shot, edited, and prepared for

shipping as a one-reel Triangle Comedy, the film described above was never released in this format. Studio politics intervened to take the film's production in an entirely new direction. Mack Sennett had, by this time, entered into negotiations with Paramount (eventually signing with them at the end of June) and was looking for ways to fulfill his contractual obligations to Triangle as quickly as possible.[85] One way to do that, he realized, was to "pad out" all of the single-reel Triangle Comedies then in production and release them as two-reel Keystone subjects. ("Try to stretch all single reelers possible into two reelers regardless of quality," Sennett instructed the new studio manager, J. A. Waldron. "[The] most essential thing now is speed and quantity.")[86] The Turpin vehicle was one of the Triangle Comedies selected for this treatment, and, on June 11, the production went back before the cameras for filming of the second reel.

This time, Keystone's filmmakers took a different approach to the comic representation of the automaton. The film's original dialectic of social comedy and technological spectacle was now recast exclusively in favor of the latter. For the film's second-reel action, Keystone's writers entirely abandoned the class dynamics of the existing footage: events in the film's final reel have nothing to do with either the janitor's interactions with the inventor or his desire for the inventor's daughter. Instead, the filmmakers exploited what had proved to be the obvious comic highpoint of the existing footage: Turpin's robotic impersonation. A new ending to the first reel was devised, in which the vaudeville magnates, unaware that the "Motoman" is really a janitor, arrange to have the device shipped to their theater for the evening show. In this way, the janitor, qua robot, is removed from the realm of labor and resituated in the realm of entertainment: the plot of the second reel requires that he continue impersonating the automaton, only this time on the stage of a crowded vaudeville house. Once again, his "act" involves a series of staccato, machine-like gestures; but, in this instance, the janitor's identity is quickly discovered, instigating a climactic donnybrook in which a mob of angry audience members chase him out of the theater and beat him up. Only in these last moments does the film's narrative fully revert to its earlier basis in class difference: the unmasking of the lowly janitor sets in motion the long-delayed cycle of humiliation and expulsion with which the proletariant must pay for his transgressions. Fade out with the janitor running off into the distance.

The film's second reel marks an evident weakening of the narrative's social discourse. For one thing, many of the film's earlier characters simply disappear: neither the inventor nor his daughter make an appearance after the first reel; instead, in what appears to have been an attempt to boost the film's marketability, the second reel surrounds Turpin at the vaudeville house with some of Keystone's best-known performers in minor roles. Chester Conklin makes a brief appearance as a theatrical property man, Wallace Beery appears as the house manager, and Juanita Hansen—among the more popular of Sennett's "Bathing Beauties"—plays a chorus girl. Where the first reel had created an integrated structure of characters defined in terms of class difference, the second offers only an atomistic, disconnected series of cameos within a theatrical setting. The pattern is further reflected in the changing articulations of space across the course of the film. The topography of the opening reel is, fundamentally, a *social* topography, organized in terms of physical distance between the classes: the inventor's laboratory is located above street level, the janitor's bed-sitter below. The two realms are, further-more, linked across the axis of class, tied to one another both in a socially normative relation of dependency (the janitor works for the inventor) and through a socially transgressive dynamic of desire (the janitor lusts after the inventor's daughter). Mediating between these spaces, the stairwell becomes a privileged site for the film's comic cross-class interactions, a liminal region in between the designations of class identity: it is here, for instance, that the janitor first declares his love to the daughter; and it is here that he devises his plot to take the automaton's place.

In all these ways, the film's social dynamics are inscribed onto the apart-ment building's very architecture. But none of this matters for the action of the second reel. The primary spatial dynamic here is defined not in *social* terms, but by the *scopic* relation between the vaudeville spectators and the "Motoman" onstage (a relation underlined in the film by cutting between the janitor's performance and the audience's enthusiastic response). Again, that topography is traversed by desire; only, here, the desire takes the form of technical fascination, of the audience's operational interest in mechani-cal invention. The vertical, upstairs-downstairs dynamic of the film's initial narrative situation has been replaced by the lateral dynamic of theatrical dis-play. The passage between the reels thus unfolds a series of displacements—a displacement in the worker's identity (from employee to automaton), a displacement in the worker's function (from instrument of labor to vaude-ville attraction), and a displacement in space (from workplace to the realm of entertainment). The force of Keystone's operational aesthetic thus reveals itself in the act of shutting down the narrative momentum of the film's opening reel, plucking the janitor out of his social context, and repo-sitioning him as a theatrical novelty: all that remains, following the move to the vaudeville house, is the comedy of the robotic dance and the discovery of the janitor's imposture.

For over eight months, Keystone's writers had struggled with different narrative situations and roles for a comic automaton, choosing in the end simply to foreground its appeal as a technological curiosity. The resulting film, like its production history, traces a transition from social comedy to the comedy of mechanical contrivance; it is divided upon this transformation and by the displacements it entails, substituting the comic attraction of an automatic man for a comic situation of class conflict. Looked at this way, the film provides an almost diagrammatic illustration, in microcosm, of the broader transformation in Keystone's output that this chapter has described: for, insofar as Keystone made mechanization one of its privileged themes, it also partook of the integrative schema of an emergent mass culture that, as later outlined by Adorno, evaded representations of social conflict by directing its energies toward "mechanical and astonishing display."[87]

In Keystone's comedies, as in the broader cultural context, the operational aesthetic formed an inevitable part of the self-expression of a society both committed to technological progress and disturbed by its consequences. Submarines could be made funny, but only by disavowing the trauma and devastation of modern warfare. Janitors could be funny too, only more for their resemblance to automata than as emblems of class difference. Keystone's comedies thus provide a kind of advance figure for the ideological conservatism that would flourish in American film following the country's entry into World War I (in April 1917), when an unprecedented interest in military machinery existed side by side with fears of Bolshevism at home and renewed government attempts to suppress "unpatriotic" representations of class difference.[88] The context of technological devastation and conservative reactionism that would mark America's experience of the war was already presaged in the technicist fascinations of modernity, of which Keystone's mechanical contrivances were such vivid symptoms. Indeed, technology is so vivaciously celebrated in Keystone's later comedies that the necessary political criticism is almost too obvious to need making. "Uproarious inventions" provided Keystone's filmmakers with a means of satisfying collective desires, but they did so by mystifying technological process and obfuscating the material social differences on which the new mass culture was founded. Not only did they update the "old slapstick effect" formerly achieved with the "familiar pie," as one critic wrote; they also uprooted the American slapstick tradition from its origins in popular, working-class culture and experience. Still, it would be on the issue of gender that the studio's engagement with mass culture would effect its most profound transformations, and it is to this that I now turn.

6. From "Diving Venus" to "Bathing Beauties"

Reification and Feminine Spectacle,
1916–1917

> The modern bathing suit . . . symbolized the new status of women
> even more than the short skirts and bobbed hair of the jazz age or
> the athleticism of the devotees of tennis and golf. It was the final
> proof of their successful assertion of the right to enjoy whatever
> recreation they chose, costumed according to the demands of the
> sport rather than the tabus of an outworn prudery, and to enjoy it
> in free and natural association with men.
>
> FOSTER RHEA DULLES, America Learns to *Play* (1940)

The story behind Keystone's Bathing Beauties was one of Mack Sennett's
favorites. As he told the tale in later years, inspiration came from a newspaper
some time in the mid-1910s. "One morning as I went through the *Times*,"
he recalled, "I noticed a three-column picture on Page One of a pretty girl
who had been involved in a minor traffic accident. The picture made the
front page for two obvious and attractive reasons. The young lady's knees
were showing. . . . I called in the staff. 'Boys, take a look at this. This is how
to get our pictures in the papers. Go hire some girls, any girls, so long as
they're pretty. Especially around the knees. . . . ' When we had the girls, we
posed them with our comedians. . . . The results were highly satisfactory.
Mack Sennett pictures began to get more space in the press than all the studios in Hollywood combined." The next step was to feature the women in
the studio's films: " 'Get those kids on the screen,' I told our people. 'Sure, I
know they can't act, but they don't have to act. Put them in bathing suits
and just have them around to be looked at while the comics are making
funny."[1] The Mack Sennett Bathing Beauties had been born.

Whether it happened exactly this way is unclear. What is certain is that
the Beauties were primarily important to Keystone as publicity tools.
Convinced, by late 1916, of the need to extricate his product from Triangle's
dwindling fortunes, Sennett seized on the Bathing Beauties as a means of
bolstering exhibitor loyalty to Keystone during this troubled period. In

April 1917, the studio's promotional newsletter, the *Mack Sennett Weekly*, began encouraging exhibitors to create lobby displays featuring "photographs of Keystone girls taken on the beach"; and similar images soon made their way into trade advertisements promising "A Splash of Beauty" in every Keystone comedy (fig. 27).[2] Yet the extraordinary success of this campaign had consequences that outstripped the needs of product placement, contributing to the Beauties' popularization as icons of modern femininity. Although other companies were quick to jump on Keystone's bandwagon—witness, for example, Fox Comedies' "Sunshine Girls"—it would be the Bathing Beauties who took strongest hold on the public imagination, even inspiring a song in 1919 titled "Help, Help, Mr. Sennett (I'm Drowning in a Sea of Love)."[3] As a basis for newspaper illustrations and promotional displays, images of Keystone's bathing-suited girls were widely circulated and brought the Beauties off the cinema screens and into the hands and imaginations of individuals, who could amass their own private collections. They even drew praise from Theodore Dreiser, who described them as "a national and even international feature—the only successful rival[s] . . . to Mr. Ziegfeld and his Follies Girls that [have] ever appeared in America or elsewhere."[4]

There were good reasons why the Beauties became the nationally recognized face of Sennett's comedies during this period. The years immediately prior to America's entry into World War I marked a high tide in the expansion of corporate advertising campaigns, and the Beauties were clearly part of that development. In particular, they registered the growth of advertising practices in which female beauty was exploited as a strategy for creating brands and projecting corporate identities.[5] To the extent that Keystone participated in this process, it helped popularize a consumerist imagery of youthful womanhood that defined women's appropriate role as that of decorative, titillating spectacle. At a time when cultural formulations of femininity were being redefined through the figure of the "New Woman," Keystone's bathing girl publicity translated changing paradigms of female behavior into commercial spectacle and relegated women's modernity to the realm of beauty and fashion aids.

This final chapter thus builds on the argument, advanced throughout *The Fun Factory*, that popular, working-class comic traditions were decisively transformed by their encounter with, and participation in, the reifying pressures of an emergent mass culture. But it departs from the book's overall chronological framework to examine female comic performance across the entirety of Keystone's five-year career, recapping the major terms of my argument through a single case history. What images of womanhood

FIGURE 27. "A Splash of Beauty," trade press advertisement for Keystone. From *Motion Picture News,* May 26, 1917. Courtesy of the Academy of Motion Picture Arts and Sciences.

had preceded the Beauties at Keystone? What kinds of experience did those images interpret and how did they change? These are questions that lead again to the issue of class, this time in its changing significance for Keystone's depictions of gender; but they also require examining how Keystone's comediennes were associated with radical shifts in women's roles in turn-of-the-century American society. If, as recent scholars have suggested, female comic performance has served historically to express alternative models of femininity, then Keystone's "funny ladies" offer a particularly rich site for exploring how modern conceptions of femininity played out on cinema screens of the 1910s.[6] What their performances revealed, however, was perhaps less the freedom of women "to enjoy whatever recreation they chose"—as Foster Rhea Dulles puts it—than the limitations of female modernity within the space of a new consumer society.

"WILD AND POOR": MABEL NORMAND, THE NEW WOMAN, AND WORKING-CLASS CULTURE

Such issues lead to the thorny concept of the "New Woman," a term first popularized by Henry James in the 1880s and that referred, initially, to affluent, college-educated women who rejected conventions, marrying late, and often pursuing social causes outside the home.[7] A sign of profound change regarding the practice of separate spheres for the sexes, the New Woman represented a break with the Victorian ideology of "true womanhood" and its accompanying precepts of domesticity, purity, and moral guardianship: whereas traditional discourse sacralized the duties of housework and childcare, the New Woman expanded the notion of women's place, charting new paths leading out of the privatized household. Whereas the "true woman" was emotionally invested in homosocial relationships within her class, the New Woman began to express new attitudes to sexuality, forming heterosocial (that is, mixed-sex) relationships both at the workplace and at new sites of commercial leisure. As America moved into modernity, a sentimental ideology of female dependence thus shifted to a cultural image of female autonomy. "The energetic, independent woman of culture is frequently caricatured as the 'New Woman,'" commented one writer in 1902. "The key-note of her character is self-reliance and the power of initiation. She aims at being in direct contact with reality and forming her own judgement upon it."[8]

A popular buzz-image, the New Woman nonetheless remained a nebulous concept within discourse of the time, and it has been left to contemporary women's historians to return it to precision. For one thing, the label was applied to two successive generations, differing from each other in critical ways: on the one hand, those women who attended colleges in the 1870s and 1880s and invested their energies into feminist issues and social activism; on the other, those who came into their own in the years around World War I and placed greater emphasis on personal flamboyance and self-fulfillment, repudiating bourgeois sexual norms to become pals in companionate marriages.[9] Further complications have been uncovered by historians who address questions of class formation. Was the New Woman a function of a consumer culture that, as Sumiko Higashi argues, invited middle-class women into palatial department stores where they learned to abandon economic reserve for the pleasures of consumer spending?[10] Or was she, as Margaret Gibbons Wilson avers, primarily a symptom of a growing white-collar employment sector that offered respectable career paths for young women?[11] Significantly, Wilson assumes that such jobs would have been taken by middle-class women, although research exists to suggest that white-collar female workers were more likely the daughters of immigrant, blue-collar families.[12] Does it make sense, then, to view the New Woman simply as a phenomenon of the "affluent new bourgeoisie," as Carroll Smith-Rosenberg claims?[13] Or did lower-class, immigrant women, as Kathy Peiss contends, contribute to changes in gender roles by participating in a heterosocial culture centered around the new world of dance halls, amusements parks, and other commercialized amusements?[14]

One way in which these complexities were voiced at the time was through the era's fascination with multiple images of the American woman. The development of a manifold and contradictory iconography of female "types" spoke to the profound alterations of meaning that were taking place, pointing to new forms of femininity in the throes of being born. There was, of course, the free-spirited Gibson Girl, as penned by illustrator Charles Dana Gibson; generally depicted in upper-class surroundings and engaged in high society pursuits, the Gibson Girl graced the pages of "quality" magazines targeting a similar class of readership, such as *Life, Harper's Weekly,* and *Collier's.* There was also the Chorus Girl, the glamorous embodiment of modern girlhood displayed in the cabaret revues that prospered in the mid-1910s; generally coming from poor families, Chorus Girls nurtured the Cinderella myth of the single working woman on her way to a life of theatrical fame and wealthy admirers.[15] Technological advances in the printing industry, a surge of new magazines and papers, and the growth of promotional techniques in advertisements and posters contributed countless other types to the list. (Martha Banta lists the "New England Woman," the "Beautiful Charmer," and the

"Outdoors Pal"—her own labels—as three further variations in the cultural imagery of modern womanhood.)[16] Small wonder that commentators of the time had trouble identifying the New Woman with any precision. "Which Is the American Princess?" the *New York Journal* asked in 1896, above an image that paired "Gertrude Vanderbilt, of Fifth Avenue" with "Bertha Krieg, of the Bowery." Was it Miss Vanderbilt, the "millionaire's child," described in the accompanying article as charitable, accomplished, and "above all, thoroughly American"? Or was it Bertha, a second-generation immigrant, "who is contented with her lot and does not envy Miss Vanderbilt a bit"?[17] The point, of course, was that there was no answer. Changes in turn-of-the-century womanhood were emerging from a multifaceted set of interactions across the socioeconomic sphere, drawing energies from different centers of gravity within different class cultures.

A case in point can be found in the sporting activities and physical culture that infused modern gender ideals. A sign of instability in Victorian constructions of femininity, women's new interests in sports threatened the model of separate spheres by transplanting the arena of female accomplishment from the spiritual realm to the physical, and, in so doing, provoked a reactionary discourse that sought to convince women that exercise was a threat to their biological inheritance. Contemporary fiction, magazine articles, and medical discourse voiced a chorus of fears that sports would leave women with masculinized bodies or, worse still, crush their uteri and threaten their reproductive capacities. ("Are athletics a menace to motherhood?" a magazine article asked in 1912.)[18] Yet despite such fears, the popularization of female athletic pursuits cut across social divisions, unifying women in a burgeoning physical culture in which all classes could participate. By the 1870s and 1880s, schools and colleges were teaching physical education to the daughters of middle-class families, and, by the turn of the century, many working-class women were regularly exercising at gymnastic facilities offered at factory plants and YWCAs.[19] For young women across the social spectrum, the growth of female physical culture not only provided a means to keep healthy, it became a way of affirming their refusal of traditional gender norms and participating in a modernizing process. Women's sporting activities thus came to imply solidarity with cultural narratives of female modernity.

But it would be in the growth of women's aquatic pursuits—both swimming and bathing—that turn-of-the-century culture found its most loaded symbols of the athletic female body. In their confident affirmation of the female body, the new figure-hugging swimsuits and short-skirted bathing costumes became embedded in the very concept of New

Womanhood.[20] In a short story of the time, for example, the female protagonist wears a "bathing suit so scanty it seemed a mere gesture flung . . . to the proprieties" and describes herself as a modern woman; in another, the villainess sits on the beach wearing an old-fashioned taffeta costume, while the heroine wears a one-piece suit and splashes around in the water.[21] But the image of the bathing girl also highlighted links between the era's iconography of female modernity and the cultural practices of young working women. As several scholars have suggested, the popularization of recreational bathing drew energies from wage-earning women who articulated personal style through the bodily freedoms and expressiveness encouraged in the realm of commercial leisure.[22] Claudia Kidwell suggests that a "trickle-up" theory of fashion is needed to account for developments in bathing costumes during this period, and other scholars have concurred, noting the role of working women in popularizing the modern sensibilities of sports clothing.[23] In the new world of amusement parks and seaside resorts, young working women led the way in embracing more daring fashions, prompting concerns among middle-class reformers who passed ordinances governing appropriate bathing costumes. Those too poor to afford their own swimwear could rent the latest styles—as early as 1880, Coney Island had installed a laundry for the thousands of bathing suits rented each day. In an age demanding symbols of modern womanhood, the new amusement resorts also supplied postcard images of young women posed coquettishly in bathing gear. A stereoscopic view of 1897 titled "Ah, There! Coney Island" featured five young ladies raising the hems of their bathing dresses and playfully thrusting out their buttocks, a far cry from the standards of decorum expected of middle-class women.[24]

There were ambiguities here, to be sure, for such images naturally played to male erotic interests, a fact that sensational sex-and-sports journals like the *National Police Gazette* exploited in numerous cover photos of women athletes in one-piece swimsuits. Touring vaudeville shows likewise appropriated the bathing girl to patriarchal discourse, in chorus lines displaying the bodies of "diving nymphs" or "diving belles" on the pretext of athletic display. Thus the figure of the bathing girl that played such a central role in working-class perceptions of New Womanhood was far from being an innocent or consensually unproblematic category. The key to its popularity arguably depended on its capacity to address different needs based on gender and sexuality—both working women's desire to assert their modernity and working men's heterosexual interests—and to unite them in a figure firmly grounded in the vibrant plebeian culture of beaches, burlesque, and amusement parks.

One who knew that culture well was Mabel Normand, a founding member of Keystone and a star whose popularity proved a key factor in the studio's initial success. Born into a carpenter's family in 1893, Normand grew up on Staten Island in conditions that Mack Sennett later recalled as having been "wild and poor."[25] According to her biographers, Normand was, from her early teens, a devotee of the working-class world of popular amusements, regularly frequenting cheap vaudeville houses and dance halls and, apparently, picking up several medals in amateur swimming contests.[26] (Her class environment was something she shared with many of Keystone's early comediennes: Minta Durfee, for example, was the daughter of a railroad brakeman and a seamstress; Marie Dressler apparently supported her immigrant parents by entering the workforce at the age of thirteen.)[27] For Normand, however, the path of economic necessity intersected early with a burgeoning visual culture responsible for the era's most paradigmatic icons of modern womanhood. After finding employment during her teens as a model in New York, Normand worked for several famous illustrators—James Montgomery Flagg, Penrhyn Stanlaws, and even Charles Dana Gibson, for whose "Gibson Girl" illustrations she posed several times. She also made money posing for newspaper advertisements and modeling in fashion shows for local department stores.[28]

At once a skilled swimmer and an experienced model, Normand was a harbinger for Keystone's later publicity practices. The "Bathing Beauty" campaign launched in 1917 was not, in fact, unrehearsed. In 1912, when the fledgling studio was first trying to drum up enthusiasm for its output, Keystone had promoted Normand as the "beautiful Diving Venus" circulating advertisements showing her in a one-piece swimsuit (as popularized by Annette Kellerman) (fig. 28).[29] True, Keystone was hardly the first studio to profit from Normand's aquatic abilities—her debut appearance for Biograph had been in the titular role of D. W. Griffith's *The Diving Girl* (1911)—but it was the first to market her films in those terms, openly promoting Normand's appearances as vehicles for "graceful diving feats."[30] Fan magazines responded in kind, praising Normand as "one of the most popular actresses on the picture stage and also one of the most shapely" and "a wonderful swimmer."[31]

Her very first role in a Keystone film—*The Water Nymph* (September 1912)—is important in this analysis. Not only does it provide a cameo of Normand's screen persona, it also indicates how the forms and practices of working women's culture could be translated into comic spectacle. In essence, the film's basic situation unfolds as a type of prank narrative common to Keystone's early output.[32] A young man (Sennett) persuades

FIGURE 28. Trade press advertisement for Keystone. From *Moving Picture World*, September 14, 1912.

FIGURE 29. Frame enlargements from *The Water Nymph* (September 1912). Mabel displays her acrobatic dives, and father tries to show off. Courtesy of the UCLA Film and Television Archive.

his fiancée (Normand) to flirt with his lecherous father (Sterling) at the beach before introducing her to his parents; when the young woman's identity is subsequently revealed, the embarrassed father immediately assents to his son's engagement. Although questions of social class are not explicitly addressed, details of costuming indicate some kind of middle-class status for the protagonists: the son, for example, sports a light summer suit, and the father, a frock coat and bow tie. The seaside excursion thus becomes a situation freighted with social uncertainties, in which the coherence of the middle-class family is tested by its association with the free and easy sexuality of working-class beach culture. The lures of erotic opportunity swiftly disrupt the family unit when the father sneaks off in amorous pursuit of bathing girls.

That pursuit leads to a confrontation with the female body, in which the father watches Mabel performing acrobatic dives off the pier and tries to match her with his own diving "skills." Consisting of thirteen shots, the pier sequence—structurally and thematically the centerpiece of the film—juxtaposes Mabel's athleticism and poise with the father's uncoordinated pomposity (fig. 29).[33] By foolishly attempting to emulate Mabel's accomplishments, the father undermines his own authority and makes himself a laughing stock for Mabel's bathing chums. Bound in a web of visual power, Mabel has used her athleticism to reverse its terms, making a spectacle of the gazer.[34] The bathing girl becomes the emblem of a new world of popular amusements in which the genteel paterfamilias can participate only at the cost of humiliation.

The principle would be repeated in Normand's subsequent appearance as Keystone's "Diving Venus," *Mabel's Lovers* (November 1912). As

Moving Picture World's summary of this lost film suggests, Mabel again turns the tables on her voyeurs, this time appearing with "welts inside her stockings, as she walks along the beach, in order to get rid of all her admirers but one."[35] The ambiguity of the bathing girl—at once a symbol of women's modernity and an object of male erotic interest—is here resolved in favor of the former, as Mabel wards off untoward advances and selects her own partner. Taken together, the two films suggest clearly how Normand's early seaside roles went beyond the cheesecake publicity to which the later Bathing Beauties would be submitted, engaging instead with the comic implications of changing gender roles. The new visibility of women who participated in a heterosocial public sphere certainly subjected them to voyeuristic predations—and no doubt Normand's "Diving Venus" persona appealed to heterosexual male audiences in a similar way—but the star's earliest roles also depicted quick-thinking women who devise comic strategies against such harassment, opening up an arena in which the complexities of women's modernity could be negotiated with laughter.

But this was only an initial step in a career that, during her first few years at Keystone, would establish a unique cinematic template for modern femininity. Normand's initial appearances as the "Diving Venus" were soon superseded by rough-and-tumble portrayals of working-class womanhood that became the cornerstone of her stardom. And, in the process, she put paid to one of the most cherished tenets of traditional patriarchal discourse: that pretty women could not be funny.

"A SLAP FROM A PERFUMED HAND": THE SCREEN COMEDY OF MABEL NORMAND

The decidedly physical nature of slapstick comedy made it an apposite site for exploring changing patterns of gendered behavior. As Peter Stallybrass and Allon White observe, it is in terms of the body that social categories are defined and imposed, and the task of understanding social change tends, in consequence, to focus upon physical symbols ("the elements of social classification itself").[36] The point is doubly appropriate for considering turn-of-the-century discourse on gendered change. For the New Woman had defined herself, in large part, by reclaiming the right to her own embodiment against the morally and spiritually defined—hence quintessentially *dis*embodied—ideal of true womanhood. Hence, the growth of women's sporting pursuits; hence, the flamboyance and flirtations encouraged in the new world of commercial recreation. And hence, too, the growing number of female performers who openly proclaimed their sensuous physicality on the stages of vaudeville theaters, burlesque houses, and cabaret revues. The dominant female ideal of early twentieth-century vaudeville took shape in a cohort of ragtime divas who combined self-command with representations of female material aspiration and libidinal desire. In the early 1900s, Eva Tanguay had brought brassy sexuality onto the stage with songs such as "I Want Some One to Go Wild with Me" and "Go as Far as You Like"; and, as vaudeville entered its period of greatest expansion in the 1910s, the number of female performers grew too, yielding such comic headliners as Elsie Janis, Sophie Tucker (the "Last of the Red Hot Mamas"), and, of course, Mae West.[37]

The phenomenon of female comic performance contributed to the somatic iconography through which gendered change was understood. We see this in Tanguay's performances of the time, in which she would shimmy on stage, singing her theme song: "I don't care! I don't care! what they may think of me." Female comicality—especially in its slapstick dimensions—offered potent symbols of gender disorder, and was viewed by conservative observers as an alarming prospect. To laugh at a woman was a refusal of the respect required by her traditional virtues. "Woman is rarely ridiculed in comedy," a *Moving Picture World* editorial declared. "It does not please the better class to see her held up to scorn."[38] Even female writers spoke critically of women who "imitate the facetiousness of men," denouncing their performances as beyond the pale of societal norms.[39] The dominant female ideal of Victorian culture had emphasized feminine spirituality and transcendence, bracketing off the body as a locus of woman's self-expression: female comic performance upset such distinctions, proposing instead a species of bodily excess, a grotesque negation of the nurturing qualities that informed sentimental ideals of womanhood.

It was precisely in their handling of gender that Keystone films proved most vulnerable to the repressive agenda of industry censors, showing again how class-based concerns about "low" slapstick were enmeshed with gendered discourses of respectability. Straightforward evidence for this is found in the actions of Chicago's police censorship board, which, between March 1914 and January 1916, regularly published its reports in the pages of the *Chicago Tribune*. During this period, the board demanded cuts in forty-eight Keystone films, at least twenty-one of which concerned the comic depiction of women. The lengthy report on *Tillie's Punctured Romance* reads like a litany of the offences for which Keystone was routinely penalized, demanding the excision of "All scenes of men kicking women and vice versa; all scenes of woman bumping into men and women; two scenes of man wiggling back in vulgar manner; man poking girl with cane in vulgar manner; man lifting tail of girl's coat in suggestive manner; woman lifting her dress to above knees; man lifting girl's dress to above her knees; . . . girl falling over couch and exposing her legs; woman doing wiggle dance; man kicking woman in abdomen; subtitle: 'The effect of Tillie's first drink.' "[40]

Yet direct censorship was only one strategy for regulating female comicality. Elsewhere—including in the pages of movie magazines—funny ladies were frequently disparaged as an aberration from standards of true womanhood, their comic performances regarded as proofs of biological deficiency or dubious female identity.[41] Women, from this perspective, could be objects of laughter only to the extent that they lacked qualities more "appropriate" to their sex, a pervasive attitude that even shaped the experiences of the comediennes themselves. For Marie Dressler, for instance, the decision to enter comedy stemmed from the painful self-awareness of her own unattractiveness: "[I]t was pleasanter to have folks laugh at you than to have them ignore you. . . . I deliberately began to imitate a yearling in a china shop. And I basked in the sunshine of the laughter and attention I drew."[42] At Keystone, it was enough for a woman to be large-boned or corpulent for her to become a comic foil: Phyllis Allen and Alice Davenport were examples of the type during the studio's Mutual period; and Blanche Payson, a former policewoman, would join their ranks at Triangle. Studio publicity on Payson implied that her outsize proportions made her unfit for male desire. "She is 6 feet 4 inches tall, and weighs 234 pounds," noted an article in *The Triangle,* adding: "She is single and lives with her mother and two brothers."[43] Such assumptions further shaped the kinds of roles in which these women appeared—petticoat tyrants and Amazonian battleaxes whose mannish demeanor and atrophied sexuality tied their comic meaning to the specter of gender abnormality.

Female comicality thus indicated a problem in the female body itself. Signifying contradictions in the Victorian construction of gender, the female clown suggested both a bodily excess (a negation of the spiritual standards that informed sentimental ideals of womanhood) *and* a bodily lack (a failure to match up to normative standards of beauty). In Bakhtinian terms, the body of the comedienne served as a species of the "grotesque," defined in contrast with the "classical" body of the true woman.[44] This straightforward antinomy permitted women to be laughable only to the extent that they deviated from specific gender norms; yet it reinforced those norms by implying that it was only their transgression that deserved laughter, not the norms themselves. Normand's significance in this context lay in her ability to go beyond these antinomies, to yoke her beauty *to* her comicality, and to fuse both in a violently physical performative style. She was, as fan magazines were fond of pointing out, "pretty, shapely, and talented"; but she also participated freely in scenes of out-and-out knockabout, whether receiving a pie in the face (in *That Ragtime Band*, May 1913), punching a man in the jaw (in *Barney Oldfield's Race for a Life*, June 1913), throwing herself into an all-out fistfight (in *Mabel's Busy Day*, June 1914), or tumbling around in her pajamas with her drunken husband (in *Mabel's Married Life*, June 1914).[45] "Philosophers who write on feminine psychology on the women's page of daily papers tell us we must not expect to find a pretty woman with a sense of humor," the *New York Telegraph* noted in 1916. "In living refutation of these theories is Mabel Normand . . . [who has] proved to the world in general that it is quite as possible to laugh at a pretty woman as to sigh for her."[46] Her screen persona thus offered a heterodox merging of elements typically perceived as incompatible: at once "classical" (in her beauty) and "grotesque" (in her slapstick), Normand's screen image unsettled the binarism that sought to contain the spectacle of female comicality. For writers of the time, Normand became an object of fascination *precisely* as such a hybrid: in *Photoplay*, Julian Johnson lyrically called her screen persona "a kiss that explodes in a laugh; cherry bon-bons in a clown's cap; sharing a cream puff from your best girl; a slap from a perfumed hand; the sugar on the Keystone grapefruit."[47]

As Normand herself knew perhaps best of all, it was this paradox that distinguished her from other comic actresses of the era. Asked once whether it was hard for a woman to succeed in film comedy, Normand distinguished her own achievements from those of "pretty girls" who, as she put it, "are content to be merely pretty." "Anyone who photographs well," Normand noted, "can walk on a scene and flirt with the comedian which is all that most good-looking girls are required to do in comedies. It takes very little ability on their part for all they have to do is follow direction. . . . But to make a farce heroine more than a mere doll, you must think out the situation yourself."[48] Her own self-directed films reflect this assessment, containing some of the most violent scenes of any of her Keystone appearances.[49] *Mabel's Busy Day* is a notable example, climaxing with a minute-long free-for-all in which Mabel, Chaplin's tramp, and a policeman (Chester Conklin) kick, punch, and throw things at each other. ("The usual strenuous work of the Keystone artists," noted a review of the film, "almost makes the screen on which it is thrown visibly wobble.")[50] Certainly, Normand's enthusiasm for this kind of performance provides a context for understanding the formal properties of her early directing work, much of which indicates a greater concern for slapstick spectacle than narrative coherence. Although the first three of her self-directed films are lost, trade press commentary suggests a consistent foregrounding of physical action over story logic: *Mabel's Stormy Love Affair* (January 1914) was an "eccentric comedy offering" with "not quite enough plot"; *Won in a Closet* (January 1914) was "a nonsense number"; and *Mabel's Bear Escape* (January 1914) was "truly a scream," especially during a sequence featuring "Mabel Normand's being chased by a very lively bear."[51] Again, though, it is in *Mabel's Busy Day* that these tendencies reach their fullest expression, shaping a unique formal structure in which scenes of narrative development and sequences of sheer slapstick alternate in counterpoint, following independent trajectories that intersect only in the climactic chase. As is typical of Keystone films of the period, the plot itself is modest: Mabel arrives at a racetrack to sell hotdogs and Charlie robs her of her wares. Structurally, the film cuts between two distinct types of scene: studio-shot sequences that bear the narrative burden; and location footage in which Chaplin and Normand, both in character, perform solo comic turns before actual crowds at a racetrack—simply dashing hither and thither, assaulting policemen and troublesome bystanders (presumably played by actors), and so forth. The result is a discontinuous patterning—both formally, in the pronounced shifts between scenes of plot development and bursts of nonintegrated physical spectacle, and stylistically, in the alternation of studio sets and location scenes. Removed from the demands of story development, the location footage becomes a space in which Normand and Chaplin give free rein to their slapstick abilities.

What is revealed in *Mabel's Busy Day* is a sense of Normand's willingness to shape a comic structure that showcased her own roughhouse antics in parity with those of her male co-stars. But it also contains clues about the specific social dimension of Normand's comedy. Like a number of Keystone's location-shot pictures—Chaplin's *Kid Auto Races* (February 1914) is a famous example—the costuming of the comic leads here blends with the milieu of the everyday people who observe them. The interactions between performers and the racetrack crowds consequently imply a social symbiosis that grounds the comedy in the realities of popular culture, directly engaging the horizon of experience of lower-class moviegoers who constituted Keystone's major audience at this time. As such, *Mabel's Busy Day* explicitly figures a complicity with working-class culture in its setting that is also evident elsewhere in Normand's comedy. Certainly, young wage-earning women who attended nickelodeons during these years would have found much to relate to in Normand's performances. The star's early screen vehicles repeatedly construct narratives that exploit her persona as a young working girl: to cite a handful of examples, she appears as a laundry worker in *The Riot* (August 1913), a domestic servant in *Mabel's Dramatic Career* (September 1913), the careworn wife of a drunken no-good in *Mabel's Married Life*, and an out-of-work maid in *Mabel's Latest Prank* (September 1914). The tendency is particularly marked during 1914: out of the thirty-one films in which she appeared that year, at least eight can be identified in which she portrays a poor working girl, two in which her character holds a low-rung office job, and two in which she appears as a simple country maid.[52] Several of her 1914 films—*The Fatal Mallet, Mabel's Married Life, Mabel's Latest Prank*, and *Gentlemen of Nerve* (October 1914)—translate working women's heterosocial culture into comic form, placing Normand in mixed-sex settings (most often public parks) where she contends against the advances of assorted "mashers."[53] Sennett himself commented upon the social dimension of Normand's screen roles in his autobiography, observing that she "was always shown on the screen as a comely girl, usually poor and unfashionable."[54]

Normand's performances from this period can, and have been, glibly labeled "subversive." More relevant, though, is to define that label in terms of the star's social appeal: after all, over a quarter million *Photoplay* readers voted her their favorite film personality in 1914—and the magazine at that time seems to have drawn a substantial female working-class readership.[55] (By contrast, in a similar poll conducted the same year in *Motion Picture Magazine*—a fan periodical whose content was geared more to middle-class tastes—Normand ranked much lower, in forty-first place.)[56] The case can, in fact, be made that working women identified with Normand's screen persona precisely as an emblem of their own cultural values and experiences, a star in whom the boisterous, flamboyant assertiveness of working-class femininity was hypostasized in her unrestrained, knockabout performance style.[57] There seems, for example, to have been particularly deep public investment in Normand's films in Rhode Island, where a measure of local celebrity (she had family in the state) likely made Normand a powerful symbol for the identifications of female moviegoers.[58] A specific example would be the Star Theatre in the textile mill town of Pawtucket, where the majority of the population were either foreign or born of foreign or mixed parents, where women seem to have comprised nearly half the labor force, and where Normand's films were unusually prominent from late 1912 through much of 1913. Star Theatre publicity routinely identified films in which she appeared as "Mabel comedies" (e.g., *That Ragtime Band*, which was promoted as an "uproariously funny new Mabel comedy," despite Ford Sterling's lead performance), while press reviews commonly indicated the intensity of audience response to her films (e.g., *Mabel's Adventures* "had the audience in screams"; *Mabel's Awful Mistake* was judged "the funniest of all the Mabel comedies").[59]

Outside of her films, fan magazines offered a further avenue for movie-goers to engage with the qualities Normand displayed in her screen roles. From early on, trade press interviews and promotional pieces constructed her star persona in opposition to sentimental ideologies of womanhood. "What's the use of making plans to go places or marry people," Normand was quoted as saying, "when like as not you will have to write a note saying, 'Excuse me. I did want to become your blushing bride today, but it's no go.'"[60] In the face of reactionary fears about the health costs of women's physical activities, fans were repeatedly told of the skill and stamina she displayed as a participant in Keystone's trademark knockabout. "Mabel says she is going to offer a prize to anyone who can think up something [Keystone's filmmakers] haven't made her do," *Photoplay* noted in October 1913. "She has been run over with everything possible, and dropped off of everything, and has been tied to trees and clocks, shot at, and dumped out of any number of boats in all kinds of water—so what in the world is left to be done?"[61] In a way that was elemental to the early star system, Normand was also said to exhibit the same athleticism in her off-camera activities as was required of her at Keystone. Thus, she was said to be an "in her element behind the wheel of a fast car" and, in May 1914, was reported to have taken part in a competitive auto race in Los Angeles's Ascot Park.[62] In every instance, Normand's ethos of derring-do conveyed the value of adventure as a pleasurable end in itself, rather than a warning about female overexertion. "As might be expected, this clever comedienne puts as much ginger into managing her car as she does into her fun-making before the camera," *Reel Life* proclaimed in November 1914. "To keep a moderate pace in anything she does is a temperamental impossibility for Miss Normand."[63]

But the specific social dimensions of Normand's appeal were nowhere more apparent than in her widely reported decision, in the spring of 1913, to campaign for the Socialist ticket through appearances before working-class audiences at Los Angeles's nickelodeons. "Miss Mabel Normand, said to be the most popular woman in the 'movie' acting profession, is an avowed Socialist," declared the *Los Angeles Citizen*, the local labor journal. "And to prove this, she intends to take the stump for the Socialists during the Los Angeles campaign."[64] Exemplifying the lines of intersection through which popular culture occasionally impinged upon class politics, Normand's association with nonconformist models of femininity was here parlayed into active lobbying for social change. Available evidence indicates that Normand may, in fact, have spoken directly on the issue of women's suffrage. A *Photoplay* issue from the period quotes from a letter she had supposedly written about her campaign experiences: "[B]elieve me, I am getting to be some speech maker. I have been making impromptu speeches at all of the picture houses in Southern California and feel very proud of myself. I really think when women's suffrage invades California I shall run for mayor of Los Angeles on the suffrage ticket."[65] In such reports, one glimpses the potential political force that Normand possessed during her early years at Keystone. Conflating feminine beauty with comic vulgarity, her star persona channeled this heterodoxy into violent, nonconformist depictions of gender and class. That she appealed to young working women who were themselves experimenting with new cultural forms is not surprising; that her appeal transformed so quickly in subsequent years merits further investigation.

. . .

For roughly the first half of her Keystone career, Normand had given boisterous expression to the flamboyant physicality of working-class women's culture; then, beginning around 1915, a combination of personal and professional motives led to significant career changes, substantially transforming her star persona and the roles she played. One possible factor behind those transformations was Normand's own class background, which seems to have left her with a symptomatic desire for self-improvement. As Mack Sennett recalled, she "became studious" during her time at Keystone and began to seek out "the handful of people in the motion-picture business who were reasonably literate."[66] These changes in Normand's lifestyle soon filtered into fan discourse. Celebrity profiles now downplayed Normand's boisterous athleticism, emphasizing instead her interests in high culture, from German philosophy and opera to the Ballet Russe and Comédie-Française.[67] Where once her stardom had emblematized the practices and experiences of her working-class female fans, it now spoke to their dreams of upward mobility. What was demonstrated, in the process, was the malleability of class identity in a culture that had come to equate refinement with commodity goods. Now, for example, her fans could read that "[c]ollecting odd bits of furniture is one of Miss Normand's hobbies" and that she lived in a "big, two-story house in semi-colonial style."[68] They also learned that she was a devotee of polo, having received a gift of "a famous polo pony once owned by Lord Tweedmouth."[69]

The impulses that drove Normand toward the pursuit of self-culture also transformed her attitude to film comedy. Already by 1915, she was voicing hopes for "improvements" in film comedy. "The comedy of four or five years ago was a very different affair from those made today," Normand observed in a *Photoplay* interview, "but I think there is still plenty of room for improvement, and the next few years will witness as great a development."[70] Within months those aspirations seem to have coalesced around the genteel ideal of narrative-based, or "situation," comedy. "More Plots and Fewer Pies for Miss Normand," a February 1916 newspaper article announced, quoting her hope "that all the pictures we do in the future will have plots."[71] In what appears to have been an implicit renouncement of her previous work for Keystone, Normand now claimed to be "tired of slapstick" and "capable of better things." Such attitudes accorded well with the film industry's middle-brow pretensions during these crucial years in the courting of a middle-class audience—but they also registered a major reversal for a star whose early persona had charted a trajectory away from older ideals of women's propriety. "She says comedy does not altogether consist of falling downstairs and throwing custard pies," a 1916 article in *Film Fun* observed, "and she believes that she can be just as funny in more dignified situations."[72]

More was at stake here than a desire for uplift. Events in Normand's personal life drove a permanent wedge between herself and Mack Sennett when, in the summer of 1915, their on-off romance culminated in a violent episode that kept her from acting for several months.[73] Fearful of losing one of its biggest stars, Keystone's management quickly negotiated a temporary compromise in the form of a new Keystone unit at the New York Motion Picture Company's facilities in Fort Lee, New Jersey. On December 26, Normand boarded a train out of Los Angeles—and away from Sennett—to begin work as star of the new unit, accompanied by director and co-star Roscoe Arbuckle, manager Ferris Hartman, publicity man Joe Murray, and supporting comedians Al St. John (Arbuckle's nephew), Minta Durfee (Arbuckle's wife), and Joe Bordeaux.[74] The Fort Lee unit quickly achieved product differentiation for its films with its debut release, *He Did and He Didn't* (January 1916), which employed a carefully sculpted, chiaroscuro visual style, tinting and toning color effects, and an ambitious narrative construction, in which dream sequences and reality are indistinguishably interlaced, forcing the viewer to puzzle out the "truth" of the depicted events.[75] As Normand proudly announced in an interview, the film was "just a little bit different from most of the comedies we have been doing because it really had a plot."[76]

Despite Normand's satisfaction with her first Fort Lee film, further career changes soon followed. After completing one more picture on the East Coast (*The Bright Lights*, February 1916), Normand announced her departure from Keystone, claiming once again that she wanted "to do more serious work" and to be "a trifle more . . . dignified" than was possible in slapstick comedy.[77] Her original intention was to join Ince's Kay-Bee brand to star in five-reel "light comedy dramas" for release through Triangle; and, by May 1916, the Mabel Normand Feature Film Company had been launched as a subsidiary of Kay-Bee "under the supervision of Thomas Ince."[78] Yet, despite Ince's nominal participation, it was, ironically, Normand's estranged former boss who contributed most to the project. Sennett had begun transferring funds from Keystone's coffers to the new company as early as April 1916, and the following September, he entered into a formal agreement to cover the costs of production and publicity on the company's first feature.[79] "Mack Sennett and his entire staff are lending their aid to make this subject the greatest success possible," *Motion Picture News* commented.[80]

Work on the feature—working title "Mountain Bred"—had begun almost immediately, but was delayed by complications concerning production personnel. The film's original director, James Young, resigned less than a month into production; his replacement, J. Farrell MacDonald, lasted only a little longer, and the job eventually fell to Richard F. Jones, one of Keystone's leading directors under Triangle.[81] Normand's continuing ill health also contributed to the slow progress, and, by the new year, Keystone's publicity staff found itself with the difficult task of promoting a movie—now titled *Mickey*—without a completion date in sight. The marketing strategies they chose are nonetheless revealing about the transformations taking place in Normand's celebrity image. The film, exhibitors learned from a January advertisement, was "a vivid and appealing comedy drama with real living characters, told without squash pies, battles or the seduction of the innocent heroine." Normand's role, meanwhile, was that of "a quaint little mountain girl who runs the gamut of life."[82] As presaged by this announcement, Normand's entry into the field of feature-length "comedy drama" was accompanied by a publicity campaign that redefined her star persona according to a sentimental paradigm akin in many respects to the image of playful girlhood popularized by Mary Pickford (fig. 30).[83] Readers of the *Mack Sennett Weekly* learned, week after week, of Normand's special affinity with nature. Like the mountain girl she portrayed in the film, she was said to be particularly at home with her pets: a May 1917 report on the completion of principal shooting stressed the star's sadness upon leaving her supporting cast of animal performers.[84] Other reports declared that "Children of the Studio Love Mabel Normand," explaining how "Every child around the studio goes straight to her from pure instinct."[85] Formerly an exemplar of female modernity, Normand's

FIGURE 30.   Mabel Normand in a publicity still for *Mickey,* "The Little Girl You Will Never Forget." From *Motion Picture News,* February 10, 1917. Courtesy of the Academy of Motion Picture Arts and Sciences.

star image was here inscribed within the openly recuperative framework of Victorian gender ideologies, linking her to children and animals as Nature's innocents. In a sense, a critical line in the sand was being drawn, divorcing Normand's screen persona from the boisterous physicality of her early roles and tying it to a sentimental emphasis on female sanctity, associated with notions of separate, gendered spheres and essential gender differences.

Given that the film was not released by the Keystone Film Company, a brief analysis of *Mickey* is somewhat out of place within the present study. Nevertheless, the film is instructive with respect to the weakening salience of social class in Normand's screen roles, and it provides a useful entry point to understanding Keystone's changing discourse of modern womanhood. As in her earlier films, Normand's performance manifests a vitality that belies outmoded notions of "ladylike" behavior and decorous femininity; yet here, that performance is placed largely outside the web of class relationships within which her early roles found their meaning. As "Mickey," Normand portrays a tomboyish orphan who has grown up apart from the influences of social institutions and a normal family life. Raised in a small western town by a poor old miner and his Native American maid, Mickey personifies the "natural" tendencies and freedoms that sentimental thinking regularly counterposed to the artificiality and restrictions of developed society. The film's first half thoroughly develops this aspect of her character, repeatedly connecting her lack of regard for societal norms to her kinship with a realm of nature—once, for example, in a sequence in which Mickey frolics naked on a forested bluff (modestly filmed in extreme long shot), later when she rescues her dog from the abuses of a cruel sheriff.

Such scenes typify sentimental discourse on nature, referring the film's protagonist to the idea of an unspoiled innocence liberated from the laws of social existence. The film's second half develops these contrasts by placing Mickey in a more structured social setting, when she is sent east to the opulent home of her gold-digging, but impecunious, aunt, Mrs. Drake. From the outset, the Drakes' mansion is presented as a place of greed and artifice. "Mrs. Drake," a title informs the viewer, "is desperately trying to maintain a millionaire's front"—an ambition she pursues by attempting to marry her children to money. When Mickey arrives at the mansion, Mrs. Drake welcomes her warmly, mistakenly believing her to be the heiress to a vast mining fortune—and thus a potential wife for her son. Once it is discovered that she will inherit only a disused mineshaft, Mrs. Drake angrily puts her to work as a maid for the remainder of her stay. Although Normand's subsequent scenes as the Drakes' housemaid establish continuity with her earlier screen roles, *Mickey* nevertheless indicates a drastic shift with respect to the depiction of class in Normand's films. The organizing content of *Mickey* is the contrast between nature, conceived broadly, and society, similarly conceived. It is only when nature enters society that class differences are created: the innocent simplicity of the rural life is now redefined as culpable penury, a redefinition that Mrs. Drake confirms by forcing her niece into domestic drudgery. Class difference thus becomes a contingent conflict in the film, a secondary function of the organizing contrast between the social and natural orders. The film's resolution consequently requires that the realms of nature and society be separated once more, erasing the injustice done to Mickey by returning her to a world of bucolic simplicity, a happy ending confirmed in the deus ex machina discovery that Mickey's mine has hit a rich seam of gold.

By drawing on the legacy of genteel sentimentalism, *Mickey* clearly sought to fulfill Normand's own ambitions for "improvements" in screen comedy. When eventually released in August 1918, the film proved the single greatest commercial success in Normand's career.[86] Critical response was nothing short of adulatory. " 'Mickey' is a digest of the science of producing motion pictures," *Moving Picture World* declared. "It has everything imaginable that might be conceived by the most inventive producer, past or present."[87] Other reviews joined the refrain, singling out the film's diversity of appeal for particular praise. "If someone asked you, Mr. Exhibitor, what sort of a picture would please everybody, wouldn't your answer be a film that combined pathos, humor, tense dramatic action, thrills and a bit of slapstick comedy, all so blended as to make a story that runs smoothly, upholds the interest and has been well produced?" *Exhibitor's Trade Review* asked. "You just bet you would, and just such an opportunity presents itself, for in 'Mickey' the above combination is to be found at its very best."[88] *Motion Picture News* thought likewise: "[The film] contains comedy, pathos, suspense, in fact almost everything that could in anyway contribute toward making 'Mickey' an entertaining picture."[89]

That the film proved such a broad success—gaining a reputation as a "mortgage lifter" for exhibitors during its remarkable four-year opening run[90]—testifies to the characteristic operations of a mass culture that hybridized social symbols by translating them into alternative narrative and ideological systems. A paradoxical union of genteel narrative values and modern gender norms, *Mickey* absorbed Normand's screen persona within the discursive conventions of Victorian sentimentalism and, in so doing, transplanted it from the web of social relations in which the New Woman first achieved her meaning. For all that working women's culture and female comicality may have challenged older constructions of female identity, *Mickey* exemplifies sentimentalism's persistence in resituating expressions of women's modernity in terms of traditional gendered ideologies. Sentimental and sensational projections of femininity were not, then, completely separate spheres, but overlapping discourses—perhaps especially so for working-class filmgoers who, like Normand herself, came to aspire to, or at least mentally identify with, standards of respectability proposed within genteel culture. So, far from contesting cultural representations of working women's modernity, those standards became a way of assimilating gendered change to the forms of an emergent mass culture.

But they were not the only way. For, during *Mickey*'s lengthy production, Keystone had also begun exploiting the Bathing Beauties as the cornerstone of its publicity practices. Like *Mickey*, discourse on the Bathing Beauties abstracted symbols of modern womanhood from social contexts; but where *Mickey* looked back to the waning ideologies of a previous era, Sennett's bathing-suited girls looked forward to the new consumer culture, accommodating changing patterns of gendered behavior to the reifying discourse of contemporary advertising techniques.

"WHOLESOME, YOUNG AMERICAN GIRLHOOD": THE BATHING BEAUTIES AND CONSUMER CULTURE

A growing conservatism in Keystone's handling of gender can, in retrospect, be traced to Normand's departure from the company. A hybrid of beauty and vulgarity, Normand's early screen image had merged elements traditionally perceived as incompatible; yet, in her absence, those antinomies could be imposed afresh. The classificatory distinction between the "grotesque" and the "classical" was reinstated within the ranks of the studio's female performers, and only those whose bodies fell short of classical standards were suitable objects of laughter.

This helps explain the success of two comediennes who, after appearing in small roles in the studio's Mutual releases, came into their own as comic leads under Triangle: Louise Fazenda and Polly Moran. A former principal of the "Twentieth-Century Maids" burlesque troupe, Moran had joined Keystone in 1913, where her rubber face and swaggering performances won her a reputation as a "distinctly sleazy" character comedienne, predominantly in lower-class roles.[91] Fazenda, meanwhile, had been recruited from Joker in 1915, and, in her Keystone films, put her elfin features in the service of eccentric—and often ethnic—character parts, from the mysterious fortuneteller, Mme de Seeresky, in *Maid Mad* (September 1916) to the impassioned Italian maiden of *Bombs!* (October 1916). A profile in the *Mack Sennett Weekly* distinguished her energetic work from that of Keystone's "pretty heroines," and implied a direct connection between Fazenda's physical appearance and her suitability as a comic foil. "Being a character comedienne in a Keystone isn't the softest berth in the world," the article began. "The 'pretty' heroines find the work none too slow, but when one plays the sort of parts in which Miss Fazenda is cast, it is dollars

FIGURE 31.   Polly Moran as "Sheriff Nell" (left) and Louise Fazenda as "Maggie" (right). Courtesy of the Academy of Motion Picture Arts and Sciences.

to doughnuts that before 'Finis' appears, she has been subjected to almost every form of abuse."[92] In effect, Fazenda and Moran filled a need created by Normand's absence—namely, for female performers willing and able to participate in knockabout action—and their success in this respect made them the highest-paid comediennes on the Keystone lot, receiving weekly paychecks of $115 (Fazenda) and $175 (Moran) throughout 1917.[93] Each was showcased in a series of her own—Moran appearing as a western town's spirited "Sheriff Nell" and Fazenda as "Maggie," an Irish servant girl with ribboned pigtails and a pronounced spit curl (fig. 31)—making them the first Keystone comediennes to achieve this distinction since Normand's "Mabel" films. Yet, unlike Normand, their distance from traditional standards of beauty tended to neutralize their transgressive potential as female comics. Even in sympathetic profiles, Fazenda's comicality was condescended to as the natural expression of daffy girlishness: she was "the most impish sprite of screen comedy," whose performances revealed nothing more challenging than a sense of "spontaneous fun."[94] Moran's outrageous burlesque was meanwhile written off as a gender aberration. As a *Motion Picture Classic* profile of the star asked in later years: "Wouldn't any woman rather be known for her beauty than for her wit? When woman's whole aim in life is to be attractive, how must it feel to play the buffoon?"[95]

The polarization that divided the studio's "pretty heroines" from its character comediennes was reinforced by hiring policies introduced in early 1916, when it was reported that Sennett had "taken it upon himself" to recruit "a number of young and attractive" players.[96] Generally lacking prior experience in film or on stage, these new signings—including the future stars Juanita Hansen, Marie Prevost, and Mary Thurman—were put to work in roles requiring scant participation in the studio's trademark knockabout.[97] The typical role was that of the flirtations stenographer, manicurist, or cabaret girl who attracts the philandering eye of a married man—as performed by Dora Rodgers in *A Love Riot* (March 1916) and Louella Maxam in *His Lying Heart* (August 1916). They also played heroines in comedies structured upon a novelistic framework of courtship and romance: portraying the daughters of assorted mayors, capitalists, and other wealthy patriarchs, actresses like Mary Thurman in *Bombs!* or Juanita Hansen in *His Pride and Shame* (February 1916) appeared as romantic objects in narratives of male rivalry, sexual trophies to be dispensed to the hero as part of his acceptance into the social order.

One key to the growing cleavage in the ranks of Keystone's female performers lay in the realm of social stratification. Stories of the Beauties' family lives routinely presented their careers as exemplars of female independence and social mobility, even as they articulated those careers as expressions of uniquely middle-class privilege. As the *Mack Sennett Weekly* reported in 1917, most of its new female signings "live at home with their families" and "have been recruited from schools and colleges."[98] Although doubtless an exaggeration, the claim contained a kernel of truth, as evidenced by the performers' biographies. There is good reason to presume that many of these women had entered the industry with the aim of putting aside the restrictions of middle-class upbringing and living unconventional lives, free from their families and economically self-sufficient. Several belonged to the growing demographic of educated young women who were venturing forth into the working world. Ora Carew, a doctor's daughter, was born into a respectable family in Salt Lake City, where she had received a high-school education at Rowland Hall.[99] Marie Prevost had completed high school in Denver and Los Angeles, and, prior to joining Keystone, was employed as a stenographer (a popular choice for young middle-class women).[100] But it was in Mary Thurman that the imprint of social privilege was deepest. The daughter of well-to-do Danish Mormons, Thurman not only graduated from high school but attended the University of Utah, eventually finding work as an elementary school teacher in the Utah town of Salina.[101] Such accomplishments were far removed from the life experiences of Polly Moran and Louise Fazenda, who, like Normand herself, were the children of working-class Catholic immigrants. Fazenda's father, born in Mexico, was apparently of mixed Italian, Portuguese, and French descent; her mother was a native Chicagoan. Put to work at her father's grocery store during her childhood, Fazenda accepted a number of jobs to supplement the family income. "I was always a business woman of some sort," she later recalled. "There was my delivery job, for one thing. After school [St. Mary's Convent in Los Angeles] I'd hitch up our old horse and deliver groceries. . . . In the afternoon I'd watch people's babies, made jellies and jams to sell, and even washed dishes."[102] Moran's early career followed a different route, though not one without precedent for working-class women: she abandoned her education—at a Chicago convent for children of Irish descent—to pursue a career in burlesque.[103]

The dominant ideals of female modernity at Keystone thus shifted across the fault lines of class, even as those ideals were now exploited as occasions for titillating display. What was occurring was a division of labor that allotted active comic duties to a number of character comediennes while employing the pretty new recruits simply as erotic objects. Themselves of working-class background, Moran and Fazenda specialized in burlesque characterizations of working women: to the extent that they invited laughter at their performances, they thereby reduced working women's culture to risible eccentricity. The "young and attractive" female talent, meanwhile, appeared in roles consigning them the wholly passive role of being fought over, looked at, and flirted with. Keystone's engagement with the forms of women's modernity thus took on increasingly reified dimensions—at once a marginalization of working women's contributions to modern gender ideals and a foregrounding of erotic spectacle. And it meant the polarization of feminine display as either objectified eroticism or objectified grotesquery, without mediating alternatives.

The commercial exploitation of the Bathing Beauties would mark the fulfillment of that process, and, in so doing, would confirm the New Woman's incorporation into the symbolic universe of the emergent consumer society. Time and again, Keystone's publicity discourse blurred the lines between modern femininity and commercial imagery. "There are now in stock a collection of photographs of Keystone girls taken on the beach which we believe are the most striking and beautiful pictures ever turned out as publicity for any motion picture company," the *Mack Sennett Weekly* asserted in 1917. "[W]e cannot imagine a more brilliant lobby display than could be made of these veritable gems of the photographer's art.

And gems, we may add parenthetically, of wholesome, young American girlhood."[104] The rhetorical rhyme here—linking "gems of the photographer's art" to "gems of young American girlhood"—succinctly encapsulates the Bathing Beauties' dual nature as, simultaneously, emblems of modernity and emblems of commerce.

The modernity of Keystone's bathing girls was sufficiently broad in definition to encompass diverse cultural and behavioral forms. In an age defined by the rise of corporate cultural hegemony, the Bathing Beauties were reported to be "remarkably keen little business women."[105] In an age that defined individual personality through consumer goods acquired in a fashion cycle, the Bathing Beauties were style experts, freely dispensing their wisdom to female fans. "From my observation and actual experience in pictures, I have found that a great part of a girl's success lies in her ability to dress appropriately," Maude Wayne was quoted as saying. "Individuality—let that be the keynote."[106] More important, however, was the relationship linking the Beauties' modernity to their alleged athleticism. Week after week, the *Mack Sennett Weekly* loudly proclaimed the studio's bathing-suited girls to be, one and all, accomplished athletes—"splendid wholesome young athletes," in fact, "upon whom the gods have smiled and given them beauty."[107] Typically, the *Weekly* paired brief articles celebrating the girls' athletic achievements with large photographs of them clad in daring swimming costumes, a publicity strategy that capitalized on the ambivalent associations of women's sports clothing. The streamlined, functional styles in modern women's sportswear may have challenged sentimental ideas of female delicacy; but they also exposed more of the female body, something the *Weekly*'s editors turned to commercial advantage. "Sennett-Keystone Gymnasium Popular with Keystone Brigade," a representative publicity piece proclaimed in 1917, alongside a picture of the starlet Marvel Rea sitting provocatively, bare legs spread, astride a wooden horse.[108]

But the Bathing Beauties were not only wonderful athletes: they were also, or so the *Weekly* would have had its readers believe, pioneers in women's sports. According to one report in January, "the Keystone girls" had established "a new winter sport . . . in California—surf-board riding" (apparently a variant of water-skiing). Marie Prevost, the report continued, "is one of the most expert surf-board riders in California—which is saying a good deal considering how wonderfully well the outdoor girls of California swim."[109] Earlier that same month, the *Weekly* proudly listed Aileen Aitken—the "1916 woman's amateur diving champion"—among the studio's female talents.[110] Just a few weeks later, it was recorded that

Mary Thurman was in training under the instruction of an Olympic gold-medalist, had broken athletics records set by the co-eds at Vassar College, and had become the first woman to take up "the ancient Grecian sport of javelin throwing" (fig. 32).[111] Such claims were, of course, pure ballyhoo: years later, Harry Carr, the *Weekly*'s editor, recalled with amusement his role in trumping up Thurman's athletic accomplishments. "We rigged Mary up in a pair of short running pants and posed her with javelins, vaulting poles and what not," Carr remembered. "With the valiant assistance of a couple of college coaches, we invented a fine line of athletic records for her. Also we tactfully graduated her from Vassar. I don't know how much Miss Thurman's running pants had to do with it, but the story was sent around the world and they are still sending postcards with her athletic pictures."[112]

Thus it was that the Bathing Beauties, for all their much-touted modernity, contributed to the devaluation of gendered change. A consumer culture in which advertising was a crucial element of economic life was also a culture in which visual symbols were severed from actual social references, circulating instead as consumer images that promised nothing more than a vague feeling of sensuous excitement.[113] As vividly exemplified by Mary Thurman's "record-breaking" feats, modern paradigms of female behavior could be stripped from any basis in real individual accomplishment, the better to be exploited as publicity for the Keystone brand. Promotional discourse on the Bathing Beauties thus constituted a form of reification in which social forms and meanings were displaced by consumer images, a numinous erotics of athletic bodies substituting for the class-oriented conception of New Womanhood found in Normand's early films.[114] As the class basis of women's bathing and athletic pursuits—in particular, their relation to working women's culture—became increasingly invisible and abstract, so women's modernity was interpreted, not in social terms, but as a decorative addition to studio advertising.

We see this also in Keystone's films, which made use of the Beauties, not as individualized, socially defined narrative agents, but rather as undifferentiated clusters of bodies whose presence in any film generally served the needs of publicity more than the requirements of narrative. *Her Nature Dance* (April 1917), for example, was advertised as boasting "fifty of the loveliest of the famous Keystone beauties . . . in the airiest of attire"; *Oriental Love*, meanwhile, was recommended for scenes of "harem beauties" at play in a "perfumed pool."[115] In such films, the Bathing Beauties take on the structure of commodities, shedding their qualitative differences and freezing into quantifiable, interchangeable "things" to be grouped within the film frame—an orderly and static mass of bodies quite unlike

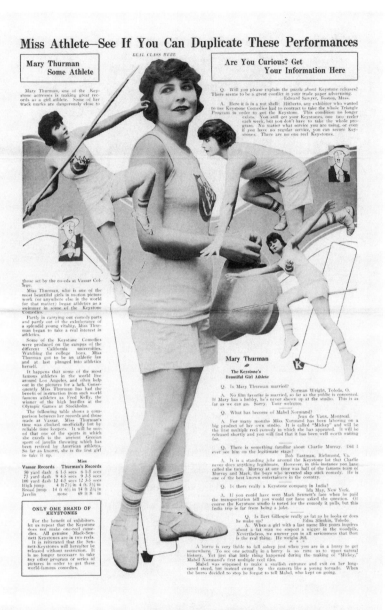

FIGURE 32. Miss Athlete—Mary Thurman in the *Mack Sennett Weekly*, January 29, 1917. Courtesy of the Academy of Motion Picture Arts and Sciences.

FIGURE 33.   Production still from *Whose Baby?* (July 1917). Courtesy of the Academy of Motion Picture Arts and Sciences.

the distinctly *disorderly* mass movements of the earlier Keystone Kops.[116] This is clear, for example, in *Whose Baby?* (July 1917), a Swanson-Vernon comedy in which the director, Clarence Badger, repeatedly arranges the girls in groups extending across the frame (fig. 33), a strategy that effectively reduces them to an element of setting, before which the main protagonists carry the burden of narrative. There is thus an impulse in these films to accumulate the display of young bodies to a point at which they congeal as visual surplus value, a form of scopic pleasure produced as a supplement to the comic action, and an adumbration of the gendered division of spectacle and narrative familiar from later classical cinema.[117]

One is, in fact, tempted to see here a precise harbinger of the phenomenon described by Siegfried Kracauer in his famous 1927 essay, "The Mass Ornament." For Kracauer, the "mass ornament" was the paradigmatic expression of the new culture industry, a phenomenon that, for him, was best represented by the Tiller Girls, a dancing troupe from England that had performed to Berlin audiences to great acclaim in the 1920s. In their synchronized dance steps, the precision of their tap-dancing, and their symmetric resemblance to one another, the Tiller Girls struck Kracauer as the "aesthetic reflex" of industrial rationality—"no longer individual girls, but indissoluble girl clusters whose movements are demonstrations of mathematics." In the mass ornament, Kracauer observed, individual (female) bodies are deeroticized, subsumed within abstract patterns, which they serve as "mere building blocks, nothing more." The structure of the mass ornament is, thus, "that of the entire contemporary situation," the index of a society in which individuals are objectified as components of a mechanized, rational system.[118]

Kracauer's argument provides one way of understanding the Bathing Beauties' broader significance. They too were envisioned as "girl clusters"; they too can be seen as emblems of mass society's commodity form. Yet the limitations of this reading—limitations typifying much Frankfurt School thought—lie in the tendency to interpret cultural forms merely as epiphenomenal manifestations of underlying social currents, "reflections" of contemporary situations but not actively involved in creating those situations.[119] The Bathing Beauties were certainly more than an "aesthetic reflex" of modern mass culture: in their tremendous popularity, they productively mapped out shared cultural experiences that transcended traditional patterns of cultural consumption. Relevant here, for example, is the comparison, often drawn at the time, of Keystone's Bathing Beauties to the Ziegfeld Follies, a New York-based revue famed for the elaborate chorus girl productions first introduced by Florenz Ziegfeld in early 1915. "Recently there appeared in a magazine of wide and national circulation an article pointing out that the Sennett-Keystone company is to the movies what Ziegfeld's Follies are to the stage," the *Mack Sennett Weekly* proudly reported in May 1917.[120] A *Photoplay* article the following month repeated the analogy, describing Keystone as "the silent Follies" and praising its output as "infinitely more eye-filling than misdirected meringue and catapulting custard."[121] Yet where the Follies catered to the New York carriage trade, charging a $3 cover for its midnight shows, Keystone's Bathing Beauties offered identical pleasures on a less exclusive basis, a point that was not lost on contemporary observers. "[T]he cost [of watching a Keystone film] is trifling as compared with the electric-lighted, grease-painted Follies of the noisy stage," the *Photoplay* article observed. "[N]o self-respecting tired businessman would think of attending [the Follies] unless first injected into so-called evening clothes. Conversely, no tired anybody would think of attiring himself in other than his ordinary garb to take his optical treatment of the Screen Follies in his own little cinema."[122] In sum, the Bathing Beauties were actively collapsing distinctions within cultural practice, recasting the exclusive satisfactions of New York nightlife in democratized form and so contributing to a mass culture based on the liquidation of cultural hierarchies.

The appeal of the Bathing Beauties also crossed lines defined by gender and sexuality, though here they were open to a wide range of—often contradictory—responses. They obviously attracted heterosexual men, authorized to gaze guiltlessly on the bodies of young women who, Sennett's publicity team reassured them, were "healthy" and "wholesome," girls whose poses lacked "any suggestion of offense."[123] In March 1917, the Beauties even graced the front page of the sensational *National Police Gazette* (fig. 34), whose covers were more typically devoted to tightly corseted burlesque queens, thus affirming their status as male working-class entertainment.[124] But, in all likelihood, they fascinated women at a far deeper level, appealing to them as exemplars as they negotiated their own relation to modern women's culture. In 1926, for example, the secretary of a "Ladies Amateur Athletic and Sport Club" wrote Sennett's studio to ask for photos of the Beauties "in either bathing suits or gymnasium suit [sic]"—presumably to give its customers something to look at, perhaps even aspire to, as they trained.[125] Earlier that year, an Iowan theater owner contacted the studio to propose a "working girl contest" in which the winner would travel to California to appear in a Sennett comedy.[126]

Photographs of the Beauties thus performed a double legitimation: of the scantily clad female body as a "healthy" object of male desire and of young women's own desires for self-transformation. Whether for the patrons of a ladies' sports club or for working girls dreaming of a trip to California, the Bathing Beauties had become role models who mediated modern gender ideals for a consumer society. In the women's pages of the nation's newspapers, the Beauties often advised on questions of health and physique, and, in the process, redefined women's physical pursuits simply as a means to the pursuit of beauty. "If you were not born with a good figure," one advised, "swim and dance to get one."[127] In the same tone with which they advocated outdoor pursuits, so did they advocate their commitment to personal beauty. "I have always wondered why girls tolerate ugly, dark hair on their arms when it is simply and easily removed without injuring the skin," Anita Barnes speculated in a 1927 piece. "Just get a bottle of double strength peroxide and apply it evenly to the arms. The hair will bleach to a neutral shade . . . and after continued applications will thin and finally disappear entirely."[128] Sally Eilers, meanwhile, advocated a particularly pungent remedy for "flabby" skin: a half cup of sauerkraut juice followed by a glass of hot water.[129]

FIGURE 34. Cover of the March 31, 1917 issue of the *National Police Gazette*. Courtesy of the Clements Library, University of Michigan.

Implicit in these assertions was something of the "perfectionist agenda" that the historian T. J. Jackson Lears sees as a fundamental feature of the new consumer society.[130] Where Normand's films articulated gender through images of unruly bodily excess, the Beauties advocated the pursuit of physiological perfectionism. Beauty, which, in the case of Mabel Normand, had formed part of a perversive hybridization of classical attractiveness and grotesque physicality, was, in the case of the Bathing Beauties, hypostasized as a spectacular commodity, something to be attained through rigorous physical training. Increasingly, beauty shed its qualitative nature and became a quantifiable possession to be compared across different women. Even before the first Miss America pageant in 1921 established the beauty contest as a permanent feature of American mass culture, Keystone was routinely sending out its bathing girls to participate in local pageants, such as the "Great Bathing Parade" in Venice, California, in 1917, in which the Bathing Beauties walked away with first, second, and third places (respectively, Mary Thurman, Juanita Hansen, and Marie Prevost and Maude Wayne, tied for third).[131] By the mid-1920s, organizers of such events routinely wrote Sennett either to ask for his participation as a judge or to invite his bathing girls to compete.[132] Beauty had become a measurable value and Sennett one of its most well known appraisers.

·   ·   ·

As a letter from his publicity director indicates, Sennett had tired of the Bathing Beauty promotions by the spring of 1927. "As you must know," Agnes O'Malley wrote to the studio manager, J. A. Waldron, "[Mack Sennett] is not very keen about bathing girl publicity any longer—says he is tired of being called a beauty expert—wants more dignified publicity. . . . Also the fact that these stills usually publicize little nobodies whom we may not use once a month in our comedies."[133] A fitting epitaph to a promotional campaign so firmly grounded in the devaluation of modern ideals of womanhood, this dismissive reference to "little nobodies" illuminates the ironies in Keystone's changing discourse on gender. Keystone's Bathing Beauty publicity popularized ideals of female physicality, but in the process surrendered the assertions of working-class distinctiveness that had frequently accompanied those ideals. It contributed to the iconography of New Womanhood, but in the process redefined women's modernity to accord with a commercial conception of bodily perfectionism.

Having learned to identify themselves with the exchange value of their own bodies, several of Sennett's original bathing girls were left psychologically unprepared to deal with the loss of their own beauty. After finding modest success in the early 1920s as a heroine in serial melodramas and five-reel westerns, Juanita Hansen abandoned her screen career in 1928 when an accident in a hotel shower left her face burned and disfigured. A hopeless morphine addict for much of the rest of her life, she made headlines in the 1950s when she was discovered working as an operator for the Southern Pacific railroad line.[134] Marie Prevost, meanwhile, paid a yet more tragic toll on her own commodification. Of the original troupe of Beauties that came to prominence in 1917, it was she who had gone on to greatest fame in the 1920s, starring in flapper roles in sophisticated sex comedies, including Ernst Lubitsch's *The Marriage Circle* (1924) and E. Mason Hopper's *Up in Mabel's Room* (1926). However, her career took a downward turn in the late 1920s when weight problems prevented her from taking on starring roles. During the early 1930s, fan magazines occasionally reported on her dieting attempts—a liquid diet that landed her in the hospital in 1932 and a stringent exercise program that, it was announced, would start her "on the comeback road" in 1934.[135] Then, on January 23, 1937, she was found dead in her Hollywood apartment in circumstances indicating extreme malnutrition. Bite marks on her body had been caused by her pet dachshund, Sinner, probably attempting to wake her—or perhaps trying to eat its dead owner, as Kenneth Anger reports in his trivia classic *Hollywood Babylon*.[136] The female body, a site for carnivalesque, comic expressions of new gender ideals, was also the site of women's exploitation within the new economy—a consumer image, itself consumed.

How, in the space of a few years, had Keystone so completely marginalized the carnivalesque enactment of working-class femininity in its films? What does it say about the new mass culture that Normand's appearances on behalf of socialist causes gave way to appearances by the Bathing Beauties as contestants in beauty pageants? One series of probing answers is suggested in the work of Jürgen Habermas, whose famous portrait of the "public sphere" provides a parallel scenario of decline associated with commercial dynamics. Prior to the growth of a consumer society, Habermas argues, the institutions of the public sphere—the press, communal meeting places, and so on—preserve a kind of social intercourse, allowing its participants to debate issues of public concern. However, the invasion of these institutions by advertising practices transforms channels of social communication into channels for the stimulation of commercial desire: characteristics of public sphere debate such as rationality and equal exchange now dissolve as cultural industries seek to marshal larger publics. To the extent that media become commercialized, Habermas concludes, "the threshold between the circulation of a commodity and the exchange of communications among the members of a public [is] leveled."[137]

Habermas's observation invites us to interpret Keystone's changing discourse on gender as a fundamental shift in how the studio communicated to its audiences. Where Normand's films imaged modern womanhood as a nonconformist expression of working-class culture, the Bathing Beauties conformed that image to the economic underpinnings of the new mass culture. The implications of this shift were threefold. First, it contained the troubling spectacle of female comicality, replacing it with the spectacle of passive, nubile bodies. Second, it separated one of the paradigmatic images of modern femininity from its association with popular cultural practices: shorn of plebeian overtones, the image of the bathing girl became more reified, hence assimilable to commodity form. Third, it reinterpreted women's modernity in consumer terms: as performed by the Bathing Beauties, women's modernity implied obedience to a commercial discourse of physiological perfectionism and a fashion cycle of purchasing beauty accessories. That this was a characteristic tactic of the new consumer culture is a point made by most historians of advertising.[138] That Keystone participated in these shifts indicates how profoundly it had internalized that culture's commercial rhetoric. Fun at the carnivalization of social categories had become fun in the service of mass consumption.

Conclusion

It is easiest to begin with the fate of the Keystone brand name.

When Triangle began to show signs of impending collapse in early 1917, Adam Kessel and Charles Baumann sold out to Harry Aitken, in a deal finalized in early March. For just $500,000, Triangle acquired control of the New York Motion Picture Co., together with rights to all Kay-Bee, Broncho, Domino, and Keystone pictures, past and present. Kessel and Baumann, in return, received peace of mind in knowing that, when the final collapse came, they would have no financial interests at stake. Kessel remained active in the company's affairs for a few more years, but Baumann retired immediately from pictures and embarked on a yearlong round-the-world trip, apparently in a state of nervous exhaustion.[1]

The Keystone label became a casualty of this deal when, in June 1917, Mack Sennett commenced his own withdrawal from Triangle. With only a one-third interest in Keystone, Sennett had little leeway for negotiating with Aitken, who, having acquired Kessel and Baumann's majority share in the company (57 percent), might have been expected to dictate terms.[2] Yet Aitken stood firm only on his rights to the Keystone brand name and relinquished ownership of all studio facilities to Sennett. Along with the Edendale lot, Sennett also kept almost all his major stars (including Chester Conklin, Charles Murray, Ford Sterling, Mack Swain, Gloria Swanson, Mary Thurman, and Ben Turpin), while Aitken assumed the contracts of a dozen or so lesser luminaries.[3]

Without either Sennett's supervision or any of Keystone's familiar stars, Aitken tried to exploit the studio brand name in a series of two-reel

"Keystone" comedies made at Triangle's Culver City studios—"false" Keystones, they have been called—but they did poor business and were discontinued the following spring. (Outlining scenarios of marital mix-ups in white-collar settings, extant production documents suggest a stronger adherence to the domestic "situation"–style of comedy than in any of the Sennett-supervised Keystones.)[4] Finis was thus written to Keystone's career as an active production concern, although Aitken would keep the name familiar to filmgoers in subsequent years by flooding the market with reissues. Sennett, meanwhile, had moved quickly to relaunch his company, finalizing a distribution deal with Paramount in late June 1917 and renaming his brand label "Mack Sennett Comedies." On June 29, four days after settling with Triangle, Sennett telegrammed the studio manager, J. A. Waldron, to announce the next chapter in the studio's career: "Have signed up with Paramount releasing one Mack Sennett comedy every two weeks starting releasing September 15th. Have made very fine contract. Figure starting full swing July 15th."[5]

What did the new deal entail with respect to developments in the studio's comic style? Evidently, Paramount recognized the value of the Keystone formula, since Sennett's contract stipulated that the new pictures were simply to be continuations of the studio's recent work—"humorous or farcical" stories of the "quality of the productions directed by the Lessor [i.e., Sennett] for two years last past."[6] Although Gloria Swanson's early resignation led to the discontinuation of the studio's romantic comedies, most other production trends remained firmly in place. "There will be no difference except the trademark," Sennett explained to exhibitors in the July 30 issue of the *Mack Sennett Weekly*. "The comedies will be made by the same actors at the same studio under the same supervision. . . . [M]any of the directors who have been my associates and co-workers in the making of comedies will still be with me in the making of comedies under the new trade name. The same comedians you have laughed at and the pretty girls you have admired will still be there. It will be the same old rose which the late Mr. Shakespeare assured us would smell as sweet under any other name."[7]

The emphasis on mechanical contrivance remained a cornerstone of the studio's comic form, both in the Paramount releases (1917–23) and during Sennett's subsequent association with Pathé Exchange (1923–29). Under the tutelage of the cinematographer Fred Jackman, the former Keystone stunt driver Del Lord supplanted Walter Wright as the studio's expert in mechanical stunts and trick effects and, by the mid-1920s, Lord was Sennett's highest-paid house director. Ben Turpin, meanwhile, would go on to become one of the studio's most successful comic stars, second only to Harry Langdon at mid-decade and well known for spoofing the matinee idols of 1920s cinema—a phony Valentino in *The Shriek of Araby* (1922), a mock Von Stroheim in *Three Foolish Weeks* (1924), the debonair "Rodney St. Clair" in *A Harem Knight* (1926). The ranks of the Bathing Beauties continued to swell, eventually spawning their own series of "Girl Comedies" in 1928, and Sennett reluctantly acquired the mantle of a Jazz Age beauty connoisseur, a frequent guest of honor at the beauty contests that flourished across the American cultural landscape of the 1920s.

It was the "same old rose" indeed; and, while the films remained profitable, the Sennett name itself became a throwback. In a decade that witnessed the successes of Buster Keaton and Harold Lloyd, the launching of the Hal Roach "All-Star" comedies, the continued ascendancy of Charlie Chaplin, and the institutionalization of the slapstick feature, Sennett's approach to comedy changed little. In 1928, at the end of the silent era, a *Photoplay* writer dubbed him the "Professor," and the Edendale lot, "the old school house"; yet few pupils remained to learn the old lessons.[8] Long after his producing career ended in the 1930s, Sennett remained hopeful that his clowns and comic policemen might once more return to the spotlight of mass culture, but a string of unrealized projects only underscored their growing obsolescence. As late as 1960, one newspaper reported that Sennett, then eighty years old, was planning to relaunch Keystone-style slapstick in the medium of commercial television. "It'll all be shot new—not old film clips," Sennett declared. "The girls will wear the newest bathing suits. The Kops will be the same."[9] The show never proceeded beyond an idea. On November 5 of that year, Mack Sennett died of a coronary thrombosis.

. . .

Keystone's larger cultural legacy is more difficult to specify. Writing of the changes in popular culture that occurred between the 1880s and the 1920s, Stuart Hall has suggested that it is in this period that the "matrix of factors and problems" that constitute our present history, and our particular deadlocks, arise. "Everything changes," he writes, "not just a shift in the relations of forces but a reconstitution of the terrain of political struggle itself."[10] What, finally, might Keystone tell us about this topography of change?

This book has argued that the history of Keystone is, in its various developments, the history of a nascent mass culture. The hybridizing of previous cultural traditions (e.g., the fusion of sentiment and knockabout), the substitution of new "classless" aesthetic forms (e.g., the machine), the reification of popular symbols (e.g., the Bathing Beauty): these processes can be explained in terms neither of a successful "top-down" incorporation of popular culture nor of a fully articulated "bottom-up" resistance. If it would be misguided to describe cinema's development during this period as a straightforward process of "embourgeoisement"—witness the failure of the Triangle Film Corporation—it would be equally wrong to interpret the resulting commercial culture as, in Miriam Hansen's suggestion, a site for engaging authentically "liberatory impulses" and "radical possibility."[11] Rather, mass culture operated as a solvent of class interests because it belonged to precisely none of the preexisting class formations, neither the genteel nor the popular, the classes nor the masses, the high nor the low. The account that this book has stressed is thus one in which commercial considerations outmatched the integrity of previous class cultures: if mass culture "belonged" to anyone, it was to the new class of leisure entrepreneurs who had, in many instances, emerged from local plebeian cultures (like Sennett), but who ultimately subverted those cultures to commercial ends.[12] We need to speak, then, of the modern hegemony of a commercial culture industry, born from the dissolving point of traditional class hierarchies.

But, if this is so, then it also becomes clear why the dynamic of popular comedy was necessarily altered in the new era. The authority of the genteel order that slapstick had challenged was crumbling rapidly; but so also was the autonomy of the popular culture in which American slapstick had its roots. The points of social reference on which slapstick had been founded were being dispersed in an age of shared commercial pleasure. With the genteel culture no longer a real opponent, the elements of farce, travesty, and nonsense gave way to the embellishments and formal variations of 1920s screen comedy. Slapstick had, by this point, long lost its ability to offend. It is no wonder, then, that a kind of amnesia clouds our image of the Keystone Film Company: the process of reification, which had already begun to extend its arthritic influence through Keystone's later films, eventually reduced the studio's legacy to a banal token of cultural nostalgia, epitomized in the tall tales and mythmaking of Sennett's 1954 autobiography, *King of Comedy*. The image that has dominated almost all subsequent histories and criticism is an image of custard pies, Bathing Beauties, and Keystone Kops—to quote Sennett, "the funny fellows and pretty girls . . . [whose] like may never walk, tumble, or pratt-fall again."[13] Sennett's contribution to early film comedy has likewise been remembered chiefly in the abstract—the "king of comedy," the "sultan of slapstick"—with little concern for how his films once inscribed working-class cultural practice during a historic moment of transition. A filmmaker who had once written opinion pieces on "Labor and the Movies," Sennett was, in his old age, more commonly asked for opinions on trends in women's swimwear.

Keystone slapstick appears dated now, because its class context has long been displaced. But Sennett himself seems to have sensed this and, following the decline of his filmmaking career, he often harped on the gulf that divided modern film comedy from its original audience. "Slapstick," he proclaimed in 1939, "is a lost art. . . . Do you think that people who've been working all day in a mine want to go and see a lot of dressed-up actors talking like Englishmen? We may understand all that fly talk, but the people who see pictures don't give a damn about it."[14] There is exaggeration here, to be sure—particularly the suggestion that the 1930s audience was largely comprised of miners and laborers—but the terms of Sennett's analysis point unmistakably to the importance of a social perspective on comic pleasure. To defer to the laughter of a film's original audience is perhaps only the first step in a social historiography of early comedy; the second, as Sennett's remark implies, requires thinking about the ties binding that laughter to the material conditions of particular groups and class formations, whether as chortling evasion, derisive mockery, or, perhaps, ribald protest. A historiography like this, such as this book has attempted, will also then be a mode of political understanding, an appreciation of past laughter as a clue to discerning the dilemmas of the present.

Notes

INTRODUCTION

1. Theodor Dreiser, "The Best Motion Picture Interview Ever Written," *Photoplay*, August 1928, 32.

2. Ibid., 32, 33, 128. Aside from the comparison with Rabelais in the quoted passage, Dreiser also speaks of Sennett's "Rabelaisian gusto and vitality" and "that ribald Rabelaisian gusto and gaiety that has kept a substantial part of America laughing with him all of these years" (ibid., 35, 128).

3. Mary Douglas, "The Social Control of Cognition: Some Factors in Joke Perception," *Man* 3.3 (1968): 366.

4. Ben Singer, *Melodrama and Modernity: Early Sensational Cinema and Its Contexts* (New York: Columbia University Press, 2001), 19.

5. Dates and figures taken from Robert C. Allen, *Vaudeville and Film, 1895–1915: A Study of Media Interaction* (New York: Arno, 1980), 36–37; John F. Kasson, *Amusing the Million: Coney Island at the Turn of the Century* (New York: Hill & Wang, 1978), 34; and Eileen Bowser, *The Transformation of Cinema, 1907–1915* (Berkeley: University of California Press, 1990), 179. One could even make the case that comedy played a determining role in the expansion of nickelodeons from 1905 onward. For if, as has frequently been claimed, it was the popularity of fiction filmmaking that fueled the early nickelodeon boom, then, given the ratio cited by Bowser, this must have been due in no small part to comedy (at least until 1908, when the proportion of comic films began to decline). For fuller discussions of the growing market for humor in turn-of-the-century America, see Albert V. McClean Jr., *American Vaudeville as Ritual* (Louisville: University of Kentucky Press, 1965), chap. 6, and Henry Jenkins, *What Made Pistachio Nuts? Early Sound Comedy and the Vaudeville Aesthetic* (New York: Columbia University Press, 1992), chap. 2. I draw on these accounts for some of the references in this and the following two paragraphs.

6. James L. Ford, "Stage Humor and Comedy," *Harper's Weekly*, November 19, 1904, 1774.

7. H. H. Boysen, "The Plague of Jocularity," *North American*, November 1895, 528, quoted in Walter Blair and Hamilan Hill, *America's Humor: From Poor Richard to Doonesbury* (Oxford: Oxford University Press, 1978), 370.

8. Harrigan quoted in McClean, *American Vaudeville as Ritual*, 106.

9. See Warren Susman's classic essay, " 'Personality' and the Making of Twentieth-Century Culture," in *Culture as History: The Transformation of American Society in the Twentieth Century* (New York: Pantheon Books, 1984), 271–85. Works by a number of historians have linked genteel configurations of morality to the process of nineteenth-century middle-class formation and the demands of a producers economy. See, e.g., Stuart Blumin, "The Hypothesis of Middle-Class Formation in Nineteenth-Century America: A Critique and Some Proposals," *American Historical Review* 90.2 (1985): 299–338; Karen Halttunen, *Confidence Men and Painted Women: A Study of Middle-Class Culture in America, 1830–1870* (New Haven: Yale University

Press, 1982); and Mary Ryan, *Cradle of the Middle Class: The Family in Oneida County, New York, 1790–1865* (Cambridge: Cambridge University Press, 1981).

10. George Meredith, *An Essay on Comedy and the Uses of the Comic Spirit* (New York: Scribner, 1897), 82; based on a London lecture published in the *New Quarterly Magazine*, April 1877. The distinction between popular and genteel discourses on humor is examined further in chapter 3 of this book.

11. "The Dominant Joke," *Atlantic Monthly*, March 1903, 432.

12. "A Plea for Seriousness," *Atlantic Monthly*, May 1892, 630.

13. Robert Snyder, *The Voice of the City: Vaudeville and Popular Culture in New York* (New York: Oxford University Press, 1989), 26.

14. Bowser, *Transformation of Cinema*, 179.

15. Statistics from Patrick Loughney, "Leave 'em Laughing: The Last Years of the Biograph Company," in Eileen Bowser, ed., *The Slapstick Symposium* (Brussels: Fedération internationale des archives du film, 1988), 20. Despite the overall decline in domestic comedy production from 1907 to 1909, however, imports of the popular French comedies made by Pathé, Gaumont, Éclair, and Eclipse remained high. Judging from ads and listings in the trade journal *Views and Films Index*, I estimate that comedies accounted for just over half of Pathé's fiction film imports each year during this period. The annual ratio of comedies to dramas from Gaumont seems to have been even higher, ranging from 60 to 70 percent. For more on French comedies and the American market, see chapter 1. See also Richard Abel, *The Ciné Goes to Town: French Cinema, 1896–1914* (Berkeley: University of California Press, 1994), 215–45.

16. John Bunny, "How It Feels to Be a Comedian," *Photoplay*, October 1914, 111.

17. See Peter Krämer, " 'Clean, Dependable Slapstick': Comic Violence and the Emergence of Classical Hollywood Cinema," in J. David Slocum, *Violence and American Cinema* (New York: Routledge, 2001), 103–16.

18. T. J. Jackson Lears, "The Concept of Cultural Hegemony: Problems and Possibilities," *American Historical Review* 90.3 (June 1984): 581.

19. Mack Sennett, with Cameron Shipp, *King of Comedy* (Garden City, N.Y.: Doubleday, 1954; reprint, San Jose, Calif.: toExcel Press, 2000), 12.

20. Kalton C. Lahue and Terry Brewer, *Kops and Custards: The Legend of Keystone Films* (Norman: University of Oklahoma Press, 1968); Kalton C. Lahue, *Mack Sennett's Keystone: The Man, the Myth and the Comedies* (South Brunswick, N.J.: A. S. Barnes, 1971); Simon Louvish, *Keystone: The Life and Clowns of Mack Sennett* (New York: Faber & Faber, 2003).

21. Steve Seidman, *Comedian Comedy: A Tradition in Hollywood Narrative Film* (Ann Arbor, Mich.: UMI Research, 1981).

22. Donald Crafton, "Pie and Chase: Gag, Spectacle and Narrative in Slapstick Comedy," in Kristine Brunovska Karnick and Henry Jenkins, eds., *Classical Hollywood Comedy* (New York: Routledge, 1995), 106–19. Similar definitions of comedy are offered by Peter Brunette, "The Three Stooges and

the (Anti-)Narrative of Violence: De(con)structive Comedy," in A. Horton, ed., *Comedy/Cinema/Theory* (Berkeley: University of California Press, 1991), 174–87; Peter Krämer, "Derailing the Honeymoon Express: Comicality and Narrative Closure in Buster Keaton's *The Blacksmith*," *Velvet Light Trap* 23 (Spring 1989): 101–16; Steve Neale and Frank Krutnik, *Popular Film and Television Comedy* (London: Routledge, 1990), chaps. 2 and 3; and Jerry Palmer, *The Logic of the Absurd* (London: BFI, 1987), chap. 7.

23. On comedy and "embodied" spectatorship, see Lauren Rabinovitz, "The Coney Island Comedies: Bodies and Slapstick at the Amusement Park and the Movies," in Charlie Keil and Shelley Stamp, eds., *American Cinema's Transitional Era: Audiences, Institutions, Practices* (Berkeley: University of California Press, 2004), 171–90; Steven Shaviro, *The Cinematic Body* (Minneapolis: University of Minnesota Press, 1993), chap. 3; Linda Williams, "Film Bodies: Gender, Genre, and Excess," *Film Quarterly* 44.4 (Summer 1991): 2–13.

24. See Jenkins, *What Made Pistachio Nuts?* 10–11.

25. This is not to say that a methodological focus on the body necessarily excludes questions of history, as any Foucauldian knows. In this respect, Jennifer Bean's ongoing work on early action genres (including serials and slapstick) is exemplary in linking "embodied" spectatorship to the experience of turn-of-the-century modernity. See Jennifer Bean, "Technologies of Early Stardom and the Extraordinary Body," *Camera Obscura* 16.3 (2001): 9–57; and "The Art of Falling Apart: Keystone Slapstick" (paper delivered at Society for Cinema and Media Studies Conference, Vancouver, 2006).

26. Raymond Williams, *Marxism and Literature* (New York: Oxford University Press, 1977), 124.

27. An "alternative" culture is that of "someone who simply finds a different way to live and wishes to be alone with it"; an "oppositional" culture that of "someone who finds a different way to live and wants to change society in its light." Raymond Williams, "Base and Superstructure in Marxist Cultural Theory," *New Left Review* 82 (December 1973): 11.

28. See Paul Dimaggio, "Cultural Entrepreneurship in Nineteenth-Century Boston: The Creation of an Organizational Base for High Culture in America," *Media, Culture and Society* 1 (January 1982): 33–50; Lawrence W. Levine, *Highbrow/Lowbrow: The Emergence of Cultural Hierarchy in America* (Cambridge, Mass.: Harvard University Press, 1988).

29. Stuart Hall, "Notes on Deconstructing 'The Popular,'" in Raphael Samuel, ed., *People's History and Socialist Theory* (London: Routledge & Kegan Paul, 1981), 227–40. This is not, of course, the only possible definition of "popular" culture. A different, though perhaps more self-evident, understanding has been provided by Lawrence Levine, who describes popular culture as simply "culture that is *popular*; culture that is widely accessible and widely accessed; widely disseminated, and widely viewed or heard or read." Levine, "The Folklore of Industrial Society: Popular Culture and its Audiences," *American Historical Review* 97 (December 1992): 1373. There are two major

limitations to this definition. First, this meaning runs into difficulties when applied to the historical context under consideration: the very notion of a "widely accessible" culture is inapposite for a period in which cultural accessibility was differentiated by class. Second, this definition has nothing to say about any relation that may exist between so-called popular culture and the traditions or values of the groups that use it. For Levine, popular culture is created solely out of choices made at the cultural marketplace; this, in turn, makes it difficult to see how the term can refer to anything but the top-down manipulation of consumers by the producers of cultural goods. What is lost—and what Hall's account seeks to retain—is not only the distinction between "popular" and "mass" culture, but also any sense of the popular as a space of difference and contestation. See also n. 47 below.

30. Alan Trachtenberg, *The Incorporation of America: Culture and Society in the Gilded Age* (New York: Hill & Wang, 1982), 99.

31. David Roediger, *Working toward Whiteness: How America's Immigrants Became White* (New York: Basic Books, 2005), 11.

32. My definition of class thus mediates between a "classical" definition that looks for the objective sources of class division in relations of capitalist production and a "poststructuralist" view that locates class distinction in language and culture. A richer understanding of class requires a nuanced perspective that accounts for how class membership is created and maintained through a range of interlocking factors, including economic, social, *and* cultural processes (e.g., patterns of consumption, leisure practices, etc.), a process Anthony Giddens calls "class structuration." See Anthony Giddens, *The Class Structure of the Advanced Societies* (New York: Harper & Row, 1975), 177–97. As Giddens argues, it is the degree to which these structuring factors converge or diverge within a given society that determines the salience of class for that society.

33. Roy Rosenzweig, *Eight Hours for What We Will: Workers and Leisure in an Industrial City, 1870–1920* (Cambridge, Mass.: Cambridge University Press, 1983), chap. 2.

34. Figures cited in Steven J. Ross, *Working-Class Hollywood: Silent Film and the Shaping of Class in America* (Princeton, N.J.: Princeton University Press, 1998), 13.

35. The phrase "cult of domesticity" originates in Aileen S. Kraditor's introduction to *Up from the Pedestal: Selected Writings in the History of American Feminism* (Chicago: Quadrangle Books, 1968). On sentimentalism and middle-class culture, see Ann Douglas, *The Feminization of American Culture* (New York: Knopf, 1977); Halttunen, *Confidence Men and Painted Ladies*; Ryan, *Cradle of the Middle Class*; Shirley Samuels, "Introduction," in Shirley Samuels, ed., *The Culture of Sentiment: Race, Gender, and Sentimentality in Nineteenth-Century America* (New York: Oxford University Press, 1992), 3–8.

36. Rollin Lynde Hartt, *The People at Play: Excursions in the Humor and Philosophy of Popular Amusements* (Boston: Houghton Mifflin, 1909), 27, 30.

37. Walter Rauschenbusch, *Christianizing the Social Order* (New York: Macmillan, 1912), 248–49, quoted in Kasson, *Amusing the Million*, 100.

38. See Shelley Streeby, *American Sensations: Class, Empire, and the Production of Popular Culture* (Berkeley: University of California Press, 2002), 31.

39. My point here derives from Michael Denning, *Mechanic Accents: Dime Novels and Working-Class Culture in America* (London: Verso, 1987), 59–60.

40. Figures cited in Snyder, *Voice of the City*, 105.

41. Denning, *Mechanic Accents*, 60. See also Francis C. Couvares, "The Triumph of Commerce: Class Culture and Mass Culture in Pittsburgh," in Michael H. Frisch and Daniel J. Walkowitz, eds., *Working-Class America: Essays on Labor, Community, and American Society* (Urbana: University of Illinois Press, 1983), 123–52; Rosenzweig, *Eight Hours for What We Will*, chap. 7. The commercialization of popular culture was in stark contrast with the largely non-profit orientation of high cultural institutions, many of which were organized on a basis of private philanthropy. See Dimaggio, "Cultural Entrepreneurship in Nineteenth-Century Boston," 35–38.

42. Couvares, "Triumph of Commerce," 123–24.

43. See Snyder, *Voice of the City*, chaps. 2 and 4.

44. See David Nasaw, *Going Out: The Rise and Fall of Popular Amusements* (New York: Basic Books, 1993), chap. 8.

45. The term "culture industry" comes from the work of Frankfurt School theorists Max Horkheimer and Theodor Adorno. See Max Horkheimer and Theodor Adorno, *Dialectic of Enlightenment*, trans. John Cumming ([1944] New York: Continuum, 2001).

46. Max Weber, *Economy and Society: An Outline of Interpretive Sociology*, vol. 2, trans. Ephraim Fischoff ([1924] New York: Bedminster Press, 1968), 937. I am indebted to Paul DiMaggio's analysis of highbrow culture for this reference to Weber. See DiMaggio, "Cultural Entrepreneurship in Nineteenth-Century Boston," 36.

47. Although the terms "mass" and "popular" culture are often used as synonymous in common parlance, I draw a distinction based on structural relations between class and cultural form: thus "popular" signifies forms derived directly from the material conditions of lower-class life, while "mass" signifies forms that suppress class meanings in order to appeal to a cross-class audience. On definitions of mass culture, see Raymond Williams, *Culture & Society: 1780–1950* (New York: Columbia University Press, 1958), 297–312.

48. Dreiser, "Best Motion Picture Interview Ever Written," 35, 124.

49. On the concept of reification, see Georg Lukács, "Reification and the Consciousness of the Proletariat," in *History and Class Consciousness: Studies in Marxist Dialectics*, trans. Rodney Livingstone (Cambridge, Mass.: MIT Press, 1971), 83–222. Lukács links the phenomenon of reification to that of commodity-structure, that is, the process whereby "a relation between people takes on the character of a thing" (83). See also chapter 6, n. 114, in this book.

50. Sennett, *King of Comedy*, 90.

1. "THE FUN FACTORY"

Epigraph: Siegfried Kracauer, "Artistisches und Amerikanisches," *Frankfurter Zeitung,* January 29, 1926, quoted in Miriam Bratu Hansen, "America, Paris, the Alps: Kracauer (and Benjamin) on Cinema and Modernity," from Leo Charney and Vanessa Schwartz, eds., *Cinema and the Invention of Modern Life* (Berkeley: University of California Press, 1995), 373.

1. W. Stephen Bush, "Factory or Studio?" *MPW,* September 21, 1912, 1153.

2. *MPW,* December 4, 1909, 837, quoted in Eileen Bowser, *The Transformation of Cinema, 1907–1915* (Berkeley: University of California Press, 1990), 179.

3. A. W. Thomas, "The Photoplaywright and His Art," *Photoplay,* October 1912, 91.

4. A. W. Thomas, "The Photoplaywright and His Art," *Photoplay,* February 1913, 120.

5. "Reflections of the Critic," *Photoplay,* December 1912, 106; "Players' Personalities," *Photoplay,* January 1913, 5.

6. Kalton C. Lahue, *World of Laughter: The Motion Picture Comedy Short, 1910–1930* (Norman: University of Oklahoma Press, 1966), 7; Bowser, *Transformation of Cinema,* 181.

7. "Pathé Notes," *MPW,* July 9, 1910, 113; ibid., March 26, 1910, 469. Other French comic series that fared well on the American market include Pathé's "Betty" and "Rigadin" films (the latter released as "Whiffles" in America), Gaumont's "Bébé" and "Calino" comedies, and Lux's "Patouillard" series ("Bill" in America).

8. " 'Alkali Ike' in Demand," *MPW,* October 26, 1912, 345; "Big Demand for 'Alkali' Ike Dolls," *MPW,* May 24, 1913, 814; "Want an 'Alkali' Ike Doll?" *MPW,* May 31, 1913, 926.

9. See Patrick Loughney, "Leave 'em Laughing: The Last Years of the Biograph Company," in Eileen Bowser, ed., *The Slapstick Symposium* (Brussels: Fedération internationale des archives du film, 1988), 20.

10. Epes Winthrop Sargent, "The Photoplaywright," *MPW,* November 11, 1913, 490.

11. Mack Sennett, with Cameron Shipp, *King of Comedy* (Garden City, N.Y.: Doubleday, 1954; reprint, San Jose, Calif.: toExcel Press, 2000), 141, 29.

12. The 1910 Russell Sage survey is cited in Russell Merritt, "Nickelodeon Theaters, 1905–1914: Building an Audience for the Movies," in Tino Balio, ed., *The American film Industry* (Madison, Wisconsin: Wisconsin University Press, 1985), 87. The class composition of early film audiences has, of course, been a subject of much controversy. At the risk of oversimplifying, that debate has been waged between two basic positions—on the one hand, a traditional understanding of early cinema as a predominantly lower-class amusement and, on the other, a revisionist interpretation of the centrality of the middle-class audience. The key proponents of the revisionist position argue that nickelodeons

attracted a middle-class audience virtually from the start. See, e.g., ibid., 83–102, and Robert C. Allen, "Motion Picture Exhibition in Manhattan, 1906–1912: Beyond the Nickelodeon," *Cinema Journal* 18.2 (Spring 1979): 2–15. Ben Singer has, however, queried the evidential basis for many of Allen's claims, arguing that moviegoers remained largely lower-class even into the teens. Ben Singer, "Manhattan's Nickelodeons: New Data on Audiences and Exhibitors," *Cinema Journal* 34.3 (1995): 5–35. Social historians tend to support Singer's findings, indicating that, in urban areas at least, regular middle-class attendance occurred at a significantly later date than has generally been assumed. Roy Rosenzweig, for example, suggests that filmgoing remained a working-class activity until at least 1914, while Lizabeth Cohen and Steven J. Ross argue that it was not until the 1920s that the movies became a genuinely "cross-class" entertainment. See Lizabeth Cohen, *Making a New Deal: Industrial Workers in Chicago, 1919–1939* (Cambridge: Cambridge University Press, 1990), chap. 3; Steven J. Ross, *Working-Class Hollywood: Silent Film and the Shaping of Class in America* (Princeton, N.J.: Princeton University Press, 1998), chap. 7; and Roy Rosenzweig, *Eight Hours for What We Will: Workers and Leisure in an Industrial City, 1870–1920* (Cambridge: Cambridge University Press, 1983), chap. 8. For further critique of the revisionist position, see Robert Sklar, "Oh! Althusser! Historiography and the Rise of Cinema Studies," *Radical History Review* 41 (Spring 1988): 10–35.

13. I am paraphrasing Raymond Williams's call for a new "sociology of culture" in which "the active and formative relationships of a [social] process, right through to its still active 'products,' are specifically and structurally connected: at once a 'sociology' and an 'aesthetics.'" Raymond Williams, *Marxism and Literature* (New York: Oxford University Press, 1977), 141.

14. Sennett, *King of Comedy*, 26.

15. Simon Louvish, *Keystone: The Life and Clowns of Mack Sennett* (New York: Faber & Faber, 2003), 11–12.

16. Sennett, *King of Comedy*, 27.

17. For the saloon as a space of working-class male recreation, see Rosenzweig, *Eight Hours for What We Will*, chap. 2. For burlesque and male working-class culture, see Robert C. Allen, *Horrible Prettiness: Burlesque and American Culture* (Chapel Hill: University of North Carolina Press, 1991).

18. Kathy Peiss, *Cheap Amusements: Working Women and Leisure in Turn-of-the-Century New York* (Philadelphia: Temple University Press, 1986).

19. Matthew Arnold, *Culture and Anarchy* (New York, 1875), 47, quoted in Lawrence W. Levine, *Highbrow/Lowbrow: The Emergence of Cultural Hierarchy in America* (Cambridge, Mass.: Harvard University Press, 1990), 223. On the rise of sensationalism in late nineteenth-century popular amusements, see Ben Singer, *Melodrama and Modernity: Early Sensational Cinema and Its Contexts* (New York: Columbia University Press, 2001), 90–96; Shelley Streeby, *American Sensations: Class, Empire, and the Production of Popular Culture* (Berkeley: University of California Press, 2002), 27–37.

20. Sennett, *King of Comedy*, 28–29.

21. Sennett refers to the "Bowery Burlesque" in his autobiography (ibid., 28). The reference must be to Miner's, among the most famous of all New York's burlesque theaters and the only one with the words "Bowery Burlesque" in its name. "If any single institution could be said to epitomize the spirit of the Bowery," write Armond Fields and L. Marc Fields, "it was Miner's. Many of the most prominent variety and vaudeville artists were alumni of Harry Miner's informal academy: Pat Rooney. . . , McIntyre & Heath, the Cohans, Ross and Fenton, Kitty O'Neil (champion jig-dancer), Gus Williams, Jennie Yeamans, [and] Sam Bernard." See Armond Fields and L. Marc Fields, *From the Bowery to Broadway: Lew Fields and the Roots of American Popular Theater* (New York: Oxford University Press, 1993), 42–43.

22. "The Circus in America," *NYT*, March 12, 1882, 14. On English clowning, see Annette Bercut Lust, *From the Greek Mimes to Marcel Marceau and Beyond: Mimes, Actors, Pierrots, and Clowns* (Lanham, Md.: Scarecrow Press, 2000), 49–52.

23. On the growth of comic acts and sketches in the postbellum concert saloon, see Brooks McNamara, *The New York Concert Saloon: The Devil's Own Nights* (Cambridge: Cambridge University Press, 2002), 55–57. A succinct history of the "stage Irishman" in nineteenth-century U.S. theater is provided by Maureen Murphy, "Irish-American Theatre," in Maxine Schwartz Seller, ed., *Ethnic Theatre in the United States* (Westport, Conn.: Greenwood Press, 1983), 222–27.

24. Douglas Gilbert, *American Vaudeville: Its Life and Times* (New York: McGraw-Hill, 1940), 62–63.

25. On the aesthetic of "popular realism" in late-nineteenth-century popular culture, see Kathryn Oberdeck, *The Evangelist and the Impresario: Religion, Entertainment, and Cultural Politics in America, 1884–1914* (Baltimore: Johns Hopkins University Press, 1999), 71–72, 101.

26. James L. Ford, "Stage Humor and Comedy," *Harper's Weekly*, November 19, 1904, 1774, 1778.

27. The "common calamity" citation is from Rollin Lynde Hartt, *The People at Play: Excursions in the Humor and Philosophy of Popular Amusements* (Boston: Houghton Mifflin, 1909), 22.

28. "Says Sunday Shows Cannot Be Stopped," *NYT*, October 21, 1907, 7.

29. Minnie Marx quoted in Robert W. Snyder, *The Voice of the City: Vaudeville and Popular Culture in New York* (New York: Oxford University Press, 1989), 46. Charles Chaplin, a future Keystone performer himself, remembered his first acting job in similar terms: "I had suddenly left behind a life of poverty and was entering a long-desired dream. . . . I was to become an actor! . . . No longer was I a nondescript of the slums; now I was a personage of the theatre, I wanted to weep." Charles Chaplin, *My Autobiography* (London: Penguin Books, 1964), 78.

30. Sennett, *King of Comedy*, 16.

31. Amy Bridges, "Becoming American: The Working Classes of the United States before the Civil War," in I. Katzenelson and A. Zolberg, eds., *Working-Class*

Formation: Nineteenth-Century Patterns in Western Europe and the United States (Princeton, N.J.: Princeton University Press, 1986), 157–96; Noel Ignatiev, *How the Irish Became White* (New York: Routledge, 1995).

32. Sennett, *King of Comedy*, 20, 19.

33. Review of *A Chinese Honeymoon, NYDM*, June 14, 1902, 14.

34. Review of *The Boys of Company B, NYDM*, April 20, 1907, 3.

35. Sennett, *King of Comedy*, 27.

36. See Catherine Sennett folder, General Files, MSC; Kalton Lahue, *Mack Sennett's Keystone: The Man, the Myth, and the Comedies* (South Brunswick, N.J.: A. S. Barnes, 1971), 249–52. Sennett's mother was, in fact, a frequent guest at his Los Angeles home throughout the 1910s and 1920s and, during her visits, would make daily trips to the studio lot to see her son at work.

37. *NYDM*, January 12, 1907, 16.

38. Sennett, *King of Comedy*, 43.

39. Ford Sterling's biography and pre-Keystone career are discussed in Wendy Warwick White, *Ford Sterling: The Life and Films* (Jefferson, N.C.: McFarland, 2007), chaps. 1 and 2. Further information is drawn from the Ford Sterling clippings file, Robinson Locke Collection of Dramatic Scrapbooks, envelope 2157, BRTC, and Louvish, *Keystone*, 62–63. According to a review in New York's *Dramatic Mirror*, Sterling appeared on Broadway with the Frank Keenan Players in the spring of 1905: the reviewer singled Sterling out for praise, noting that he "had sincerity and force, and was an earnest lover" (*NYDM*, April 1, 1905, 16). Elsewhere, his role as "Orphis Noodle, Prime Minister" in *King Casey* in 1909 drew praise from the *Indianapolis Star*, which noted his "clever character work in the fantastic German role" (*Indianapolis Star*, September 21, 1909, Robinson Locke Collection of Dramatic Scrapbooks, Envelope 2157, BRTC).

40. Biographical information on Henry Lehrman derives from Kalton C. Lahue and Terry Brewer, *Kops and Custards: The Legend of Keystone Films* (1968; reprint, Norman: University of Oklahoma Press, 1972), 28–31.

41. "Brief Biographies of Popular Players," *MPSM*, October 1914, 108.

42. Carolyn Lowry, *The First One Hundred Noted Men and Women of the Screen* (New York: Moffat, Yard, 1920), 140, quoted in Christina Marie Mugno, "The Cinema of Mabel Normand" (Ph.D. diss., Wayne State University, 1998), 1. Normand's pursuit of elite culture became a major trope of fan discourse on the star during the mid- to late-1910s; see chapter 6 in this book. For more on Normand's early years, see Betty Harper Fussell, *Mabel* (New Haven, Conn.: Ticknor & Fields, 1982), 20–29; Louvish, *Keystone*, 42–44; and William Thomas Sherman, *Mabel Normand: A Source Book to Her Life and Films* (Seattle: Cinema Books, 1994), chap. 1.

43. This kind of reinvention was rather common among early screen stars who, in accord with the film industry's middlebrow pretensions, frequently claimed distinguished social pedigree. Sumiko Higashi, "Vitagraph Stardom: Constructing Personalities for Lower Middle-Class Consumption" (MS) discusses this.

44. Sennett, *King of Comedy,* 40.

45. Biographical information on Mace is drawn from the following sources: "Fred Mace," *Billboard,* August 18, 1906, Robinson Locke Collection of Dramatic Scrapbooks, ser. 2, vol. 272, BRTC; Epes Winthrop Sargent, "The Photoplaywright," *MPW,* November 2, 1912, 447; "Chats with the Players," *MPSM,* April 1913, 113–14; "Fred Mace, Comedian, Keystone," *MPN,* January 29, 1916, 36; Kalton C. Lahue and Samuel Gill, *Clown Princes and Court Jesters* (South Brunswick, N.J.: A. S. Barnes, 1971), 230–33; Louvish, *Keystone,* 21–22, 41–42.

46. I am thinking here primarily of Vitagraph, a production company that seems to have hired predominantly white, middle-class employees. A late article on the company described it as "the only one of the original motion picture companies that was founded entirely by Anglo-Saxons" (William Basil Courtney, "History of Vitagraph," *MPN,* February 7, 1925, 342, quoted in Siobhan B. Somerville, "The Queer Career of Jim Crow: Racial and Sexual Transformation in *A Florida Enchantment,*" in Jennifer M. Bean and Diane Negra, eds., *A Feminist Reader in Early Cinema* [Durham, N.C.: Duke University Press, 2002], 258).

47. Sennett, *King of Comedy,* 77–79.

48. Louvish, *Keystone,* 50.

49. Thanks to Jennifer Putzi and Simon Joyce for the information on Adam Kessel.

50. Francis Couvares, "The Triumph of Commerce: Class Culture and Mass Culture in Pittsburgh," in Michael H. Frisch and Daniel J. Walkowitz, eds., *Working-Class America: Essays on Labor, Community, and American Society* (Urbana: University of Illinois Press, 1983), 123–51.

51. See Richard Abel, *The Red Rooster Scare: Making Cinema American, 1900–1910* (Berkeley: University of California Press, 1999), 126–28.

52. Fred Mace was also signed on to the new company, although he had already quit the Biograph unit early in 1912. He joined the Keystone team after its arrival in Los Angeles that fall. See Lahue and Brewer, *Kops and Custards,* 32–33. On the battles between the Trust and the independents, see Bowser, *Transformation of Cinema,* chaps. 2, 5, and 9.

53. The Film Supply Co. meanwhile proved less competitive: Aitken withdrew his interest in the failing organization in late 1912, and its few surviving remnants were reorganized in April 1913 as the Exclusive Supply Company.

54. For a more comprehensive account of these disputes among the independents, see Bowser, *Transformation of Cinema,* chap. 13.

55. Keystone Film Company stock certificate book, 1912, ABP.

56. For the exact date when Keystone began production, see Lahue, *Mack Sennett's Keystone,* 15–42. The official commencement date of July 6 is not mentioned by Lahue but is cited in the Keystone Film Company journal, September 1912 to October 1915, ABP. Sennett himself claimed that the first Keystone production—which he identified as *Cohen at Coney Island* (actual

release title *At Coney Island*)—was shot during one of the "hottest July Fourths on record," and, in 1915, he hosted an extravagant third birthday party for Keystone on that date. Sennett, *King of Comedy*, 84; "Keystone, 3 Years Old, Enters Ranks of Veterans," *MPN*, July 24, 1915, 40. Synthesizing the data, one may hypothesize that production did, in fact, begin on July 4, 1912 (which was a Sunday), but that an official commencement date could not be entered until after the holiday weekend.

57. For trade press reports on the arrival of the Keystone players in California, see "Doings at Los Angeles," *MPW*, September 14, 1912, 1067; "Doings at Los Angeles," *MPW*, September 21, 1912, 1160.

58. Sennett, *King of Comedy*, 85.

59. Advertisements for Keystone, Bison, and Broncho, *MPW*, August 31, 1912, 832–34, and September 7, 1912, 942–44. As part of its acrimonious split with Universal, the New York Motion Picture Co. gave up rights to the Bison brand name but retained the production unit, eventually renamed "Kay-Bee," from Kessel and Baumann's initials. Subsequent "Bison" releases were produced by a new production company at Universal.

60. Although the original contract has been lost, it is possible to calculate its financial provisions from the studio's existing ledgers. See the Keystone Film Company journal, September 1912 to October 1915, ABP.

61. Advertisement for Keystone, *MPW*, August 31, 832.

62. Advertisement for *At It Again*, *MPW*, November 2, 1912, 421.

63. "Doings at Los Angeles," *MPW*, September 21, 1912, 1160.

64. As late as November 1912, in fact, a Mutual ad for Keystone promised "High Class Comedy and Dramatic Subjects." Advertisement for Keystone, *Photoplay*, November 1912, 143.

65. In return for his supervisory services, Ince received 10 percent shares in Keystone. See Keystone stock certificate book, 1912, ABP.

66. See Janet Staiger, "The Central Producer System: Centralized Management after 1914," in David Bordwell, Janet Staiger, and Kristin Thompson, *The Classical Hollywood Cinema: Film Style and Mode of Production to 1960* (New York: Columbia University Press, 1985), 128–41.

67. "Reflections of the Critic," *Photoplay*, December 1912, 106.

68. "Doings at Los Angeles," *MPW*, February 15, 1913, 668; "Doings at Los Angeles," *MPW*, March 15, 1913, 1090.

69. On Stout's association with Keystone, see Lahue, *Mack Sennett's Keystone*, 244–54.

70. On the new construction at Keystone, see Epes Winthrop Sargent, "The Photoplaywright," *MPW*, February 14, 1914, 803; Lahue and Brewer, *Kops and Custards*, 70–73.

71. Interview with Mack Sennett, April 15, 1955, TPI.

72. "'You Can't Put a Stop Watch on Brains'—Says Mack Sennett," *MSW*, February 12, 1917, 1.

73. "Doings at Los Angeles," *MPW*, October 26, 1912, 331.

74. "Doings at Los Angeles," *MPW*, November 23, 1912, 761.

75. "More Big 'Bison-101' Pictures," *MPW*, October 5, 1912, 32; "Chaos at Keystone," *MPW*, November 30, 1912, 870; "Doings at Los Angeles," *MPW*, September 7, 1912, 969; "Doings at Los Angeles," *MPW*, July 26, 1913, 415.

76. Sennett, *King of Comedy*, 137.

77. Advertisement for *Mabel's Dramatic Career*, *MPW*, September 20, 1913, 1245.

78. Review of *Tillie's Punctured Romance*, *MPN*, November 14, 1914, 40.

79. Sennett describes his office bath in his autobiography: "I had my office, my tub, and my masseur installed there. Thus I could bathe and soap and splash and shout any time of the day, and simultaneously keep an eye on my outrageous employees. Most of my story and business conferences were held there" (93). Felix Adler, one of Sennett's later gagmen, recalled the "tremendous bathtub" as being "about eight feet long, five feet wide, and five feet high". (Interview with Felix Adler, May 12, 1955, TPI.)

80. "Doings at Los Angeles," *MPW*, January 18, 1913, 251.

81. Interview with Felix Adler, TPI.

82. Herbert G. Gutman, "Work, Culture, and Society in Industrializing America, 1815–1919," *American Historical Review* 78.3 (June 1973): 531–88.

83. "The 'Movies' in the Making," *Los Angeles Citizen*, February 5, 1915, 1, 3.

84. Jennifer M. Bean, "The Imagination of Early Hollywood: Movie-Land and the Magic Cities, 1914–1916," in Richard Abel, Giorgio Bertellini, and Rob King, eds., *Early Cinema and the "National"* (Eastleigh, UK: John Libbey Publishing, 2008), 332–41.

85. Mabel Condon, "Keystone: The Home of Mack Sennett and the Film Comedy," *NYDM*, September 9, 1916, 32 (emphasis added). Thanks to Jennifer Bean for bringing this article to my attention.

86. Foucault defines a heterotopia as a "counter-site"—a "kind of effectively enacted utopia in which the real sites, all the other real sites that can be found within the culture, are simultaneously represented, contested, and inverted." Michel Foucault, "Of Other Spaces," *Diacritics* 16.1 (Spring 1986): 24, quoted in Miriam Hansen, *Babel and Babylon: Spectatorship in American Silent Film* (Cambridge, Mass.: Harvard University Press, 1991), 107.

87. Douglas Riblet, "The Keystone Film Company, 1912 to 1915" (Ph.D. diss., University of Wisconsin-Madison, 1998), 55, 78. My argument in this section is indebted to Riblet's excellent analysis. See Riblet, chap. 3.

88. See Lee Grieveson, *Policing Cinema: Movies and Censorship in Early-Twentieth-Century America* (Berkeley: University of California Press, 2004), 117–120.

89. See Loughney, "Leave 'em Laughing," 21.

90. For fuller description of Vitagraph's comedy output, see Jon Gartenberg, "Vitagraph Comedy Production," in Bowser, ed., *Slapstick Symposium*, 45–48; Peter Krämer, "Vitagraph, Slapstick and Early Cinema," *Screen* 29.2 (Spring 1988): 98–104; Lahue, *World of Laughter*, 11–26.

91. On the "comedy of marital combat," see Henry Jenkins, *What Made Pistachio Nuts? Early Sound Comedy and the Vaudeville Aesthetic* (New York: Columbia University Press, 1992), 248–56. Such comedies expressed real tensions created by the "feminization" of middle-class culture, which, as Richard Stott claims, made middle-class men marginal to their own culture and attracted them to working-class recreational pursuits (e.g., prizefights, burlesque, saloons). Richard Stott, *Workers in the Metropolis: Class, Ethnicity and Youth in Antebellum New York City* (Ithaca, N.Y.,: Cornell University Press, 1990), 272.

92. Tom Gunning, "The Cinema of Attractions: Early Film, Its Spectator and the Avant-Garde," in Thomas Elsaesser and Adam Barker, eds., *Early Cinema: Space, Frame, Narrative* (London: BFI, 1990), 56–62.

93. William Lord Wright, "The True Worth of Humor," *MPSM*, March 1914, 101.

94. Epes Winthrop Sargent, "The Photoplaywright," *MPW*, April 12, 1913, 157.

95. Tom Gunning, "Crazy Machines in the Garden of Forking Paths: Mischief Gags and the Origins of American Film Comedy," in Kristina Karnick and Henry Jenkins, eds., *Classical Hollywood Comedy* (New York: Routledge, 1995), 87–105.

96. The leader of the League was played by Flora Finch, in what was apparently her screen debut.

97. Riblet, "The Keystone Film Company, 1912 to 1915," 60–61.

98. For more on Biograph's use of the "farce comedy" label, see Loughney, "Leave 'em Laughing," 24.

99. For a history of "farce comedy" on the American stage, see Cecil Smith and Glenn Litton, *Musical Comedy in America* (New York: Theater Arts Books, 1981), 31–38.

100. Raymond Schrock, "Reflections of the Critic," *Photoplay*, January 1913, 103.

101. Raymond Williams, *Marxism and Literature*, 122, defines as "residual practices" those that have been "effectively formed in the past, but [are] still active in the cultural process"; they may also have "an alternative or even oppositional relation to the dominant culture." See also Introduction, n. 27, above.

102. Review of *The Curtain Pole*, *MPW*, February 20, 1909, 202, quoted in Tom Gunning, *D. W. Griffith and the Origins of American Narrative Film: The Early Years at Biograph* (Urbana: University of Chicago Press, 1991), 133.

103. In its use of an actual parade, *Stolen Glory*'s climactic chase replicates a comic strategy from of one of Sennett's Biograph films, *The Would Be Shriner* (1912), released earlier that summer. In that film, "Hank Hopkins"—a rube played by Sennett—tries to participate in a real Shriners' Parade, shot on the streets of Los Angeles. The filming of this Biograph picture undoubtedly provided the basis for one of Sennett's favorite tall tales about Keystone's early days. As Sennett liked to tell it, the Keystone company happened upon a parade

immediately upon arriving at Los Angeles station and began shooting an improvised comic sequence. "'Now take this doll,'" Sennett supposedly told Mabel Normand, "'It's your baby. . . . Run up and down the line of march and embarrass those Shriners.' . . . Mabel put on the comicalest act you ever clapped eyes on, pleading, stumbling, holding out her baby—and the reactions she got from those good and pious gentlemen in the parade were something you couldn't have caught on film after six days of D. W. Griffith rehearsals. . . . One kind soul dropped out and tried to help Mabel. . . . Ford [Sterling] leaped in and started a screaming argument with the innocent Shriner. . . . The police moved in on Ford and Mabel. Ford fled, leaping, insulting the police, and they . . . chased him. I helped the cameraman and we got it all" (Sennett, *King of Comedy*, 87). For further discussion of this apocryphal tale, see Lahue and Brewer, *Kops and Custards*, 35–39; Louvish, *Keystone*, 54..

104. Parallel-edited rescues are, however, not without precedent in Sennett's earlier work at Biograph—notable examples being *A Dash through the Clouds* and *Help! Help!* (both 1912). On the latter film, see my analysis later in this chapter.

105. For Griffith's use of the parallel-edited, race-to-the-rescue climax, see Gunning, *D. W. Griffith and the Origins of American Narrative Film*, chap. 4.

106. Although *The Man Next Door* is the first extant appearance of this madcap group of law officers, it appears that previous Keystone films had occasionally included one or more comic policemen. Kalton Lahue and Terry Brewer cite *Hoffmeyer's Legacy* (December 23, 1912) as "the first recorded existence of a Kop picture" (Lahue and Brewer, *Kops and Custards*, 47), and the *Moving Picture World*'s summary of this lost film indeed suggests the appearance of a group of policemen in some kind of chase sequence: "A legacy of five hundred dollars lead [sic] Hoffmeyer and his wife into a series of eccentric situations. They are pursued through the streets in night attire, and are haled [sic] into court, where the judge fines them the exact amount of the legacy" ("Comments on the Films," *MPW*, December 28, 1912, 1293). Surviving production stills in the Margaret Herrick Library's Sennett Collection point to an even earlier appearance of a group of comic policemen in *Pat's Day Off* (December 2, 1912) and show that, in this film and in *Hoffmeyer's Legacy*, the role of police chief was played by Mack Sennett himself. Whatever the case, the oft-made claim that the Keystone Kops first appeared in *The Bangville Police* (April 1913)—a claim made at the beginning of the Blackhawk print of this film and recently repeated by Simon Louvish (*Keystone*, 63)—is simply incorrect: *The Bangville Police* had not even been readied for distribution by the time *The Man Next Door* was released (March 17). See "Keystone Releases," General Files, MSC. According to my research, the earliest use of the term "Keystone cops" in the trade press occurs in "In and out of West Coast Studios," *MPN*, November 20, 1915, 72, where it is reported that "The uniforms of the Keystone cops . . . [are to be] replaced by foxy new uniforms of the style of those worn by the cops of New York." The first reference to the "Keystone Kops" (with the "Kops" spelling) appears to be in *Photoplay*, February 1916, 58.

107. Sennett candidly admitted the influence of French comedies in his autobiography. "It was those Frenchmen who invented slapstick and I imitated them. I never went as far as they did, because give a Frenchman a chance to be funny and he will go the limit—you know what I mean. But I stole my first ideas from the Pathés" (Sennett, *King of Comedy*, 65). On the popularity of early French comedies in America, see n. 7 above.

108. The films are *The Man Next Door* (March), *Hide and Seek, The Bangville Police* (April), *Mabel's Awful Mistake, A Little Hero* (May), *Barney Oldfield's Race for a Life* (June), *Love and Rubbish, A Noise from the Deep* (July), *The Riot, Mabel's New Hero* (August), *A Healthy Neighborhood, Two Old Tars* (October), *A Muddy Romance, Cohen Saves the Flag* (November), and *His Sister's Kids* (December). Of these, *Hide and Seek, A Little Hero, A Healthy Neighborhood,* and *Cohen Saves the Flag* do not feature policemen as the rescuers: *A Little Hero* is a novelty film with an animal cast, while *Hide and Seek, A Healthy Neighborhood,* and *Cohen Saves the Flag* feature firemen, doctors, and soldiers as the respective rescuing groups. I have not been able to view the Munich Film Archive's print of *The Gusher* (December), which may have ended with a parallel-edited rescue from an oil-well fire. (The film is included on Kino Videos's 2008 release of *The Extra Girl*.)

109. Shot numbers refer to the Library of Congress's incomplete 35 mm print (missing the opening).

110. "Comments on the Films," *MPW*, March 22, 1913, 1222.

111. On average shot lengths, see Riblet, "The Keystone Film Company, 1912 to 1915," 115.

112. Gunning, *D. W. Griffith and the Origins of American Narrative Film*, 105.

113. Lukács describes the experience of industrial labor thus: "[T]ime sheds its qualitative, variable, flowing nature; it freezes into an exactly delimited, quantifiable continuum filled with quantifiable 'things' (the reified, mechanically objectified 'performance' of the worker, wholly separated from his total human personality)." Georg Lukács, *History and Class Consciousness: Studies in Marxist Dialectics*, trans. Rodney Livingstone (Cambridge, Mass.: MIT Press, 1971), 90.

114. "The Exhibitor's End of It," *RL*, October, 1914, 23.

115. Chaplin, *My Autobiography*, 148. Chaplin's films under Nichols are *A Film Johnnie, His Favorite Pastime, Cruel, Cruel Love* (March 1914), and *The Star Boarder* (April 1914).

116. Riblet, "The Keystone Film Company, 1912 to 1915," 115, gives the average shot length for Keystone's surviving films for this period as 12.4 seconds. I have factored into Riblet's calculations the shot lengths for *At Coney Island*, recently rediscovered at the Netherlands Filmmuseum. Thanks to Elif Rongen-Kaynakci for making this film available to me.

117. "Tempo—The Value of It," *Wid's Films and Film Folk*, October 7, 1915, 1, quoted in Riblet, "The Keystone Film Company, 1912 to 1915," 99.

118. Interview with Mack Sennett, TPI.

119. "Comments on the Films," *MPW*, December 7, 1912, 977.

120. "Comments on the Films," *MPW*, April 5, 1913, 49, 50; ibid., April 26, 1913, 381.

121. Of course, there were exceptions. The first daily newspaper in America to publish a weekly page devoted to film was New York's *Morning Telegraph*, beginning as early as January 1910; two years later, the same paper gave motion pictures their own separate supplement, eventually running six to eight pages and comprising interviews, articles, listings, and theater ads. Several newspapers in smaller towns also introduced detailed listings around this time—for instance, the *Cleveland Leader*, which, in December 1911, began a full page headlined "Photo-Plays and Players." Even in these instances, however, smaller neighborhood theaters were listed only infrequently, when they were not omitted altogether. See the entry on the *Morning Telegraph* in Richard Abel, ed., *Encyclopedia of Early Cinema* (London: Routledge, 2005), 472. See also Richard Abel, *Americanizing the Movies and "Movie-Mad" Audiences, 1910–1914* (Berkeley: University of California Press, 2006), 215–26.

122. See, e.g., "The 'Movies' in the Making," *Los Angeles Citizen*, February 5, 1915, 1, 3; "Savoy Theatre," ibid., February 19, 1915, 6; and "Superba Theatre," ibid., June 25, 1915, 8.

123. "Main Street—the Bowery of Los Angeles," *Los Angeles Citizen*, January 31, 1913, II, 1.

124. An exception here would be the New Windsor Theater, a 1,500-seater located in the fashionable residential area north of the Loop. For a brief period at the end of May, patrons at the New Windsor could watch first-run Keystone comedies, backed by a fourteen-piece orchestra, for the regular admission of twenty cents. My account of Chicago, Los Angeles, and New York theaters draws from listings in the *Chicago Tribune*, the *Los Angeles Times*, and the *New York Times*, September 1912 through December 1914.

125. Quotations taken from "Star Theatre," *Pawtucket Times*, November 19, 1912, 9; Star Theatre ads, ibid., July 12, 1913, 5, and July 19, 1913, 7.

126. "The Exhibitor's End of It," *RL*, August 29, 1914, 20.

127. "The Movies," *Des Moines News*, December 31, 1912, 3.

128. "Photo Plays to Come Next," *Toledo Daily Blade*, June 7, 1913, 10.

129. The ad was for *Zuzu, the Band Leader*, Keystone's 1913 Christmas special, which played at the Hart Theater in March 1914. See ad for Hart Theatre, *Toledo Daily Blade*, March 20, 1914, 3. Unlike Keystone's regular releases, *Zuzu* was distributed on an unrestricted basis, allowing theaters not contracted with Mutual—like the Hart—to screen the film in their area. On *Zuzu, the Band Leader*, see also chapter 2. Thanks to Richard Abel for sharing his research on Des Moines, Rhode Island, and Toledo theaters.

130. "Doings at Los Angeles," *MPW*, March 29, 1913, 1323.

131. "Comments on the Films," *MPW*, April 5, 1913, 49.

132. "Independent Film Stories," *MPW*, March 29, 1913, 1364.

133. Ibid. A fuller discussion of *The Fatal Hour* in relation to Griffith's use of parallel editing is offered in Gunning, *D. W. Griffith and the Origins of American Narrative Film*, 95–106.

134. "Comments on the Films," *MPW*, April 5, 1913, 49.

135. Gertrude M. Price, "Makes Comedy Out of Melodrama," *Des Moines News*, May 19, 1913, 4; advertisement for New York Motion Picture Co., *MPW*, April 12, 1913, 182. For more on Price, a pioneering movie columnist in newspapers, see Abel, *Americanizing the Movies*, 223–26, 239–52.

136. In fact, as Allen, *Horrible Prettiness*, esp. chaps. 4 and 6, has shown, the leg shows were an offshoot of the parodies. Ever since the Broadway success of Lydia Thompson and her "British Blondes" in *Ixion* in 1868, theatrical burlesque had emphasized female spectacle as an essential element of its high culture travesties.

137. Simon Dentith, *Parody* (London: Routledge, 2000), 150.

138. Karen Halttunen, *Confidence Men and Painted Women: A Study of Middle-Class Culture in America, 1830–1870* (New Haven: Yale University Press, 1982), chap. 6.

139. Buster Keaton recalled taking the stage of vaudeville theaters and improvising hastily contrived travesties of the dramatic sketches on which the curtain had just fallen. Buster Keaton and Charles Samuels, *My Wonderful World of Slapstick* (New York: Doubleday, 1960), 52–53.

140. See T. J. Jackson Lears, *No Place of Grace: Antimodernism and the Transformation of American Culture, 1880–1920* (Chicago: University of Chicago Press, 1981), chap. 1. I borrow the term "weightless" from Lears's analysis (32).

141. Peter Brooks, *The Melodramatic Imagination: Balzac, Henry James, Melodrama, and the Mode of Excess* (New York: Columbia University Press, 1976), 20.

142. See Singer, *Melodrama and Modernity*, 145–48.

143. D. W. Griffith, "Unfinished Autobiography" (MS, Museum of Modern Art Film Library, New York), quoted in Lary May, *Screening out the Past: The Birth of Mass Culture and the Motion Picture Industry* (Chicago: University of Chicago Press, 1980), 71.

144. Griffith quoted in May, *Screening out the Past*, 73.

145. The locus classicus for Griffith's condemnation of social reform is, of course, the modern story in *Intolerance* (1916).

146. On Griffith's indebtedness to the sensationalist conventions of "blood and thunder" melodrama, see Singer, *Melodrama and Modernity*, 195: "[O]f the roughly seventy films released during [Griffith's first] seventh months [at Biograph], about half (or two-thirds if one excludes comedies) contained some combination of extreme moral polarity, abduction, assault, brawling, brutality, binding-and-gagging, murder, and 'infernal machines' (intricate death-delaying contraptions used to prolong suspense)."

147. On middle-class ideologies of domesticity, see esp. Mary Ryan, *Cradle of the Middle Class, 1790–1865* (Cambridge: Cambridge University Press,

1981). On the role of the family in Griffithian melodrama, see Nick Browne, "Griffith's Family Discourse: Griffith and Freud," in Christine Gledhill, ed., *Home Is Where the Heart Is: Studies in Melodrama and the Woman's Film* (London: British Film Institute, 1987), 223–34.

148. Griffith quoted in May, *Screening out the Past*, 77.

149. Sennett, *King of Comedy*, 60. According to his autobiography, Sennett regularly submitted story ideas at Biograph to supplement his five-dollar-a-day actor's salary.

150. Sennett, *King of Comedy*, 51–52, 54–55.

151. "Sennett Has Big Army at Laugh Factory," *TT*, March 11, 1916, 3.

152. Margaret A. Rose, *Parody/Meta-Fiction: An Analysis of Parody as a Critical Mirror to the Writing and Reception of Fiction* (London: Croom Helm, 1979), 25–26.

153. Shot numbers refer to the print held at the UCLA Film and Television Archive.

154. See Ann Douglas, *The Feminization of American Culture* (New York: Knopf, 1977), esp. chap. 4.

155. "Comments on the Films," *MPW*, May 3, 1913, 485.

156. The average shot length for the film's first half is calculated from the fifty-seven shots and eight title cards up to the intertitle "The Race for a Life" (in the Kino Video version of the film). The average shot length for the second half is calculated from the subsequent forty-three shots (uninterrupted by intertitles).

157. This point is suggested in Riblet, "The Keystone Film Company, 1912 to 1915," 113–14.

158. Harry D. Carr, manager, Lyric Theatre, to Bert Ennis, publicity director, New York Motion Picture Company, n.d., quoted in "This Comedy Too Good," *Toledo Daily Blade*, September 24, 1913, 7 (emphasis added). In contrast, a newspaper ad for Pawtucket's Star Theatre promoted *Barney Oldfield* as a "Sensational Keystone *Drama*," with no indication of the film's comic overtones. Advertisement for the Star Theatre, *Pawtucket Times*, June 14, 1913, 7 (emphasis added).

159. Advertisement for *Barney Oldfield's Race for a Life*, *MPW*, May 31, 1913, 880; advertisement for *For the Love of Mabel*, *MPW*, July 5, 1913, 12.

160. The compatibility of pastiche and affect is discussed in Richard Dyer, *Pastiche* (London: Routledge, 2007), esp. chap. 5.

161. Price, "Makes Comedy Out of Melodrama."

162. Epes Winthrop Sargent, "The Photoplaywright," *MPW*, January 17, 1914, 283.

163. Chester Conklin, interview, May 19, 1955, TPI.

164. Sargent, "Photoplaywright."

165. "West Coast Studio Jottings," *Photoplay*, February 1914, 108.

166. Advertisement for the Keystone Film Company, *MPN*, June 17, 1916, 3704–5.

167. Stuart Hall, "Notes on Deconstructing 'The Popular,'" in Raphael Samuel, ed., *People's History and Socialist Theory* (London: Routledge & Kegan Paul, 1981), 238.

168. "Pretty 'Movie' Actress Will Stump for the Socialist Ticket," *Los Angeles Citizen*, April 18, 1913, II, 1; Mack Sennett, "Labor and the Movies," ibid., February 25, 1916, II, 1. That Sennett and Normand took these steps, rather than any of Keystone's other founding members, should perhaps be linked to the traditional importance of labor organizing in nineteenth-century Irish American communities. See Ignatiev, *How the Irish Became White*, chap. 4.

169. Peter Krämer, "'Clean, Dependable Slapstick': Comic Violence and the Emergence of Classical Hollywood Cinema," in J. David Slocum, ed., *Violence and American Cinema* (New York: Routledge, 2001), 103–16.

2. "FUNNY GERMANS" AND "FUNNY DRUNKS"

Epigraph: Chester Conklin, interview, May 19, 1955, TPI.

1. Universal Film Manufacturing Co. advertisement, *MPW*, March 7, 1914, 1196–97.

2. While still employed as general manager of NYMP's West Coast studios, Balshofer apparently made arrangements with Laemmle whereby the latter promised to hire him if he could entice either Sterling or Normand to join Universal. See Kalton C. Lahue and Samuel Gill, *Clown Princes and Court Jesters* (South Brunswick, N.J.: A. S. Barnes, 1970), 346–49. Sterling's company at Universal was eventually named "Sterling Comedies." See "'Sterling' Adopted as Universal Brand," *MPW*, April 11, 1914, 223.

3. On the development of the "star system" in the American film industry, see Richard Decordova, *Picture Personalities: The Emergence of the Star System in America* (Urbana: University of Illinois Press, 1990).

4. Mack Sennett, with Cameron Shipp, *King of Comedy* (Garden City, N.Y.: Doubleday, 1954; reprint, San Jose, Calif.: toExcel Press, 2000), 150, 151.

5. Charles J. Maland, *Chaplin and American Culture: The Evolution of a Star Image* (Princeton, N.J.: Princeton University Press, 1989), 5. "The essential difference between the Keystone style and Chaplin's comedy is that one depends on *exposition*, the other on *expression*," David Robinson observes in *Chaplin: His Life and Art* (New York: McGraw-Hill, 1985), 113.

6. In the light of the concerns of this chapter, a word on definitions is appropriate. Throughout, I differentiate ethnicity, as a category of identity perceived as assimilable, from race, as a category perceived as immutable. My usage derives from Manning Marable, who draws a distinction between race as "passive affiliation," a category into which one happens to be born and which cannot be changed, and ethnicity as "active affiliation," something that is maintained only by active practice (e.g., a sustained commitment to the traditions, linguistic idioms, etc., of the ethnic community). Marable's views are discussed in Robert Stam and Ella Shohat, *Unthinking Eurocentrism: Multiculturalism*

and the Media (London: Routledge, 1994), 20. Historically, as David Roediger has shown, the concept of ethnicity as distinct from that of race emerged only gradually during the early twentieth century, becoming widely accepted only after the 1924 immigration restrictions undercut the usefulness of "immigrant" as a social category. See David R. Roediger, *Working toward Whiteness: How America's Immigrants Became White* (New York: Basic Books, 2005), chap. 1. If I have chosen, somewhat anachronistically, to distinguish between these concepts here, it is because changes within the ranks of Keystone's clowns implied some sense of the distinction, as I later argue. See also page 82 in this chapter.

7. See Louis A. Hieb, "Meaning and Mismeaning: Toward an Understanding of the Ritual Clown," in Alfonso Ortiz, ed., *New Perspectives on the Pueblo* (Albuquerque: University of New Mexico Press, 1972), 190, quoted in Henry Jenkins, *What Made Pistachio Nuts? Early Sound Comedy and the Vaudeville Aesthetic* (New York: Columbia University Press, 1992), 223.

8. Mikhail Bakhtin, *Rabelais and His World,* trans. Helene Iswolsky (Cambridge, Mass.: MIT Press, 1968), 26.

9. Peter Stallybrass and Allon White, *The Politics and Poetics of Transgression* (New York: Cornell University Press, 1986), 25.

10. See David R. Roediger, *The Wages of Whiteness: Race and the Making of the American Working Class* (London: Verso, 1991).

11. Susan Gray Davis, *Parades and Power: Street Theatre in Nineteenth-Century Philadelphia* (Philadelphia: Temple University Press, 1986), chap. 4.

12. Figures on immigration taken from Paul Boyer, *Urban Masses and Moral Order in America, 1820–1920* (Cambridge, Mass.: Harvard University Press, 1978), 123–25.

13. For more on vaudeville traditions of ethnic stereotyping, see Laura Browder, *Slippery Characters: Ethnic Impersonators and American Identities* (Chapel Hill: University of North Carolina Press, 2000); Paul Distler, "The Rise and Fall of the Racial Comics in American Vaudeville" (Ph.D. diss., Tulane University, 1963); Albert McClean, *American Vaudeville as Ritual* (Louisville: University of Kentucky Press, 1965), chap. 6; Robert Snyder, *The Voice of the City: Vaudeville and Popular Culture in New York* (New York: Oxford University Press, 1989), chap. 6.

14. On the commodification of ethnic identity in turn-of-the-century popular culture, see Browder, *Slippery Characters,* 47–51.

15. This model, derived from Henri Bergson, is suggested by Charles Musser in his essay "Ethnicity, Role-Playing, and American Film Comedy: From *Chinese Laundry Scene* to *Whoopee,*" in Lester Friedman, ed., *Unspeakable Images: Ethnicity and the American Cinema* (Chicago: University of Illinois Press, 1991), 39–81.

16. See Roediger, *Wages of Whiteness,* chaps. 5 and 6.

17. Sam Bernard, "Twenty Years—and More—of Stage Laughs," *Theatre Magazine,* May 1920, Sam Bernard Scrapbooks, 11,161a, BRTC.

18. As such, Dutch comedy corresponded to perceived class differences among immigrant groups. Germans were, in general, often more successful

than other immigrants in finding skilled labor and were commonly among the first to move out of immigrant ghettoes in large cities. See Hartmut Keil, "Immigrant Neighborhoods and American Society: German Immigrants on Chicago's Northwest Side in the Late Nineteenth Century," in Hartmut Keil, ed., *German Workers' Culture in the United States, 1850 to 1920* (Washington, D.C.: Smithsonian Institution Press, 1988), 25–58.

19. See William R. Linneman, "Immigrant Stereotypes: 1880–1900," *Studies in American Humor* 1.1 (April 1974): 28–39.

20. Ethnic stereotyping "rests upon the reasonable conviction that whoever seeks asylum among us—whether Hebrew or Celt or Saxon or Latin—owes us the tribute of conformity to American standards," Rollin Lynde Hartt asserted in *The People at Play: Excursions in the Humor and Philosophy of Popular Amusements* (Boston: Houghton Mifflin, 1909), 34. See also Mark Winokur, *American Laughter: Immigrants, Ethnicity, and 1930s Hollywood Film Comedy* (New York: St. Martin's Press, 1996), 71.

21. Musser, "Ethnicity, Role-Playing, and American Film Comedy." See also Thomas Cripps, "The Movie Jew as an Image of Assimilationism, 1903–1927," *Journal of Popular Film* 4.3 (1974), 190–207.

22. Keystone was not, of course, the only studio to exploit ethnic stereotyping in the early 1910s, though it was perhaps the most prominent. In an era when film producers were signing renowned stage actors to appear in their films, several manufacturers made widely publicized attempts to acquire the services of some of vaudeville's most famous ethnic impersonators. In September 1913, it was announced that Joe Weber and Lew Fields, the two most successful Dutch comedians of early-twentieth-century vaudeville, had been signed to appear in a Kinemacolor five-reel feature. See "Weber and Fields in Pictures," *MPW*, September 6, 1913, 1051. (Weber and Fields later joined Keystone in 1915, appearing in two films for the company; see chapter 4.) The following month, the fledgling Warner's Features company signed the famed Jewish impersonator Joe Welch to appear in a three-reel comic feature titled *The Struggle for Wealth*. See "Joe Welch in Pictures," *Toledo Blade*, October 23, 1913, 13.

23. The output of the studio's first twelve months is taken to include every release from the studio's debut reel, featuring *Cohen Collect a Debt* and *The Water Nymph* (released September 23, 1912), to the one-reel comedy *When Dreams Come True* (released September 22, 1913). Of these, the following feature ethnic or racial impersonation: (German) *Stolen Glory, Hoffmeyer's Legacy, A Strong Revenge, The Two Widows, The Man Next Door, On His Wedding Day, A Game of Poker, His Chum the Baron, That Ragtime Band, The New Conductor, His Ups and Downs, A Game of Pool;* (Jewish) *Cohen Collects a Debt, A Deaf Burglar, A Wife Wanted, Toplitsky and Co., The Peddler, The Firebugs;* (Italian) *A Landlord's Troubles, The Chief's Predicament, A Life in the Balance, The Fatal Taxicab;* (blackface) *A Double Wedding, The Deacon Outwitted, The Elite Ball, The Darktown Belle, Rastus and the Gamecock;* (French) *The Ambitious Butler, The Duel;* (Spanish/Mexican) *Pedro's*

Dilemma, A Red Hot Romance, At Twelve O'Clock; (Native American) *Forced Bravery, The Sleuth's Last Stand;* (Irish) *Pat's Day Off.* A handful of other films feature conflicts between Irish characters and other immigrant groups: (Irish and Jewish) *Murphy's IOU, Cohen's Outing, The Riot, The New Baby;* (Irish and German) *Riley and Schultz, Heinze's Resurrection, A Dollar Did It.* I have determined these titles from analysis of extant prints and plot descriptions in *Moving Picture World.*

24. Advertisement for *The Riot, MPW,* August 16, 1913, 703.

25. Advertisement for *The Fire Bug, MPW,* August 23, 1913, 801.

26. See Noel Ignatiev, *How the Irish Became White* (New York: Routledge, 1995); Eric Lott, *Love and Theft: Blackface Minstrelsy and the American Working Class* (New York: Oxford University Press, 1993); Roediger, *Wages of Whiteness,* esp. chaps. 5, 6, and 7.

27. "Facts and Comments," *MPW,* October 25, 1913, 355.

28. Lottie Briscoe, "The Great War," *MPSM,* February 1915, 81–84.

29. "Comments on the Films," *MPW,* October 12, 1912, 144.

30. On Sterling's biography, see chapter 1.

31. "Ford Sterling Using Vaudeville Stunts," *MPW,* April 26, 1913, 361.

32. Sterling had certainly portrayed a Dutch character in *Hoffmeyer's Legacy* (December 1912) and probably in *Riley and Schultze* (September 1912). Earlier still, Sterling had assayed the type in one of his Biograph films, *Tragedy in a Dress Suit* (1912).

33. "Photoplay Magazine's Great Popularity Contest," *Photoplay,* July 1913, 61; "The Exhibitor's End of It," *RL,* October 2, 1914, 23.

34. Advertisement for the Mutual Film Corporation, *CT,* January 4, 1914, 8.

35. "A New Author," *Photoplay,* June 1914, 94. Similar anecdotes can be found in *Photoplay,* August 1913, 102–103; September 1913, 72; October 1913, 63; December 1913, 114, 116; February 1914, 79, 97; and April 1914, 148.

36. "Chats with the Players: Ford Sterling," *MPSM,* December 1914, 115.

37. *MPSM,* October 1914, 130.

38. See the advertisements for *Zuzu* in *MPW,* November 29, 1913, 1069; December 13, 1913, 1303; December 20, 1913, 1477; and December 27, 1913, 1619.

39. Review of *Zuzu, the Band Leader, MPW,* December 13, 1913, 1262.

40. See the ad for the Hart Theatre, *Toledo Blade,* March 20, 1914, 3. I am indebted to Richard Abel for this reference.

41. Financial figures calculated from the Keystone Film Company cash book, September 28, 1912, to April 24, 1924, and the Keystone Film Company ledger, September 1912 to January 1916, ABP.

42. "Keystone Plant Enlarged," *MPW,* February 7, 1914, 689.

43. "Ford Sterling Using Vaudeville Stunts."

44. Review of *Love and Vengeance, MPW,* April 18, 1914, 341.

45. "Comments on the Films," *MPW,* January 31, 1914, 545; review of *Zuzu, the Band Leader, MPW;* "Comments on the Films," *MPW,* March 15, 1915, 1106.

46. "Ford Sterling Using Vaudeville Stunts."

47. Advertisement for *Love and Vengeance, MPW,* April 11, 1914, 153.

48. The average shot length of Keystone's extant 1913 releases (8.6 seconds) is derived from figures cited in Douglas Riblet, "The Keystone Film Company, 1912 to 1915" (Ph.D. diss., University of Wisconsin-Madison, 1998), 64, 115. The average shot lengths of *Double Crossed* and *A False Beauty* are calculated from my own viewings of prints held at the Library of Congress. Sterling's only other self-directed films prior to his departure from Keystone were *A Thief Catcher* (February 1914) and *Across the Hall* (March 1914, co-directed with Sennett). See "Keystone Releases."

49. My analysis here borrows from Pierre Bourdieu's category of the "pure gaze" that "implies a break with the ordinary attitude toward the world, which, given the conditions in which it is performed, is also a social separation." Pierre Bourdieu, *Distinction: A Social Critique of the Judgement of Taste,* trans. Richard Nice (Cambridge, Mass.: Harvard University Press, 1984), 4.

50. "Comments on the Films," *MPW,* May 3, 1913, 485.

51. Umberto Eco, "The Frames of Comic 'Freedom,'" in Thomas A. Sebeok, ed., *Carnival!* (Berlin: Mouton, 1985), 2.

52. Ibid., 3.

53. Musser, "Ethnicity, Role-Playing, and American Film Comedy," 52.

54. For a statistical analysis of these changes, see the survey of acts at Sylvester Poli's New Haven vaudeville houses in Kathryn Oberdeck, *The Evangelist and the Impresario: Religion, Entertainment, and Cultural Politics in America, 1884–1914* (Baltimore: Johns Hopkins University Press, 1999), 341–49.

55. Cripps, "Movie Jew," 190–91; Distler, "Rise and Fall of the Racial Comics," 188–94.

56. James Latham's study of "German-ness" in early film makes the case that, during the war, Germans were strongly coded as less "white" than other immigrants, even as warmongering Asiatic Huns as opposed to more "civilized" Europeans. Latham also shows that during the same period, fictional representations of German characters declined in favor of propagandist references to real German military and political leaders, primarily Kaiser Wilhelm II. See James R. Latham, "The Promotion of Early Hollywood: Racial, Ethnic, and National Identity in Text and Context," (Ph.D. diss., New York University, 2003), chap. 6.

57. The comment on Al Shean comes from an undated clipping (ca. 1915) in the Billy Rose Theatre Collection of the New York Public Library for the Performing Arts, quoted in Simon Louvish, *Monkey Business: The Lives and Legends of The Marx Brothers* (New York: Thomas Dunne Books, 1999), 99.

58. "Censors Reject Six Films," *CT,* May 26, 1914, 11.

59. "In and Out of Los Angeles Studios," *MPN,* January 16, 1915, 31.

60. On the substitution of comic eccentricity for earlier traditions of ethnic comedy, see the discussion of the 1930s "Thin Man" series in Winokur, *American Laughter,* chap. 4.

61. As Conklin explained in a later interview: "In those days, a Dutch comedian always wore a cropped wig and a chin piece. . . . Well before I started [in vaudeville], I worked for a Dutch baker by the name of Schultz and Schultz had this long droopy mustache. So I says to myself, 'Chester, why be like all the rest of them? Schultz is Dutch, why don't you just take his mustache?' And I says, 'All right, I will.'" Interview with Chester Conklin, TPI.

62. A signal exception here would be *The Battle of Ambrose and Walrus* (August 1915), where Conklin and Swain play soldiers in the Mexican army. Arguably, however, much of the film's humor plays off the *disjunction* between the characters' familiar identities and their atypical roles here as Mexican infantrymen (for which Swain and Conklin appear—absurdly—in tanned makeup).

63. Roy Rosenzweig, *Eight Hours for What We Will: Workers and Leisure in an Industrial City, 1870–1920* (Cambridge: Cambridge University Press, 1983), 172. See also Kathy Peiss, *Cheap Amusements: Working Women and Leisure in Turn-of-the-Century New York* (Philadelphia: Temple University Press, 1986), esp. Conclusion.

64. Roediger, *Working toward Whiteness*, 83.

65. For an insightful study of the work of the Chicago School, see Stow Persons, *Ethnic Studies at Chicago, 1905–1945* (Chicago: University of Illinois Press, 1987). See also David Ward, *Poverty, Ethnicity, and the American City, 1840–1925: Changing Conceptions of the Slum and the Ghetto,* (Cambridge: Cambridge University Press, 1989), chap. 5.

66. On the persistence of blackface performance in early twentieth-century popular culture, see David Nasaw, *Going Out: The Rise and Fall of Public Amusements* (New York: Basic Books, 1993), chap. 5.

67. See n. 6 above.

68. Advertisement for the New York Motion Picture Co., *MPW*, March 21, 1914, 1557.

69. Advertisement for the New York Motion Picture Co., *MPW*, March 28, 1914, 1628.

70. "Comments on the Films," *MPW*, February 7, 1914, 678.

71. Given the film's completion date of March 31, it is likely that *Mabel at the Wheel* was put into production immediately in the wake of Universal's aggressive ad campaign. See "Keystone Releases," General Files, MSC. The production of the film was a notoriously bad experience for all involved, with Chaplin storming off the set after Mabel Normand, the film's director, supposedly refused to listen to his gag ideas. Chaplin himself provides a colorful account of the making of the film in his *My Autobiography* (1964; London: Penguin Books, 1992), 149–51.

72. The films in which Chaplin does not appear in the tramp characterization are, in order of release, *Making a Living* (February 1914, in which he sports a frock coat, top hat and handlebar mustache), *Tango Tangles* (March 1914, in which he appears without distinguishing makeup), *Cruel, Cruel Love* (March 1914, in which he appears as an upper-class toff), *Mabel at the Wheel* (April 1914,

where he plays a burlesque villain in the Ford Sterling mold), *A Busy Day* (May 1914, where he appears in drag), *Mabel's Married Life* (June 1914, in which he sports a top hat as Mabel's husband), *The Rounders* (September 1914, where he plays an upper-class drunk), and *Tillie's Punctured Romance* (December 1914, in which he plays a city slicker). A fascinating and detailed account of the genesis of Chaplin's tramp is provided by Bo Berglund in "The Day the Tramp Was Born," *Sight and Sound* 58.2 (Winter 1988–89): 106–12.

73. "Live News of the Week," *MPN*, March 21, 1914, 37.

74. "The Exhibitor's End of It," *RL*, August 29, 1914, 20; "Great Cast Contest," *MPSM*, November 1915, 124.

75. Review of *Dough and Dynamite*, *MPW*, October 24, 1914, 497; "Notes of the Trade," *MPW*, October 31, 1914, 662.

76. Harry Carr, "Charlie Chaplin's Story, Part III," *Photoplay*, September 1915, 107. In a 1955 TPI interview, Conklin provided a similar account of the tramp's eclectic origins, describing Chaplin's costume as an amalgamation of Sterling's shoes, a "piece of hair off the makeup bench" (the mustache), and Roscoe Arbuckle's hat. Conklin's account is also found in Mack Sennett's autobiography, with slight variations. See Sennett, *King of Comedy*, 156–59.

77. Michael Davis, "Forced to Tramp: The Perspective of the Labor Press, 1870–1900," in Eric H. Monkonnen, ed., *Walking to Work: Tramps in America, 1790–1935* (Lincoln: University of Nebraska Press, 1984), 142.

78. On popular cultural representations of tramping, see Tim Cresswell, *The Tramp in America* (London: Reaktion Books, 2001), chap. 6; Michael Denning, *Mechanic Accents: Dime Novels and Working-Class Culture in America* (London: Verso, 1987), chap. 8; Douglas Gilbert, *American Vaudeville: Its Life and Times* (New York: Dover, 1940), 269–78.

79. Charles Musser, "Work, Ideology, and Chaplin's Tramp," in Robert Sklar and Charles Musser, eds., *Resisting Images: Essays on Cinema and History* (Philadelphia: Temple University Press, 1990), 40.

80. Ibid., 42–49.

81. On tramping and ethnicity, see John C. Schneider, "Tramping Workers, 1890–1920: A Subcultural View," in Monkkonen, ed., *Walking to Work*, 212–34.

82. "No Foreign-Born Hoboes," *Los Angeles Citizen*, November 28, 1913, 8.

83. "The Hobo," *Los Angeles Citizen*, November 29, 1914, 11.

84. Jack London, *The Road* (1907; reprint, Santa Barbara, Calif.: Peregrine Press, 1970), 53.

85. Nels Anderson, *The Hobo: The Sociology of the Homeless Man* (1923; reprint, Chicago: University of Chicago Press, 1961), xiv. See also Browder, *Slippery Characters*, 178–83.

86. Oberdeck, *The Evangelist and the Impresario*, 96, 198–203.

87. "Vaudeville," *NYDM*, February 10, 1915, 17.

88. Caroline Caffin, *Vaudeville* (New York: M. Kennerley, 1914), 205.

89. See my essay " 'A Purely American Product': Tramp Comedy and White Working-Class Formation in the 1910s," in Richard Abel, Giorgio Bertellini,

and Rob King, eds., *Early Cinema and the "National"* (Eastleigh, UK: John Libbey Publishing, 2008), 236–47.

90. Leslie T. Peacocke, "Hints on Photoplay Writing," *Photoplay*, August 1915, 133.

91. Leslie T. Peacocke, "Hints on Photoplay Writing," *Photoplay*, June 1915, 131.

92. Epes Winthrop Sargent, "The Photoplaywright," *MPW*, November 11, 1913, 490, quoted in Jenkins, *What Made Pistachio Nuts?* 49–50.

93. Chaplin, *My Autobiography*, 147–54.

94. "Comments on the Films," *MPW*, February 7, 1914, 678.

95. Harry Carr, "Charlie Chaplin's Story, Part II," *Photoplay*, August 1915, 46.

96. Chaplin, *My Autobiography*, 146–47.

97. My discussion of the long-take style in Chaplin's films draws on Riblet, "The Keystone Film Company, 1912 to 1915," 164–79. In his biography of Chaplin, David Robinson discusses *His Musical Career* as a bold experiment in the long-take style: with this film, argues Robinson, Chaplin "declared . . . that cutting was not an obligation but a convenience" (*Chaplin: His Life and Art*, 127).

98. Eco, "Frames of Comic 'Freedom,'" 7.

99. "Essanay Signs Charles Chaplin," *MPW*, December 26, 1914, 1822.

100. Review of *His Trysting Place*, *MPW*, October 31, 1914, 645 (emphasis added).

101. *National Labor Tribune*, November 11, 1915, quoted in Francis C. Couvares, "The Triumph of Commerce: Class Culture and Mass Culture in Pittsburgh," in Michael H. Frisch and Daniel J. Walkowitz, eds., *Working-Class America: Essays on Labor, Community, and American Society* (Urbana: University of Illinois Press, 1983), 143 (emphasis added).

102. "Thousands Will Attend Carnival," *Los Angeles Citizen*, February 9, 1917, 1 (emphasis added).

103. "The Exhibitor's End of It," *RL*, August 29, 1914, 20.

104. Letter reprinted in "The Exhibitor's End of It," *RL*, November 7, 1914, 18.

105. "To Be Frank About It," *Police Gazette*, August 28, 1915, 2.

106. Keystone Film Company cash book, September 28, 1912–April 24, 1924, ABP.

107. The quoted characterization of the Strand is taken from W. Stephen Bush, "Opening of the Strand," *MPW*, April 18, 1914, 371. It is unclear why the Strand's management paid the additional $100 for *His Prehistoric Past*, since Keystone's pictures had played regularly at the theater since its opening. See Keystone Film Company cash book, ABP.

108. This, surely, was an example of what the Soviet theorist of language V. N. Voloshinov would describe as the "multiaccentuality" of all ideological signs, the process whereby meanings are differentially inflected (or "accented") based on the class assumptions that different readers bring to their reading.

V. N. Voloshinov, *Marxism and the Philosophy of Language* (1930; New York: Seminar Press, 1973), 23, cited in Denning, *Mechanic Accents*, 82.

109. "Warning to Exhibitors," *MPW*, November 7, 1914, 845. Although the duping of Keystone's films was less than welcome from Mutual's perspective, it has produced benefits for film historians. To protect the studio's output against unlicensed copies, Mutual began to register paper prints of the films at the Library of Congress, starting in late October 1914, and did so until the end of Keystone's affiliation with Mutual. As a result, there is a higher ratio of surviving prints from this period than for any other point during Keystone's five-year history.

110. Charles Chaplin to Syd Chaplin, August 9, 1914, quoted in Robinson, *Chaplin: His Life and Art*, 132.

111. Review of *Dough and Dynamite*, *MPW*, October 24, 1914, 497; review of *Dough and Dynamite*, *CT*, October 27, 1914, 14.

112. "Charlie Chaplin's Story, Part III," 109. In his autobiography, Mack Sennett claims that *Dough and Dynamite* was "Charlie's first personal triumph as a comedian. His name was important after that picture" (*King of Comedy*, 178). Chester Conklin similarly described the film as "the picture to make Chaplin a star." Interview with Chester Conklin, TPI.

113. Chaplin, *My Autobiography*, 157.

114. Conklin, interview, TPI.

115. Review of *Dough and Dynamite*, *MPW*.

116. Robinson, *Chaplin: His Life and Art*, 127.

117. On the Los Angeles bakers' unions, see Louis B. Perry and Richard S. Perry, *A History of the Los Angeles Labor Movement, 1911–1941* (Berkeley: University of California Press, 1963), chap. 2.

118. On conservative depictions of labor during this period, see Steven J. Ross, *Working-Class Hollywood: Silent Film and the Shaping of Class in America* (Princeton, N.J.: Princeton University Press, 1998), 63–69.

119. Review of *His Trysting Place*, *MPW*.

120. Charles Baumann to Mack Sennett, June 4, 1915, correspondence folder (1915–1917), General Files, MSC.

121. These are *Mabel and Fatty's Wash Day*, *Hogan's Mussy Job* (January 1915), *The Home Breakers*, *Fatty's New Role*, *Hogan the Porter*, *Hogan's Romance Upset*, *Hogan's Aristocratic Dream*, *Hearts and Planets*, *A Lucky Leap*, *Hogan Out West* (February 1915), *From Patches to Plenty*, *Beating Hearts and Carpets*, *Ambrose's Little Hatchet*, *Fatty's Faithful Fido*, *A One Night Stand* (March 1915), *Droppington's Devilish Deed*, *The Beauty Bunglers*, *Do-Re-Mi-Boom!*, *Ambrose's Nasty Temper*, *Their Social Splash* (April 1915), *Those College Girls* (May 1915), *Those Bitter Sweets*, and *A Hash House Fraud* (June 1915). This list has been determined from analysis of extant prints and plot summaries in *Moving Picture World*.

122. "The Shadow Stage," *Photoplay*, May 1916, 108–9.

123. See Ross, *Working-Class Hollywood*, chap. 2 and 293, n. 22.

124. As Oskar Negt and Alexander Kluge have suggested, each class creates a specific perception of society based upon its horizon of experiences. "An

individual worker . . . has 'his own experiences.' The horizon of these experiences is the unity of the proletarian context of living. . . . It is via this unified context, which he 'experiences' publicly and privately, that he absorbs 'society as a whole.'" Oskar Negt and Alexander Kluge, *Public Sphere and Experience: Toward an Analysis of the Bourgeois and Proletarian Public Sphere*, trans. Peter Labanyi, Jamie Owen Daniel, and Alexander Oksiloff (Minneapolis: University of Minnesota Press, 1993), 6.

125. Quoted in Denning, *Mechanic Accents*, 153 (emphasis added). Denning also cites a Knights of Labor lecture in Rutland, Vermont, in 1887: "We [the Knights] stand today as the conservators of society. We have watched the growth of a privileged class and of a vast army of tramps. If these extremes come together there will be a crash" (ibid., 154).

126. Denning, *Mechanic Accents*, 81.

127. William Taylor, "The Launching of a Commercial Culture: New York City, 1860–1930," in John H. Mollenkopf, ed., *Power, Culture, and Place: Essays on New York City* (New York: Russell Sage Foundation, 1988), 122.

128. Louis Reeves Harrison, "A Comedy to Those Who Think," *MPW*, July 31, 1915, 788.

129. Review of *Hearts and Planets, MPW*, March 16, 1915, 1457.

130. The term "eccentric" was one of the most frequent terms in *Moving Picture World* reviews of Keystone's output during this period, appearing in no fewer than eight pieces between September 1914 and January 1915.

131. "Comments on the Films," *MPW*, May 15, 1915, 1072 (emphasis added).

132. "Savoy Theatre," *Los Angeles Citizen*, February 19, 1915, 6. On the Superba, see "Superba Theatre," ibid., June 25, 1915, 8; "Superba Theater Is Now Strictly Union," ibid., July 2, 1915, 5.

133. A *Motion Picture News* article on the Strand's opening mistakenly lists the film as "The Bathing Beauty," which does not correspond to the title of any known Keystone release. The reference must be to *A Bath House Beauty*, an Arbuckle one-reeler released on April 13. See "Crowds Flock to Strand Opening," *MPN*, April 25, 1914, 18.

134. "Stories of the New Photoplays," *RL*, November 21, 1914, 22.

135. "Keystone Pictures on Broadway," *Motography*, October 24, 1914, 566.

136. Information on the Gaiety and the Palace is drawn from theater listings in, respectively, the *Toledo Daily Blade* and the *Des Moines News*. Thanks, again, to Richard Abel for sharing his research.

137. "When the Lofty Temples Tumbled," *Photoplay*, April 1915, 86.

3. "THE IMPOSSIBLE ATTAINED!"

Epigraph: Rollin Lynde Hartt, *The People at Play: Excursions in the Humor and Philosophy of Popular Amusements* (Boston: Houghton Mifflin, 1909), 15–16.

1. Mack Sennett, interview, April 15, 1955, TPI. Sennett made a similar observation in a 1915 interview with the *Chicago Tribune*: "[G]oing beyond more than two reels in comedy is taking your life in your hands. Gosh, you have to be careful. You have to have it growing all the time and have everybody with something lively to do every minute, or else your audience will sit back and say, 'Why, see that fellow. What's he in there fore *[sic]*? He hasn't done anything to raise a laugh for the last ten minutes.'" See Kitty Kelly, "How Sennett Makes Keystone Comedies," *CT*, April 15, 1915, 10.

2. See Steve Neale and Frank Krutnik, *Popular Film and Television Comedy* (London: Routledge, 1990), 119.

3. For a fuller account of these developments, see Eileen Bowser, *The Transformation of Cinema, 1907–1915* (Berkeley: University of California Press, 1990), chap. 12; Michael Quinn, "Distribution, the Transient Audience, and the Transition to the Feature Film," *Cinema Journal* 40.2 (Winter 2001): 35–56; Ben Singer, "Feature Films, Variety Programs, and the Crisis of the Small Exhibitor," in Charlie Keil and Shelley Stamp, eds., *American Cinema's Transitional Era: Audiences, Institutions, Practices* (Berkeley: University of California Press, 2004), 76–100.

4. Carl Laemmle, "Doom of Long Features Predicted," *MPW*, July 11, 1914, 185.

5. W. Stephen Bush, "The Single Reel—II," *MPW*, July 4, 1914, 36.

6. *United States of America* v. *Motion Pictures Patent Company et al.*, 4: 2002 (December 1913), quoted in Bowser, *Transformation of Cinema*, 212.

7. See Douglas Riblet "The Keystone Film Company, 1912 to 1915" (Ph.D. diss., University of Wisconsin–Madison, 1998), 198–209, from which I draw some of the quotations in this paragraph.

8. Bush, "Single Reel—II."

9. Review of *This Is the Life, Variety*, July 17, 1914, 17, quoted in Riblet, "Keystone Film Company," 204.

10. Charles R. Condon, "A Six-Reel Keystone Comedy," *Motography*, November 14, 1914, 657.

11. "Notes of the Trade," *MPW*, May 2, 1914, 683.

12. Mack Sennett, with Cameron Shipp, *King of Comedy* (Garden City, N.Y.: Doubleday, 1954; reprint, San Jose, Calif.: toExcel, 2000), 184; review of *Tillie's Punctured Romance, MPN*, November 14, 1914, 40.

13. Review of *Tillie's Punctured Romance, MPN*.

14. "Comments on the Films," *MPW*, November 16, 1912, 660 (emphasis added).

15. Donald Crafton, "Pie and Chase: Gag, Spectacle and Narrative in Slapstick Comedy," in Kristine Karnick and Henry Jenkins, eds., *Classical Hollywood Comedy* (London: Routledge, 1995), 106–19.

16. Al E. Christie, "The Elements of Situation Comedy" (Los Angeles: Palmer Photoplay Corporation, 1920), 4–5 (emphasis in original).

17. Shot numbers refer to the Grapevine Video release of this film, in "Chaplin Keystones Volume #2."

18. "Comments on the Films," *MPW*, June 13, 1914, 1541.

19. Henry Jenkins, *What Made Pistachio Nuts? Early Sound Comedy and the Vaudeville Aesthetic* (New York: Columbia University Press, 1992), chap. 2. See also Introduction, above, pages 2–5. I am indebted to Jenkins's superb analysis for some of the citations and most of the interpretive framework of my following two paragraphs.

20. George Meredith, *An Essay on Comedy and the Uses of the Comic Spirit* (New York: Scribner, 1897), 82.

21. W. L. Courtney, "The Idea of Comedy," *Living Age,* August 8, 1914, 348–59, quoted in Jenkins, *What Made Pistachio Nuts?* 31.

22. Ibid.

23. See Albert McClean, *American Vaudeville as Ritual* (Louisville: University of Kentucky Press, 1965), 112.

24. Figures cited in Jenkins, *What Made Pistachio Nuts?* 38–39. On the growing market for joke books in the late nineteenth century, see also Laurence Senelick, "Variety into Vaudeville: The Process Observed in Two Manuscript Gagbooks," *Theatre Survey* 19.1 (May 1978): 1–15.

25. Wilfred Clarke, "The Vaudeville Novelty," *Variety,* December 12, 1908, 43, quoted in Jenkins, *What Made Pistachio Nuts?* 78.

26. Brett Page, *Writing for Vaudeville* (Springfield, Mass.: The Home Correspondence School, 1915), 147, quoted in Jenkins, *What Made Pistachio Nuts?* 33.

27. See chapter 1 above.

28. Christie, "Elements of Situation Comedy," 3, 5, 19.

29. William Lord Wright, "The True Worth of Humor," *MPSM*, March 1914, 101.

30. Alfred A. Cohn, " 'Writing' Slapstick," *Photoplay*, September 1917, 116.

31. Robert Wagner, "You—At the Movies," *American Magazine* 90.6 (December 1920): 42–44, quoted in Ben Singer, *Melodrama and Modernity: Early Sensational Cinema and Its Contexts* (New York: Columbia University Press, 2001), 97.

32. Raymond Schrock, "Reflections of the Critic," *Photoplay,* January 1913, 103.

33. Hutchison quoted in Epes Winthrop Sargent, "The Photoplaywright," *MPW*, May 16, 1914, 962.

34. Review of *The Little Teacher, MPW,* July 3, 1915, 79.

35. See Janet Staiger's chapter "The Central Producer System: Centralized Management after 1914," in David Bordwell, Janet Staiger and Kristin Thompson, *The Classical Hollywood Cinema: Film Style and Mode of Production to 1960* (New York: Columbia University Press, 1985), 128–41.

36. "Ince and Sennett Coming East," *MPW*, August 1, 1914, 686 (emphasis added).

37. Synopsis, *Mabel's Strange Predicament,* Production Files, MSC.

38. "The 'Movies' in the Making," *Los Angeles Citizen,* February 5, 1915, 3.

39. Scenario, "The Eavesdropper," *He Loved the Ladies,* Production Files, MSC.

40. Kalton C. Lahue and Terry Brewer, *Kops and Custards: The Legend of Keystone Films* (1968; reprint, Norman: University of Oklahoma Press, 1972), 98.

41. That this process was in place some time in 1915 is indicated by a peculiar studio document from the period titled "Scenario Staff Report." The document, a questionnaire on scenario preparation, asks at one point "whether Gag Sheet accompanies report." See "Scenario Staff Report," General Files, MSC.

42. Smith quoted in Sennett, *King of Comedy,* 128–29.

43. See Fredric Jameson, *The Political Unconscious: Narrative as a Socially Symbolic Act* (Ithaca, N.Y.: Cornell University Press, 1981): "[T]he individual text or cultural artifact . . . is here restructured as a field of force in which the dynamics of sign systems of several distinct modes of production can be registered and apprehended. These dynamics . . . make up what can be termed the ideology of form, that is, the determinate contradiction of the specific messages emitted by the varied sign systems which coexist in a given artistic process" (98–99).

44. Scenario, "Fire Insurance Story," *When Ambrose Dared Walrus,* Production Files, MSC.

45. *The Cannon Ball, The Little Teacher, Fatty's Plucky Pup* (June 1915), *When Ambrose Dared Walrus, Dirty Work in a Laundry, Fatty's Tintype Tangle* (July 1915), *The Battle of Ambrose and Walrus,* and *Only a Messenger Boy* (August 1915).

46. See chapter 1 above.

47. Sennett, *King of Comedy,* 183–84.

48. Unidentified clipping, January 4, 1910, Robinson Locke Collection of Dramatic Scrapbooks, vol. 163, BRTC.

49. "News of Music and the Theaters," *CT,* January 3, 1910, 7.

50. Marie Dressler, with Mildred Harrington, *My Own Story* (Boston: Little, Brown, 1934), 167.

51. Louella O. Parsons, "Seen on the Screen," *Chicago Herald,* September 15, 1915, Robinson Locke Collection of Dramatic Scrapbooks, vol. 164, BRTC.

52. Accounts differ concerning Dressler's salary. A *Variety* article from April 1914 lists $2,800 a week for twelve weeks, while Sennett's autobiography cites $2,500 weekly. See "Dressler in Pictures," *Variety,* April 17, 1914, 20; Sennett, *King of Comedy,* 184. Although the facts of her contract cannot be recovered with certitude, company documents support Sennett's figure: Keystone's ledgers for this period indicate a sum of $30,000 paid into a "Marie Dressler advanced account" at the end of the year, an amount consistent with twelve payments of $2,500. See the Keystone Film Company ledger, September 1912 to January 1916, ABP.

53. "Notes of the Trade," *MPW* May 2, 1914, 683.

54. Additional information on Dressler's contract taken from Dressler, *My Own Story,* 168; Matthew Kennedy, *Marie Dressler: A Biography, with a Listing of Major Stage Performances, a Filmography and a Discography*

(Jefferson, N.C.: McFarland, 1999), 80; Lahue and Brewer, *Kops and Custards*, 82; Betty Lee, *Marie Dressler: The Unlikeliest Star* (Lexington: University of Kentucky Press, 1997), 105.

55. See Riblet, "Keystone Film Company," 213–14.

56. Sennett, *King of Comedy*, 185.

57. Ibid., 186 (emphasis added).

58. *Tillie's Nightmare* script (Tams-Witmark Collection, Mills Music Library, University of Wisconsin–Madison), i.

59. Ibid., 7.

60. Review of *Tillie's Nightmare*, NYDM, May 14, 1910, 6.

61. *Tillie's Nightmare* script, 59, 71.

62. Review of *Tillie's Nightmare*, NYDM.

63. *Tillie's Nightmare* script, 14–15.

64. On the city/country contrast in American melodrama, see Christine Gledhill, "The Melodramatic Field: An Investigation," in id., ed., *Home Is Where the Heart Is: Studies in Melodrama and the Woman's Film* (London: BFI, 1987), 24–25. By basing the plot to his film on the lyrics to "Heaven Will Protect the Working Girl," Sennett perhaps also hoped to capitalize on the song's popularity. Based on the 1901 English tune "I'm a Respectable Working Girl," the song had in fact featured in Dressler's vaudeville act as early as 1908. With the success of *Tillie's Nightmare*, the sheet music sold thousands of copies, and Dressler exploited the number as her theme song in subsequent stage appearances. See Dressler, *My Own Story*, 153–54; Kennedy, *Marie Dressler*, 65.

65. Condon, "Six-Reel Keystone Comedy," 657.

66. "Mack Sennett Talks of His Work," *MPW*, August 15, 1914, 968.

67. These opening shots, missing from all previous circulating prints, are preserved in the UCLA–National Film and Television Archive's 2003 restoration, which incorporates all known surviving footage. All my references to shot lengths, order of shots, etc., are based upon this restoration.

68. Quotes taken from Percy Hammond, "Concerning Musical Comedies That Are Now in Our Midst," *CT*, January 9, 1911, II, 2 and James O'Donnell Bennett, "Tillie's Nightmare Is Rightly Named," *Chicago Record*, January 4, 1910, Robinson Locke Collection of Dramatic Scrapbooks, vol. 163, BRTC.

69. Sennett, *King of Comedy*, 186.

70. Condon, "Six-Reel Keystone Comedy," 657 (emphasis added).

71. This, incidentally, is how another Keystone film, *Leading Lizzie Astray* (November 1914), ends. A one-reel burlesque of the same "city slicker" narrative that provides the narrative template of *Tillie's Punctured Romance*, the film concludes with a chaotic fight sequence in which the city gent is pummeled senseless and the country girl rescued.

72. Tom Gunning, "From the Opium Den to the Theatre of Morality: Moral Discourse and the Film Process in Early American Cinema," *Art and Text* 30 (September–November 1988): 37. See also Lee Grieveson, *Policing Cinema: Movies and Censorship in Early-Twentieth-Century America* (Berkeley: University of California Press, 2004), 110–14.

73. Review of *Tillie's Punctured Romance, MPW*, November 14, 1914, 914.

74. The UCLA–NFTVA 2003 restoration here includes a scene missing from previous versions: a twelve-shot sequence in which Tillie is returned to her uncle's home, makes a nuisance of herself (more inebriated dancing), and is thrown out.

75. Kelly, "How Sennett Makes Keystone Comedies."

76. The number of shots comprising the chase is taken to include every shot from Tillie's discovery of Charlie with Mabel to the shot when Tillie, having tumbled into the ocean, is brought safely back onto Santa Monica pier.

77. Review of *Tillie's Punctured Romance, MPW*.

78. Kelly, "How Sennett Makes Keystone Comedies."

79. Again, this sequence is missing from previous circulating versions of the film.

80. Peter Krämer, "Vitagraph, Slapstick and Early Cinema," *Screen* 29.2 (Spring 1988): 101.

81. Advertisement for *Tillie's Punctured Romance, MPW*, November 7, 1914, 738–39.

82. The New York Motion Picture Company's "Film Release Book" lists the film's production dates as April 14 to June 9, a period of exactly eight weeks. See New York Motion Picture Company, Film Release Book, ABP. The July 25 shipping date for "Dressler No. 1" (the working title for *Tillie's Punctured Romance*) is given in "Keystone Releases," General Files, MSC.

83. "Mack Sennett Talks of His Work."

84. For the picture's production expenses, see the Keystone Film Company journal, September 1912–October 1915, and ledger, September 1912–January 1916, ABP. According to a handwritten note in the former, the $14,000 represented "14 weeks production exp[enses] at $1000 per week."

85. See "Marie Dressler Picture Sold to Alco," *MPW*, December 12, 1914, 1528, and "Special Feature Service Organized by Famous Co.," *Variety*, January 30, 1915, 3. The number of prints sold to Alco is given in the Keystone Film Company journal, ABP.

86. Keystone Film Company journal, ABP.

87. " 'Tillie's Punctured Romance' in Court," *MPW*, June 5, 1915, 1581.

88. Shubert quoted in Lee, *Marie Dressler*, 82.

89. "Marie Dressler Picture Sold to Alco."

90. Figures on publicity expenses taken from the Keystone Film Company journal, ABP. According to this, $1,106.49 was spent on advertising and $2,651.92 on posters in preparation for the film's December release.

91. "Show Reviews," *Variety*, January 1, 1915, 20.

92. "Harry Lauder at Majestic," *LAT*, October 11, 1914, III, 1.

93. "Gates Play for the Mason," *LAT*, December 27, 1914, III, 3.

94. "Tillie's Romance Makes Record in Pittsburgh," *MPN*, February 20, 1915, 36.

95. Review of *Tillie's Punctured Romance, MPN*.

96. Condon, "Six-Reel Keystone Comedy," 657.

97. Review of *Tillie's Punctured Romance, NYDM*, November 4, 1914, 36.

98. Review of *Tillie's Punctured Romance, MPN*.

99. Review of *Tillie's Punctured Romance, MPW*.

100. "Film Flashes," *Variety*, March 19, 1915, 20; "Keystone Film Wins Marie Dressler Suit," *MPN*, March 27, 1915, 48; "Keystone Upheld by Court," *Motography*, March 27, 1915, 484; "Court Upholds Keystone Company," *MPW*, March 27, 1915, 1944.

101. "Marie Seeks Accounting," *Variety*, May 14, 1915, 20.

102. "Keystone Wins Dressler Suit," *MPN*, August 21, 1915, 75. See also "Marie Dressler Wins Against Keystone," *MPN*, August 14, 1915, 1141.

103. "Mack Sennett to Head New Production Company," *MPN*, January 23, 1915, 31.

104. Advertisement for *Tillie's Punctured Romance, MPN*, January 23, 1915, 59.

105. "Doings at Los Angeles," *MPW*, February 20, 1915, 1126.

106. "Rebuilding of Keystone Interior under Way," *MPN*, February 27, 1915, 42.

107. "Brevities of the Business," *Motography*, May 1, 1915, 709; ibid., May 15, 1915, 793.

108. As Douglas Riblet has shown, footage from the second feature project eventually saw the light of day in 1922 when it was released under the title *Oh, Mabel Behave* by the remnants of the Triangle Film Corporation. The *Moving Picture World* review of the film provides the following synopsis: "Squire Peachem [Sterling] used the mortgage he holds on the innkeeper's property as a lever to win his daughter [Normand], but the daughter cannot see it that way as she loves a young swell, Randolph Roanoke [Owen Moore]. The squire, with the aid of his trusty but ignorant henchman, Blaa Blaa [Sennett], seeks to sidetrack Roanoke which leads to complications, but how poorly he succeeds and how the daughter brings things around so that she has her own way furnishes the action for the burlesque which contains fights, a comedy duel, stunts and thrills." Review of *Oh, Mabel Behave, MPW*, December 17, 1921, 855, quoted in Riblet, "Keystone Film Company," 244. As Riblet notes (ibid., 243–45), this cast list conforms exactly with earlier trade press descriptions of Keystone's second feature.

109. Charles O. Baumann to Mack Sennett, June 4, 1915, correspondence folder (1915–1919), General Files, MSC.

110. Ibid.

111. "Though the formation of Triangle ultimately ended Sennett's ambitions of moving into feature film production, that process . . . [was not] determined by slapstick genre's immaturity or Keystone-style comedy's inability to sustain a feature film," Riblet contends ("Keystone Film Company," 248).

4. "MADE FOR THE MASSES WITH AN APPEAL TO THE CLASSES"

Epigraph: Van Wyck Brooks, " 'Highbrow' and 'Lowbrow,' " in *America's Coming-of-Age* (1915; reprint, New York: Doubleday Anchor Books, 1958), 15–16.

1. Harry Aitken, "Out of Quantity—Quality," *MPW*, July 11, 1914, 211.

2. Ibid.

3. See Richard Koszarski's analysis of Triangle in his *An Evening's Entertainment: The Age of the Silent Feature Picture, 1915–1928* (Berkeley: University of California Press, 1990), 63–69.

4. "Triangle Completes First Releasing Plan," *MPN*, September 4, 1915, 41–42.

5. "'Sig,' $4,000,000 Production Company Is Launched," *MPN*, July 17, 1915, 87. For more information about Triangle's corporate structure, see Kalton C. Lahue, *Dreams for Sale: The Rise and Fall of the Triangle Film Corporation* (South Brunswick, N.J.: A. S. Barnes, 1971), chap. 3. Although Triangle set a precedent for the vertical integration of the film industry, it differed from later companies in not actually owning any of the theaters in which its product was shown.

6. The figure for Triangle's debts ($711,634.07) is taken from the agreement between F. S. Smithers and Company, Knauth, Nachod, and Kuhne, and Richard A. Rowland, October 11, 1916, ABP.

7. Stuart Hall, "Notes on Deconstructing 'The Popular,'" in Raphael Samuel, ed., *People's History and Socialist Theory* (London: Routledge & Kegan Paul, 1981), 227–40.

8. "The Fourth Knickerbocker Triangle Program," *MPN*, November 6, 1915, 86.

9. See Lawrence Levine, *Highbrow/Lowbrow: The Emergence of Cultural Hierarchy in America* (Cambridge, Mass.: Harvard University Press, 1988), esp. chaps. 2 and 3.

10. Thorstein Veblen, *The Theory of the Leisure Class: An Economic Study of Institutions* (1899; reprint, New York: Random House, 1934), 167.

11. The role of inflation in fostering new patterns of middle-class spending is argued by Daniel Horowitz, *The Morality of Spending: Attitudes toward the Consumer Culture in America, 1875–1940* (Baltimore: Johns Hopkins University Press, 1985), chap. 6.

12. See Lewis Erenberg, *Steppin' Out: New York Nightlife and the Transformation of American Culture, 1890–1930* (Westport, Conn.: Greenwood Press, 1981), chap. 2.

13. Veblen, *Theory of the Leisure Class*, 84.

14. Aitken quoted in Al P. Nelson and Mel R. Jones, *A Silent Siren Song: The Aitken Brothers' Hollywood Odyssey, 1905–1926* (New York: Cooper Square Press, 2000), 8.

15. See ibid., 7–10, 27–29.

16. Harry Aitken to D. W. Griffith, April 15, 1914, D. W. Griffith Collection, Museum of Modern Art, New York, quoted in Richard Schickel, *D. W. Griffith: An American Life* (New York: Simon & Schuster, 1984), 211.

17. Roy E. Aitken, with Al P. Nelson, *The Birth of a Nation Story* (Middleburg, Va.: Denlinger, 1965), 33, 38.

18. "Editorial," *TT*, October 23, 1915, 2.

19. "The Great Triangle Idea—Its Full Scope and Purpose," *TT*, October 23, 1915, 1.

20. Keystone production expenses are calculated from the Keystone Film Company journals, September 1912–October 1915 and November 1915–December 1922, ABP. Other production figures taken from Lahue, *Dreams for Sale*, 85, 127.

21. Information on the Knickerbocker lease is taken from the contract between Klaw and Erlanger, Al Hayman, Charles Frohman, Inc., and Harry Aitken, August 9, 1915, ABP. Kalton Lahue incorrectly gives a figure of $65,000 for the Knickerbocker's annual rental (Lahue, *Dreams for Sale*, 53).

22. "Local Theatre Owners Start Big Special Letter-Writing Campaign," *TT*, April 15, 1916, 1 (emphasis added).

23. "Movies Take Over the Knickerbocker," *NYT*, September 24, 1915, 11. Even in the early 1920s, the majority of theaters in the United States still charged less than a quarter for an evening show, while those charging a dollar or more accounted for less than 1 percent of all exhibition venues. See Koszarski, *Evening's Entertainment*, 15.

24. "Triangle Blazes the Way for Regular $2 Seats," *MPN*, October 9, 1915, 41.

25. "The First Knickerbocker Program," *MPN*, October 9, 1915, 84.

26. "Movies Take Over the Knickerbocker," *NYT*.

27. "Flickerings from Film Land," *CT*, October 4, 1915, 14.

28. "Two-Dollar Admission Price Is Triangle's Aim," *MPN*, August 14, 1915, 43.

29. "What They Really Get—NOW!" *Photoplay*, March 1916, 27–30.

30. My discussion of Triangle's theatrical stars, both here and in the following paragraphs, combines my own research with material from the following sources: Aitken, *Birth of a Nation Story*, 72–73; Lahue, *Dreams for Sale*, 56–60, 134–48; Nelson and Jones, *Silent Siren Song*, 166–69; and Anthony Slide, *The Kindergarten of the Movies: A History of the Fine Arts Company* (Metuchen, N.J.: Scarecrow Press, 1980), chaps. 4 and 7. Further information on star salaries during this period can be found in Koszarski, *Evening's Entertainment*, 114–16.

31. "Sir Herbert Tree Dead," *Variety*, July 6, 1917, 4.

32. Advertisement for Keystone Film Company, *MPN*, May 22, 1915, 84–85.

33. "Weber and Fields Sign with Keystone Film," *MPN*, July 10, 1915, 64.

34. Review of *Macbeth*, *Variety*, June 9, 1916, 23.

35. Julian Johnson, "The Shadow Stage," *Photoplay*, September 1916, 127.

36. Synopsis (5 pp.), *Fatty and the Broadway Stars*, Production Files, MSC.

37. Review of *Her Painted Hero*, *MPW*, October 30, 1915, 809.

38. "What They Really Get," *Photoplay*, 29. According to Kalton Lahue and Terry Brewer, Foy ultimately filed a lawsuit against Keystone, demanding $2,000 to cover outstanding salary payments and transportation back to New York for himself and his children. Although the hearing was set for April 25,

1916, Foy dropped his suit when Sennett's lawyers filed a counterclaim, accusing him of delaying production and refusing to follow the instructions of his director. See Kalton C. Lahue and Terry Brewster, *Kops and Custards: The Legend of Keystone Films* (1968; reprint, Norman: University of Oklahoma Press, 1972), 121–22.

39. "In and Out of West Coast Studios," *MPN*, January 8, 1916, 73; "News from the Three Big California Studios," *TT*, March 4, 1916, 7.

40. "Close-Ups," *Photoplay*, November 1916, 63.

41. "Editorial," *TT*, June 10, 1916, 2.

42. "The Great Triangle Idea," *TT*, 7.

43. "Rothapfel Takes Hold of Knickerbocker Theatre," *MPN*, January 22, 1916, 347; "Triangle Leaves Knickerbocker Theatre," *MPN*, May 13, 1916, 2908; "Loew Gets Knickerbocker, New York," *MPN*, June 17, 1916, 3729.

44. Receipts calculated from Triangle's cash books for 1915 and for November 1, 1915–April 22, 1916, ABP.

45. "Local Theatre Owners Start Big Special Letter-Writing Campaign," *TT*, April 15, 1916, 1.

46. Strand Amusement Co. to Mack Sennett, January 15, 1917, correspondence folder (1915–1919), General Files, MSC; "Why One Exhibitor Plunged on Triangle," *TT*, October 23, 1915, 2.

47. Indeed, extant Triangle business records include an exhibition contract that explicitly forbade the screening of Triangle films "in theaters seating less than 400 people and charging less than ten cents." Contract between Triangle Film Corporation and Big "T" Film Corporation, February 21, 1916, ABP. On neighborhood theaters and working-class audiences, see Lizabeth Cohen, *Making a New Deal: Industrial Workers in Chicago, 1919–1939* (Cambridge: Cambridge University Press, 1990), 120–47.

48. My overview of Triangle's New York theaters is compiled from the following reports: "Editorial," *TT*, February 12, 1916, 2; "Ten Big Theatres Signed Up in One Week by New York Office," *TT*, April 8, 1916, 1; "Rothapfel Opens Two Million Dollar Rialto with Triangle," *TT*, April 29, 1916, 1, 3; "Triangle Conspicuous in Columns of Dailies," *TT*, May 20, 1916, 2; "Activities at 14 Theatres on Broadway," *TT*, June 3, 1916, 8.

49. Data on Triangle's Chicago exhibition is drawn from theater listings in the *Chicago Tribune*, February to April, 1916, and from the following *Triangle* reports: "Biggest Chicago Theatre Owners Talk Triangle," *TT*, January 29, 1916, 1, 7; "Triangle Scores New Triumph in Chicago," *TT*, March 4, 1916, 2; "Chicago Strand Opens with Triangle Plays," *TT*, April 8, 1916, 3; "Exhibitors Organizing Local Advertising Clubs," *TT*, May 6, 1916, 2. For useful statistics on Chicago land use during this period, see Homer Hoyt's *One Hundred Years of Land Values in Chicago* (Chicago: University of Chicago Press, 1933).

50. Financial figures drawn from the Triangle Film Corporation cash record, April 29, 1916–July 28, 1917, ABP.

51. Harry Aitken to Mack Sennett, September 28, 1916, Triangle Film Corp.–Keystone Film Co. folder, Contract Files—General, MSC.

52. See "Triangle Rumors Set at Rest by Griffith, Ince, and Sennett," *MPN*, October 28, 1916, 2654. For a more detailed account of the events described in this paragraph, see Lahue, *Dreams for Sale*, chaps. 10 and 11.

53. Strand Amusement Co. to Mack Sennett.

54. Excerpts from letters regarding the distribution of Keystone pictures, correspondence folder (1915–1919), General Files, MSC.

55. So precipitous was the decline of Aitken's exhibition empire that, in March and April 1917 alone, Triangle was forced to cease distribution of its films in no fewer than seven states (in chronological order, Michigan, Colorado, Ohio, Massachusetts, Illinois, Minnesota, and Washington). See Coleman C. Vaughan, secretary of state (Michigan), to Walter N. Seligsberg, March 5, 1917; George E. Tralles, attorney at law, to Walter N. Seligsberg, March 28, 1917; William D. Fulton, secretary of state (Ohio), to Triangle Film Corporation, April 11, 1917; William D. T. Trefry, commissioner of corporations (Mass.), to W. N. Seligsberg, April 16, 1917; "A. L. S.," memo to F. Lipnick, April 23, 1917; Julius A. Schmahl, secretary of state (Minnesota), to Triangle Film Corporation, April 27, 1917; I. M. Howell, secretary of state (Washington), to Triangle Film Corporation, May 1, 1917, ABP.

56. Keystone Film Company journal, November 1915–December 1922, ABP.

57. Lahue, *Dreams for Sale*, 161.

58. Paul DiMaggio, "Cultural Entrepreneurship in Nineteenth-Century Boston: The Creation of an Organizational Base for High Culture in America," *Media, Culture and Society* 1 (January 1982): 33–50.

59. Max Weber, *Economy and Society: An Outline of Interpretive Sociology*, vol. 2, trans. Ephraim Fischoff (1924; reprint, New York: Bedminster Press, 1968), 937. See DiMaggio, "Cultural Entrepreneurship," 36.

60. "Movies Take Over the Knickerbocker," *NYT*, September 24, 1915, 11.

61. Francis G. Couvares, "The Triumph of Commerce: Class Culture and Mass Culture in Pittsburgh," in Michael H. Frisch and Daniel J. Walkowitz, eds., *Working-Class America: Essays on Labor, Community, and American Society* (Urbana: University of Illinois Press, 1983), 123–52.

62. Average production times calculated from thirty-eight extant "Complete Production Reports" on Keystone's Triangle films, held at the Margaret Herrick Library and the Wisconsin Historical Society. Using these reports, I calculate the average time for story preparation as 10.5 days; for rehearsals, 2.5; and for filming, 46.6. For production statistics on *Tillie's Punctured Romance*, see chapter 3 above.

63. Information on the new buildings is collated from the following sources: "Keystone Laughs Itself into a New $100,000 Studio," *MPN*, September 25, 1915, 58; "Keystone Enlarges Stage Space," *MPN*, October 23, 1915, 50; "In and out of West Coast Studios," *MPN*, November 6, 1915, 69; ibid., December 18, 1915, 74; "Rebuild Keystone Studio by Aid of Laughs," *MPN*, July 22, 1916, 402–3.

64. "Mack Sennett Is in New York Conferring with Triangle Heads," *MPN*, July 29, 1916, 589.

65. On Waldron, see Lahue and Brewer, *Kops and Custards,* 118.

66. For Keystone's Triangle directors, see advertisement for Keystone Film Company, *MPN,* January 29, 1916, Studio Directory, 34; "Their Lieutenants," *Photoplay,* March 1916, 42–48; "Rebuild Keystone Studio by Aid of Laughs," *MPN.*

67. One of the exceptions appears to have been Keystone's very first Triangle release, the Sennett-directed *My Valet.* Although the Library of Congress print preserves only one reel of the original four, surviving footage shows an extreme use of long takes (average shot length 9.2 seconds) focused in particular on Sennett's own portrayal of the eponymous valet. In fact, a reviewer of the time criticized Sennett's direction on just this count: "By reason of his inability to resist the temptation to feature himself, Mr. Sennett has lost a chance to live up to his past performance as a great director. . . . One is impelled to the view that if Mr. Sennett wanted to be the feature, he should have allowed Mr. Hitchcock to direct him" ("The First Knickerbocker Program," *MPN,* October 9, 1915, 84). On the use of long takes in Keystone's Mutual pictures, see Douglas Riblet, "The Keystone Film Company, 1912 to 1915" (Ph.D. diss., University of Wisconsin-Madison, 1998), 164–79.

68. Information on Keystone's new writers is drawn from "In and out of Los Angeles Studios," *MPN,* March 13, 1915, 41–42; advertisement for Keystone Film Company, *MPN,* January 29, 1916, Studio Directory, 34–35; "In and out of Los Angeles Studios," *MPN,* July 8, 1916, 86–87; Clarence Badger clippings file, AMPAS. For William Jerome, see Anthony Slide, *The Vaudevillians: A Dictionary of Vaudeville Performers* (Westport, Conn.: Arlington House, 1981), 56–57.

69. William Uricchio and Roberta E. Pearson, *Reframing Culture: The Case of the Vitagraph Quality Films* (Princeton, N.J.: Princeton University Press, 1993), 46.

70. Advertisement for Keystone Film Company, *MPN,* Studio Directory, January 29, 1916, 34–35.

71. Unidentified clipping, ca. early 1904, Sam Bernard Scrapbooks, 11,160, BRTC. On turn-of-the-century musical comedy, see Cecil Smith and Glenn Litton, *Musical Comedy in America* (New York: Theater Arts Books, 1981), esp. chaps. 10 and 11.

72. A similar development occurred somewhat earlier in vaudeville, where the influence of musical comedy inspired the emergence of the "ensemble act," popularized around 1906 and featuring beautiful chorus girls, glossy sets and costumes, and high budgets. See Kathyrn Oberdeck, *The Evangelist and the Impresario: Religion, Entertainment, and Cultural Politics in America, 1884–1914* (Princeton, N.J.: Princeton University Press, 1999), 207.

73. "Three Companies for Keystone, Making Fifteen," *MPN,* March 25, 1916, 1730.

74. "Coming Keystones with Great Comedy Stars," *TT,* December 18, 1915, 5.

75. Howells quoted in Michael Denning, *Mechanic Accents: Dime Novels and Working-Class Culture in America* (London: Verso, 1987), 79.

76. See Lee Grieveson, *Policing Cinema: Movies and Censorship in Early-Twentieth-Century America* (Berkeley: University of California Press, 2004), conclusion.

77. Steven J. Ross, "Beyond the Screen: History, Class, and the Movies," in David James and Rick Berg, eds., *The Hidden Foundation: Cinema and the Question of Class* (Minneapolis: University of Minnesota Press, 1996), 43.

78. Scenario, "His Dream Girl," *The Late Lamented*, Production Files, MSC.

79. The pattern exemplifies the "allegorical" displacements discussed by Fredric Jameson in a famous essay on mass culture: since mass-cultural narrative is unable to represent "the political logic of daily life" as an overt political message, the representation of social class must be displaced to a secondary—as Jameson terms it, allegorical—level of meaning. Fredric Jameson, "Class and Allegory in Contemporary Mass Culture: *Dog Day Afternoon* as a Political Film," in *Signatures of the Visible* (London: Routledge, 1992), 38.

80. Denning, *Mechanic Accents*, 61. In a similar vein, Ann Douglas analyzes sentimentalism as an evasive response to late-nineteenth-century social change in her book, *The Feminization of American Culture* (New York: Knopf, 1977).

81. "Respectability," writes Richard Butsch, "was at its core a gendered concept," a point that Butsch explores in his own study of the "re-gendering" of American theater in the nineteenth century. Richard Butsch, "Bowery B'hoys and Matinee Ladies: The Re-Gendering of Nineteenth-Century American Theater Audiences," *American Quarterly* 46.3 (September 1994): 375.

82. "Promotion Ideas in Releases of Jan 16th," *TT*, January 8, 1916, 4.

83. On the sentimentalization of Chaplin's tramp persona, see Charles Maland, *Chaplin and American Culture: The Evolution of a Star Image* (Princeton, N.J.: Princeton University Press, 1989), chap. 1.

84. Synopsis (3 pp.), *Gypsy Joe*, Production Files, MSC.

85. Continuity (8 pp.), *Gypsy Joe*, Production Files, MSC.

86. Final synopsis, *Gypsy Joe*, Production Files, MSC.

87. Synopsis (1 p.), *Gypsy Joe*, Production Files, MSC.

88. Final synopsis, *Gypsy Joe*, MSC.

89. Ibid.

90. Rehearsal, "Tramp Story," *A Modern Enoch Arden*, Production Files, MSC.

91. "Mace Is Back With Keystone," *MPN*, July 3, 1915, 53. The date for Mace's departure from Keystone is given in "Mace Quits Keystone," *MPN*, April 5, 1913, 33.

92. "The Second Knickerbocker Triangle Program," *MPN*, October 16, 1915, 83; "Triangle Program," *MPW*, November 18, 1916, 1001; "Triangle Program," *MPW*, May 27, 1916, 1531.

93. "Comments on the Films," *MPW*, October 30, 1915, 793; ibid., June 9, 1917, 1628.

94. "Triangle Program," *MPW*, June 2, 1917, 1459; ibid., July 14, 1917, 255.

95. Ibid., February 5, 1916, 798.

96. Kalton Lahue, *Mack Sennett's Keystone: The Man, The Myth, and the Comedies* (South Brunswick, N.J.: A. S. Barnes, 1971), 179.

97. Gloria Swanson, *Swanson on Swanson* (New York: Random House, 1980), 49.

98. On Parrott's career at Keystone, including salary details, see Brian Anthony and Andy Edmonds, *Smile When the Raindrops Fall: The Story of Charley Chase* (Lanham, Md.: Scarecrow Press, 1998), chap. 4. Additional salary information is from the Clarence Badger, Eddie Cline, Fred Fishback, and Victor Heerman folders, Contract Files, MSC.

99. Swanson, *Swanson on Swanson*, 51.

100. "Cutting Notes," *A Dash of Courage*, Production Files, MSC. As well as indicating Sennett's concern with the unit's success, this document also reveals his growing unfamiliarity with the comedians under his employ. As Sennett writes at one point, "That shot should wake up what you call him."

101. Figures for Swanson's salary are taken from Lahue and Brewer, *Kops and Custards*, 154–57, and "Employment—Idle Time," Financial Files, MSC.

102. "In and out of West Coast Studios," *MPN*, December 23, 1916, 4028.

103. "Comments on the Films," *MPW*, November 25, 1916, 1189.

104. The quote is from Harry Gribbon's studio biography, Biography Files, MSC. Further information on Gribbon is drawn from "In and out of Los Angeles Studios," *MPN*, January 9, 1915, 35.

105. Review of *The Little Teacher*, *MPW*, July 3, 1915, 79.

106. Fredric Jameson, *The Political Unconscious: Narrative as a Socially Symbolic Act* (Ithaca, N.Y.: Cornell University Press, 1981), 188.

107. Swanson, *Swanson on Swanson*, 49–50.

108. Final Synopsis, *Haystacks and Steeples*, Production Files, MSC.

109. Ibid.

110. Ibid.

111. Harry Carr, "An Interview in Great Danish," *Photoplay*, July 1917, 29.

112. "The Nick of Time Baby," *MSW*, January 1, 1917, 3.

113. "First Independent Release Now on the Market," *MSW*, January 29, 1917, 2.

114. W. Stephen Bush, "Scenarios by the Bushel," *NYT*, December 5, 1920, quoted in Koszarski, *Evening's Entertainment*, 30. For further statistics on the female audience of the 1910s, see also Richard Abel, *Americanizing the Movies and "Movie-Mad" Audiences, 1910–1914* (Berkeley: University of California Press, 2006), 90–92; Shelley Stamp, *Movie-Struck Girls: Women and Motion Picture Culture after the Nickelodeon* (Princeton, N.J.: Princeton University Press, 2000), 6–7.

115. Within the broader industry, appeals to female and family audiences had gathered pace during the 1910s as one of the central strategies for connecting cinema to gendered standards of respectability, although this was not without its contradictions. Shelley Stamp has shown how trade publications and fan magazines often expressed unease about female moviegoers, who, despite being much-prized by exhibitors, were also associated with behaviors

seen as disruptive and distracting. Stamp, *Movie-Struck Girls,* chap. 1. On the role of romance in fostering a commodified female fan culture, see Gaylyn Studlar, "The Perils of Pleasure? Fan Magazine Discourse as Women's Commodified Culture in the 1920s," *Wide Angle* 13.1 (January 1991): 6–33.

116. "Mickey Is Almost Ready and Is Certain To Make a Real Hit," *MSW,* March 26, 1917, 1.

117. T. J. Jackson Lears, *No Place of Grace: Antimodernism and the Transformation of American Culture, 1880–1920* (Chicago: University of Chicago Press, 1983), 144–49. For more on middle-class attitudes to childhood, see Viviana A. Zelizer, *Pricing the Priceless Child: The Changing Social Value of Children* (Princeton, N.J.: Princeton University Press, 1994); Rob King, "The Kid from *The Kid:* Jackie Coogan and the Consolidation of Child Consumerism," *Velvet Light Trap* 48 (Fall 2001): 4–19. See also Martha Wolfenstein's classic essay, "Fun Morality: An Analysis of Recent American Child-Training Literature," in Margaret Mead and Martha Wolfenstein, eds., *Childhood in Contemporary Culture* (Chicago: University of Chicago Press, 1955), 168–78.

118. Quoted in T. J. Jackson Lears, *Fables of Abundance: A Cultural History of Advertising in America* (New York: Basic Books, 1994), 178.

119. See Ileen Devault, *Sons and Daughters of Labor: Class and Clerical Work in Turn-of-the-Century Pittsburgh* (Ithaca, N.Y.: Cornell University Press, 1990).

120. See Warren Susman's essay, "'Personality' and the Making of Twentieth-Century Culture," in *Culture as History: The Transformation of American Society in the Twentieth Century* (New York: Pantheon Books, 1984), 271–85. Richard Abel has recently reintroduced the concept of "personality" for a consideration of early stardom in his *Americanizing the Movies,* 232–39.

121. Clarence Badger, interview in *Image,* May 1957, quoted in Lawrence J. Quirk, *The Films of Gloria Swanson* (Secaucus, N.J.: Citadel Press, 1984), 11 (emphasis added).

122. Nor was this formula limited to the Swanson-Vernon films. Probably its clearest statement comes in one of the Carew-Belmont romantic comedies, *Skidding Hearts* (June 1917). "In these modern times," reads the film's opening title card, "there lived a friendly couple with old-fashioned ideas about providing a husband for their daughter." "But their daughter," reads the second, "was determined to hold the reins." On marriage as a strategy of social advancement, see Mary Ryan's insightful analysis of antebellum middle-class culture, *Cradle of the Middle Class: The Family in Oneida County, New York, 1790–1865* (Cambridge: Cambridge University Press, 1981).

123. See, e.g., Sumiko Higashi, "The New Woman and Consumer Culture: Cecil B. DeMille's Sex Comedies," in Jennifer Bean and Diane Negra, eds., *A Feminist Reader in Early Cinema* (Durham, N.C.: Duke University Press, 2002), 298–332; Koszarski, Evening's Entertainment, 181–190; Lary May, *Screening Out the Past: The Birth of Mass Culture and the Motion Picture Industry* (Chicago: University of Chicago Press, 1980), chaps. 5 and 8; Steven J.

Ross, *Working-Class Hollywood: Silent Film and the Shaping of Class in America* (Princeton, N.J.: Princeton University Press, 1998), chap. 7.

124. "Mack Sennett Contends Fair Sex Is Essential to Success of Plays" (n.d., n.s., ca. mid-1920s), Press Clippings Folder, General Files, MSC.

125. *The Pullman Bride*, Production Files, MSC.

126. Swanson, *Swanson on Swanson*, 77–79.

127. See Joan Rubin, *The Making of Middlebrow Culture* (Chapel Hill: University of North Carolina Press, 1992), chap. 1.

128. D. W. Griffith to Harry Aitken, October 16, 1916, D. W. Griffith Collection, Museum of Modern Art, New York, quoted in Schickel, *D. W. Griffith*, 338.

129. Aitken, *Birth of a Nation Story*, 12–13.

130. Ibid., 83.

5. "UPROARIOUS INVENTIONS"

Epigraph: Lewis Mumford, *Technics and Civilization* (New York: Harcourt & Brace, 1934), 101.

1. Alfred A. Cohn, " 'Writing' Slapstick," *Photoplay*, October 1917, 117.

2. "Three-Minute Visit to Keystone Studio," *TT*, November 27, 1915, 6.

3. Review of *Bathtub Perils*, *MPW*, June 24, 1916, 2259; "The Seventh Knickerbocker Triangle Program," *MPN*, November 27, 1915, 92; "The Shadow Stage," *Photoplay*, May 1916, 109.

4. John F. Kasson, *Amusing the Million: Coney Island at the Turn of the Century* (New York: Hill & Wang, 1978), 8, calls the amusement parks "laboratories of the new mass culture." The role of mechanical spectacle in turn-of-the-century popular culture is examined in detail in Ben Singer, *Melodrama and Modernity: Early Sensational Cinema and Its Contexts* (New York: Columbia University Press, 2001), chap. 3.

5. Figures taken from John F. Kasson, *Civilizing the Machine: Technology and Republican Values in America, 1776–1900* (New York: Penguin Books, 1976), 183–84; Alan Trachtenberg, *The Incorporation of America: Culture and Society in the Gilded Age* (New York: Hill & Wang, 1983), 64.

6. "Triangle Program," *MPW*, January 1, 1916, 91 (emphasis added).

7. The budget increase has been calculated from the Keystone Film Company cash book, September 28, 1912–April 24, 1924, ABP. The original contract documents are no longer extant.

8. Advertisement for *The Cannon Ball*, *MPW*, June 5, 1915, 563.

9. "Comments on the Films," *MPW*, June 19, 1915, 1940.

10. "Work on New Keystone Studio Is a Rush Job," *MPN*, May 29, 1915, 44. My description of the new Keystone studio facilities also draws on the following: "Sennett Razes Mountain for Keystone Studio," *TT*, October 30, 1915, 7; "In and out of West Coast Studios," *MPN*, November 6, 1915, 69; "Rebuild Keystone Studio by Aid of Laughs," *MPN*, July 22, 1916, 402–3; "Facts about

the Sennett Studios" (ca. 1923–24), General Files, MSC. See also Kalton C. Lahue and Terry Brewer, *Kops and Custards: The Legend of Keystone Films* (1968; reprint, Norman: University of Oklahoma Press, 1972), 93, 110; Kalton C. Lahue, *Dreams for Sale: The Rise and Fall of the Triangle Film Corporation* (South Brunswick, N.J.: A. S. Barnes, 1971), 77.

11. "In and out of West Coast Studios," *MPN*, November 27, 1915, 76.

12. Coy Watson Jr., *The Keystone Kid: Tales from Early Hollywood* (Santa Monica, Calif.: Santa Monica Press, 2001), 110. Information on the "Cyclorama," ibid., 110–15, and "Facts about the Sennett Studios," MSC. The Cyclorama features prominently in the 1927 behind-the-scenes comedy *Crazy to Act*, released in 2005 as part of Kino Video's *Oliver Hardy Collection* DVD.

13. "Three-Minute Visit to Keystone Studio," *TT*.

14. *New York Tribune* review quoted in "Telegram Predicts Long Run for 'Quixote,'" *TT*, January 8, 1916, 8.

15. See "Keystoners Preparing Thrills and Laughs," *TT*, December 11, 1915, 4; "In and out of Los Angeles Studios," *MPN*, December 18, 1915, 73.

16. "Triangle Program," *MPW*, January 1, 1916, 91.

17. Randolph Bartlett, "Why Aren't We Killed?" *Photoplay*, April 1916, 84.

18. "Triangle Program," *MPW*, January 1, 1916, 91; "Triangle Turns the First Birthday Mark," *MPN*, November 18, 1916, 3128.

19. See Singer, *Melodrama and Modernity*, 182.

20. See Donald Crafton, *Before Mickey: The Animated Film, 1898–1928* (Chicago: Chicago University Press, 1993), esp. chaps. 1 to 3.

21. For basic information on Larry Semon, see Jon Gartenberg, "Vitagraph Comedy Production," in Eileen Bowser, ed., *The Slapstick Symposium* (Brussels: Fedération internationale des archives du film, 1988), 45–48; Kalton C. Lahue, *World of Laughter: The Motion Picture Comedy Short, 1910–1930* (Norman: University of Oklahoma Press, 1966), 150–56.

22. Mack Sennett to Adolph Zukor, December 13, 1917, correspondence folder (1915–1919), General Files, MSC.

23. On the "operational aesthetic," see Neil Harris, *Humbug: The Art of P. T. Barnum* (Boston: Little, Brown, 1973), chap. 3.

24. Certainly, one catches the spirit of Goldberg's inventions in the following description of Sennett's films, from a 1918 *Photoplay* review: "If it is funny for a tipsy man to stumble against a diner, it is funnier still if he makes the diner spill a cup of hot coffee; and not merely spill the coffee, but spill it on an impetuous passer by; this victim swings at the original offender, who dodges and the blow lands upon the anatomy of a fourth; nor is it sufficient that the three disturbed persons hurl the original offender into the street—he must land in a passing automobile, finding himself comfortably seated in the tonneau, without effort on his part, and thus, in state, be driven to a fashionable reception, and hailed as the guest of honor, who has meanwhile been disposed of by a similar chain of incidents" ("The Shadow Stage," *Photoplay*, February 1918, 66).

25. "Triangle Program," *MPW*, July 7, 1917, 80; ibid., July 14, 1917, 255.

26. Ibid., June 16, 1917, 1798; July 7, 1917, 80; July 14, 1917, 255. The average shot length (ASL) cited in this paragraph should be taken as a very rough estimate only. Only around 36 percent of Keystone's Triangle releases survive (according to my findings, 43 out of 119), and, of these, many exist only in heavily reedited and/or fragmentary form. The reasons for the large number of lost films are unclear (especially when compared with the 48 percent survival rate for Keystone's Mutual releases). The reediting of the surviving prints can, however, be confidently attributed to the policies of W. H. Productions and the Tower Film Corporation, two companies that reissued Triangle films during the late 1910s. As Kalton Lahue explains, these companies were set up by Harry Aitken in the fall of 1917 as a way of squeezing money out of his back catalog while Triangle crumbled around him. See Lahue, *Dreams for Sale*, chap. 12. Although many of Keystone's Triangle releases exist now only because of these reissues, the extensive reediting to which they were subjected makes it very difficult to achieve accurate statistical analysis of the films.

27. "Comments on the Films," *MPW*, October 12, 1912, 144.

28. "Triangle Program," *MPW*, December 4, 1915, 1848 (emphasis added).

29. Ibid., January 1, 1916, 91 (emphasis added).

30. Ibid., November 27, 1915, 1679.

31. "Sennett Gets Open Letter from Keystone Fan," *TT*, November 27, 1915, 1.

32. Michael M. Davis, *The Exploitation of Pleasure* (New York: Russell Sage Foundation, 1911), quoted in Singer, *Melodrama and Modernity*, 65.

33. See Stephen Kern, *The Culture of Time and Space, 1880–1918* (Cambridge, Mass.: Harvard University Press, 1983), 124–30.

34. Leo Marx, *The Machine in the Garden: Technology and the Pastoral Ideal in America* (London: Oxford University Press, 1964). On dystopian motifs in turn-of-the-century magazines, see Singer, *Melodrama and Modernity*, 69–90. For the image of modernity as juggernaut, see Anthony Giddens, *The Consequences of Modernity* (Stanford, Calif.: Stanford University Press, 1990), 139.

35. "Production Report," *A Submarine Pirate*, ABP.

36. "Seventh Knickerbocker Triangle Program," *MPN*, November 27, 1915, 92; review of *A Submarine Pirate*, *MPW*, November 27, 1915, 1681; "The Shadow Stage," *Photoplay*, February 1916, 104.

37. "New York Elite Gives Private Triangle Show," *TT*, December 4, 1915, 5.

38. "Prominent Comedians at Keystone Studios," *TT*, November 13, 1915, 5.

39. "Triangle Film Shows Working of Submarine," *TT*, November 13, 1915, 7.

40. "Bally-Hoo Display for Syd Chaplin Comedy, 'A Submarine Pirate,'" *TT*, December 18, 1915, 5; reviews of *A Submarine Pirate* quoted in *TT*, December 4, 1915, 5.

41. See, e.g., "War by Assassination," *NYT*, May 8, 1915, 14; "Submarines Alter Marine War Code," *NYT*, May 9, 1915, 5.

42. "Triangle Film Shows Working of Submarine." The expression "submarine pirate" was in fact British slang for a German U-boat, first appearing

after Germany began its submarine campaign in British waters in early 1915. It is tempting to hypothesize that Syd Chaplin, a Briton himself, contributed the title of the Keystone film. I am grateful to Inie Park for bringing this to my attention.

43. This original beginning is absent from the version of the film available on the *American Slapstick* DVD (Image, 2006), which preserves a later two-reel reissue. I have based my analysis on the more complete version held at UCLA's Film and Television Archive, drawing also upon the cutting continuity held at the Margaret Herrick Library (Continuity, "Submarine Story" [19 pp.], Production Files, MSC).

44. For "Shoot-the-Chutes" and the "Barrel of Fun," see Kasson, *Amusing the Million*, 60, 78–79.

45. James R. Latham, "The Promotion of Early Hollywood: Racial, Ethnic, and National Identity in Text and Context" (Ph.D. diss., New York University, 2003), 658, 685. *A Submarine Pirate* was not the first film to exploit the modern submarine as technological spectacle. In December 1914, just a few months following the outbreak of war in Europe, Universal reissued the four-year-old picture *The Submarine Spy*, with an advertisement campaign trumpeting the film's topicality: "Every newspaper is full of present war stories and naval battles wherein the Submarine plays the biggest part. What, then, could be more timely than such a subject?" (advertisement for *The Submarine Spy, MPW*, December 12, 1914, 1460–61).

46. Joseph Stella, "Discovery of America: Autobiographical Notes," *Art News* 59 (November 1960), 64, quoted in Kasson, *Amusing the Million*, 88.

47. See the oft-cited essay by Walter Benjamin, "On Some Motifs in Baudelaire," in id., *Illuminations,* trans. Harry Zohn (New York: Harcourt, Brace & World, 1968), 157–202. Lynn Kirby brilliantly discusses Benjamin's notion of "shock" in relation to early cinema; see Kirby, *Parallel Tracks: The Railroad and Silent Cinema* (Durham, N.C.: Duke University Press, 1997), chap. 1.

48. I use the term "homologous" here in the sense suggested by Raymond Williams, that is, to describe a link between different specific practices as "directly related expressions of and responses to a general historical process." Raymond Williams, *Marxism and Literature* (New York: Oxford University Press, 1977), 104.

49. Synopsis (6 pp.), *A Game Old Knight,* Production Files, MSC.

50. Review of *Bathtub Perils, MPW*, June 24, 1916, 2259. Accounts of the filming of this sequence can be found in Simon Louvish, *Keystone: The Life and Clowns of Mack Sennett* (New York: Faber & Faber, 2003), 126–27; Watson, 72–74.

51. See Lauren Rabinovitz, "The Coney Island Comedies: Bodies and Slapstick at the Amusement Park and the Movies," in Charlie Keil and Shelley Stamp, eds., *American Cinema's Transitional Era: Audiences, Institutions, Practices* (Berkeley: University of California Press, 2004), 171–90.

52. In April 1910, Kessel and Baumann had signed a three-year rental contract for the Carlton Motion Picture Laboratories, located on Neptune Avenue

and West Twentieth Street, Coney Island. (Agreement between Edison Electric Illuminating Company and New York Motion Picture Company, April 5, 1910, ABP.) Keystone's filmmakers seem to have shot location footage for *At Coney Island* during the Fourth of July holiday in 1912, prior to the company's departure for Los Angeles the following month. See chapter 1, n. 56.

53. Johan Huizinga, *Homo Ludens* (1938; trans., 1944, reprint, Boston: Beacon Press, 1955), 8–10, quoted in David Nasaw, *Going Out: The Rise and Fall of Public Amusements* (New York: Basic Books, 1993), 80.

54. See, e.g., Kathy Peiss, *Cheap Amusements: Working Women and Leisure in Turn-of-the-Century New York* (Philadelphia University Press: Temple University Press, 1986), chap. 5.

55. Alfred A. Cohn, "'Writing' Slapstick," *Photoplay*, September 1917, 117.

56. Thorstein Veblen, *The Theory of the Leisure Class: An Economic Study of Institutions* (1899; reprint, New York: Random House, 1934).

57. René Gimpel, *Journal d'un collectionneur: Marchand de tableaux* (Paris: Calmann-Lévy, 1963), quoted in Paul Virilio, *The Art of the Motor*, trans. Julie Rose (Minneapolis: University of Minnesota Press, 1995), 77.

58. Theodor Adorno, "Perennial Fashion—Jazz," in *Prisms*, trans. Samuel Weber and Shierry Weber (Cambridge, Mass.: MIT Press, 1967), 125.

59. Theodor Adorno, "The Schema of Mass Culture," in *The Culture Industry*, ed. J. M. Bernstein (London: Routledge, 1991), 79.

60. Henry Adams, *The Education of Henry Adams* (1907; reprint, New York: Modern Library, 1996), 474–88.

61. On the impact of the Armory Show, see Robert Crunden, *American Salons: Encounters with European Modernism, 1885–1917* (New York: Oxford University Press, 1993), esp. 357–82; Martin Green, *New York 1913: The Armory Show and the Paterson Strike Pageant* (New York: Scribner, 1988). Although the impact of social realism in American painting was cut short by modernism's arrival at the Armory Show, it is important not to overstate the degree to which the Ashcan painters were socially committed artists. As Sumiko Higashi argues, they may have "sympathized with the urban poor, and, at various times in their careers, contributed to the socialist publication *The Masses*"; still "there is a marked degree of middle-class voyeurism" in some of their works, a trait that Higashi links to the photographs of Jacob A. Riis. Sumiko Higashi, "The American Origins of Film Noir: Realism in Urban Art and *The Naked City*," in Eric Smoodin and Jon Lewis, eds., *Looking Past the Screen: Case Studies in American Film History and Method* (Durham, N.C.: Duke University Press, 2007), 360.

62. Peter Seixas, "Lewis Hine: From 'Social' to 'Interpretive' Photographer," *American Quarterly* 39.3 (Fall 1987): 381–409.

63. Trachtenberg, *Incorporation of America*, 55.

64. On Cohan and the "mechanics of emotion," see Henry Jenkins, *What Made Pistachio Nuts? Early Sound Comedy and the Vaudeville Aesthetic* (New York: Columbia University Press, 1992), 32–37.

65. Henri Bergson, *Laughter: An Essay on the Meaning of the Comic*, trans. Cloudesley Brereton and Fred Rothwell (1900; trans., London: Macmillan, 1911).

66. "Putting the Laugh in Laughter," *RL*, May 30, 1914, 20.

67. Quoted phrases taken from the production synopsis of *The Love Comet*, ABP; "Comments on the Films," *MPW*, July 8, 1916, 306.

68. On representations of women's driving in early film, see Jennifer Parchesky, "Women in the Driver's Seat: The Auto-Erotics of Early Women's Films," *Film History* 18.2 (2006): 174–84.

69. Scenario, "Inventor Story" (3 pp.), August 5, 1916, and scenario, "Inventor Story" (5 pp.), August 11, 1916, *A Maiden's Trust*, Production Files, MSC.

70. Note regarding "Automat Story," *A Clever Dummy*, Production Files, MSC.

71. Story Outline, "Automat Story" (2 pp.), September 8, 1916, *A Clever Dummy*, Production Files, MSC.

72. Ibid.

73. The plot outlined in the "Automat Story" synopsis bears striking similarity to an earlier Italian comedy, *Lea Bambola* (*Lea the Doll*, Ambrosio, 1913), in which a young man conceals his beloved from his relatives by having her masquerade as a mechanical doll. The later British film *Bamboozled* (Swastika Films, 1919) also features a similar plot situation, in which a mechanical woman again plays a key comic role. It is possible, as Richard Koszarski has suggested to me, that an "ur"-vaudeville act lies behind the transnational popularity of this comic device.

74. "Complete Production Report," April 11, 1917, *A Maiden's Trust*, Production Files, MSC.

75. Turpin's starting salary compares favorably even with Keystone's most established performers: Charles Murray, then the studio's longest-serving lead comedian, received $300 a week according to a contract signed in January 1917; while Polly Moran, one of Keystone's most successful comic actresses, was paid $175 for her weekly services. See the contracts between Ben Turpin and the Keystone Film Company, March 16, 1917, Charles Murray and the Keystone Film Company, January 17, 1917, and Polly Moran and the Keystone Film Company, July 23, 1917, Contract Files, MSC.

76. On the "Triangle Comedies," see chapter 4.

77. Mack Sennett, with Cameron Shipp, *King of Comedy* (Garden City, N.Y.: Doubleday, 1954; reprint, San Jose, Calif.: toExcel Press, 2000), 143, 145.

78. *RL*, July 8, 1916, quoted in Steve Rydzewski, "Ben Turpin—The Early Years, Part Three: Vogue Comedies," *Slapstick* 3 (2000); *Motography* June 24, 1916, also quoted in Rydzewski. My information on Turpin (both here and in following paragraphs) is collated from Rydzewski's article and the following sources: Ben Turpin folder, Biography Files, and Ben Turpin folder, Contract Files, MSC; R. E. Braff, "Ben Turpin Filmography" (n.d.), from the Ben Turpin clippings file, AMPAS; Kalton C. Lahue, *Mack Sennett's Keystone: The Man,*

the *Myth and the Comedies* (South Brunswick, N.J.: A. S. Barnes, 1971), 151–56.

79. Scenario, with steno notes, "The Automatic Figure" (3 pp.), May 17, 1917, *A Clever Dummy*, Production Files, MSC.

80. Ibid.

81. Rehearsal continuity, "Figure Story" (3 pp.), May 18, 1917, *A Clever Dummy*, Production Files, MSC.

82. "Complete Production Report," June 28, 1917, *A Clever Dummy*, Production Files, MSC.

83. On the "Human Dynamo," see "Luna Park," *New York Call*, August 13, 1916, 6.

84. Peter Wollen, *Raiding the Icebox: Reflections on Twentieth-Century Culture* (Bloomington: Indiana University Press, 1993), 41–42. The word robot was first coined in 1920 by Czech writer Karel Capek as a derivation from the Czech word for "forced labor."

85. Contract between Mack Sennett and Paramount Pictures Corp., June 29, 1917, Paramount Pictures folder, Contract Files—General, MSC.

86. Mack Sennett to John A. Waldron, June 29, 1917, correspondence folder (1915–1919), General Files, MSC.

87. Adorno "Schema of Mass Culture," 87.

88. As Steven Ross has shown, the Committee on Public Information (CPI), headed by George Creel, used economic incentives to encourage "wholesome" representations of American life during the war, e.g., by denying export licenses to films dealing with class conflict and political corruption. See Steven J. Ross, *Working-Class Hollywood: Silent Film and the Shaping of Class in America* (Princeton, N.J.: Princeton University Press, 1998), 123–30. Although Ross rightly points to World War I as a decisive moment in the changing ideological focus of American cinema, recent work by Lee Grieveson indicates that this was part of a longer process of legal decisions and regulatory measures—notably the Supreme Court's famous *Mutual* ruling of 1915—that progressively divorced mainstream cinema from a socially engaged role. See Lee Grieveson, *Policing Cinema: Movies and Censorship in Early-Twentieth-Century America* (Berkeley: University of California Press, 2004), esp. "Conclusion."

6. FROM "DIVING VENUS" TO "BATHING BEAUTIES"

Epigraph: Foster Rhea Dulles, *America Learns to Play, 1607–1940* (New York: D. Appleton-Century, 1940), 363.

1. Mack Sennett, with Cameron Shipp, *King of Comedy* (Garden City, N.Y.: Doubleday, 1954; reprint, San Jose, Calif.: toExcel, 2000), 167.

2. "Photographs for Your Lobby," *MSW*, April 23, 1917, 3; advertisement for Keystone, *MPN*, May 26, 1917, 3221.

3. Music folder, General Files, MSC. The chorus to the song—lyrics and music by Ray Perkins—deserves full quotation: "Help, help, Mr. Sennett,

help, / I'm drowning in a sea of love. / Just because those bathing girls of yours / Have got me always thinking of 'em. / Gee, I love 'em. / Each peach strolling on the beach won me when she winked and smiled. / If you need a lifeguard just call upon me. / I'd like to offer my services free. / Help, help, Mr. Sennett, help, / Your bathing beauties are driving me wild."

4. Theodore Dreiser, "The Best Motion Picture Interview Ever Written," *Photoplay*, August 1928, 128.

5. See Kathy Peiss, "On Beauty . . . and the History of Business," in Philip Scranton, ed., *Beauty and Business: Commerce, Gender, and Culture in Modern America* (New York: Routledge, 2001), 7–22.

6. See Henry Jenkins, *What Made Pistachio Nuts? Early Sound Comedy and the Vaudeville Aesthetic* (New York: Columbia University Press, 1992), chap. 7; Kathleen K. Rowe, *The Unruly Woman: Gender and the Genres of Laughter* (Austin: University of Texas Press, 1995).

7. On Henry James's use of the term "New Woman," see Carroll Smith-Rosenberg, *Disorderly Conduct: Visions of Gender in Victorian America* (New York: Knopf, 1985), 176.

8. Boyd Winchester, "The New Woman," *Arena*, April 1902, 367, quoted in Margaret Gibbons Wilson, *The American Woman in Transition: The Urban Influence, 1870–1920* (Westport, Conn.: Greenwood Press, 1979), 3.

9. On the different generations of New Women, see Smith-Rosenberg, *Disorderly Conduct*, 177–78.

10. Sumiko Higashi, *Cecil B. DeMille and American Culture: The Silent Era* (Berkeley: University of California Press, 1994), 87–92.

11. Wilson, *American Woman*, esp. Introduction and chap. 6.

12. See Ileen Devault, *Sons and Daughters of Labor: Class and Clerical Work in Turn-of-the-Century Pittsburgh* (Ithaca, N.Y.: Cornell University Press, 1990).

13. Smith-Rosenberg, *Disorderly Conduct*, 245.

14. Kathy Peiss, *Cheap Amusements: Working Women and Leisure in Turn-of-the-Century New York* (Philadelphia: Temple University Press, 1986).

15. On the chorus girl in early twentieth-century American culture, see Lewis Erenberg, *Steppin' Out: New York Nightlife and the Transformation of American Culture, 1890–1930* (Westport, Conn.: Greenwood Press, 1981), chap. 7.

16. Martha Banta, *Imaging American Women: Idea and Ideals in Cultural History* (New York: Columbia University Press, 1987), chap. 1.

17. "Which Is the American Princess?" *New York Journal*, January 12, 1896, discussed in Banta, *Imaging American Women*, 105–9.

18. Annette Parry, M.D., "The Athletic Girl and Motherhood," *Harper's Bazaar*, August 1912, 380, quoted in Sarah A. Gordon, " 'Any Desired Length': Negotiating Gender Through Sports Clothing, 1870–1925," in Scranton, ed., *Beauty and Business*, 26.

19. On working women's exercise, see Gordon, " 'Any Desired Length,' " 44.

20. For an excellent overview of changes in women's swimwear during this period, see Claudia B. Kidwell, "Women's Bathing and Swimming

Costume in the United States," *United States National Museum Bulletin* 250 (1968): 2–32.

21. Jane Pride, "Pick-up," *Delineator*, May 1927, 15, quoted in Kidwell, "Women's Bathing and Swimming Costume," 29.

22. Peiss, *Cheap Amusements*. See also Elizabeth Ewen *Immigrant Women in the Land of Dollars: Life and Culture on the Lower East Side, 1890–1925* (New York: Monthly Review Press, 1985).

23. Kidwell, "Women's Bathing and Swimming Costume," 30; see also Gordon, " 'Any Desired Length,' " 43.

24. "Ah, There! Coney Island" is discussed in John F. Kasson, *Amusing the Million: Coney Island at the Turn of the Century* (New York: Hill & Wang, 1978), 46–47.

25. Sennett, *King of Comedy*, 48.

26. See Betty Harper Fussell, *Mabel* (New Haven, Conn.: Ticknor & Fields, 1982), 61.

27. On Dressler, see Betty Lee, *Marie Dressler: The Unlikeliest Star* (Lexington: University of Kentucky Press, 1997), 9; on Durfee, see Fussell, *Mabel*, 68.

28. Normand herself described her early work as a model in the posthumously published interview, "Madcap Mabel Normand: The True Story of a Great Comedienne," *Liberty*, September 6, 1930, quoted in William Sherman, *Mabel Normand: A Source Book to Her Life and Films* (Seattle: Cinema Books, 1994), 361–370. "Mr. Gibson was truly a master," Normand is quoted as saying. "How I loved to watch, between poses, as he filled in the outlines of my face or body with his soft warm crayons. . . . He was so kind, always nodding when he saw me weary with the pose" (Sherman, 367).

29. Apocryphally, it was Annette Kellerman's starring performance in Universal's *Neptune's Daughter* (1914) that first seduced Hugo Münsterberg into a movie theater, leading to his writing of the landmark theoretical text *The Photoplay: A Psychological Study* (1916). The gestation of classical film theory thus owes something to women's swimwear. Thanks to Lee Grieveson for this observation.

30. The reference to "graceful diving feats" comes from the advertisement for *The Water Nymph, MPW*, September 21, 1912, 1160. Other films to feature Normand's diving displays include *Mabel's Lovers* (November 1912), *Mabel's New Hero* (August 1913), and *The Little Teacher* (June 1915).

31. "The Photoplayers," *Photoplay*, August 1913, 104; "Mabel Normand," *Photoplay*, May 1914, 8.

32. See chapter 1 above.

33. Some of the shots of Normand's diving tricks (not pictured) have intertexts in photos from working-men's magazines like *The Police Gazette*, where, as in this film, bathing girls were commonly photographed in profile, thereby accentuating breasts and buttocks.

34. In this sense, the film supports the arguments of feminist scholars who suggest that spectatorship in early film differed from the patriarchal, voyeuristic

paradigm of later narrative cinema. As Lauren Rabinovitz has written, "Early cinema routinely portrayed women either in possession of a visual gaze or overturning the male mastery of the gaze." Lauren Rabinovitz, *For the Love of Pleasure: Women, Movies, and Culture in Turn-of-the-Century Chicago* (New Brunswick, N.J.: Rutgers University Press, 1998), 81. See also Miriam Hansen's discussion of Edwin S. Porter's *The "Teddy" Bears* (Edison, 1907) in her book *Babel and Babylon: Spectatorship in American Silent Film* (Cambridge, Mass.: Harvard University Press, 1991), 44–59.

35. "Comments on the Films," *MPW*, November 16, 1912, 660.

36. Peter Stallybrass and Allon White, *The Politics and Poetics of Transgression* (Ithaca, N.Y.: Cornell University Press, 1986), 26.

37. For more on the changing models of feminity in turn-of-the-century vaudeville, see Kathryn Oberdeck, *The Evangelist and the Impresario: Religion, Entertainment, and Cultural Politics in America, 1884–1914* (Baltimore: Johns Hopkins University Press, 1999), 203–13.

38. Louis Reeves Harrison, "It Is to Laugh," *MPW*, December 21, 1912, 1166.

39. Elizabeth Stanley Trotter, "Humor with a Gender," *Atlantic*, December 1922, quoted in Jenkins, *What Made Pistachio Nuts?* 257.

40. "A Censorial Broadside," *CT*, January 9, 1915, 10. Figures on Chicago's police censors are calculated from reports in the *Chicago Tribune*, March 3, 1914–January 11, 1916.

41. See Jenkins, *What Made Pistachio Nuts?* 256–59.

42. Marie Dressler, with Mildred Harrington, *My Own Story* (Boston: Little, Brown, 1934), 3, 17.

43. "Keystone Amazon," *TT*, April 8, 1916, 3.

44. On Bakhtin and the "grotesque" body, see chapter 2 above.

45. "Mabel Normand," *Photoplay*, May 1914, 8.

46. "More Plots and Fewer Pies for Miss Normand," *New York Telegraph*, February 13, 1916, quoted in Sherman, *Mabel Normand*, 20–21.

47. Julian Johnson, "Impressions," *Photoplay*, June 1915, quoted in Sherman, *Mabel Normand*, 13.

48. "More Plots and Fewer Pies," quoted in Sherman, *Mabel Normand*, 22.

49. There is considerable doubt concerning which films Normand directed at Keystone. We know, for example, that she was promoted to director at the end of 1913. We also know that, according to existing studio documents, her first directorial efforts included *Mabel's Stormy Love Affair, Mabel's Bear Escape, Won in a Closet* (January 1914), *Mabel's Strange Predicament* (co-dir. Sennett), *Love and Gasoline* (February 1914), *Mabel at the Wheel* (co-dir. Sennett), and *Caught in a Cabaret* (April 1914, possibly co-dir. Chaplin). See "Keystone Releases," General Files, MSC. Unfortunately, studio documents provide only scant directing credits for films released after May 1914, making it difficult to identify Normand's later contributions with certainty. Other films that Normand may have directed, or had a hand in directing, include *Mabel's Busy Day, Her Friend, the Bandit* (possibly co-dir. Chaplin), *Mabel's*

Married Life (June 1914, possibly dir./co-dir. Chaplin), *Mabel's Nerve* (possibly dir. George Nichols), *Mabel's New Job* (July 1914, possibly dir. Nichols), *Mabel's Latest Prank*, *Mabel's Blunder* (September 1914), and *Hello, Mabel* (October 1914). See Betty Fussell, "The Films of Mabel Normand," *Film History* 2.4 (November–December, 1988): 373–91.

50. "Comments on the Films," *MPW*, June 27, 1914, 1829.

51. "Comments on the Films," *MPW*, January 17, 1914, 290; "Comments on the Films," *MPW*, January 24, 1914, 414; "Comments on the Films," *MPW*, February 7, 1914, 678.

52. Judging from my viewings and trade-press descriptions, I identify her working-class roles as *Mack at It Again* (April 1914), *The Fatal Mallet* (June 1914), *Mabel's Busy Day*, *Mabel's Married Life* (June 1914), *Mabel's Latest Prank* (September 1914), *Gentlemen of Nerve* (October 1914), *His Trysting Place* (November 1914), and *Tillie's Punctured Romance* (December 1914). Her appearances as an office employee are in *Mabel's Blunder* (September 1914) and *Hello Mabel* (October 1914), and as a country girl in *Those Country Kids* (August 1914) and *Lovers' Post Office* (November 1914).

53. This was a common plot in early film comedy. "Many early films delighted in street-smart women who could repel sexual advances, defend themselves in dangerous situations, and devise ingenious strategies to achieve their goals. A popular genre of movies about 'mashers' . . . often depicted quick-witted women outfoxing male harrassers" (Peiss, *Cheap Amusements*, 157).

54. Sennett, *King of Comedy*, 136.

55. "Victory on the Last Lap!" *Photoplay*, June 1914, 140–41. On *Photoplay*'s readership, see Kathryn Fuller, *At the Picture Show: Small Town Audiences and the Creation of Movie Fan Culture* (Washington, D.C.: Smithsonian Institution Press, 1996), chap. 8.

56. "Great Artist Contest," *MPSM*, October 1914, 128.

57. Normand's popularity thus supports the argument of Hansen, *Babel and Babylon*, 118, that early film "functioned as a particularly female heterotopia"—that is, as an alternative social site in which single working women could engage imaginatively in negotiating the gaps between "traditional standards of sexual behavior and modern dreams of . . . sexual expression, between freedom and anxiety."

58. Providence, Rhode Island, was home to a number of Normand's relatives, although her parents had left the state before her birth. I am grateful to Marilyn Slater for sharing this information, also available at her website, www.freewebs.com/looking-for-mabel (accessed December 27, 2007).

59. Advertisements for the Star Theatre, *Pawtucket Times*, May 10, 1913, 7, January 7, 1913, 9, and May 21, 1913, 5.

60. "Why Aren't We Killed?" *Photoplay*, April 1916, 83.

61. "From the Inside," *Photoplay*, October 1913, 100.

62. "Mabel Normand Driving Tetzlaff's Racing Car," *Photoplay*, December 1913, 44; "Doings at Los Angeles," *MPW*, May 30, 1914, 1248. The significance of motoring to Normand's star image is also evident in a number of films from

the period—*Barney Oldfield's Race for a Life* (June 1913), *The Speed Kings* (October 1913), and two of her self-directed pictures, *Love and Gasoline* (February 1914, now lost) and *Mabel at the Wheel*. In the first of these, Normand is rescued by the racing star Barney Oldfield; in the second, she chooses between two racecar drivers (again real-life racers, Teddy Tetzlaff and Earl Cooper). Tellingly, it is only under her own direction that she takes the driving seat herself (in *Mabel at the Wheel*; surviving plot information for *Love and Gasoline* is sketchy). See Jennifer Parchesky's observations on the alignment of women motorists and women directors as symbols of emancipation in early-twentieth-century feminism, in "Women in the Driver's Seat: The Auto-Erotics of Early Women's Films," *Film History* 18.2 (2006): 174–84. In addition to her automotive enthusiasms, Normand was also said to be an "ardent boxing fan" who took a "deep interest in the events of fistiana and its heroes," at a time when women were rarely permitted to attend boxing fights. See "Movie Star Is a Boxing Fan," *Reno Evening Gazette*, March 15, 1915. Thanks to Marilyn Slater for this reference.

63. "Reel Tales About Reel Folk," *RL*, November 21, 1914, 20. It is difficult not to see Normand's star image as analogous to those of the stars of "serial queen" melodramas, such as Helen Holmes, Pearl White and Kathlyn Williams. On the serial queens, see Jennifer M. Bean, "Technologies of Early Stardom and the Extraordinary Body," in Jennifer M. Bean and Diane Negra, eds., *A Feminist Reader in Early Cinema* (Durham, N.C.: Duke University Press, 2002), 404–43; Ben Singer, *Melodrama and Modernity: Early Sensational Cinema and Its Contexts* (New York: Columbia University Press, 2001), chap. 8; Shelley Stamp, *Movie-Struck Girls: Women and Motion Picture Culture After the Nickelodeon* (Princeton, N.J.: Princeton University Press, 2000), chap. 3.

64. "Pretty 'Movie' Actress Will Stump for the Socialist Ticket," *Los Angeles Citizen*, April 18, 1913, II. 1.

65. "From the Inside," *Photoplay*, August 1913, 102. The issue of suffrage is also raised in a 1917 profile of the star, in which Normand complains that women did not yet have the vote in New Jersey, where she was filming for Goldwyn. "Mabel Normand Has Lost Her Vote" (n.s., September 1917), Robinson Locke Collection of Dramatic Scrapbooks, Envelope 1629, BRTC. A similar example of a filmmaker who linked her career to the suffrage movement, though in a more sustained way, would be Lois Weber, as Shelley Stamp's work on the director has shown. See, e.g., Shelley Stamp, "Lois Weber, Progressive Cinema, and the Fate of 'The Work-a-Day Girl' in *Shoes*," *Camera Obscura* 19.2 (2004): 141–69.

66. Sennett, *King of Comedy*, 110–11.

67. "The Real Mabel Normand, by the Editor," *MSW*, March 19, 1917, 1, 3; "More Plots and Fewer Pies," quoted in Sherman, *Mabel Normand*, 20–22. As Mark Lynn Anderson has argued, these shifts in Normand's celebrity image gained pace in 1918 following her move to the Goldwyn company, when a *Photoplay* interview with the star described her personal library: "There were Gautier, Strindberg, Turgeneff, Stevenson, Walter Pater, Kipling, Oscar Wilde,

Shaw, Ibsen, John Evelyn, J. M. Barrie, Francois Coppé, Bret Harte. Of superficial best sellers there was not a single sample. Nor was there to be found in the room a copy of any of the cheap, current fiction magazines." Randolph Bartlett, "Would You Have Ever Suspected It?" *Photoplay*, August 1918, 43–44, quoted in Anderson, "Reading Mabel Normand's Library," *Film History* 18.2 (2006): 209–21. Such reports were ultimately turned against Normand after her involvement in the William Desmond Taylor scandal, when she was mocked for her supposed cultural pretensions and inability to distinguish between high and low culture. Anderson, 214–19. On the complications of "intellectual" female stardom, see also Amelie Hastie, "Louise Brooks, Star Witness," *Cinema Journal* 36.3 (Spring 1997): 3–24.

68. "Movie Royalty in California," *Photoplay*, June 1915, 127.

69. "Famous Pony Teaches Mabel How to Play Polo," *MSW*, February 19, 1917, 2.

70. "The Girl on the Cover," *Photoplay*, August 1915, 41.

71. "More Plots and Fewer Pies," quoted in Sherman, *Mabel Normand*, 21.

72. "They Will Not Remain in Comedy," *Film Fun*, May 1916, quoted in Sherman, *Mabel Normand*, 31.

73. There are many conflicting versions of this incident. Most accounts agree that Normand and Sennett had decided to marry on July 4, 1915—the third anniversary of Keystone's founding. It is similarly agreed that the incident occurred shortly before the wedding, when Normand discovered Sennett with another woman. Accounts diverge concerning subsequent events. According to Kalton Lahue, the disappointment left Normand in a weakened physical condition, whereupon she fell prey to a spell of pneumonia. See Kalton Lahue and Terry Brewer, *Kops and Custards: The Legend of Keystone Films* (1968; reprint, Norman: University of Oklahoma Press, 1972), 106–7. Sennett's autobiography asserts that Normand simply stayed away from the Keystone lot, feigning terminal illness as a way of getting revenge: "Mabel was staging a thriller to get even" (see Sennett, *King of Comedy*, 196–99). Normand's biographer, Betty Fussel suggests two other possibilities: either she threw herself off the Santa Monica pier in despair or she received a traumatic blow to the head in a fight with Sennett and his girlfriend (Fussell, *Mabel*, 79–81). Whatever the case, Sennett's publicity team worked hard to cover up the incident: fans were treated to a variety of spurious press releases claiming, alternately, that Normand was "unconscious and rapidly sinking" after a bad fall or that she had been struck by a flying shoe or brick during filming. See, e.g., "Famous Moving Picture Comedy Queen Is Battling with Death," *St. Louis Globe-Democrat*, September 21, 1915; "Mabel Normand Hit with Brick—Not Fatal," *New York Mail*, September 28, 1915; and "Mabel Normand Soon to Be Back in Films," *New Orleans Star*, October 17, 1915, Robinson Locke Collection of Dramatic Scrapbooks, envelope 1630, BRTC.

74. See "Arbuckle and Mabel Normand on Way to Eastern Studios," *MPN*, January 8, 1916, 55; "In and out of West Coast Studios," *MPN*, January 8, 1916, 73; "Keystone Stars Arrive in New York from Los Angeles," *MPN*, January 15,

1916, 248. According to existing financial records, the New York Motion Picture Company paid the Fort Lee unit $1,800 a week to cover the costs of production and payroll. See the Keystone Film Company cash book, September 28, 1912–April 24, 1924, ABP.

75. Indeed, the film features what is arguably the most complex narrative structure in Keystone's entire filmography. Whereas previous Keystone films generally based their narratives in the realm of physical action alone, *He Did and He Didn't* makes use of two distinct narrative registers in order to foreground character psychology. The basic situation concerns the romantic misunderstandings that arise between a doctor and his wife when her former boyfriend stops by for dinner. Although the story appears to be conveyed from an objective narrational perspective throughout, the closing moments reveal the entire action of the film's second half to have been a "shared" dream between the two male protagonists. The viewer is consequently required to reevaluate that action—in which the husband throttles his wife and throws her former boyfriend out of a window—as the subjective projection of the two dreamers: at once the revenge fantasy of a husband suspicious of his wife's infidelity *and* the paranoid projection of a former lover fearful of the husband's wrath.

76. "More Plots and Fewer Pies," quoted in Sherman, *Mabel Normand*, 21.

77. "They Will Not Remain in Comedy," quoted in Sherman, *Mabel Normand*, 31.

78. "Mabel Normand Leaves East to Join Ince-Triangle Forces," *MPN*, April 29, 1916, 2527; "In and out of West Coast Studios," *MPN*, May 20, 1916, 3051.

79. Keystone Film Company cash book, ABP; contract with Mack Sennett and the Keystone Film Company, re. Mabel Normand Picture, September 29, 1916, Triangle Film Corp. folder, Contract Files—General, MSC.

80. "First Subject to Star Mabel Normand Is in Production," *MPN*, June 10, 1916, 3592.

81. "In and out of West Coast Studios," *MPN*, May 20, 1916, 3051; "Young Signed to Direct Normand," *MPN*, June 3, 1916, 3382; "In and out of West Coast Studios," *MPN*, July 1, 1916, 4061; "Richard Jones Selected to Direct Mabel Normand in Feature Productions," *MPN*, October 21, 1916, 201.

82. Advertisement for *Mickey, MPN*, January 13, 1917, 221.

83. Lary May argues that Mary Pickford's star persona offered a "model of vitality" that expanded the parameters of respectable female behavior; yet, at the same time, her screen roles "still carried the . . . moral impulses of nineteenth-century women." See Lary May, *Screening Out the Past: The Birth of Mass Culture and the Motion Picture Industry* (Chicago: University of Chicago Press, 1980), 121, 211. Normand's character in *Mickey* precisely fits this model, and it is tempting to attribute this shift in her screen image to Pickford's tremendous popularity.

84. "Mabel Needs Menagerie to House Her Host of Pets," *MSW*, May 7, 1917, 1, 3.

85. "Children of the Studio Love Mabel Normand," *MSW*, January 29, 1917, 1.

86. The picture seems have been completed around April 1917, but its release was held up by complications in the wake of Sennett's departure from Triangle. As part of his separation agreement, Sennett signed over his 25 percent share in the picture, thereby forfeiting any control over the film's release. *Mickey* subsequently languished on Triangle's shelves for over a year as Aitken struggled to keep his company afloat. See contract with Triangle Film Corporation and New York Motion Picture Co., June 25, 1917, Paramount Pictures Corp. folder, Contract Files—General, MSC.

87. "Mickey," *MPW*, August 10, 1918, 880.

88. Review of *Mickey, Exhibitor's Trade Review,* August 13, 1918, 750.

89. "Mickey," *MPN*, August 3, 1918, 719.

90. Lahue and Brewer, *Kops and Custards,* 118.

91. The characterization of Moran as "distinctly sleazy" is in "Polly of the Laughs," *Photoplay,* September 1916, 99–100.

92. "Miss Fazenda O.K.'s Fishing," *MSW,* July 16, 1917, 2.

93. "Employment—Idle Time (1917)," Financial Files, MSC; contract with Polly Moran and Mack Sennett Films Corporation, July 23, 1917, Polly Moran folder, Contract Files, MSC.

94. "Louise Fazenda," *Photoplay,* March 1914, 18; "The Most Impish Sprite of Screen Comedy," *TT,* September 30, 1916, 8.

95. Gladys Hall, "Is It Tragic to Be Comic?" *Motion Picture Classic,* May 1931, 48, quoted in Jenkins, *What Made Pistachio Nuts?* 258.

96. "Sennett Has Big Army at Laugh Factory," *TT,* March 11, 1916, 3.

97. The relatively undemanding nature of their roles was reflected in low weekly wages, which by 1917 ranged from $20 to $75. See "Employment—Idle Time (1917)," Financial Files, MSC.

98. "Keystone Beauties Victors at Great Bathing Parade in Venice," *MSW,* June 25, 1917, 1–2.

99. See Ora Carew clippings file, AMPAS.

100. See Marie Prevost clippings file, AMPAS.

101. A concise biographical essay on Thurman has been written by her grand-niece, Lisa Huber. See Lisa Huber, "Mary Thurman," *Slapstick,* no. 3 (2000).

102. Howard Strickling, "Life Story of Louise Fazenda," undated press release, in Louise Fazenda clippings file, AMPAS.

103. See Polly Moran clippings file, AMPAS.

104. "Photographs for Your Lobby," *MSW.*

105. "How Mack Sennett-Keystone Beauties Invest Their Earnings," *MSW,* May 28, 1917, 1.

106. "Fashion Tips from Keystone Style Expert," *MSW,* April 23, 1917, 4.

107. "Lobby Displays That Will Delight You and Startle Your Competitors," *MSW,* May 21, 1917, 4.

108. "Sennett-Keystone Gymnasium Popular with Beauty Brigade," *MSW,* May 14, 1917, 4.

109. "'Aquaplaning' Supplies Thrills to Keystone Nymphs," *MSW,* January 22, 1917, 4.

110. "Athletes Plentiful," *MSW*, January 1, 1917, 4.

111. "Miss Athlete—See If You Can Duplicate These Performances," *MSW*, January 29, 1917, 4.

112. Harry Carr, "Untold Tales of Hollywood," *Smart Set*, January 1930, quoted in *Taylorology* 43 (July 1996), http://www.public.asu.edu/~ialong/Taylor43.txt (accessed December 27, 2007).

113. See T. J. Jackson Lears, "From Salvation to Self-Realization: Advertising and the Therapeutic Roots of the Consumer Culture, 1880–1930," in Richard Wightman Fox and T. J. Jackson Lears, eds., *The Culture of Consumption: Critical Essays in American History, 1880–1980* (New York: Pantheon Books, 1983), 3–38.

114. As defined by Georg Lukács, reification "requires that a society should learn to satisfy all its needs in terms of commodity exchange. . . . Consumer articles no longer appear as the products of an organic process (as for example in a village community). They now appear . . . as abstract members of a species identical by definition with its other members." Georg Lukács, *History and Class Consciousness: Studies in Marxist Dialectics*, trans. Rodney Livingstone (Cambridge, Mass.: MIT Press, 1971), 91.

115. "Next Keystone Is a Picture of Startling Beauty," *MSW*, April 9, 1917, 2; "Peaches Play in Perfumed Pool," *MSW*, May 21, 1917, 2.

116. Such is the suggestion of Hilda D'haeyere, who draws a number of productive comparisons between the Bathing Beauties and the Keystone Kops as distinct forms of "mass" spectacle. Whereas the members of both groups were equally anonymous as individuals, the Beauties were generally present in *ordered* patterns, the Kops in *chaotic* arrangements. Likewise, D'haeyere argues, the bathing girls featured as *counterpoints* to slapstick violence, not as participants, a point that clearly relates to gender difference. Hilda D'haeyere, "Sea, Sex, and Slapstick: Sennett's Bathing Beauties" (paper delivered at "(Another) Slapstick Symposium," Brussels, 2006).

117. I am referring, of course, to Laura Mulvey's now-canonical analysis of the patriarchal dynamics of classical cinema, "Visual Pleasure and Narrative Cinema," *Screen* 16.4 (1975): 6–18. See, however, n. 34 above.

118. Siegfried Kracauer, "The Mass Ornament," in *The Mass Ornament: Weimar Essays*, trans. Thomas Levin (Cambridge, Massachusetts: Harvard University Press, 1995), 75, 78.

119. For this critique of Frankfurt School thought, see Raymond Williams, *Marxism and Literature* (New York: Oxford University Press, 1977), 101–7.

120. "Lobby Displays That Will Delight You," *MSW*.

121. Alfred A. Cohn, "The 'Follies' of the Screen," *Photoplay*, June 1917, 85–86.

122. Ibid.

123. "Lobby Displays That Will Delight You," *MSW*.

124. This was not the Beauties' only appearance in the *Police Gazette* in 1917. Other examples include a photospread featuring Ruth Churchill in fencing gear and an article on Alice Maison's charitable work knitting socks

for Belgian soldiers. See *Police Gazette*, April 14, 1917, 2, and August 4, 1917, 16.

125. E. H. Stringer to managing director, Mack Sennett Studios, December 3, 1926, Publicity Dept. Correspondence (1926), General Files, MSC.

126. H. L. Davidson to publicity director, July 24, 1926, Publicity Dept. Correspondence (1926), General Files, MSC.

127. Undated press release, Natalie Kingston folder, Biography Files, MSC.

128. "Beauty Hints," Anita Barnes folder, Biography Files, MSC.

129. "Beauty Hints," Sally Eilers folder, Biography Files, MSC.

130. T. J. Jackson Lears, *Fables of Abundance: A Cultural History of Advertising in America* (New York: Basic Books, 1994), 162–77.

131. "Keystone Beauties Victors at Great Bathing Parade," *MSW*.

132. For example, in July 1926, the American Legion of Santa Monica invited Sennett to send "young ladies" to participate in a "Water Carnival, Mardi Gras and Bathing Beauty Parade." Over the next two years, Sennett would be an invited judge in at least three further local beauty contests—the "Queen of Hollywood," "Miss Hollywood," and "Miss Studio City" pageants—the top prizes for which all included trial employment at Mack Sennett Comedies for periods ranging from eight to twelve weeks. See E. L. Sullivan to Mack Sennett Comedies, July 17, 1926, Publicity Dept. Correspondence (1926), General Files and "Beauty Contests" folder, Contract Files—General, MSC.

133. Agnes O'Malley to John A. Waldron, April 29th, 1927, Publicity Dept. Correspondence (1927), General Files, MSC.

134. See Juanita Hansen clippings file, AMPAS.

135. "Marie Prevost on Liquid Diet to Lose 20 Lbs" (n.s.), January 28, 1932, and unidentified clipping, October 29, 1934, from the Marie Prevost clippings file, AMPAS.

136. Kenneth Anger, *Hollywood Babylon* (San Francisco: Straight Arrow Books, 1975), 146.

137. Jürgen Habermas, *The Structural Transformation of the Public Sphere: An Inquiry into a Category of Bourgeois Society*, trans. Thomas Burger (Cambridge, Mass.: MIT Press, 1989), 181.

138. In his study of American advertising before World War II, Roland Marchand notes how commercial illustrations "interpreted woman's modernity primarily in a 'fashion' sense . . . and defined her status as 'decorative object' as one of her natural and appropriate roles." Roland Marchand, *Advertising the American Dream: Making Way for Modernity, 1920–1940* (Berkeley: University of California Press, 1985), 185. See also Lears, *Fables of Abundance*, 162–95.

CONCLUSION

1. "Bauman [sic] Quits N.Y.M.P. for Trip 'Round World,'" *MPN*, February 17, 1917, 1040; "Aitken Buys Controlling Interest in Kessel and Bauman [sic]," *MPN*, March 10, 1917, 1521.

2. Keystone Film Company stock certificate book, 1912, ABP.

3. For more detail on the terms of Sennett's withdrawal, see the contract between Triangle Film Corp. and New York Motion Picture Co., June 25, 1917, Paramount Pictures Corp. folder, Contract Files—General, MSC.

4. See, e.g., the production synopses for *Haunted by Himself* (November 1917), *Dimples and Dangers* (January 1918), *A Lady Killer's Doom* (March 1918), *I Love Charles Albert* (April 1918), and *Mr. Miller's Economics* (April 1918), ABP. Flagging its allegiance to the situation style, advertising copy for the third of these described how "the comedy is not forced and touches on actual conditions," adding that "such pictures always touch the heartstrings as well as the laughter muscles." Synopsis, *A Lady Killer's Doom*, ABP.

5. Mack Sennett to J. A. Waldron, June 29, 1917, correspondence folder (1915–1919), General Files, MSC. According to this contract, the studio would receive payments of $12,000 per week, in addition to a 65 percent share of the domestic gross for the films and a 60 percent share of international receipts. See the contract between Mack Sennett and Paramount Pictures Corp., June 29, 1917, Paramount Pictures Corp. folder, Contract Files—General, MSC.

6. Contract between Mack Sennett and Paramount Pictures Corp. (emphasis added).

7. "Great Paramount Company Will Release Mack Sennett Comedies," *MSW*, July 30, 1917, 1.

8. *Photoplay*, June 1928, 76.

9. *Morning Telegraph*, July 4, 1960, quoted in Simon Louvish, *Keystone: The Life and Clowns of Mack Sennett* (New York: Faber & Faber, 2003), 292.

10. Stuart Hall, "Notes on Deconstructing 'The Popular,'" in Raphael Samuel, ed., *People's History and Socialist Theory* (London: Routledge & Kegan Paul, 1981), 229.

11. "[W]e have to understand the material, sensory conditions under which American mass culture, including Hollywood, was received and could have functioned as a powerful matrix for modernity's liberatory impulses—its moments of abundance, play, and radical possibility, its glimpses of collectivity and gender equality," Miriam Hansen observes in "The Mass Production of the Sense: Classical Cinema as Vernacular Modernism," *Modernism/Modernity* 6.2 (1999): 69. Ironically, slapstick is Hansen's privileged example for these claims, although Keystone's own later development indicates a degree of utopianism in her reading.

12. Francis C. Couvares, "The Triumph of Commerce: Class Culture and Mass Culture in Pittsburgh," in Michael H. Frisch and Daniel J. Walkowitz, eds., *Working-Class America: Essays on Labor, Community, and American Society* (Urbana: University of Illinois Press, 1983), 123–52.

13. Mack Sennett, with Cameron Shipp, *King of Comedy* (Garden City, N.Y.: Doubleday, 1954; reprint, San Jose, Calif.: toExcel Press, 2000), 275.

14. Unidentified clipping, ca. 1939, Mack Sennett Clippings File (1900–1979), BRTC.

Filmography

This filmography includes only those titles discussed in the main text of this book. They are listed chronologically with information (where available) on release dates, production dates, length, casts, and directors.

Data for this filmography have been synthesized from a number of sources—the Aitken Brothers Papers in the Wisconsin Historical Society, Madison; the Mack Sennett Collection at the Margaret Herrick Library, Los Angeles; numerous trade journals (in particular, *Moving Picture World*, *Motography*, and *The Triangle*); and, of course, the prints themselves. I have also drawn upon information from a number of existing filmographies, notably Brian Anthony and Andy Edmonds's *Smile When the Raindrops Fall: The Story of Charley Chase* (Lanham, Md.: Scarecrow Press, 1998); the British Film Institute's superb online Chaplin resource, http://chaplin.bfi.org.uk (accessed December 27, 2007); Betty Fussell's "The Films of Mabel Normand," *Film History* 2.4 (1988): 373–391; Kalton Lahue and Terry Brewer's *Kops and Custards: The Legend of Keystone Films* (Norman: University of Oklahoma Press, 1968); and Warren Sherk's *The Films of Mack Sennett: Credit Documentation from the Mack Sennett Collection at the Margaret Herrick Library* (Lanham, Md.: Scarecrow Press, 1998).

None of this means, however, that the entries are necessarily complete or perfect, although I have tried to limit data to what can be empirically verified. Space constraints and the frequent difficulties of identifying individual performers from surviving prints have meant that my cast listings are unavoidably selective, in each case limited to no more than five principal performers. Furthermore, for a number of Keystone films released in 1916, the archival record is deeply contradictory, with release dates for individual films sometimes preceding the date given for the end of shooting.

In these instances, I have kept the contradictions in my entries, citing references for the relevant information. Finally, I use the following acronyms to indicate sources when I have been unable to verify credit data: Anthony and Edmonds: [AE]; British Film Institute: [BFI]; Fussell: [BF/MN]; Lahue and Brewer: [LB]; and Sherk: [WS].

MUTUAL FILM CORPORATION RELEASES

1912   *Cohen Collects a Debt*
        Release date: September 23, 1912
        Length: split-reel
        Cast: Fred Mace, Mabel Normand, Ford Sterling
        Director: Mack Sennett

        The Water Nymph
        Release date: September 23, 1912
        Length: split-reel
        Cast: Mabel Normand, Mack Sennett, Ford Sterling
        Director: Mack Sennett

        Riley and Schultz
        Release date: September 30, 1912
        Length: split-reel
        Cast: Fred Mace, Ford Sterling [LB]
        Director: Mack Sennett

        Stolen Glory
        Release date: October 14, 1912
        Length: one reel
        Cast: Alice Davenport, Fred Mace, Mabel Normand, Ford Sterling
        Director: Mack Sennett

        The Grocery Clerk's Romance
        Release date: October 28, 1912
        Length: split-reel
        Cast: Fred Mace, Mabel Normand, Ford Sterling
        Director: Mack Sennett

        At Coney Island
        Release date: October 28, 1912
        Production dates: shooting, ca. July 4, 1912
        Length: split-reel
        Cast: Mabel Normand, Mack Sennett, Ford Sterling
        Director: Mack Sennett

        Mabel's Lovers
        Release date: November 4, 1912
        Length: split-reel

Cast: Alice Davenport, Fred Mace, Mabel Normand
Director: Mack Sennett

At It Again
Release date: November 4, 1912
Length: split-reel
Cast: Alice Davenport, Fred Mace, Mabel Normand, Mack
  Sennett, Ford Sterling
Director: Mack Sennett

A Desperate Lover
Release date: November 25, 1912
Length: split-reel
Cast: Fred Mace, Mabel Normand
Director: George Nichols [BF/MN]

Pat's Day Off
Release date: December 2, 1912
Length: split-reel
Cast: Alice Davenport, Fred Mace, Mabel Normand,
  Mack Sennett, Ford Sterling [BF/MN]
Director: Mack Sennett

Mabel's Adventures
Release date: December 16, 1912
Length: split-reel
Cast: Fred Mace, Mabel Normand, Ford Sterling
Director: Mack Sennett

Hoffmeyer's Legacy
Release date: December 23, 1912
Length: split-reel
Cast: Fred Mace, Mack Sennett, Ford Sterling
Director: Mack Sennett

1913   *The Cure That Failed*

Release date: January 13, 1913
Length: split-reel
Cast: Henry Lehrman, Fred Mace, Mabel Normand, Ford Sterling
Director: George Nichols [BF/MN]

The Deacon Outwitted
Release date: January 27, 1913
Length: split-reel
Cast: Harry McCoy, Mabel Normand, Betty Schade,
  Ford Sterling [BF/MN]
Director: Henry Lehrman [BF/MN]

The Sleuths at the Floral Parade
Release date: March 6, 1913
Length: split-reel
Cast: Henry Lehrman, Fred Mace, Mabel Normand, Mack
  Sennett, Ford Sterling
Director: Mack Sennett

A Strong Revenge
Release date: March 10, 1913
Length: one reel
Cast: Nick Cogley, Dot Farley, Mabel Normand, Mack Sennett,
  Ford Sterling
Director: Mack Sennett

The Two Widows
Release date: March 13, 1913
Length: split-reel
Cast: Dot Farley, Ford Sterling

The Man Next Door
Release date: March 17, 1913
Length: split-reel
Cast: Charles Avery, Nick Cogley, Dot Farley, Ford Sterling
Director: Mack Sennett

A Wife Wanted
Release date: March 20, 1913
Length: split-reel
Cast: Nick Cogley, Dot Farley, Fred Mace, Ford Sterling

At Twelve o'Clock
Release date: March 27, 1913
Length: one reel
Cast: Fred Mace, Mabel Normand, Mack Sennett
Director: Mack Sennett

Her New Beau
Release date: March 31, 1913
Length: split-reel
Cast: Fred Mace, Mabel Normand, Mack Sennett [LB]

On His Wedding Day
Release date: March 31, 1913
Length: split-reel
Cast: Nick Cogley, Dot Farley, Ford Sterling

Hide and Seek
Release date: April 3, 1913
Length: split-reel

Cast: Nick Cogley, Helen Holmes, Mabel Normand, Ford Sterling
[BF/MN]
Director: George Nichols

Cupid in a Dental Parlor
Release date: April 21, 1913
Production dates: shipped, March 12, 1913
Length: one reel
Cast: Fred Mace, Joseph Swickard
Director: Henry Lehrman

The Bangville Police
Release date: April 24, 1913
Production dates: shipped, March 17, 1913
Length: split-reel
Cast: Nick Cogley, Dot Farley, Edgar Kennedy,
  Fred Mace, Mabel Normand
Director: Henry Lehrman

His Chum, the Baron
Release date: April 28, 1913
Production dates: shipped, March 21, 1913
Length: split-reel
Cast: Edgar Kennedy, Hank Mann, Ford Sterling
Director: Mack Sennett

That Ragtime Band
Release date: May 1, 1913
Production dates: shipped, March 27, 1913
Length: one reel
Cast: Nick Cogley, Alice Davenport, Edgar Kennedy,
  Mabel Normand, Ford Sterling
Director: Mack Sennett

The Darktown Belle
Release date: May 8, 1912
Production dates: shipped, April 1, 1913
Length: split-reel
Cast: Fred Mace
Director: Henry Lehrman

A Little Hero
Release date: May 8, 1913
Production dates: shipped, April 1, 1913
Length: split-reel
Cast: Mabel Normand
Director: Mack Sennett

Mabel's Awful Mistake
Release date: May 12, 1913

Production dates: shipped, April 5, 1913
Length: one reel
Cast: Edgar Kennedy, Mabel Normand, Mack Sennett,
  Ford Sterling
Director: Mack Sennett

Toplitsky and Co.
Release date: May 26, 1913
Production dates: shipped, April 12, 1913
Length: one reel
Cast: Nick Cogley, Alice Davenport, William Hauber,
  Edgar Kennedy, Ford Sterling
Director: Henry Lehrman

Barney Oldfield's Race for a Life
Release date: June 2, 1913
Production dates: shipped, April 24, 1913
Length: one reel
Cast: William Hauber, Mabel Normand, Barney Oldfield,
  Mack Sennett, Ford Sterling
Director: Mack Sennett

For the Love of Mabel
Release date: June 30, 1913
Production dates: shipped, June 6, 1913
Length: one reel
Cast: Roscoe Arbuckle, Mabel Normand, Ford Sterling
Director: Henry Lehrman

Rastus and the Game Cock
Release date: July 3, 1913
Production dates: shipped, June 6, 1913
Length: one reel
Cast: Roscoe Arbuckle, Charles Avery, Nick Cogley, Mack
  Sennett, Ford Sterling
Director: Mack Sennett

Love and Rubbish
Release date: July 14, 1913
Production dates: shipped, June 20, 1913
Length: one reel
Cast: Roscoe Arbuckle, Charles Avery, Alice Davenport, Billy Jacobs,
  Ford Sterling
Director: Henry Lehrman

The Peddler
Release date: July 31, 1913
Production dates: shipped, June 25, 1913
Length: split-reel

Cast: Henry Lehrman, Ford Sterling
Director: Henry Lehrman

The Riot
Release date: August 7, 1913
Production dates: shipped, July 25, 1913
Length: one reel
Cast: Roscoe Arbuckle, Mabel Normand, Ford Sterling
Director: Mack Sennett

The Fire Bug
Release date: August 21, 1913
Production Dates: shipped, May 28, 1913
Length: two reels
Cast: Nick Cogley, Alice Davenport, Edgar Kennedy,
    Mack Sennett, Ford Sterling
Director: Mack Sennett

Mabel's New Hero
Release date: August 28, 1913
Production dates: shipped, August 2, 1913
Length: one reel
Cast: Roscoe Arbuckle, Charles Inslee, Edgar Kennedy,
    Virginia Kirtley, Mabel Normand
Director: Mack Sennett

Mabel's Dramatic Career
Release date: September 8, 1913
Production dates: shipped, August 12, 1913
Length: one reel
Cast: Roscoe Arbuckle, Alice Davenport, Mabel Normand,
    Mack Sennett, Ford Sterling
Director: Mack Sennett

A Healthy Neighborhood
Release date: October 16, 1913
Production dates: shipped, September 23, 1913
Length: one reel
Cast: Virginia Kirtley, Mack Sennett, Ford Sterling
Director: Mack Sennett

The Speed Kings
Release date: October 30, 1913
Length: one reel
Cast: Roscoe Arbuckle, Earl Cooper, Mabel Normand,
    Ford Sterling, Teddy Tetzlaff
Director: Wilfred Lucas [BF/MN]

A Muddy Romance
Release date: November 20, 1913

Production dates: shipped, October 25, 1913
Length: one reel
Cast: Charles Avery, William Hauber, Mabel Normand, Ford
    Sterling, Mack Swain
Director: Mack Sennett

Zuzu, the Band Leader
Release date: December 24, 1913
Production dates: shipped, October 16, 1913
Length: two reels
Cast: Charles Haggerty, Hank Mann, Mabel Normand, Ford
    Sterling [BF/MN]
Director: Mack Sennett

1914   *Love and Dynamite*

Release date: January 3, 1914
Production dates: shipped, December 6, 1913
Length: one reel
Cast: Ford Sterling
Director: Mack Sennett

Mabel's Stormy Love Affair
Release date: January 5, 1914
Production dates: shipped, December 14, 1913
Length: one reel
Cast: Nick Cogley, Alice Davenport, Edgar Kennedy, Hank Mann,
    Mabel Normand [BF/MN]
Director: Mabel Normand

Won in a Closet
Release date: January 22, 1914
Production dates: shipped, December 30, 1913
Length: one reel
Cast: Alice Davenport, Edgar Kennedy, Harry McCoy, Hank
    Mann, Mabel Normand [BF/MN]
Director: Mabel Normand

Double Crossed
Release date: January 26, 1914
Production dates: shipped, January 7, 1914
Length: one reel
Cast: Chester Conklin, Al St. John, Ford Sterling, Mack Swain
Director: Ford Sterling

Mabel's Bear Escape
Release date: January 31, 1914
Production dates: shipped, January 11, 1914
Length: one reel

Cast: Mabel Normand
Director: Mabel Normand

Making a Living
Release date: February 2, 1914
Production dates: shooting, ca. December 17, 1913–January 9,
  1914 [BFI]; shipped, January 14, 1914
Length: one reel
Cast: Charles Chaplin, Chester Conklin, Alice Davenport, Minta
  Durfee, Henry Lehrman
Director: Henry Lehrman

Kid Auto Races
Release date: February 7, 1914
Production dates: shooting, January 10, 1914 [BFI]; shipped,
  January 17, 1914
Length: split-reel
Cast: Charles Chaplin, Henry Lehrman, Frank Williams [BFI]
Director: Henry Lehrman

Mabel's Strange Predicament
Release date: February 9, 1914
Production dates: shooting, ca. January 6–12, 1914 [BFI]; shipped,
  January 20, 1914
Length: one reel
Cast: Charles Chaplin, Chester Conklin, Alice Davenport, Harry
  McCoy, Mabel Normand
Director: Mabel Normand (with Mack Sennett)

Between Showers
Release date: February 28, 1914
Production dates: shooting, ca. January 27–31, 1914; shipped,
  February 7, 1914
Length: one reel
Cast: Charles Chaplin, Chester Conklin, Emma Clifton, Sadie
  Lampe, Ford Sterling [BFI]
Director: Henry Lehrman

A Film Johnnie
Release date: March 2, 1914
Production dates: shooting, ca. February 1–6, 1914 [BFI]; shipped,
  February 11, 1914
Length: one reel
Cast: Roscoe Arbuckle, Charles Chaplin, Minta Durfee, Edgar
  Kennedy, Virginia Kirtley
Director: George Nichols

A False Beauty
Release date: March 5, 1914

Production dates: shipped, February 14, 1914
Length: one reel
Cast: Alice Davenport, Hank Mann, Ford Sterling, Mack Swain
Director: Ford Sterling

His Favorite Pastime
Release date: March 16, 1914
Production dates: shooting, ca. February 11–17, 1914 [BFI];
   shipped, February 19, 1914
Length: one reel
Cast: Roscoe Arbuckle, Charles Chaplin, Edgar Kennedy, Harry
   McCoy, Peggy Pearce
Director: George Nichols

Mabel at the Wheel
Release date: April 18, 1914
Production dates: shooting, ca. February 26–March 16, 1914
   [BFI]; shipped, March 31, 1914
Length: two reels
Cast: Charles Chaplin, Chester Conklin, Harry McCoy, Mabel
   Normand, Mack Sennett
Director: Mabel Normand (with Mack Sennett)

Caught in a Cabaret
Release date: April 27, 1914
Production dates: shooting, ca. March 27–April 2, 1914 [BFI];
   shipped, April 11, 1914
Length: two reels
Cast: Charles Chaplin, Chester Conklin, Edgar Kennedy, Harry
   McCoy, Mabel Normand
Director: Mabel Normand (with Charles Chaplin?)

The Fatal Mallet
Release date: June 1, 1914
Production dates: shooting, ca. May 10–12, 1914 [BFI]; shipped,
   May 16, 1914
Length: one reel
Cast: Charles Chaplin, Mabel Normand, Mack Sennett,
   Mack Swain
Director: Mack Sennett

Mabel's Busy Day
Release date: June 13, 1914
Production dates: shooting, ca. May 17–26, 1914 [BFI]; shipped,
   May 30, 1914
Length: one reel
Cast: Charles Chaplin, Chester Conklin, Harry McCoy, Mabel
   Normand, Slim Summerville
Director: Mabel Normand

Mabel's Married Life
Release date: June 20, 1914
Production dates: shooting, ca. May 30–June 2, 1914 [BFI];
  shipped, June 6, 1914
Length: one reel
Cast: Charles Chaplin, Alice Howell (?), Hank Mann, Mabel
  Normand, Mack Swain
Director: Charles Chaplin (with Mabel Normand?)

Laughing Gas
Release date: July 9, 1914
Production dates: shooting, ca. June 15–22, 1914 [BFI]; shipped,
  June 26, 1914
Length: one reel
Cast: Charles Chaplin, Alice Howell (?), Fritz Schade, Slim
  Summerville, Mack Swain
Director: Charles Chaplin

The Property Man
Release date: August 1, 1914
Production date: shooting, ca. June 25–July 11, 1914 [BFI];
  shipped, July 18, 1914
Length: two reels
Cast: Phyllis Allen, Charles Bennett, Charles Chaplin, Fritz
  Schade, Joseph Swickard
Director: Charles Chaplin

The Masquerader
Release date: August 27, 1914
Production dates: shooting, ca. July 25–August 1, 1914 [BFI];
  shipped, August 12, 1914
Length: one reel
Cast: Roscoe Arbuckle, Charles Chaplin, Chester Conklin, Minta
  Durfee, Charles Murray
Director: Charles Chaplin

Mabel's Latest Prank
Release date: September 10, 1914
Production dates: shipped, August 22, 1914
Length: one reel
Cast: Hank Mann, Mabel Normand, Mack Sennett, Slim
  Summerville [BF/MN]
Director: Mabel Normand [BF/MN]

He Loved the Ladies
Release date: September 21, 1914
Production dates: shipped, September 2, 1914
Length: one reel

Cast: Alice Davenport, Edgar Kennedy, Charles Murray, Charles
  Parrott
Director: Charles Parrott (?)

The New Janitor
Release date: September 24, 1914
Production dates: shooting, ca. August 18–26, 1914 [BFI];
  shipped, September 3, 1914
Length: one reel
Cast: Glen Cavender, Charles Chaplin, Jack Dillon, Minta Durfee,
  Al St. John [BFI]
Director: Charles Chaplin

Dough and Dynamite
Release date: October 26, 1914
Production dates: shooting, ca. August 29–September 11, 1914
  [BFI]; shipped, September 18, 1914
Length: two reels
Cast: Charles Chaplin, Chester Conklin, Vivian Edwards, Edgar
  Kennedy, Fritz Schade
Director: Charles Chaplin

Gentlemen of Nerve
Release date: October 29, 1914
Production dates: shooting, ca. September 20–27, 1914 [BFI];
  shipped, October 7, 1914
Length: one reel
Cast: Phyllis Allen, Charles Chaplin, Chester Conklin, Mabel
  Normand, Mack Swain
Director: Charles Chaplin

His Musical Career
Release date: November 7, 1914
Production dates: shooting, ca. October 1–10, 1914 [BFI]; shipped,
  October 17, 1914
Length: one reel
Cast: Charles Chaplin, Frank Hayes, Charles Parrott, Fritz
  Schade, Mack Swain
Director: Charles Chaplin

His Trysting Place
Release date: November 9, 1914
Production dates: shooting, ca. September 19–26, 1914 [BFI];
  shipped, October 1, 1914
Length: two reels
Cast: Phyllis Allen, Glen Cavender, Charles Chaplin, Mabel
  Normand, Mack Swain
Director: Charles Chaplin

His Prehistoric Past
Release date: December 7, 1914
Production dates: shooting, ca. October 14–27, 1914 [BFI];
   shipped, October 31, 1914
Length: two reels
Cast: Cecile Arnold, Charles Chaplin, Gene Marsh, Fritz Schade,
   Mack Swain
Director: Charles Chaplin

The Plumber
Release date: December 10, 1914
Production dates: shipped, November 25, 1914
Length: one reel
Cast: Charles Murray, Joseph Swickard

Fatty's Magic Pants
Release date: December 14, 1914
Production dates: shipped, December 2, 1914
Length: one reel
Cast: Roscoe Arbuckle, Minta Durfee, Charles Parrott, Bert
   Roach, Al St. John
Director: Roscoe Arbuckle

Hogan's Annual Spree
Release date: December 17, 1914
Production dates: shipped, December 3, 1914
Length: one reel
Cast: Charles Murray
Director: Charles Avery [LB]

Fatty and Minnie-He-Haw
Release date: December 21, 1914
Production dates: shipped, October 8, 1914
Length: two reels
Cast: Roscoe Arbuckle, Minnie Devereaux, Eddie Dillon, Minta
   Durfee, Harry McCoy
Director: Roscoe Arbuckle

Tillie's Punctured Romance
Release date: December 21, 1914
Production dates: shooting, April 14–June 9, 1914; shipped,
   July 25, 1914
Length: six reels
Cast: Charles Bennett, Charles Chaplin, Nick Cogley, Chester
Conklin, Marie Dressler, Edgar Kennedy, Charles Murray, Mabel
   Normand, Charles Parrott, Mack Swain
Director: Mack Sennett

Hogan's Wild Oats
Release date: December 31, 1914
Production dates: shipped, December 18, 1914
Length: split reel
Cast: Phyllis Allen, Bobby Dunn, Charles Murray
Director: Charles Avery [LB]

1915   *A Dark Lover's Play*

Release date: January 2, 1915
Production dates: shipped, December 19, 1914
Length: one reel
Cast: Mack Swain

Hash House Mashers
Release date: January 16, 1915
Production dates: shipped, January 5, 1915
Length: one reel
Cast: Virginia Chester, Chester Conklin, Frank Opperman,
   Charles Parrott, Fritz Schade
Director: Nick Cogley and Edwin Frazee [AE]

Hogan's Mussy Job
Release date: January 21, 1915
Production dates: shipped, January 10, 1915
Length: one reel
Cast: Alice Davenport, Bobby Dunn, Frank Hayes, Harry McCoy,
   Charles Murray
Director: Charles Avery [LB]

Colored Villainy
Release date: January 25, 1915
Production dates: shipped, January 15, 1915
Length: one reel
Cast: Mae Busch, Nick Cogley, Charles Parrott, Frank Opperman,
   Fritz Schade
Director: Nick Cogley [AE]

Fatty's New Role
Release date: February 1, 1915
Production dates: shipped, January 22, 1915
Length: one reel
Cast: Roscoe Arbuckle, Bobby Dunn, Edgar Kennedy, Slim
   Summerville, Mack Swain
Director: Roscoe Arbuckle

Hogan the Porter
Release date: February 4, 1915
Production dates: shipped, January 24, 1915

Length: one reel
Cast: Bobby Dunn, Frank Hayes, Charles Murray
Director: Charles Avery [LB]

A Bird's a Bird
Release date: February 8, 1915
Production dates: shipped, January 27, 1915
Length: one reel
Cast: Chester Conklin, Alice Davenport, Minta Durfee, Harry Ward

Hogan's Romance Upset
Release date: February 13, 1915
Production dates: shipped, February 1, 1915
Length: one reel
Cast: Roscoe Arbuckle, Bobby Dunn, Louise Fazenda, Charles Murray, Ford Sterling
Director: Charles Avery [LB]

Hogan's Aristocratic Dream
Release date: February 15, 1915
Production dates: shipped, January 21, 1915
Length: two reels
Cast: Bobby Dunn, Charles Murray
Director: Charles Avery [LB]

Hogan Out West
Release date: February 27, 1915
Production dates: shipped, February 3, 1915
Length: one reel
Cast: Bobby Dunn, Billy Gilbert, Charles Murray
Director: Charles Avery [LB]

Wilful Ambrose
Release date: March 1, 1915
Production dates: shipped, February 20, 1915
Length: one reel
Cast: Joe Bordeaux, Dixie Chene, Vivian Edwards, Louise Fazenda, Mack Swain

From Patches to Plenty
Release date: March 6, 1915
Production dates: shipped, February 26, 1915
Length: one reel
Cast: Bobby Dunn, Vivian Edwards, Ethel Madison, Dave Morris, Charles Murray

Settled at the Seaside
Release date: March 29, 1915
Production dates: "finished," March 18, 1915

Length: split reel
Cast: Mae Busch, William Hauber, Charles Parrott, Fritz Schade, Vera Steadman
Director: Walter Wright [AE]

Ambrose's Lofty Perch
Release date: April 3, 1915
Production dates: shipped, March 26, 1915
Length: one reel
Cast: Don Barclay, Louise Fazenda, Harry McCoy, Dave Morris, Mack Swain

The Rent Jumpers
Release date: April 8, 1915
Production dates: shipped, April 1, 1915
Length: one reel
Cast: Mae Busch, Frank Opperman, Charles Parrott, Fritz Schade
Director: Frank Griffin [AE]

Do-Re-Mi-Boom!
Release date: April 15, 1915
Production dates: shipped, April 6, 1915
Length: one reel
Cast: Charles Arling, Harry Booker, Chester Conklin
Director: Charles Parrott [AE]

Ambrose's Nasty Temper
Release date: April 17, 1915
Production dates: shipped, April 8, 1915
Length: one reel
Cast: Cecile Arnold, Don Barclay, Louise Fazenda, Dave Morris, Mack Swain
Director: Walter Wright (?)

Mabel's Wilful Way
Release date: May 1, 1915
Production dates: shipped, April 23, 1915
Length: one reel
Cast: Roscoe Arbuckle, Joe Bordeaux, Alice Davenport, Edgar Kennedy, Mabel Normand
Director: Roscoe Arbuckle

A Hash House Fraud
Release date: June 10, 1915
Production dates: shipped, June 2, 1915
Length: one reel
Cast: Harry Bernard, Chester Conklin, Hugh Fay, Louise Fazenda, Fritz Schade

The Cannon Ball
Release date: June 14, 1915
Production dates: shipped, May 14, 1915
Length: two reels
Cast: Charles Arling, Peggy Pearce, Harry Booker, Chester Conklin
Director: Walter Wright

The Little Teacher
Release date: June 21, 1915
Production dates: shipped, May 25, 1915
Length: two reels
Cast: Roscoe Arbuckle, Frank Hayes, Owen Moore, Mabel Normand, Mack Sennett
Director: Mack Sennett

Fatty's Plucky Pup
Release date: June 28, 1915
Production dates: shipped, June 10, 1915
Length: two reels
Cast: Phyllis Allen, Roscoe Arbuckle, Luke (dog), Al St. John, Josephine Stevens
Director: Roscoe Arbuckle

Court House Crooks
Release date: July 5, 1915
Production dates: shipped, June 15, 1915
Length: two reels
Cast: Charles Arling, Billie Bennett, Minta Durfee, Harold Lloyd, Ford Sterling
Director: Charles Parrott

When Ambrose Dared Walrus
Release date: July 12, 1915
Production dates: "finished," June 19, 1915
Length: two reels
Cast: Billie Brockwell, Chester Conklin, Vivian Edwards, Mack Swain, Joseph Swickard
Director: Walter Wright

The Battle of Ambrose and Walrus
Release date: August 16, 1915
Production dates: shipped, August 8, 1915
Length: two reels
Cast: Harry Bernard, Chester Conklin, Dora Rodgers, Mack Swain
Director: Walter Wright

Only a Messenger Boy
Release date: August 23, 1915
Production dates: shipped, August 19, 1915
Length: two reels
Cast: Nick Cogley, Bobby Dunn, Minta Durfee, Charles Parrott,
  Ford Sterling
Director: Charles Parrott

TRIANGLE FILM CORPORATION RELEASES*

1915 *My Valet*
Release date: November 7, 1915
Production dates: shipped, September 9, 1915
Length: four reels
Cast: Alice Davenport, Raymond Hitchcock, Fred Mace, Mabel
  Normand, Mack Sennett
Director: Mack Sennett

A Game Old Knight
Release date: November 7, 1915
Production dates: shipped, September 10, 1915
Length: two reels
Cast: Harry Booker, Louise Fazenda, Charles Murray, Slim
  Summerville, Wayland Trask
Director: Richard F. Jones

A Favorite Fool
Release date: November 14, 1915
Production dates: shipped, September 22, 1915
Length: two reels
Cast: Charles Arling, Mae Busch, Eddie Foy (and the Seven Little
  Foys), Polly Moran, Joseph Swickard
Director: Edwin Frazee

Her Painted Hero
Release date: November 21, 1915
Production dates: shipped, September 18, 1915
Length: two reels
Cast: Harry Booker, Hale Hamilton, Polly Moran, Charles
  Murray, Slim Summerville
Director: Richard F. Jones

---

*Release dates for Triangle films are derived primarily from *The Triangle* and *The Mack Sennett Weekly* and refer to the films' nationwide releases, not their model theater debuts.

Saved by Wireless
Release date: November 21, 1915
Production dates: shipped, October 14, 1915
Length: two reels
Cast: Ora Carew, Nick Cogley, Chester Conklin, Harry McCoy,
  Mack Swain
Director: Walter Wright

A Janitor's Wife's Temptation
Release date: December 5, 1915
Production dates: shooting, ca. mid-August–October 1915;
  shipped, November 23, 1915
Length: two reels
Cast: Marta Golden, Harry Gribbon, Joy Lewis, Fred Mace, Betty
  Marsh
Director: Del Henderson

The Great Vacuum Robbery
Release date: December 12, 1915
Production dates: shipped, November 5, 1915
Length: two reels
Cast: Louise Fazenda, Edgar Kennedy, Charles Murray, Slim
  Summerville, Wayland Trask
Directors: Harry Williams (?) and Clarence Badger (?)

Crooked to the End
Release date: December 19, 1915
Production dates: shipped, November 20, 1915
Length: two reels
Cast: Hugh Fay, Dale Fuller, Anna Luther, Fred Mace, Earl
  Rodney
Director: Edwin Frazee (with Walter Reed)

Fatty and the Broadway Stars
Release date: December 19, 1915
Production dates: shipped, November 23, 1915
Length: two reels
Cast: Roscoe Arbuckle, Ivy Crosthwaite, Mack Sennett, Al St.
  John, Weber and Fields
Director: Roscoe Arbuckle

A Submarine Pirate
Release date: December 26, 1915
Production dates: shooting, May 5-October 14, 1915; shipped,
  November 24, 1915
Length: four reels
Cast: Phyllis Allen, Cecile Arnold, Glen Cavender, Syd Chaplin,
  Wesley Ruggles
Directors: Charles Avery and Syd Chaplin

The Hunt
Release date: December 26, 1915
Production dates: shooting, mid-October–November 1915
Length: two reels
Cast: May Emory, Polly Moran, Ford Sterling, Bobby Vernon, Guy Woodward
Directors: Ford Sterling and Charles Parrott

1916   *Dizzy Heights and Daring Hearts*

Release date: January 2, 1916
Production dates: shooting, October 19–December 10, 1915
Length: two reels
Cast: Cora Anderson, David Anderson, Nick Cogley, Chester Conklin, William Mason
Director: Walter Wright

The Worst of Friends
Release date: January 2, 1916
Production dates: shipped, December 18, 1915
Length: three reels
Cast: Mae Busch, Alice Davenport, Lew Fields, Joe Weber
Director: Frank Griffin

The Great Pearl Tangle
Release date: January 9, 1916
Production dates: shooting, October 26–December 9, 1915; shipped, December 22, 1915
Length: two reels
Cast: Mildred Adams, Sam Bernard, Minta Durfee, Harry Gribbon, Harry McCoy
Director: Dell Henderson

Fatty and Mabel Adrift
Release date: January 9, 1916
Production dates: shipped, December 24, 1915
Length: two reels
Cast: Roscoe Arbuckle, Frank Hayes, Mabel Normand, Al St. John, May Wells
Director: Roscoe Arbuckle

A Modern Enoch Arden
Release date: January 16, 1916
Production dates: shooting, October 12–December 31, 1915; shipped, January 6, 1916
Length: two reels
Cast: Vivian Edwards, Joe Jackson, Betty Marsh, Dora Rodgers, Mack Swain
Director: Clarence Badger and Charles Avery

He Did and He Didn't
Release date: January 30, 1916
Production date: shooting, January 10–19, 1916
Length: two reels
Cast: Roscoe Arbuckle, Joe Bordeaux, William Jefferson, Mabel Normand, Al St. John
Director: Roscoe Arbuckle

Better Late Than Never
Release date: February 13, 1916
Production dates: shooting, December 23, 1915–January 25, 1916; shipped, February 8, 1916
Length: two reels
Cast: Joseph Belmont, Mae Busch, William Collier, Frank Opperman, Marie Prevost
Director: Frank Griffin and Jean Havez

The Bright Lights
Release date: February 20, 1916
Length: two reels
Cast: Roscoe Arbuckle, James Bryant, William Jefferson, Mabel Normand, Al St. John
Director: Roscoe Arbuckle

His Pride and Shame
Release date: February 27, 1916
Production dates: shipped, February 18, 1916
Length: two reels
Cast: Bobby Dunn, Juanita Hansen, Ford Sterling, Bobby Vernon, Guy Woodward
Directors: Ford Sterling and Charles Parrott

Gypsy Joe
Release date: March 19, 1916
Production dates: shooting, January 9–March 4, 1916; shipped, March 9, 1916
Length: two reels
Cast: Marion de la Parelle, Joe Jackson, Betty Marsh, Louis Morrison, Dora Rodgers
Director: Clarence Badger

A Love Riot
Release date: March 19, 1916
Production dates: "finished or shipped," February 19, 1916
Length: two reels
Cast: Harry Booker, Alice Davenport, Louise Fazenda, Charles Murray, Dora Rodgers
Director: Richard F. Jones

By Stork Delivery
Release date: March 26, 1916
Production dates: shooting, February 25–March 17, 1916;
  shipped, March 19, 1916
Length: two reels
Cast: Ivy Crosthwaite, Bobby Dunn, May Emory, Polly Moran,
  Mack Swain

The Lion and the Girl
Release date: April 30, 1916 [*Moving Picture World,* May 27,
  1916]
Production dates: shipped, May 1, 1916 ["Keystone Releases,"
  Mack Sennett Collection]
Length: two reels
Cast: Phyllis Allen, Claire Anderson, Joe Jackson, Louis Morrison,
  May Wells
Director: Glen Cavender

A Dash of Courage
Release date: May 7, 1916
Production dates: shooting, February 25–April 27, 1916; shipped,
  May 3, 1916
Length: two reels
Cast: Wallace Beery, Harry Gribbon, Gloria Swanson, Bobby
  Vernon, Guy Woodward
Director: Charles Parrott

Bath Tub Perils
Release date: May 14, 1916 [*The Triangle,* May 20, 1916]
Production dates: shooting, April 24–May 22, 1916 ["Complete
  Production Report," Aitken Brothers Papers]; shipped, May 27,
  1916 ["Keystone Releases," Mack Sennett Collection]
Length: two reels
Cast: Claire Anderson, Hugh Fay, Dale Fuller, Anna Luther,
  Fred Mace
Director: Edwin Frazee

The Love Comet
Release date: May 21, 1916 [*The Triangle,* June 10, 1916]
Production dates: shooting, May 10–29, 1916 ["Complete
  Production Report," Aitken Brothers Papers]; shipped, May 31,
  1916 ["Keystone Releases," Mack Sennett Collection]
Length: two reels
Cast: Joseph Belmont, Joseph Callahan, Ora Carew
Director: Walter Wright

Ambrose's Cup of Woe
Release date: June 4, 1916 [*The Triangle,* June 24, 1916]

Production dates: shooting, May 15–June 7, 1916 ["Complete
  Production Report," Aitken Brothers Papers]; shipped, June 13,
  1916 ["Keystone Releases," Mack Sennett Collection]
Length: two reels
Cast: May Emory, Joey Jacobs, Edgar Kennedy, Mack Swain,
  Joseph Swickard
Director: Fred Fishback

His First False Step
Release date: June 18, 1916 [*The Triangle*, July 22, 1916]
Production dates: shipped, July 5, 1916 ["Keystone Releases,"
  Mack Sennett Collection]
Length: two reels
Cast: Chester Conklin, Charles F. Reisner, Dora Rodgers, Mary
  Thurman, Mae Wells
Directors: William Campbell and Harry Williams

The Surf Girl
Release date: July 9, 1916 [*The Triangle*, July 29, 1916]
Production dates: shipped, July 20, 1916 ["Keystone Releases,"
  Mack Sennett Collection]
Length: two reels
Cast: Glen Cavender, Ivy Crosthwaite, Julia Faye, Ray Griffith,
  Fritz Schade
Director: Harry Edwards

Hearts and Sparks
Release date: July 16, 1916 [*Motography*, July 15, 1916; *Moving
  Picture World* gives a release date of June 4]
Production dates: shipped, June 21, 1916 ["Keystone Releases,"
  Mack Sennett Collection]
Length: two reels
Cast: Billie Bennett, Nick Cogley, Hank Mann, Gloria Swanson,
  Bobby Vernon
Director: Charles Parrott

A Social Club
Release date: July 16, 1916 [*The Triangle*, August 5, 1916]
Production dates: shooting, ca. June–July, 1916 [production files,
  Mack Sennett Collection]; shipped, July 26, 1916 ["Keystone
  Releases," Mack Sennett Collection]
Length: two reels
Cast: Elizabeth DeWitt, Harry Gribbon, Reggie Morris, Gloria
  Swanson, Bobby Vernon
Director: Clarence Badger

His Lying Heart
Release date: August 20, 1916 [*Moving Picture World*, October 7,
  1916]

Production dates: shooting, July 7–August 12, 1916 [production files, Aitken Bros. Papers]; shipped, August 30, 1916 ["Keystone Releases," Mack Sennett Collection]
Length: two reels
Cast: Vivian Edwards, Louella Maxam, Charles F. Riesner, Joseph Singleton, Ford Sterling
Directors: Ford Sterling and Charles Avery

Maid Mad
Release date: September 3, 1916 [LB]
Production dates: shipped, September 15, 1916 ["Keystone Releases," Mack Sennett Collection]
Length: two reels
Cast: Sylvia Ashton, Harry Booker, Louise Fazenda, Charles Murray, Wayland Trask
Director: Frank Griffin

Haystacks and Steeples
Release date: October 1, 1916 [*Moving Picture World*, November 25, 1916]
Production dates: shooting, September 1–October 4, 1916 [production files, Aitken Brothers Papers]; shipped, October 17, 1916 ["Keystone Releases," Mack Sennett Collection]
Length: two reels
Cast: Reggie Morris, Della Pringle, Gloria Swanson, Eva Thatcher, Bobby Vernon
Director: Clarence Badger

Bombs!
Release date: October 8, 1916 [LB]
Production dates: shooting, September 20–October 23, 1916 [production files, Mack Sennett Collection]; shipped, October 31, 1916 ["Keystone Releases," Mack Sennett Collection]
Length: two reels
Cast: Harry Booker, Louise Fazenda, Charles Murray, Mary Thurman, Wayland Trask
Director: Frank Griffin

His Busted Trust
Release date: November 9, 1916 [LB]
Production dates: shooting, August 22–October 3, 1916; shipped, October 10, 1916
Length: two reels
Cast: Bobbie Dunn, Vivian Edwards, Shorty Hamilton, Peggy Pearce, Slim Summerville
Director: Edward Cline

A Scoundrel's Toll
Release date: November 9, 1916 [LB]
Production dates: shooting, July 2–September 20, 1916; shipped,
    September 29, 1916
Length: two reels
Cast: Dale Fuller, Ray Griffith, Edgar Kennedy, Gene Rogers,
    Mary Thurman
Director: Glen Cavender

1917   *The Nick of Time Baby*

Release date: February 15, 1917
Production dates: shipped, December 22, 1916
Length: two reels
Cast: Sylvia Ashton, Earl Rodney, Gloria Swanson, Teddy (dog),
    Bobby Vernon
Director: Clarence Badger

Her Nature Dance
Release date: April 8, 1917
Production dates: shooting, November 23, 1916–March 16, 1917;
    shipped, March 21, 1917
Length: two reels
Cast: Alice Lake, Gene Rogers, Marie Prevost, Fritz Schade, Eva
    Thatcher
Director: William Campbell

Teddy at the Throttle
Release date: April 15, 1917
Length: two reels
Cast: Wallace Beery, May Emory, Gloria Swanson, Teddy (dog),
    Bobby Vernon
Director: Clarence Badger

A Maiden's Trust
Release date: April 29, 1917
Production dates: shooting, November 28, 1916–March 31, 1917;
    shipped, April 11, 1917
Length: two reels
Cast: Alice Davenport, Hugh Fay, Don Likes, Myrtle Lind, Ford
    Sterling
Director: Victor Heerman

His Naughty Thought
Release date: May 6, 1917
Production dates: finished, February 4, 1917 [WS]
Length: two reels

Cast: Larry Lyndon, Polly Moran, Dora Rodgers, Mack Swain, Eva Thatcher
Director: Fred Fishback

A Royal Rogue
Release date: May 20, 1917
Production dates: shooting, ca. early February 1917
Length: two reels
Cast: William Armstrong, Hal Cooley, Ray Griffith, Juanita Hansen, Jack Henderson
Directors: Robert Kerr and Ferris Hartman

Oriental Love
Release date: May 27, 1917
Production dates: shooting, ca. February 13–March 16, 1917
Length: two reels
Cast: Joseph Belmont, Joseph Callahan, Ora Carew, Edgar Kennedy, Blanche Payson
Director: Walter Wright (with Clarence Badger?)

Cactus Nell
Release date: June 3, 1917
Production dates: shooting, March 7–April 19, 1917; shipped, May 16, 1917
Length: two reels
Cast: Wallace Beery, Joey Jacobs, Polly Moran, Dora Rodgers, Wayland Trask
Director: Fred Fishback

A Dog Catcher's Love
Release date: June 24, 1917
Production dates: shooting, February 12–June 6, 1917; shipped, June 9, 1917
Length: two reels
Cast: Glen Cavender, Peggy Pearce, Gene Rodgers, Slim Summerville, Teddy (dog)
Director: Edward Cline

Whose Baby?
Release date: July 1, 1917
Production dates: shooting, ca. March, 1917.
Length: two reels
Cast: Tom Kennedy, Gloria Swanson, Ethel Teare, Teddy (dog), Bobby Vernon
Director: Clarence Badger

A Clever Dummy
Release date: July 15, 1917

Production dates: shooting, May 21–June 23, 1917; shipped, June 28, 1917
Length: two reels
Cast: Wallace Beery, Chester Conklin, James DeLano, Juanita Hansen, Ben Turpin
Director: Herman Raymaker, with Ferris Hartman and Robert Kerr

Thirst
Release date: July 29, 1917
Length: two reels
Cast: Cliff Bowes, Joey Jacobs, Mack Swain, Ethel Teare, Eva Thatcher
Director: Fred Fishback

The Late Lamented
Release date: September 23, 1917
Production dates: finished, ca. mid-July 1917
Length: two reels
Cast: George Binns, William P. DeVaull, Robert Milliken, Mack Swain, Mary Thurman
Director: Harry Williams

The Sultan's Wife
Release date: September 30, 1917
Length: two reels
Cast: Gonda Durand, Blanche Payson, Gloria Swanson, Teddy (dog), Bobby Vernon
Director: Clarence Badger

Index

Text: 10/13 Aldus
Display: Aldus
Compositor: International Typesetting and Composition
Printer: Sheridan Books, Inc.